Kinds of Literature

Kinds of Literature

An Introduction to the
Theory of Genres and Modes

ALASTAIR FOWLER

Harvard University Press · *Cambridge, Massachusetts* · *1982*

Library of Congress Cataloging in Publication Data

Fowler, Alastair.
    Kinds of literature.

    Bibliography: p.
    Includes index.
    1. Literary form. I. Title.
PN45.5.F6   801'.95   81-23962
ISBN 0-674-50355-4   AACR2

Preface

For quite some time now, it has been taken for granted that the old order of historical kinds has irrevocably gone. If we are to have genres, they must be arrived at *de novo* rather than *ab ovo*. And in the main, critics have preferred to talk about genres—or "modes"—in a very broad, unhistorical way. Such theory is sometimes interesting. But it seldom seems to make for better reading of literature. And since it deals with a very small repertoire of modes, it has tended to narrow the literary canon.

This book springs from the conviction that it is time to enlarge the critical repertory: to recover a sense of the variety of literary forms. It inquires whether genre in the traditional sense may not still have a place in literature. How do genres function? How are they formed? What is the relation of "fixed genre" to mode? My aim has not been to build systems of genres (there are all too many of those already), but to discuss problems and issues that arise when literary groupings are considered in terms of genre. In particular, I have tried to follow out some of the implications of treating genres not as permanent classes but as families subject to change. I have tried always to keep diachronic considerations in mind. Not that literature cannot sometimes transcend external history. But to do so it must accept its own history.

The book will seem too audacious to some, to others pedestrian. With few exceptions, for example, it deals specifically with English literature. I am aware of the comparatists' objections to genre studies on a national basis, and agree with them. But I have had to weigh against this the great differences between the orders of genres in different literatures. Some kinds, indeed, occur exclusively in one, without equivalent elsewhere. Many are international, however, and the decision to concentrate on a single literature was primarily a choice of scale. But although I have focused on English literature and the ideas that bear on it, I have introduced other literatures where it seemed helpful to do so. Considering the relevant sources, models, analogues, formative traditions, and theoretical influences inevitably involves a genre critic in some comparative work. Allowing for such involvements, we may think that English literature would not be a disablingly inadequate sample to take, if one knew how to take it. The generic nature of literature may be such that one extensive literature may stand as an exemplar of literature itself. If I am thought wrong in this, the book may be mentally retitled *Kinds of English Literature*. In any event, this is not a history of criticism. If it were, it would have to find far more space for Continental theorists: for Brunetière and Lukács, for Russian formalists, for Hans Robert Jauss, perhaps even for French structuralists.

As many have noticed, discussions of genre easily become chimerical. This is partly at least because of the paucity of examples of practicable length. I have tried, therefore, to illustrate as much as possible, if only from short forms. Such examples are not, I hope, atypical: others from longer kinds could have been given. Many of the examples come from the Renaissance and the eighteenth century. But the disproportion may be allowed, since in those periods genre criticism was especially energetic and illuminating.

In dealing with so many different periods in a book of this character, some compromise in treatment of orthography was unavoidable. Normally, the spelling has been modernized but not the punctuation. Occasionally, however, original spelling has been retained where it is significant; then the whole quotation is treated in the same way.

Earlier versions of parts of Chapters 5 and 6 were read as lectures, particularly a Churchill lecture at Bristol University and a David Nichol Smith Seminar at the Humanities Research Centre, Canberra—opportunities for which I am grateful. Chapter 12 appeared in a somewhat different form in *New Literary History* 11 (1979); I wish to thank the editor and publisher for permission to reprint parts of it here. Acknowledgments are due to Martin Brian and O'Keeffe, Édouard Champion, Yale University Press, the National Council of Teachers of English, and Gerald Duckworth for permission to reprint the epigraph and the diagrams on pages 240, 244, 245, and 247, respectively.

In forming the ideas and writing the book, I incurred more debts than can be acknowledged. Most of my colleagues and many of my students at Oxford, Edinburgh, and elsewhere contributed. But I particularly wish to thank E. D. Hirsch, Jr., Ralph Cohen, and Wallace Robson for their patience and kindness in arguing me out of at least some errors. Paul Barolsky, Ian Donaldson, Sam Goldberg, John Hardy, Jack Levenson, Alastair Minnis, and James Turner all gave generous assistance on particular points.

In a more practical sense, completion of the book would not have been possible without periods of study leave at the Institute for Advanced Study, Princeton, and the Humanities Research Centre at the Australian National University, Canberra. There and at Edinburgh, parts of the manuscript were typed by Betty Horton, Sandy Lafferty, Julie Barton, Pearl Moyseyenko, Sheila Strathdee, and Jill Strobridge with much skill and care. Special thanks are due to Peter McIntyre, who prepared the index. The debt to my wife, who read proof and tolerated the vexations of authorship, belongs to a large genre that can only be mentioned here.

University of Edinburgh   A.F.

To E. D. Hirsch, Jr.

Contents

1. Literature as a Genre

The bewildered foreigner can only say:
"But if the Diary is all you assert of it,
It must be literature, or, if it is not literature,
It cannot be all you assert of it."

HUGH MACDIARMID

To the question "What is literary theory a theory of?" no simple answer can be returned. Indeed, there is no permanent answer at all, and perhaps not even a temporary one satisfying to everyone. Some will say that literary theory deals with the criticism of literature, or directly with literature. But literature cannot be counted the material of a critical science in the way that machines form the material of mechanical engineering, or puddings of a branch of domestic science. There are gods in literature's machines, who are said to metamorphose and multiply beyond knowing. That is, criticism treats a distinctive sort of experimental evidence: the results of reading. The *materia critica* should not be thought of as a group of objects. It is literature subjectively encountered, individually and in part variously constructed, interpreted, and valued, within the institutions of societies that change. We can reach objective conclusions about it; but our best chance of doing so is to allow for its variety and its variation.

Even with this limitation, literary theorists are now the fortunate possessors of a wealth of criticism dealing with a wide variety of literature. Is, then, a general theory of literature at last possible? We may think that to have explanatory power, theories must explain specific problems.[1] Of these, contemporary literary theory has succeeded in identifying several. There is no single question fundamental to literary theory.[2] The old and new problems—validity of interpretation, value of literature, taxonomy of kinds, genetics of invention, responsibility of writers, reality of the heterocosm—all these and others call for attention. This book treats one particular problem: the function of genre in literature.

Limits of Literature

Some are perplexed that literature should have an uncertain extent. But this should not be surprising. Produced by diverse societies, variously conceived and valued at different times, and never known except in small part, literature inevitably elicits disparate ideas of itself. For a man who reads only modern novels, or who thinks history to be fact (or bunk), literature is going to differ from Gibbon's literature, or Vinaver's. Nevertheless, one response to this flux has been to define "literature" as the class of works that are, or have been, generally accepted as literary. In the brahminical version of this notion, literature is set as a unique canon, to which new members occasionally gain admittance.

Attractively simple as this idea may seem, it has provoked disagreements about which works are canonical, without leading to much theoretical construction. Moreover, the monumentality it stresses easily recalls that of a cemetery, so that it may have exacerbated hostility to the very idea of literature. The sensitive Rivière (himself a defender of literature) could feel positively grateful for the onslaughts of Dada and of the surrealists.[3] As for the structuralist Jacques Ehrmann, he exults over "the death of literature": "What is literary is not one text to the exclusion of another, but the texts that the reader decides to qualify as such . . . A certain conception of 'literature'—the one that makes of certain signs an aristocracy of discourse . . . loses all validity, all foundation, on losing its privileges. Thus 'literature,' a dumping ground for fine feelings, a museum of 'belles lettres,' has had its day."[4] The expression "aristocracy of discourse" reflects a common view that the idea of literature is elitist in a bad sense. And this would almost be justified, if literature were an immutable institution. A literary museum that could only be extended might well call for the destructive attentions of a terrorist-critic, just as

> literature
> that gouty excrement of human intellect
> accumulating slowly and everlastingly
> depositing, like guano on the Peruvian shore[5]

—as Robert Bridges described it—might need Ehrmann's and Beaujour's "stirring up shit." But in fact, literary traditions and literary change are far too complex to be contained by any merely incremental concept. It would certainly be foolish to provoke Clio by regarding literature as a single class of works. No sooner are literature's sacred cows branded with the iron of definition than Apollo wants a new sacrifice, perhaps of goats.

There are also logical difficulties in asserting literature to be a class, as later chapters will try to show. One feels uneasy, Beardsley remarks, about the phrase "poor literature"—which indicates an honorific element in the term. But, he continues, literature is also connected with the concept of genres, since any work that belongs to a genre belongs in some sense to literature. And here is a difficulty. For we freely speak of *poems* as bad, and "if . . . every poem is a literary work, then 'literary work,' it would seem, is not honorific."[6] Although the reasoning could be closer, Beardsley is right to oppose the argument (of Colin Lyas and others) that literature is a purely normative term. From their argument, moreover, he interestingly notes in passing, "the alternative conclusion could be drawn that literature is not after all simply the class of literary works—since one of these terms is normative, the other not." This "escape," which Beardsley rejects without examination, seems an avenue worth exploring. When one considers the various senses of *literature*— "good writing," "edifying writing," "memorable writing," "great writing," "whatever is written," and so forth—and the various implied contrasts—"not subliterature," "not writing that tries and fails to be great," and so on—it is hard to think that the term refers to a single class.

Literature should not be regarded as a class at all, but as an aggregate. It is not what literary works have in common, but constitutes, rather, the cultural object of which they are parts. And by no means the only parts: we are not to think of works as like bricks forming a wall. Some of the literary object is highly structured, yet it is also flexible (as F. W. Bateson was fond of saying). Now it expands from the *Dunciad* into classical influences or epic conventions; now it contracts to "Maeotis sleeps" or the choice of "skulking" as an epithet for Truth. It also varies in a disconcertingly protean fashion, from time to time, place to place, reader to reader. It constitutes different things for different individuals and nations, and even different social groups or educational cadres.

To parts of this mass of writing (and oral literature), many groupings in various ways partly correspond, such as:
1. works currently considered literature
2. works formerly canonical
3. canonical passages
4. literary oeuvres
5. genres, subgenres, and similar groupings
6. works surviving in human memory
7. literary conventions, devices, motifs, and so forth
8. great classics
9. literary traditions
10. literary diction
11. the words that have occurred in literature.

Even if some of these groupings could be regarded as classes, this is plainly not true of all. Again, some of the groupings intersect or are included within another. But we can see intuitively that a single class including all of them would be an impossibility. To a large extent, they exist independently. A nonliterary word such as "phenylalanine" or "penstock" may occasionally occur in a literary work, without abrogating group 1 or 10. Technical manuals with many words not belonging to group 10 are still unlikely to belong to 1—or, indeed, to form any part of the literary aggregate. Each class, it seems, has its own validity, its own appropriate applications. In evaluation the aggregate is normally thought of as works (group 1 or 2) or oeuvres (group 4). When a brief passage is discussed, however, it may be referred to some other class, such as 3, 7, 9, or 10. An essay by Montaigne will not always be primarily considered in relation to the symmetrically ordered *Essais;* an Elizabethan sonnet "sequence" can legitimately be treated as a collection of love lyrics, a long poem in quatorzains, or an embodiment of Petrarchism.

This is not to say that such groupings have equal explanatory power, or that it makes no difference which we favor. If we make a habit of considering the aggregate in terms of literary diction (group 10), we are likely to opt for a "language concept of literature."[7] Determining literature's extent then resolves itself into distinguishing (or not) between literary and nonliterary discourse. But if we think mainly of works (groups 1, 2, and the like), we shall probably adopt a broader art concept taking other elements besides language into account; or a concept based on fiction; or a value concept. It is mainly in works, not in words, that literature embodies values.

It cannot have been to deny this, surely, that Northrop Frye made his famous affirmation, "Literature is not a piled aggregate of 'works,' but an order of words."[8] Still, the dictum is not a very happy one. When we read literature, what we read are groups of works, or works, or parts of works: not words. True, critics may be much more than readers. But what they study comes into existence for them through readings of works. Most of these works have, to be sure, a rhetorical order, an order of words. But some have a sublexical order of sounds (metrical or other), and others—such as Ian Hamilton Finlay's concrete poems, or Ernest Vincent Wright's lipogrammatic novel without *e*'s—have an order of letters. In still other works, notably in probable report novels, the words may be so indifferent, so little organized in a literary sense, that they could be extensively replaced without disordering or changing the work. In *Act without Words,* words are absent altogether. Yet an idea of literature that excluded Beckett's play would carry its own minimalism to deficiency. (Nor could the missing discourse be supplied merely by invoking the notion of side-text.)[9] Many such cases become problematic, if we identify literature, as the structuralists do, with its discourse. It is better to allow that literary order need not inhere primarily in words. Discourse is an order of words, but literature is an order of works.

Those who think of literature purely as language or "discourse" face a dilemma. They are obliged to exclude novels from literature (if literary discourse is distinctive), or else (if it is not) to deny literature's existence as a distinct entity. For a realistic novelist may choose to put little or no effort into selecting or forming his language, but concentrate instead on forming the imitated life. In certain documentary genres, indeed, the words may be the writer's only in a very weak sense. Considered merely as discourse, without reference to any integrated work, literature is not always distinguishable from other writing. Understandably, then, those loyal to modern fiction have preferred to resolve the dilemma by the bold course of assassinating literature. Thus, criticism's recent concentration on prose fiction is indirectly linked with rejections of the concept of literature.

Similar problems arise with individual literary genres. Their extent, too, is problematic; their existence, likewise, has the complexity of historical development. And we find the same contemporary impulse to deny their validity. This is no coincidence. Indeed, the so-called central concept of literature practically identifies—or confuses—the literary aggregate with the class of genres.[10]

According to the central conception, "literature" refers to a certain group of genres, whose exemplars are therefore by definition literary, at least in aspiration. These central genres comprise the poetic kinds, the dramatic, and some of the prose kinds. The canon has varied a good deal, but has always included satire, for example, and fictional narrative. Round this nucleus spreads a looser plasma of neighboring forms: essay, biography, dialogue, history, and others. They are, so to say, literature *in potentia*. By criteria that seem to vary from kind to kind, a history, perhaps, or a philosophical work will come to be singled out as belonging to literature. This is without prejudice to the remaining, nonliterary, histories, which may enjoy a high reputation in their own field. Farther still from the nucleus lie those technical specialized kinds in which it is hard to imagine a literary work occurring. Modish talk about cut up *textes* cannot conceal the fact that uncut plumber's manuals, telephone directories, or treatises on Boolean algebra are never regarded as literary works—not even as worthless attempts at literature. Some great works that are undeniably part of our literature stand outside the nuclear genres and constitute partial anomalies. But the central conception has obvious intuitive force.

Literature as Fiction

The conception has commonly been developed by presupposing fixed historical kinds at the center, and by asking what these have in common. A plausible answer is "fiction." It should not be thought, however, an easy answer. Aristotle's theory that fiction is a characteristic of literature was for centuries lost sight of, while literary studies were the province of grammarians. Only after a long, painful course of difficult thought and sharp controversy was the idea that fiction differs from falsehood as well as from truth arrived at. Not until Sidney do we reach a full defense of poesy's ideal truth, and even then it is couched in enigmas—as that the literary artist "nothing affirms, and therefore never lieth."[11] More recently, fiction has often been regarded as a defining characteristic of literature. Bennison Gray makes it the sole basis. And Tzvetan Todorov—although, to be sure, he sees fiction as "one of the properties of literature rather than its definition"[12]—hammers the idea out so finely as to extend it to nonfiction: a true story can be viewed " 'as if' it were literature." But it may turn out that fiction is not so distinct a concept, or not so related to literature, as to settle its definition very firmly.

　　Attempts have been made to distinguish precisely between fiction and nonfiction by applying Austin's theory of speech acts. This distinguishes between the locutionary act (utterance), the propositional act (including reference and predication), the illocutionary act (asserting, promising, and so forth with respect to the proposition), and the perlocutionary effect upon the recipient. The speech act theorists separate fiction and nonfiction not at the locutionary level (by grammatical rules) but at the propositional and subsequent levels. The distinction is supposed to reside: (1) in fiction's suspension of the "propositional-act and the illocutionary-act rules of non-fiction," such as its restriction of reference to real existents; and (2) in fiction's obligation to pretend to perform a real propositional and illocutionary act—or to report that someone else performed it.[13] Literary discourse, they say, has mimetic force alone.

　　This line of argument is not without taxonomic attractions. It seems at first to achieve a clean division between an extended literature—in which, for example, propositions are asserted—and a central literature, which only imitates their assertion. Expository prose has included some great literature: no fit reader would deny the profound literary value of Ruskin's *Stones of Venice,* say. But he would not wish, either, to question its real practical value as art history—any more than he would question the value of Pater's art criticism. Or again: suppose that an essay, on the borderline, has gone beyond purporting to imitate the speech of someone arguing persuasively and has actually set the argument out and engaged in real persuasion. Then it will gain, perhaps, real propositional, assertive illocutionary and perlocutionary value, but it will lose the status of central literature.

However, these attempts to apply speech act theory do not take us far. This is partly because of the limitations of the theory itself, which uses a rather simplistic model of speech. (The different acts are not really independent.) But in part—and this is what we need to notice—the reason is that the fictional genres resist definition. Distinction 1 looks solid. But it is only a permissive rule. Nothing obliges the writer of fiction to dispense with reference. Trollope may set *The Warden* in Barsetshire, but Dickens sets *Oliver Twist* in London. As for distinction 2, it fails to apply to all cases. Many works in the central genres contain propositions really asserted by the authors. As the example of Whitman would be enough to show, didactic statements *in propria persona* find a not inconsiderable place even in poetry. In former ages, indeed, the didactic function of literature was so central that Beardsley's "difficult examples" made up a large part of the aggregate. *Piers Plowman,* Chaucer's *Parson's Tale, The Faerie Queen:* all have extensive passages meant to inform or persuade in good earnest.[14] And even after we have allowed for the distinction between writing and use (intention and uptake, creation and practical application), the real illocutionary force of certain literary expressions of love, public poetry, and the like remains uncanceled. To relegate works with this practical bearing to extended literature would deprive the central genres of all but their least serious or least engaged representatives. Again, genres such as epithalamium and epitaph have social functions of another kind. As occasional or epigraphic, their exemplars form parts of ceremonies or monuments and share their actual force. An Elizabethan wedding was made more complete as a social event by its spousal song. Third, and conversely, mimesis is by no means confined to the central genres. Many sorts of discourse have a fictive element. Todorov instances myths, and case histories that include patients' "memories"; and one might add liturgies, with their many poetic passages. Yet the larger liturgical sections (at any rate the Marriage Service) beyond question qualify as perlocutionary and even performative. It seems that central literature is not so distinct after all.

Perhaps in response to these difficulties, some have exchanged the idea of literary genres for the weaker notion of literary discourse. Todorov, who denies to literature any structural basis, goes so far as to speculate that "each type of discourse usually referred to as literary has non-literary relatives which resemble it more than do other types of literary discourse."[15] There is a truth in this idea, which derives from the Russian formalists Tynjanov and Shklovskij, and to which we shall return. We may agree that, for example, certain lyric kinds have affinities with prayer. And certain prose narrative kinds could be related to history or biography, certain subgenres of satire to the real-life hoax.[16] But such affinities do not obtain at the level of literary organization, so much as at the level of discourse. Any two neighboring or contrasting literary types (relations discussed in Chapter 13) have a far closer mutual relation in terms of genre than either has with a nonliterary type—even one from which it draws its formal material. In any event, to talk of types as Todorov does is in effect to concede that literature has a structural basis, if not the one traditionally recognized. Theories based on a terminology of "texts" and "discourse" offer at best merely rhetorical solutions. Any texts whatsoever can be treated as literary discourse, but not all can be treated as literary works.

The Changing Paideia

A different challenge to the idea of central genres has arisen from controversies about the educational canon. E. D. Hirsch delivers it most strongly: "literature" in its modern sense is a comparatively recent aberration, Victorian in origin; the earlier absence of a single term reflected the concept's lack of unitary force; and the concept itself is based on historically local assumptions about the privileged character of aesthetic criteria. Although Hirsch is obviously innocent of any Frankish rage for disorder, or wish to assassinate literature, he would like to persuade us to abandon the nineteenth-century (and New Critical) concentration on aesthetic aspects and to recognize the extraliterary, nonintrinsic bases of value. In practice this means that we should emphasize moral or instrumental values once again, desegregating the central genres and welcoming the "pedagogical expansion of literature."[17] There can be no question about the seriousness of these issues, nor about the need to view them in broad perspective. And we may have a good deal of sympathy with Hirsch's immediate aims. But an even longer historical view might not discover that literature has developed quite as he supposes.

For one thing, the recency of "literature"[18] does not prove the absence of a unitary term for the central genres earlier. They were referred to in the Renaissance as "poesy." This term was not at all equivalent to "poetry" in the modern sense that contrasts with "prose": "It is not rhyming and versing that maketh Poesy: one may be a poet without versing." Thus, Sidney frequently refers to prose writers (Plato, Xenophon, Heliodorus, Sannazaro, More) as writers of poesy, and similarly to prose works of various kinds that are characterized by fiction or imagination or "feigning" (the *Cyropedia,* "an absolute heroical poem"; *Amadis de Gaule,* "which God knoweth wanteth much of a perfect poesy").[19] It was a common position: Sidney shared it, for example, with Minturno.[20] Indeed, several of the systematic literary theories of the Renaissance, such as Scaliger's, discuss fictional prose under the head of *poesia.* The altered nomenclature that Hirsch notes cannot have signaled the first emergence of the unitary concept. Perhaps the nineteenth-century change rather indicates a reaction to the temporarily overextended concept that underlay Augustan literature, with its extreme georgic or didactic emphasis.

The extent of literature—that is, of poesy—was controversial in the Renaissance, too, however. Patrizi, Scaliger (with certain reservations), and many others took an inclusive view: literature extended to a whole *paideia* or curriculum of learning. Minturno held that philosophers such as Empedocles and Lucretius wrote poesy. On the other side, rigidly Aristotelian-Horatian theorists so defined the genres as to seal them off from extended literature.[21] It was a debate not unlike our own. Except that the different, and shifting, relations of Renaissance prose and verse kinds, the different views of didacticism, the different values: all these differences meant that the boundaries of literature were not then the same as those that critics of the present century dispute.

The recent phase of the controversy has taken a distinctly ideological form. This does not always receive acknowledgment in the United States when the expansion of "literature" is accepted as a "natural" return to a "more venerable, undifferentiated usage under which 'literature' covers everything worth preserving in written form, whether or not it has artistic merit."[22] In practice, expanded literature is far from everything worth preserving in written form (which would presumably include, for example, registers of births). Nor on the other hand does it seem in the main to add many works worth preserving for very long. Little of "the best that is known and thought in the world" comes into university courses on Women in Literature that was not already within literature's unexpanded limits. One should not expect it to. The point of thematic curricula is not to enlarge literature, but to restructure it and so challenge its values. This may be justified. The intrinsic criticism of the nineteenth century neglected ethical questions to which our own century has rightly reverted. The new *paideia* thus finds its *raison d'être* partly in correcting earlier formalism, partly in accommodating militant minorities. Our purpose here cannot be to adjust claims, or judge whether "the Arnoldian notion of culture" (as something above politics and attainable by all) serves as "an instrument for the maintenance of American class structure."[23] But we need to notice that the extent of literature varies with cultural setting.

In Britain, for example, literature is not expanding in quite the same way. But then, the British *paideia* has always extended to moral and other nonliterary writing of a sort little studied in English courses in the United States during the earlier decades of this century. In several European countries, indeed, accession to the demand that literary studies should be politically relevant has narrowed rather than enlarged literature's limits. Far from including "everything worth preserving," it has confined literature to the last century or so, until European commentators have begun to speak of a flight from the past.[24] They also notice a lowering of aesthetic standards, which is not always justified by the other values of the writing now promoted. Our age has a great appetite for studies of writing that is hardly worth studying.[25] Thrillers, detective stories, science fiction, advertisements, pop poetry, pornography: these and other kinds of *Trivialliteratur* are accorded a weighty treatment that nevertheless avoids, somehow, questions of value. In fact, some critics openly express their greater interest in the typical than in the valuable. All this is not to deny a place to sociological and political studies of low culture. But to pass these off as literary criticism endangers the very cause by which they are inspired. Shall we in the name of antielitism deprive the people of their legitimate inheritance? Is their literature to be less than the best? If we are to replace the term "literature" by "letters," it would seem that we must reintroduce the old distinction between "letters" and "humane letters."

The Mutability of Literature

Such variations in *paideia* mask a greater difficulty in the concept of literature: namely, the instability of its generic structure. The genres counted central in one historical period are not necessarily the same as those central in another. This represents a deeper challenge to the unitary concept. Even those who feel sure about the present extent of literature must concede that it was thought something else last century, and something else again the century before. Under various names, literature has held its ground for a very long time, but the ground has changed a good deal. It seems that we must either accept an impoverished Higher Common Factor, a canonical "great tradition" common to all periods but comprising very few authors besides Eliot's single classic, Virgil, or else reject the concept of literature as void of permanent content.

To questions of canon we shall return in Chapter 12. Here we need only distinguish two sorts of generic mutability. One is the continual process whereby change in the population of an individual genre gradually alters its character. Epic was not quite the same after Blackmore's *Prince Arthur* and by no means the same after *Paradise Lost*. From time to time, however, a second sort of farther-reaching alteration disturbs the interrelations of several whole genres. Thus, the familiar essay counted as a central genre in the nineteenth century, as did the closely related sketch form. But now Beardsley can say (wrongly, but not unintelligibly) that works of the genre represented by *Aes Triplex* are "not literary works."[26] The sermon, the "character," the scientific treatise, and the history (to mention obvious instances) have changed not only their own parameters but their relations to neighboring genres. Genres are thus doubly lacking in stability.

However, ambiguity of literary status is confined to a few genres, for the most part—especially letters and travel books, and nontechnical essays, histories, biographies, and philosophical and scientific treatises. These debatable lands have been thoughtfully surveyed by Graham Hough, who notes two ways in which nonfiction can "participate in the nature of literature." Its linguistic organization may give satisfaction independently, beyond the requirements of any practical purpose. Pater, Ruskin, and Gibbon, although sometimes read for information, themselves had mixed intentions and from the first gave aesthetic pleasure too. Alternatively the original purpose may have become obsolete. Browne's botany and Burton's medicine being no longer valuable (let us suppose) in a practical or scientific way, we are free to recategorize and to enjoy them for their intellectual qualities, their poetic vision, their alterity, or perhaps merely their quaintness. In this way the boundary can change by a sort of negative entropy. So long as the works seemed practically useful, they were not literature; when they ceased to function as treatises, they had a chance of coming to literature by default.

The readership (actual and imagined) is fairly decisive at the outer edge of the peripheral genres. It is commonly with the *selective* biography and with the *nontechnical* essay that ambiguity arises. Few would regard a factual research biography as literature; few would deny that an essay for the general reader has a better claim. So with histories. The specialized monograph, say, on an aspect of local administrative history, presents no problem of taxonomy. But Syme's *Roman Revolution* establishes literary claims that our successors will surely feel drawn to recognize; held in dubitancy (it may be) only by its persistent claims to continued use by ancient historians. The two works may concur in being valuable, but in interest to general readers they diverge.

Readership, then, has a bearing on the range of illocutionary acts intended. With works in the central genres, the imagined readers may extend so far beyond any immediately identifiable social group that directly practical perlocutionary effects must in part be out of the question.

Recategorizing is also bound up with the interrelation of the genres. Changes in this bring many puzzling shifts between literary and nonliterary. The treatise, as we have seen, is now commonly relegated to nonliterature. But at one time the verse treatise, at least, had a much closer relation to the central genres, with which it might share the advantages of verse. Bennison Gray might object that verse was merely a memory device and as such irrelevant now to the definition of literature. But if it was once relevant it will always be so to the theorist. And in any case, verse is no mere external adjunct that can be ignored at will, but an interpenetrating organization touching all levels of the work. Whether Hawes' *Pastime of Pleasure*—with its informative exposition of grammar as well as its magnificent apostrophe of Time—was once literature through and through is a question we may never settle. But it certainly illustrates how far a work may cease to be literature. By an opposite change, other kinds of expository and narrative writing may grow more literary, as in Browne's *Hydriotaphia*. Such recategorization has been put down to supersession of the old ideas (or, at least, of the systems determining their conceptualization). But it probably has more to do with developments in the genres themselves. The kind of treatise Browne wrote has come to be seen as an essay, in which form personal coherence and style of address may qualify a work as peripheral literature. In the same way, many would now agree that Pepys' *Diary* and Boswell's *London Journal* belong to literature. But to begin with they would not have seemed on that footing at all, not even potentially. This is partly due to the increased interest such sources of information acquire with age. But there is another reason: namely, that autobiographical writings, which enjoyed very little public esteem, formerly had a different relation to the central genres.

The question naturally arises: How free are we to recategorize at will and how far may we be prompted by inherent aesthetic qualities distinguishing the peripheral works concerned? Georg Lukács supposed that additional coding systems allowed the *De Rerum Natura* or the *Divina Commedia* to continue to communicate some "poetic form of conceptual rightness," some truths, even after their scientific content ceased to be tenable. However that may be, any valid recategorization must find warrant in features objectively attributable. Browne's literary qualities have not been invented arbitrarily: such as they are, *Hydriotaphia* always exhibited them. Here it has been customary to introduce the idea of style to supply the inherent qualities needed for validity. But we need not agree with Bennison Gray's view of style as an empty concept to see that invoking it in this way will not do. Literature is not written in a special language. If there were such, its use outside the central genres would be indecorous. Or, if literature involves a special use of language, the purpose of this goes far beyond the production of fine words. The literariness now discerned in some exemplars of the peripheral genres is far from depending on rhetorical qualities alone. The notion that obsolete nonfiction hangs on by its style cannot then be thought adequate. This is not what the best historians of style have meant by their emphasis. Indeed, in "Linguistics and Literary History" Leo Spitzer explicitly affirms that "language is only one outward crystallization of the 'inward form.'" If the "outward form" is really valuable, something of the "inward form" must qualify too. Thus, it is not merely for their style that we read Raleigh's *History* and Donne's sermons—still less the Authorized Version.

There is a danger, in fact, of false recategorization. An interpretation that ignored the Bible's spiritual challenge and put it with other works in cadenced prose "to be read as literature" would quite falsify its character. It is not that declining practical value leads to uncertain status, allowing works to be included in literature on the strength of their stylistic imaginativeness. The inclusion of works in literature need not at all mean that their practical illocutionary force has been nullified. The Bible's general authority may have weakened. But a good reader will sense its claims and recognize (for example) when promises are being made, even if he chooses—as he might have chosen in 1611—not to respond. The most far-reaching intellectual change cannot make a nonfictional work fictional. Even if Raleigh's *History* were entirely superseded—even if every bit of information in it were proved false—it would remain obstinately unmimetic.

The special case of found poetry (which seems to amount to recategorization at will) is not really an exception. True, such writing may alter the force of some of the original illocutionary acts. But it does not do so merely by the change of function. In actuality a perceived resemblance between nonliterary and literary material is also involved. Found poetry is thus a form of minimalist art, somewhat akin to that of Duchamp's museum pieces, which depends for its effect on concealed mimesis.

Language Concepts

Some of these difficulties might be resolved by a more considered formal approach. In its earliest, belles-lettristic version, the language concept posited a distinct literary dialect, including special dictions in poetry and fine (or at least idiosyncratic) style in prose. This is not a vacuous notion. It applied quite well to a great part of literature, especially but not only poetry, up to Swinburne and the early Yeats, to Doughty and even to some of Conrad. But we now value some earlier and many later writers to whom the concept is inapplicable. As we have seen, it does not work even with a central genre such as the report novel. This problem, together with modern dislike of poetic diction and alembicated prose, has led theorists to abandon the language concept altogether, or else to reformulate it in quite new ways.[27] Thus, Beardsley proposes "substantial" implicit meaning as a condition of literariness. But—Lyas points out—nonliterary speech acts may carry great weights of implicit meaning, whereas literary language may be very literal. (Large parts of *Chevy Chase*, or of *Rasselas*, mean just what they say.) Beardsley may mean to include a larger ordonnance beyond the merely grammatical and locally rhetorical, or he may even refer to the capacity to arouse imaginative response. At all events, both these possibilities are helpful. We need them in order to move beyond the cruder versions of the language concept, such as that which underlies Sartre's contrast between a utilitarian prose that *uses* words and a poetry whose words are "opaque"—substantive rather than significative.[28]

Only the broadest sense of implicit meaning could apply to a probable report novel whose effort bypasses or neglects considerations of style. In many modern novels the language is insignificant or "transparent," so that foregrounding is rare, and for the most part we look through the words to the narration—the primarily ordered level of organization for readers of such works.[29] As Wellek and Warren put it, "novelists may use words as signs." The sort of analysis of style that yields fruit with Jane Austen or Henry James would be difficult with the art-sentences of Hemingway or the heavy efforts of Dreiser, let alone the nonstyle of some of their successors. In such works it is not the language that carries implicit meaning. Consequently, we may have to modify our idea of literary art to allow for works in which stylistic organization is relatively perfunctory. The art that counts in a prose writer such as Lawrence is an art of imaginative ordonnance, presenting a persuasive, perhaps mythic vision—however fumbling and clumsily sloppy his language may be. This is arguably a rhetorical art (*inventio* and *dispositio*), but not in the sense of "rhetoric" now current. In a comparable way, writers outside the fictional genres can impart a literary experience—or, at least, an experience similar to literature's—of imaginatively ordered vision.

Still, it would be very difficult to make a convincing case for including many of the works that we cherish as literature, purely on the basis of their literary art.

Normative Concepts

In an attempt to improve the art concept, Colin Lyas proposes a list of aesthetic qualities (compactness, perceptiveness, and so on) that if present in eminent degree should qualify a work as literature.[30] And one could add other qualities, such as unusual agreement between constituent elements. These criteria are frankly normative. But normative concepts are surely indispensable in doing justice to extended literature.

Perhaps, even, it might be counted sufficient if a work gives aesthetic pleasure to some educated general readers. The work would not then belong, indeed, to "that species of composition, which is opposed to works of science, by proposing for its *immediate* object pleasure, not truth,"[31] but to the wider grouping that gives pleasure without proposing it as the primary object. "Aesthetic pleasure" needs comment. Christopher Butler notices its awkwardness as a term—too broad when it extends to word games, too narrow when each work has a different, proper pleasure. Definition of the pleasure would be an impossible, though delightful, task. But we have to think of it as extending to profound evocations of moral values, as well as to the high pleasure of very rapid satisfaction of epistemological desire. A great work of science can sometimes give even a lay reader an excitement that is hard to distinguish from imagination's leap on first reading a great poem. On the other hand, literary theory of the past decade has shown growing interest in the reader's specifically literary response. The possibility opens up of exploring the ways in which many distinct kinds of pleasure, perhaps corresponding to the literary genres, are recognized. Several important papers by Hans Robert Jauss have drawn attention to the distinctive pleasurable experiences of reading various genres.[32] This approach, a congenial one to me, seems promising in terms of results. It is surely on the scale set by Jauss that there is most hope of agreement about literary pleasures.

These criteria are subjective. But then individual subjectivity by no means invalidates literature's distinct existence as a social object. Denying the validity of literature as an aesthetic category does nothing to redress the balance of *utile* and *dulce*. Nor, on the other hand, can we dispense with value judgment in order to secure a "scientific" theory. Value judgment is part of the experience of literature that theory has to give an account of. Admittedly, it is awkward that value judgments must precede description, in that the writing to be analyzed—that is, worth analyzing as literature—must first be selected. But they also follow description, so that the theorist faces an organic situation. And the measure of agreement on value, across the ages, is impressive. At the same time, we need to recognize that no adequate account of literature could ever be based on the normative criteria of a single age. Literature is not merely a few great works of "ageless" appeal: "Parnassus has its flowers of transient fragrance, as well as its oaks of towering height, and its laurels of eternal verdure."[33]

Properly understood, the normative concept implies that what is regarded as literature must vary with values, and ultimately with views of the world.[34] If anything, this recommends the concept to those who have observed literature's actual variety through the ages. For those with fantasies of defining an immutable literature, it rules the concept out. But these fantasies are peopled with chimeras. Theorists who try to disengage from normative criticism either make literature implausibly extensive (like the structuralists), or else (like the New Critics) narrow it to short works in the central genres as these are now conceived. Normative criteria are inescapable if criticism is either to answer or to challenge society's needs.[35] Not that the social responsibility need be immediate or crudely interpreted in terms of a single generation's expediencies. Even so, it entails limitations of view, and these must from time to time be compensated.

This applies with especial force to extended literature. No doubt the value of extended "great literature" lies precisely in its long-term human significance. Such a status is not to be conferred lightly or by arbitrary regrouping. Yet it has been conferred on very various works. Extended literature varies rather widely, in fact. It exhibits less continuity and mutual coherence than literature of the central genres.

Taxonomic Problems

The taxonomic problem seems intractable. Multiple standards evidently qualify works as literature. "Some things are literature simply by virtue of being fiction ... while other things, non-fiction, only become literature by being particularly good."[36] If a work fails to get in as "fictional discourse" it can always try again as "the best that is thought or said." Besides fiction, and excellence, we have to think of a third sort of qualification, on the grounds of authenticity, or greatness. As we have seen, this has led some critics to recast the concept of literary art in an extremely general way. Most baffling of all, perhaps, membership of a central genre in itself constitutes a fourth qualification, and yet the canon of central genres can change historically. And to uncap all, there is the ever-present possibility of recategorization. Fiction, nonfiction with aesthetic qualities, human documents, intentionally generic writing: what definition could embrace all these? None, I venture to answer. Not even "textuality" can be thought a defining characteristic, as the case of oral literature, transmitted by creative performance, is sufficient to show.[37]

All serious attempts at definition have worked by allowing only one qualification (usually fiction, or art) and consequently by rejecting as unqualified large parts of what has traditionally been regarded as literature.

This is true even with the central genres. Todorov clearly recognizes as much when he decides against the legitimacy of literature as a structural category. He reflects that it has been given two independent definitions, based on different groupings: fiction (the Aristotelian definition) and poeticality of language. "Each definition can account for a great number of works usually called literary, but by no means for all . . . They are admittedly linked by mutual affinities, but not by mutual implication."[38] As we have seen, Todorov turns to considering the structural affinities of central genres with nonliterary genres, and so to denying the integrity of literature. But his interesting reflections might have taken another and more constructuve direction, had he thought that difficulties similar to those he describes are encountered at every turn in attempts to define the literary genres themselves.

Every genre, too, has multiple distinguishing traits, which however are not all shared by each exemplar. If literature is a genre, the idea of defining it is misconceived.[39] For, as I shall argue, the character of genres is that they change. Only variations or modifications of convention have literary significance.

This is not to say that literature cannot be identified. Certainly I should wish to avoid defeatism (or historical relativism) in this regard. Indeed, what a society chooses to consider as literature may be a judgment upon it. But theory has to take the historical variation into account.

Such considerations have led some to compare literature's mode of existence to that of an institution. "The concept of a literary work is dependent upon there being human institutions (of which indeed critics have become an integral part), governing its production, and guaranteeing its relationship to human purposes. We only know that a literary work has been produced if these institutional features come into play."[40] Literature conceived as a genre corresponds quite closely to the literary "institution" accompanying and fostering its tradition. Nevertheless, genre and institution are distinct. And the generic account may be more inward. So when we compare varieties of religious experience, we do this in terms of liturgical tradition and doctrinal beliefs, rather than mere affiliation to a denominational institution. The institutional concept may usefully encourage a sense of literature's ramifying social responsibilities. But it is also worth noting that the institution is not the source of literature's value.

Whether or not literature is a genre, general questions about it undeniably involve questions about the nature and extent of individual genres and about their mutual relations. To these we shall now turn. Not that individual genres are fixed or definable, either. But at least they can often be identified. And their more manageable scale may allow us to clarify something of their mode of existence—something of what it means (or ought to mean) to speak of literature as a genre.

2. Ancient Misapprehensions

Every work of literature belongs to at least one genre. Indeed, it is sure to have a significant generic element. For genre has quite a different relation to creativity from the one usually supposed, whereby it is little more than a restraint upon spontaneous expression. Rightly understood, it is so far from being a mere curb on expression that it makes the expressiveness of literary works possible. Their relation to the genres they embody is not one of passive membership but of active modulation. Such modulation communicates. And it probably has a communicative value far greater than we can ever be directly aware of.

Genre and Communication

To see how this may be, consider the form of existence of a literary work. It is the record of a specialized speech act. That is, its author communicates it in part much as a speaker might express himself, by a system of shared but more or less unconscious and unformulated grammatical rules, and in part by specialized literary conventions. The grammatical rules are similar to, but not necessarily identical with, Saussure's *langue*. Thus, from one point of view a literary work resembles the individual *parole* of ordinary speech. As with *parole,* its contingent and unique communication depends upon and embodies a previously shared system—which, however, it modifies, initiating new departures that in turn become available as conventions or material for further literary *paroles*. But there is an obvious difference between everyday and literary communication. This difference, which is so considerable as to limit the usefulness of the linguistic analogy, stems from literature's greatly extended repertoires of forms. They include not only the forms of grammar, but every feature that has in any manner whatsoever been made to serve as a literary (or antiliterary) convention. Potentially, indeed, they include an entire cosmos of forms, for there is no distinguishable feature of the world, nor of the language used to imitate or express it, whose concept may not be conventionalized and so contribute to literary communication.

Why should literature be so elaborately conventional? There is no satisfactory explanation in terms of ornamental deviation from some hypothetical directness; or of obfuscating displacement; or of inertia of custom; or of crafty elitism. Remove all these "causes" and still literature, if it is to exist at all, will require highly wrought codes.

It may help to introduce an idea from communication theory. The literary artist can be thought of as using a nonreversible communication link, like a speaker with a megaphone, say, or Roland at Roncesvalles. Now we know that a unidirectional link, since it offers no chance for questions or corrections, calls for increased "redundancy" in the message. By redundancy—a somewhat misleading term—is meant that property of communication systems "which arises from a superfluity of rules, and which facilitates communication in spite of all the factors of uncertainty acting against it."[1] Individual redundancies, such as the repetitions in phone conversation, pop poetry, and oral literature, are locally superfluous so far as information content goes. But they are necessary in the long run if the message as a whole is to be received, in spite of noise, inattention, and other impediments. Where the amount of redundancy needed can be quantified, we find that it varies widely with the situation of utterance. In particular, shared context makes a great difference. It may in itself have enough communicative power to allow fundamental grammatical rules to be dispensed with, without loss of intelligibility—as when a librarian checking a wrongly stamped book says, "This loan was renewed . . . tomorrow!"[2] If situational context matters so much, it seems that literary communication, which characteristically lacks a real situation, must work at a crippling disadvantage.

Admittedly, written language introduces certain extra rules that compensate in part. And these are often adequate for nonliterary communication. But then, it takes place in situations of utterance that are real and even in the main foreseeable, if not directly and immediately personal. For example, scientific discourse ordinarily finds scientific readers of a particular level of specialization and a known historical stage of knowledge, who really expect from it information of a narrowly defined and predictable sort. Literary works, however, commonly lack even this attenuated actuality of situation. Or if at first they are topical or occasional, the immediate situation will eventually lose communicative value when the bright local references become inaccessible and dull, under the obscuring smoke of time.

What enables literature to survive against these odds are its special re-dundancies. These make up a greatly extended *langue,* which supplies the deficiency of actual situation in two main ways. First, it provides a situa-tion of *literary* context; second, it reinforces the signal system with addi-tional coding rules. These additional codes sometimes replace codes of or-dinary language, as is obvious in the poetry of Cummings, where we may find such "ungrammatical" diction as "the of an it ignoblest he."[3] But often they supplement the ordinary rules of grammar, without subtract-ing from them. Indeed, literary communication need not involve any special conventions at the grammatical or even the lower rhetorical level. (As for poetic diction, although it may seem comparable to technical jargon, it is not really specialized in the same way. After all, it aspires to be the best part of language.) What literary coding always does is to confirm the work itself as well as its message, not so much maximizing the efficiency as the integrity and the pleasure of its communication. Thus, the effort of attention may be eased by conventions involving al-ready familiar features (the formulas of oral literature; stock characters) or by reiteration (rhetorical schemes of repetition; refrains; thematic parallels). Or the writer may introduce confirming patterns, moral and other, as in the accompaniment of sense by sound and rhythm (melo-poeia, assonance, poetic syntax). The same feature may have many differ-ent conventional functions simultaneously. And every convention the writer uses ultimately bears upon his meaning, properly considered (which is not the same as his semantic meaning). Thus, the notion that "formal" patterns such as meter make no difference to meaning rests on a misconception of literary communication.[4] To put this differently, liter-ary redundancy is an "unnecessarily" continuous aptness in manifold ways to the writer's realized intention.

Of all the codes of our literary *langue,* I have no hesitation in propos-ing genre as the most important, not least because it incorporates and or-ganizes many others. Just how many other codes are generically articu-lated remains uncertain. Probably far more than we are aware of. At any rate there is no doubt that genre primarily has to do with communica-tion. It is an instrument not of classification or prescription, but of meaning.

However, language and communciation systems offer only limited analogies for literature. Both analogies can easily be pressed too far. Perhaps we can see this happening when Jan Trzynadlowski attempts an account of genre exclusively in terms of information theory. Genre-linked features serve not only as information, he suggests, but as "instructions" for interpreting other coded information. The generic element is more than a mere result of formal components, then: it is a goal-directed "program" of interpretation, which shapes both local information and hermeneutic instructions. This hypothesis, interesting as it is (a brief summary cannot do it justice), shows the limitations of the analogy with communication systems. The communication theory model hardly provides for literature's formal values—for the valuing of "redundancy," or internal consistency, as a pleasurable end and as a means of communicating more than propositional "information." Moreover, it fails to allow for change, for the historical transformation of literature.[5] This is a serious defect. For to have any artistic significance, to mean anything distinctive in a literary way, a work must modulate or vary or depart from its generic conventions, and consequently alter them for the future. (Thibaudet was right when he said that "to create in accordance with one genre means to extend this genre"; and Croce was not *entirely* wrong.)[6] And about this innovating uniqueness, communication theory has little to say.

Every literary work changes the genres it relates to. This is true not only of radical innovations and productions of genius. The most imitative work, even as it kowtows slavishly to generic conventions, nevertheless affects them, if only minutely or indirectly. It will make one convention familiar and unambiguous, another easy and disgusting. Consequently, all genres are continuously undergoing metamorphosis. This, indeed, is the principal way in which literature itself changes. I shall mention some specific types of transformation of genre in later chapters. At present we need only notice that literary meaning necessarily involves modulations or departures from generic codes, and therefore, eventually, alterations of them. However a work relates to existing genres—by conformity, variation, innovation, or antagonism—it will tend, if it becomes known, to bring about new states of these genres. Perhaps this was part of Eliot's meaning: "What happens when a new work of art is created is something that happens simultaneously to all the works of art which preceded it."[7]

In itself, the dependence of literary meaning on generic types is a familiar idea, which received magisterial exposition in E. D. Hirsch's *Validity in Interpretation*. Meaning is such (the argument runs) that only determinate types can be communicated: "A verbal meaning is always a type since otherwise it could not be sharable. If it lacked a boundary, there would be nothing in particular to share; and if a given instance could not be accepted or rejected as an instance of the meaning . . . the interpreter would have no way of knowing what the boundary was." Hirsch's theory commands broad assent. We may not be fully satisfied, however, that he leaves us knowing enough about "intrinsic genre": the "over-arching notion" that he posits, between the exact meaning itself and the "vague, heuristic genre idea, with which an interpreter always starts."[8] Intrinsic and heuristic genres need to be explored more fully. And for this a good *point d'appui* might be their relation to genre in a more traditional sense: that is, the historical kinds and modes, about which so much has been written and about which, by now, some things are even known. These kinds and modes persist (I shall argue) in the literature of all periods, although in various ways at different times. Writers and readers of certain historical periods, for example, have ignored genre. But while doing so, they have unconsciously engaged in generic transactions all the same. In fact, ignoring genre has often meant passively accepting the conventions prescribed by custom or fashion. So medieval readers accommodatingly took allegory for granted—just as we tend to generalize, without much thought, naturalistic presuppositions and criteria appropriate only to a narrow range of novelistic genres.

The Relevance of Genre

Some think that genre theory is irrelevant, in that it fails to correspond to actual literary works. This opinion rests often on a misapprehension about genres. It assumes that they exist simply and immutably, that they are permanently established once and for all, so that they apply equally to all literature, before and after, past, present, and to come. Hence, that all genre theory has the same (lowish) value. But, as we have seen, genres are actually in a continual state of transmutation. It is by their modification, primarily, that individual works convey literary meaning. Frequent adjustments in genre theory are needed, therefore, if the forms are to continue to mediate between the flux of history and the canons of art. Thus, to expect fixed forms, immune to change yet permanently corresponding to literature, is to misunderstand what genre theory undertakes (or should undertake). The sequel must be dismay, when real genres are found to change and old accounts of their earlier states to be remote from newer literature.

At the same time, the charge of irrelevance is not without force. Much genre criticism really has been irrelevant in a damaging way. I do not mean merely that its descriptions have in the end been eluded by literature (that is inevitable with all criticism), but that it has failed to describe individual works even plausibly. Graham Hough is perfectly justified in holding that "by the middle of the eighteenth century, with the rise of new forms, especially of prose fiction, [genre legislation's] inadequacy to the actual literary facts became obvious."[9] As he clearly appreciates, however, it would be wrong to infer from this that the genres have no sound theoretical basis. To deny their existence as Stutterheim does, on the ground that attempts to describe them have failed, would be presumptuous as well as pusillanimous.[10] It would also be unjust: descriptions of genres have varied greatly in quality from age to age. The genre criticism of the period just after Croce was vacuous enough to justify all the skepticism of Wellek. But in our own time, this is no longer so. Much of our best criticism is taken up with matters of genre. Disparities between literature and its generic description can still, of course, be striking. And the limitation of even contemporary criticism to a small range of kinds must be regretted, since it is precisely variety of description and evaluation that genre theory has to offer as its main strength.[11] But the genres themselves do not cease to function just because some genre critics run short of ideas.

To confuse genres with their critical formulations is a serious error. Even the best descriptions cannot be identified with the genres themselves. For one thing, generic operations are partly unconscious. What reader is ever simultaneously aware of all he understands (to go no further than that) by "epic"? Even less are we conscious of our intuitive apprehensions of epic's more specific forms. For another thing, the changing and interpenetrating nature of the genres is such as to make their definition impossible.[12] Ben Jonson, himself a neoclassicist, is clear about this in the Prologue to *The Sad Shepherd*, where he defends comic-pastoral mixture. It would be wrong, he argues, to judge from a fixed idea of pastoral: "As if all Poesy had one Character: / In which what were not written, were not right."[13] The ideas of the genres must change with their actual operation in literature. We have also to remember that full accounts of individual genres have not even been attempted very often. Some periods, indeed, notably the Middle Ages, have passed without any considerable body of genre criticism. And "the embarrassing disparity between Augustan theory and practice" is notorious.[14]

Of all modern periods before our own, it is the Renaissance in which the most sustained development of genre theory can be discerned. Many ideas still discussed today derive from Renaissance Italian critics. Yet even their achievement, distinguished though it still seems, lacks depth and range. For the most part they concentrated on tragedy, comedy, pastoral, and romantic epic, ignoring many considerable genres altogether. True, J. C. Scaliger, the most powerful genre critic of his time, is a partial exception. He described more than a hundred genres, to say nothing of their subgenres. But even he wrote on few of these at any length, and he neglected the vernacular kinds.[15] About the sonnet, he has nothing to say; it was not an ancient form. Other Italian critics were slavishly Aristotelian (if the oxymoron is not too sharp). And as for the more modern, less historical theorists such as Antonio Sebastiano Minturno, who had ideas about emergent forms, they lacked Scaliger's range without matching him in depth. All the same, Renaissance insights into genre were sometimes penetrating. And they probably had much influence on the brilliant generic innovations that distinguish the period's literature.[16] Certainly there was close interaction between theory and practice both with tragicomedy and with pastoral drama.

Nevertheless, it would not be unreasonable to say that this most impressive body of genre criticism failed to come quite to grips with most literature, especially recent literature. It arrived at some interesting results, to which we shall return. But it cannot be regarded as having fairly tested the relevance of genre, once and for all.

Prescriptiveness and Inhibition

After the Renaissance, the next considerable body of genre theory was neoclassical. Both in France and in England, this neoclassical criticism is thought of as having been consistently and severely prescriptive in cast, which has given rise to the misapprehension that generic types are necessarily of that character. The misconception has proved inveterate. Even today, mention of the "rules" of genre is less likely to suggest communicative codes than arbitrary prohibitions. And of course we know that anything like normative criticism is to be rejected *tout à fait*. Is it not inhibiting, morally informed, challenging?

No one can dispute that much neoclassical genre criticism was crudely prescriptive. Not only the Rymers but the Rowes thought that "that way of tragicomedy was the common mistake of Shakespeare's age."[17] And although John Dennis' rules often crystallized intimate appreciations of contemporary literature, he could apply them with a somewhat chilling implacability: "Mr Cowley is certainly in the right in his Notes upon his *Davideis,* where he tells us, that God is to be introduced speaking simply."[18] If we agreed to fault *Paradise Lost,* we should still fear that so judicial a rule ("is to be") would sooner or later be used to damn some innocent portrayal of a God speaking subtly. Even Dryden and Johnson, who lived before or after the time of tightest prescription, and who are supposed to have defended literature against the rules, did so by way of exoneration. Johnson's overturning of the unities has been made much of; but in sitting light to them he is "almost frighted at [his] own temerity"[19] and at the same time beseeches us to make "some allowance for [Shakespeare's] ignorance"—hardly an excuse that would be thought necessary now, or proper.

But it is less clear just how the Augustan critics went wrong. Claudio Guillén attributes the unreality of neoclassical poetics to the assumption that "genres are sharply delimited objects 'out there.' "[20] However, this hypostatizing of genres may in practice be less destructive than two other errors of the neoclassicists. One is their belief that the genres are timelessly immutable. That delusion, which almost all the Augustan critics shared, had earlier afflicted the Ancients of the Renaissance *querelle.* These regarded the kinds "as Forms, which are always the same, which make no concessions to times or audiences, which impose upon the poet a strict obedience to unalterable rules."[21] On the other side, the Renaissance Moderns thought of the kinds as adaptable: art's universality resided in broad principles, not in particular generic forms. And Dryden, in this regard a later Modern, at times affirmed the mutability of genre rather boldly: " 'Tis not enough that Aristotle has said so, for Aristotle drew his models of tragedy from Sophocles and Euripides; and if he had seen ours, might have changed his mind."[22] Rules that could be revised in the light of infringements would stand a good chance of being unoppressive. But apparently the consensus view held by the Augustans was more rigid. Generic rules were fixed. New works had to obey old rules, or else prove themselves to embody some worthwhile additional kind, happily exempt from the old criteria.

The other great error of neoclassical genre theory was generalization from a narrow and inappropriate canon of genres. Especially, rules drawn from the genres of classical antiquity were assumed to apply to vernacular genres. This suited the revived classical forms well enough. But it had a disastrous effect on the criticism of medieval genres and their modern developments, from which we are only now recovering. When the classical epic rule calling for unity of action is applied to medieval romances, or even romantic epics, discriminating criticism is unlikely to result. For the rule of the medieval genre calls for interlaced multiplicity of action. This error, again, can be traced to the Renaissance. Minturno himself, broad as his sympathies were, was capable of dismissing the broken action of romance simply as a "vice."[23] In neoclassical criticism, however, this inappropriate prescriptiveness developed more confidently and went much further. Not only did critics cease to appreciate medieval literature but they lost sight of the very possibility that it might have genres and rules and a poetics of its own. When rules of the wrong genre are applied, they naturally seem arbitrary and oppressive.

But if we ask whether generic prescription is in itself necessarily objectionable, we may find it harder to agree. As the example of Dryden suggests, the critic's individual caliber may count for more than the degree of prescriptiveness that officially prevails. An Aristotle, a Scaliger, or a Johnson has the mind to observe and to judge soundly, whatever the rules. And to lesser critics, prescriptive rules may serve as continual reminders of the duty to evaluate—using proper criteria to do so. In any event, is it possible to dispense with prescription, even today? Modern theory and practice are wildly at variance in this respect. Theoretically, officially, prescriptive genre rules are now out. In actual practice, they continue to be enforced with scarcely abated rigor. Novels, for example, are quite commonly censured for defects of probability: a criticism that certainly implies normative ideas of genre. It is a rule of their genre that novels of a certain kind (but not other kinds) must maintain naturalistic probability.[24] And it is by applying this rule, this prescriptive rule, that critics have found fault with, say, the coincidences in Hardy's novels. When Peter Conrad condemns *Ranthorpe* as "a collection of essays in moral anatomy, literary criticism and pictorial analysis jostled together by a pair of lurid plots" he is invoking, surely, novelistic rules that exclude melodramatic plots and free mixture with the moral essay.[25] And similarly Q. D. Leavis writes that "Dickens's increasing powers as an artist incline him away from the melodramatic and even the theatrical . . . The true surprise in the novel [*Bleak House*] is a wholly novelistic one (not in the least theatrical or stagey but psychological and truly human." The exposure scenes of *Our Mutual Friend,* however, revert to an earlier manner: they are "theatrical nonsense."[26] Is this judgment unsound theoretically, just because it relies on prescriptive rules of genre? I cannot believe so. Such judgments are the stuff of criticism. Indeed, a proper defense of *Our Mutual Friend* would be couched in terms no less prescriptive than Mrs. Leavis', although it would assign the novel to a rather different sub-genre from that of *David Copperfield*. In sum, prescriptive genre rules are indispensable; without them, normative criticism of any sort would be impossible. Northrop Frye saw this, and was entirely consistent in attempting a theory that would be free not only of prescriptive rules but of evaluation itself. Consistent, but quixotic. Every aspect of literature—not least genre itself—is far too thoroughly imbued with values for any such theory to be practicable. And if it were, would it really be desirable?

The very mention of prescriptive genres will have raised specters of inhibited creativity. But these alarms are exaggerated. Even when enforcement of the neoclassical rules was at its most draconian, literature hardly dwindled away. Great writers have found a challenge in genre rules, while minor or invertebrate talents have been positively supported by them, as by armatures. As to inhibiting effects, it is impossible to prove the negative. But considering Swift's output, say, or Richardson's, or Wordsworth's, one is bound to feel that the burden of proof lies on the other side.

There are several reasons why even rigid prescriptive genre theories should be harmless. First, a writer can always have recourse to one of the many half-recognized semicanonical genres, which in any manageable theory remain largely undescribed. In the Renaissance, these included forms of dialogue, history, treatise, and parodic satire;[27] in the seventeenth and eighteenth centuries, description and English georgic in addition. Second, a writer is free to invent new kinds with rules of his own devising. And critics with an understanding of genre have welcomed such originality. Denham, Thomson, Collins, Crabbe: all invented strikingly novel "species" that were nevertheless acceptable to neoclassical critics. Johnson is not abandoning prescriptive genre when he writes that "every new genius produces some innovation, which, when invented and approved, subverts the rules which the practice of foregoing authors had established."[28] This is particularly true if the innovating genre addresses itself to some relatively unworked area of experience (such as notations of landscape in the eighteenth century). Thus, prescriptive genres encourage the writer to break new ground. He has a choice. He may go beyond the domain of established genres, or he may prefer variations within a familiar genre—but then must face progressively more detailed and demanding prescriptions for imitation.

But we should not think of prescriptive genres as harmless merely because their writ did not run far. Even in genres much legislated about, good critics have applied the rules with a certain reserve, or sense of deeper equities. They have left writers, in fact, with all the freedom that they could reasonably expect:

> Some beauties yet, no precepts can declare,
> For there's a happiness as well as care.
>
> (Pope *Essay on Criticism* 141–142)

(The wordplay in "happiness" is itself a decorous infringement; *ambiguitas* was not officially a quality of style.) In Pope's continuation, he positively recommends incorrectness, where deeper purposes require it: "Those oft are stratagems which errors seem" (l. 179). Generic rules, as he imagines them, almost form a recursive progression, whereby each successful breach of a rule itself becomes a new rule.

> If, where the rules not far enough extend,
> (Since rules were made but to promote their end)
> Some lucky LICENCE answers to the full
> Th' intent proposed, that licence is a rule.
> Thus Pegasus, a nearer way to take,
> May boldly deviate from the common track.
> Great wits sometimes may gloriously offend,
> And rise to faults true critics dare not mend;
> From vulgar bounds with brave disorder part,
> And snatch a grace beyond the reach of art,
> Which, without passing through the judgment, gains
> The heart, and all its end at once attains.
>
> (*Essay on Criticism* 146–157)

The *Essay* is not uncharacteristic of the best Augustan criticism, particularly as regards its distinction between higher and lower, or major and minor rules. With Pope's "if you must offend / Against the precept, ne'er transgress its end" (ll. 163–164) one might compare Dennis' severe *Reflections on "An Essay upon Criticism"*: " 'Tis equally the duty both of Ancients and Moderns, to break through a less important rule, when without that infringement a greater must be violated, or the great end of all the rules neglected."[29] Dennis counted the unities of time and place as minor rules of tragedy. His major rules included decorum, probability, and (more vaguely) the character of the various generic spirits— apparently, what we should call "mode." If he castigated Addison for breaking rules in *Cato,* he was just as ready to "show the absurdities with which he abounds through a too nice observing some of them, without any manner of judgment or discretion."[30] Even under the neoclassical regime of fixed prescriptive genres, rules were for breaking, a little. In accordance with the myth of liberation, some have celebrated doing away with these doubtful rules altogether. Historically, however, the liberation has never actually taken place. How could it? If it did, literary tradition and communication would cease.

Far from inhibiting the author, genres are a positive support. They offer room, as one might say, for him to write in—a habitation of mediated definiteness; a proportioned mental space; a literary matrix by which to order his experience during composition.[31] Claudio Guillén, who has developed similar ideas, suggests that the genres operate as problem-solving models. Instead of a daunting void, they extend a provocatively definite invitation. The writer is invited to match experience and form in a specific yet undetermined way. Accepting the invitation does not solve his problems of expression: "A form can never be 'taken over' . . . It must be 'achieved' all over again, from the start, with each single work."[32] But it gives him access to formal ideas as to how a variety of constituents might suitably be combined. Genre also offers a challenge by provoking a free spirit to transcend the limitations of previous examples. And there have been many instances where it directly supported original explorations in an even more intimate way. Renaissance controversies about the romantic epic provided the intellectual runway for such genre-conscious works as *The Faerie Queen* and *Don Quixote* to take off from.[33] In the same way, far from English "mongrel tragicomedy" barking in the face of contemporary criticism, as used to be said, in fact theorists discussed the mixture of comedy and tragedy by multiplication and separation of plots, before Shakespeare came on the scene. In *The Winter's Tale,* original as it is, he turned his attention to "problems of genre and structure debated with passion in the Italian polemic over Guarini's *Il Pastor Fido.*"[34] In our own time, the instances are more obvious: experimental fiction, *nouveau roman,* and theater of the absurd are all generic groupings, fashionable with reviewers, that have supported rather than threatened innovative writers, to say nothing of epigones.

Writers themselves, or the more thoughtful of them, agree on the advantage of genre. Some, like Wordsworth, have written studies of genres or poems in praise of them. If in no other way, they testify to this by practicing a craft of *imitatio,* basing their most original works on creative reinterpretation of predecessors in a genre. Thus, during the first English classicism, when the doctrine of imitation was elaborated, we find Shakespeare and Jonson, in some of their finest poems, publicly assuming in their readers a knowledge that this craft is being practiced. The paradox is only a superficial one—that the writer who cares most about originality has the keenest interest in genre. Only by knowing the beaten track, after all, can he be sure of leaving it. Or, as Eliot says, "true originality is merely development."[35] This is not just a way of putting it: in the realm of genre, revolution or complete discontinuity is impossible. An antinovel may seem to light out for completely new territory, but it requires the novel (and some other genres) for its own intelligibility. All this is not to say, of course, that writers are necessarily conscious of genre's support. But in practice they always need relevant generic models and directions of departure.[36] At the very least, they have to know which rules are worth breaking.

Obsoleteness

Literary change is sometimes said to have become so radical in our age that genre has lost its meaning. It has ceased to function, for the first time in literary history. Theorists may thus concede to genre an earlier relevance, but deny it any today. They insist on a discontinuity between contemporary literature and all that has gone before. According to Ihab Hassan, for example, form proliferates so rapidly in postmodern literature that "the history of artistic genres and forms becomes irrelevant"; and René Wellek, although adopting a less orphic stance, lends his learning to a view not dissimilar—namely, that genre study has declined because "in the practice of almost all writers of our time genre distinctions matter little: boundaries are being constantly transgressed, genres combined or fused, old genres discarded or transformed, new genres created, to such an extent that the very concept has been called in doubt."[37] But it would be wrong to suppose that generic transformation is peculiarly modern. Or rather, that modernism itself is new. In the dialectical progressions of literary history, there have been many times when the urge to go beyond existing genres has recurred.[38] To some extent, indeed, the tendency is perpetual. Boundaries have always been transgressed, genres have always been combined or discarded. This is something that Voltaire and Lord Kames, for example, already began to see.

Besides, what are those forms, exactly, whose history is supposed to be irrelevant? They always turn out to be the "fixed historical kinds." In themselves, these are of course bound to be inappropriate. When a critic persists in discovering the conventions of a historical kind outside their real limits, however plausibly, the result is like putting new wine into old generic bottles: it may produce a ferment of interest, but it shatters our confidence in the bottles. Overextending a critical type, as perhaps William Empson did in *Some Versions of Pastoral,* makes it in the end vacuous. What we have rather to do, in approaching recent literature, is to explore new groupings. But these will have taken their departure from earlier groupings. We are far less likely to find or to understand them if we abandon the study of genres.

The problem of continuity arises most often with prose fiction—the very part of literature that has come to dominate criticism. How can traditional genre theory have anything to say about forms so new and so various as those of "the novel"? But this needs to be put into perspective by recalling how genre has operated historically. Identifying emergent forms has never been easy. We think of mock epic, now, as a rather distinct genre, but we are at a remove from the creative moment. The earliest mock epicists and their critics would have been hard put to it even to distinguish the genre from burlesque. Why should we believe that contemporary fiction is any different? Novels are sometimes said to have a form quite different from that of other genres. But this seems a highly improbable, not to say provincial, view. In principle, any form that can be invented can be identified, just as any definition of it can be disproved by subsequent literature. No doubt most fictional genres have still to be identified. But that is not a very good argument for abandoning genre study.

To distinguish the types of contemporary fiction would be the work of another book. But this one is concerned with principles that at least have a bearing on the task. As we shall see, works of fiction may be grouped in several ways: by mode, for example, or with reference to various axes. There is even some validity to the obvious grouping by subject matter, as in the lazarine type (Dostoevsky's *House of the Dead,* Solzhenitsyn's *Cancer Ward,* Figes' *Days,* Bienek's *Cell*). Doubtless the more fundamental groupings will be debatable. But that hardly poses a new problem. Nor is the formal multiplicity entirely novel. "The novel," no longer new, has long included a diversity of types: picaresque, romantic, epic, comic, epistolary, reportorial, and others, all in combination with various "matters." Some types have always been elusive. Indeed, Nashe's *Unfortu-*

nate Traveller is still far more difficult to identify generically than many a modern work. It is more "open," so to say, than most thrillers bound for film adaptation, or than science fiction of the gothic, utopian, dystopian, spatial, temporal, or ESP types (subgenres as clear-cut as any in Augustan poetry).

Where novels mix older types, criticism already deals in terms of genre, up to a point. So Burgess' *Tremor of Intent* will be said to fail by vacillating between straight and burlesque espionage thriller, and Mailer's *Barbary Shore* to be unreadable because of its maladroit mixture of political treatise, diatribe, and thriller. This may not take us very far. It would not be enough to criticize Willingham's *Eternal Fire* for approaching burlesque Southern gothic without stabilizing a satiric mode; or Mann's *Doktor Faustus* for combining *Bildungsroman* with novel of ideas in an awkward proportion; or Highsmith's *They Who Walk Away* for departing too far from the crime, in the direction of the psychological novel; or Barth for using too little science fiction in *Giles Goatboy* to provide a vehicle for Varronian satire. Such superficial exercises in the Polonian manner would merely disguise rough guesses under knowing generic labels. But then, genre criticism is very much more than identification. Grouping allows the critic to interpret a work's individual contribution by discerning kindred forms and to evaluate it by distinguishing superior from inferior representatives of them. It allows comparison between similars. Thus, it would not at all do to liken *The French Lieutenant's Woman* simply to Sartre, since it mingles the philosophical or existential not with the political but with the historical novel. Adequate criticism is probably not practicable without reference to genre—although this may be far from obvious in the case of contemporary literature with its unnamed forms.

Naturally, new forms are hard to describe: it takes time to develop a critical language for exploring them. Thus, we might agree that a new genre of dystopic fiction was emerging, exemplified by Pynchon's *Crying of Lot 49* and *Gravity's Rainbow* and Vonnegut's *Cat's Cradle:* works adapting science fiction's assumption of familiarity to a new purpose, namely economical suggestion of intricate social structures presented in a satirical or alienated way. But we would have very few concepts with which to analyze this "mosaic fiction" or to describe its formal characteristics. Not until it had been more fully discussed critically would we have any firm idea as to whether its closest relations were with *Brave New World* and Menippean satire, or with collective realism and Dos Passos, or with some other grouping as yet obscure. Nevertheless, there exist many opportunities to begin such explorations of contemporary genres. Much of our best criticism, indeed, has already entered on these endeavors, without calling them genre studies.

Hierarchy and Conservatism

Another misconception about genre is that it entails a hierarchic and retrogressive social philosophy. This view has a plausible foundation in previous genre theory. There used once to be much rank ordering of the genres. Epic and tragedy, perhaps, would compete for the position of honor, with comedy and satire winning lower places, and pastoral being relegated to a humbler rank still: "Can'st write the comic, tragic strain, and fall / From these to pen the pleasing pastoral."[39] But theorists are wrong to suppose that there was ever a fixed hierarchy of genres. On the contrary, as we shall see in Chapter 11, the generic community evinced an almost hectic social mobility. This was possible because complete rank orderings were seldom worked out. Patrizi's ambitious attempt to order a large group of genres is by way of being a rare exception.[40] More typical were the paradigms of selected genres, such as the Wheel of Virgil, a scheme of only three modes (heroic, georgic, pastoral) correlated with style heights and corresponding to the divisions of feudal society.[41] This characteristically incomplete medieval *summa* can hardly have been very oppressive.

Nevertheless, it confirmed rather than challenged the established order. And it was tenacious. We can still trace its influence, probably, in Minturno's anxiety to separate dramatic characters of different rank and distribute them between high and low plots according to degree. (The *raison d'être* of the double plot was at first social decorum, rather than thematic development.) Even in more recent times, the link between genre and social decorum has persisted. Frye is not alone in detecting political bias in Arnold's cairn of generically cemented touchstones: "His demotion of Chaucer and Burns to Class Two seems to be affected by a feeling that comedy and satire should be kept in their proper place, like the moral standards and the social classes which they symbolize."[42] And a similar decorum governs our own media programming: some kinds of television plays are for peak viewing times, others are not.

But in all this there is no reason why genre theory should necessarily entail a fixed hierarchy of kinds. It is highly probable that the modern theorist would wish to revalue many traditional rank orderings. And why should we avoid the very ideas that help us to learn what values are implicit in our own unacknowledged schemes?

In any case, we should beware of dismantling the traditional hierarchies too eagerly. They are not as reactionary as they may look. In past ages, most of the greatest writers put their best efforts into the "highest" kinds, so that generic height acquired at the very least a certain *de facto* validity. To obliterate all such differences of value would be perilous indeed.

Moreover, genres may have a benignly conservationist influence, in that they partly resist period incorporation. Some of them, at any rate, embody values of very long standing, and they consequently may serve to offset the bias or oppression of a particular society. Here we need not accept the whole Braudelian doctrine of *longues durées*.[43] But we ought also to be a little skeptical toward easy correlations of genres with immediate social contexts. The relation is almost certainly far too complex to be explained by any simple model of "superstructure." However, we can be sure of one thing: the influence of genre is by no means automatically retrogressive. During the Renaissance, indeed, as Rosalie Colie did much to show, the study of genre positively assisted cultural transfer and the spread of *nova reperta*.[44] And, inversely, neglect of generic ideas earlier this century probably made modernist literature more obscure than it need have been, thus reducing its audience. Subsequently, the notion that established traditional genres were ideologically reactionary deflected many writers into using underground or experimental forms, so that they lost leverage without escaping incorporation in the literary establishment.[45]

I have argued that genre is ubiquitous in literature, as the basis of the conventions that make literary communication possible. It is thus relevant, in principle, to all literature, although the genre criticism of some periods has in fact perpetuated outmoded and irrelevant forms and applied them in inappropriately prescriptive ways. In particular, nothing about contemporary literature leads us to suppose that genre is now at last becoming obsolete—except that, as always, there is the perennial need to revise generic groupings yet again. What sort of thing is genre, then, to continue recognizable from period to period and yet always be changing? It is time to consider the nature of the grouping we call "genre."

3. Concepts of Genre

Genres are often said to provide a means of classification. This is a venerable error. It goes back to the ancient grammarians. And so fine a critic as Graham Hough can write that "in abstraction the theory of kinds is no more than a system of classification. It is given content and positive value by filling each of its pigeon holes with adequate description and adequate theory."[1] The likely concomitants of such a view are puzzlement whenever a work does not fit, vexation when partitions cannot be found, and despondency when the holes themselves shift. Fortunately, since the eighteenth century, alternative views of genre have gradually formed. From the mid-1700s, empirical and exploratory critics such as Blair and Kames were able to see that the genres have no clear dividing boundaries, and that membership of one by no means rules out membership of others. So Kames, ridiculing the chimera of definition, observes that "literary compositions run into each other, precisely like colours: in their strong tints they are easily distinguished; but are susceptible of so much variety, and take on so many different forms, that we never can say where one species ends and another begins."[2] Some have concluded that genre theory, being unhelpful in classification, is valueless. But in reality genre is much less of a pigeonhole than a pigeon, and genre theory has a different use altogether, being concerned with communication and interpretation. When that is recognized, genre's propensity to change may seem less upsetting. Of course, we need not abandon all thought of classification. If literature is generically organized, genres are likely to have some taxonomic application. But it turns out, as we shall see, to be unexpectedly limited. The main value of genres is not classificatory.

Class? Type? Family?

Indeed, genres are best not regarded at all as classes, but types. As E. D. Hirsch brings out the distinction, "A type can be entirely represented in a single instance, while a class is usually thought of as an array of instances."[3] The literary genre, moreover, is a type of a special sort. When we assign a work to a generic type, we do not suppose that all its characteristic traits need be shared by every other embodiment of the type. In particular, new works in the genre may contribute additional characteristics. In this way a literary genre changes with time, so that its boundaries cannot be defined by any single set of characteristics such as would determine a class. The matter of change we shall return to later. Here the notion of type is introduced to emphasize that genres have to do with identifying and communicating rather than with defining and classifying. We identify the genre to interpret the exemplar.

In literary communication, genres are functional: they actively form the experience of each work of literature. If we see *The Jew of Malta* as a savage farce, our response will not be the same as if we saw it as tragedy. When we try to decide the genre of a work, then, our aim is to discover its meaning. Generic statements are instrumentally critical, as Mario Fubini said: they serve to make an individual effect apprehended as a warp across their *trama* or weft. And when we investigate previous states of the type, it is to clarify meaningful departures that the work itself makes. It follows that genre theory, too, is properly concerned, in the main, with interpretation. It deals with principles of reconstruction and interpretation and (to some extent) evaluation of meaning. It does not deal much with classification.

Nevertheless, the notion that genres are classes has dominated literary theory for a very long time. Until recently, with rare exceptions such as Aristotle,[4] the common practice has simply been to take it for granted that genres are definable and mutually exclusive. Perhaps theorists lacked the terms and the logic needed to sustain a different view. Thus, Francesco Patrizi, one of the subtlest Renaissance Italian theorists, refers to the genres as "species" but also uses the term "parts" in an elusive way that might imply a different relation between works and their kinds. In modern theory, however, the assumption that if genres exist they must be definable classes is still regular. Crane, Olson, and Sacks are unusual only in the enthusiasm with which they pursue mutually exclusive generic categories.[5] Bennison Gray explicitly tackles the logical problem of describing literature and again and again presses on to explicit definition: his attempt is "to classify a phenomenon, namely literature, in terms of genus and species." Even critics not at all given to stressing the fixity of genres fall into a similar way of speaking. Claudio Guillén, whose whole drift is in another direction, makes the fatal concession: "Let us admit, with Croce, that a genre is an external class in aesthetic terms."[6] And Francis Cairns, in a leading study of rhetorical genres in ancient literature, refers throughout to classes of content, distinguished from "classifications of literature in terms of form as ... epic, lyric, elegy, or epistle." These "content" genres sometimes approximate modern subgenres, which to a limited extent resemble classes. But what we need to notice here is the wording of Cairns' generalization: "Every genre can be thought of as having a set of primary or logically necessary elements which in combination distinguish that genre from every other genre."[7] The expectation of "necessary elements" or defining characteristics is almost universal among critics writing about genre.

It is an expectation without any sufficient basis. A very few necessary elements exist (all *propemptika* refer to a departure; all comedies have characters), but not nearly enough to supply a theory of genre. No formal genres could usefully be distinguished in such a way; not even comedy and tragedy. And the rhetorical genres of antiquity present formidable problems of definition, which might well be insuperable if a greater quantity of ancient literature survived. With modern genres, boundaries are even more indistinct and shifting, overlapping and allowing intricate mixture. Necessary elements are sparse.

Consider tragedy, surely as distinct a genre as any. Looking for defining characteristics, we might begin with those that *Oedipus at Colonus* shares with *Hamlet*. But to begin is almost to end, since the common features are few and indistinct. Far more noticeable are the specific disparities: in duration of the action, in number of characters and of acts, in amount and immediacy of violent action, and in frequency of peripeteias and of anagnoroses. But set these aside, along with the difficulty of applying Aristotle's description of tragedy to Shakespeare's work (although Rymer found that decisive). Let us think simply of common features that might be necessary elements of tragedy. What could they be? Not the fall of a great man: at Colonus, Oedipus has already fallen, and in a modern tragedy the protagonist need not be great. Not an unhappy ending (Aristotle's "metabolē ex eutuchias eis dustuchian"): *Oedipus at Colonus* ends neither happily nor unhappily, and some other Greek tragedies end in happy reconciliation.[8] Not, now, the festival occasion that Richmond Lattimore puts among the "minimal, indispensable characteristics" of Athenian tragedy. Seriousness, perhaps—but even that must be qualified in view of comic and satiric modulations in the English form. Dryden was led to consider that "not only pity and terror are to be moved."[9]

The issues of Dryden's dispute with Rymer at first raise hope that we may conquer the problem by dividing tragedy diachronically, or into subgenres. Perhaps it is not one, but several classes. If so, there will have to be several definitions: of Athenian tragedy, medieval *de casibus* tragedy, domestic tragedy, revenge tragedy, modern tragedy, and many others.[10] Greek tragedy, whose form involved music and dance, probably in its entirety shared features absent from the tragedy of later periods. And Renaissance English tragedy comes close to making the representation of sudden death into a defining characteristic. But, on the whole, multiplying classes will not serve. For the same logical problem returns on a different scale. Each subgenre has too much variety too elusively and mutably distributed for definition to be feasible. We can specify features that are often present and felt to be characteristic, but not features that are always present. Most Attic tragedies avoid direct visual representation of violence, but Sophocles' Ajax kills himself on stage. Most focus on a crucial moral choice (Rivière's "décision capitale, souvent mortelle, toujours irrévocable"), but need not where the plot is mainly concerned with discovery or revenge or escape (*Oedipus Tyrannus,* Sophocles' *Electra* and *Iphigeneia in Tauris*). Such exceptions persuaded Lattimore to abandon the idea that Attic tragedy is a single class, and to propose instead a number of subclasses. Definition has receded, that is to say, to the level of subsubgenre. But works of this type, too, will turn out to have a composition such as to elude definition in a similar manner. Even the subsubgenres will have their exceptions, their overlapping anomalies, their variety.

And so with other subgenres of tragedy and other genres of literature. They never have enough necessary elements common to all members for them to be regarded as classes. Either defining characteristics are absent altogether, or they are limited to meager distinctions that do no more than subdivide the genre. In short, genres at all levels are positively resistant to definition. Definition is ultimately not a strategy appropriate to their logical nature. They have less formal resemblance to the class of solid substances, say, than to the type of solid characters. So elusive are the groupings of genre that some critics have quite understandably dismissed it as chimeric, or have argued, with Irvin Ehrenpreis, that it need imply no more than "some similarity between certain works."[11]

But others have tried for a looser concept of genre that would not dissolve altogether, by applying the theory of family resemblance. This theory, invented by Dugald Stewart, was developed by Wittgenstein in a famous analogy between language games and games in general:[12] "These phenomena have no one thing in common which makes us use the same word for all—but they are *related* to one another in many different ways." The relations are not simple: "We see a complicated network of similarities overlapping and criss-crossing . . . I can think of no better expression to characterize these similarities than 'family resemblances'; for the various resemblances between members of a family: build, features, colour of eyes, gait, temperament, etc., etc., overlap and criss-cross in the same way. And I shall say: 'games' form a family." Wittgenstein's theory has been applied to the problem of genre by several art theorists and literary theorists: for example, Robert Elliott (1962), Maurice Mandelbaum (1965), and Graham Hough (1966).[13] Literary genre seems just the sort of concept with blurred edges that is suited to such an approach. Representatives of a genre may then be regarded as making up a family whose septs and individual members are related in various ways, without necessarily having any single feature shared in common by all. The analogy proves extraordinarily suggestive. It promises to apply not only to close-knit connections within subgenres (Jacobean revenge tragedy) but also to far-flung resemblances between widely divergent works (pride in reputation in *Oedipus Tyrannus* and *Death of a Salesman;* humiliations in *Oedipus* and *Lear*). Genres appear to be much more like families than classes.

Here we should take account of Bennison Gray's view that the family resemblance approach is a mere preliminary to definition.[14] Gray is convinced that the problem of defining the literary genre might be resolved, if only we could decide on just the right class, or conduct a vigorous enough search to discover "whether or not the defining feature or features is present." However, agreeing on a defining feature is no more feasible than agreeing on the definition in advance. Gray's procedure leads in the event only to a stipulative definition, since he decides unilaterally, at the very outset, that fiction is to be the defining characteristic. That is what literature is to mean.

In any case, it is a mistake to think of family resemblance as an inferior substitute for a class. True, the urge to define is nearly irresistible. Everyone writing about a group of works seems to feel that "he must commit himself to some kind of formal definition of the genre."[15] The language of family resemblance, with its terms like "often" and "sometimes" and "typical," seems less rigorous, less capable of demonstration. But to describe a genre in such terms is not to prepare for its definition as a class, but to treat it as a different sort of grouping, not reducible to a class. Besides, as Dr. Johnson recognized,

> definitions have been no less difficult or uncertain in criticism than in law. Imagination, a licentious and vagrant faculty, unsusceptible of limitations, and impatient of restraint, has always endeavoured to baffle the logician, to perplex the confines of distinction, and burst the inclosures of regularity. There is therefore scarcely any species of writing, of which we can tell what is its essence, and what are its constituents; every new genius produces some innovation, which, when invented and approved, subverts the rules which the practice of foregoing authors had established.[16]

The undefinability of the type will be seen as a potential strength, if one considers the fertility of literary invention. Definitions of genre can hardly be stated, before they are falsified.

Family resemblance theory seems to hold out the best hope to the genre critic. But the Wittgensteinian theory needs some modification. In its primitive form, it would sweep away not only traditional genre theory but all generalizing about literature and aesthetics. Madelbaum draws attention to this danger, as well as to Wittgenstein's overemphasis on directly exhibited resemblances (compared with function, for example). How is the theory to distinguish between patience games and fortune-telling? Or fiction and lying? In the analogy, some would now wish to put more emphasis on what accounts for many family resemblances: namely, biological relations between the members.[17]

In literature, the basis of resemblance lies in literary tradition. What produces generic resemblances, reflection soon shows, is tradition: a sequence of influence and imitation and inherited codes connecting works in the genre. As kinship makes a family, so literary relations of this sort form a genre. Poems are made in part from older poems: each is the child (to use Keats' metaphor) of an earlier representative of the genre and may yet be the mother of a subsequent representative. Naturally the genetic make-up alters with slow time, so that we may find the genre's various historical states to be very different from one another. Both historically and within a single period, the family grouping allows for wide variation in the type. In its modified form, the theory of family resemblance also suggests that we should be on the lookout for unexhibited, unobvious, underlying connections between the features (and the works) of a genre. As with heredity, with generic tradition too we have to expect quite unconscious processes to be at work, besides those that readers are aware of. It would be strange if genre did not in part operate unconsciously, like other coding systems within language and literature.

One caveat, however. In generic resemblance, the direct line of descent is not so dominant that genre theory can be identified with source criticism. We need to leave room for polygenesis (a phenomenon to which Dámaso Alonso has drawn attention) and for remote influences. It is not always easy to say when generic resemblances are like immediate family resemblances, and when like atavisms. Consider the case of Spenser's *Shepherd's Calendar* March, where Willye undertakes to look after Thomalin's sheep while the latter tells about his encounter with Cupid (ll. 37–42). Editors compare this with Thyrsis' offer of help in Theocritus *Idylls* (1.14) and the delegation of a similar task by Virgil's Menalcas: "Incipe; pascentis servabit Tityrus haedos" (*Eclogues* 5.12). We might begin to think of the motif as genre-linked, as an optional feature of pastoral eclogue. But we should not be entitled to conclude that Spenser is offering an *imitatio* of his most recent predecessors in the genre. He and Virgil may even have invented the detail quite separately, from life (it would be natural to think of providing for the flocks). Or they may have attempted independent variations from Theocritus (Spenser's in that case being much the more dramatic and amusing). Or, perhaps, by Spenser's time, the motif was felt to be a trifle *passé* and in need of renewal. Deciding in just what sense a feature is generic may be difficult. For some purposes it may be necessary nonetheless. But for criticism of subsequent contributions to the genre, the source of genre-linked features may be quite irrelevant. What matters is simply the coding rule and its immediate application, not how it came to be known. Thus, Gordon Braden shrewdly observes that anti-Olympian mythological touches in Marlowe's *Hero and Leander* need not result from imitation of the School of Nonnos.[18] They may have been arrived at independently, or in response to the implications of the genre. But this might make little difference to later writers, for whom, perhaps, Musaeus, Marlowe, and others all used the code of a subsequent grouping.

Codes often come to a writer indirectly, deviously, remotely, at haphazard, rather than by simple chronological lines of descent. But this very possibility of return to earlier paradigms constitutes a difference that makes literary genres more coherent than some other families.

Acquisition of Competence

Once we introduce the idea of literary tradition's connecting links, it becomes possible to approach the question of how individuals acquire competence in genre. By what means, and through what stages in the course of our reading lives, do we all learn to recognize at least some of the genres that are current, or currently interesting? This question is not usually asked. It is as if there were nothing in the slightest puzzling about the acquisition of generic competence—as if we could take literary competence for granted. It is assumed that the production and the recognition of literary types are somehow automatically guaranteed. (E. M. Forster can say, "Donald Windham, I understand, has never learnt literature. He merely produces it.") But this convenient assumption runs counter to our actual experience. In real life we have to arrive at familiarity with such types through a learning process. That is true even of such a fundamental genre as narrative. Most would agree that story is one of the primary elements of literature. Cowley, indeed, writes as if he was able to appreciate it at a stage when he was still too imperfect a reader to appreciate metrical types: "I remember when I began to read, and to take some pleasure in it, there was wont to lie in my mother's parlour . . . Spenser's works; this I happened to fall upon, and was infinitely delighted with the stories . . . and by degrees with the tinkling of the rhyme and dance of the numbers."[19] Even narrative, however, has to be learned. Cowley perhaps forgot this, but there was once a time, long before, when he was not delighted in stories at all. As every parent knows, children may not even be prepared to listen to a story unless it is recognizably a game. For some time, perhaps, stories are the games you have to sit still for. Similarly with nursery rhymes. Somewhat later, when our memories begin, we may remember being confused by riddles, say, or puzzled by the whole notion of parody—not from inadequate knowledge of the original, merely, but because the procedure itself was baffling. Such contretemps have something to tell us about generic competence, by catching its acquirement in the act.

There is plausibility in the view that broad and "simple" generic ideas are acquired first. First games, then language games. First stories, then tales of terror and fabulations. But the reverse will seem quite as likely to be true, if one reflects on the ritualistic nature of children's games. The idea of story may emerge only after familiarity with a number of well-understood yet highly specific story-games. (Species, similarly, are easier to identify than phyla.) Either explanation, on its own, encounters difficulties. Acquisition of generic competence appears to be a complicated and lengthy process. As with language acquirement, it is never complete. A mature and competent reader of literature finds many works unidentifiable generically, at any level of consciousness, and still cannot respond to certain genres, even after they have been identified. We cannot assume, either, that acquisition is steadily progressive. True, some genres depend on the knowledge of other genres. The most gifted adult beginner must assimilate quite a few forms before he can hope to get far with the poetry of Wallace Stevens. But sometimes readers can grasp a genre with mysterious celerity, on the basis of seemingly quite inadequate samples, almost as if they were forming a hologram from scattered traces. This ease of acquisition remains problematic. The explanation may possibly be that literary types are in part learned indirectly: for example, through conversation, subliterature, advertising, films, and other interdependent forms.[20] There may also be systems of genres that assert themselves subliminally through the implications and constraints of generic relations—neighboring genres, contrasting genres, and the like (see Chapter 13). The problem admits of no immediate solution, but is mentioned as a promising subject for future research.

Instability

In their historical development, too, the genres change continually. Consequently, theorists bent on defining have had to elevate them to a level of very high abstraction, far removed from actual literature. We can arrive at permanent entities in that way, so long as we keep our descriptions vague. Then the genres remain in every age uniformly stable, equally tenuous, predictably inactive, like inert gases. But the defining characteristics are few and elusive. And if we describe the genres in fuller detail, we find ourselves coming to grips with local and temporary groupings, perpetually contending with historical alterations in them. For they everywhere change, combine, regroup, or form what seem to be new alignments altogether. This upsets the system-builder in us. But it is just the activity that genre's communicative function should have led us to expect. If literary meaning works by departing from generic forms, successions of meanings over a long period are bound to change them extensively. The wines of Helicon are all soleras.

This fact, that genres are mutable, can no longer be ignored. In 1588 Giason Denores could discuss quite seriously "The Constitution of a Most Perfect Tragedy." But we do not really think in such terms any more. Good criticism never arrives at its evaluations, now, on the basis that permanent genres are established up in heaven or in the world of ideas. No pantheon of immutable forms is any longer supposed to rest in *apatheia* on some Parnassian height above the course of literary history. Everyone agrees on this in practice. But in genre theory the implications remain largely unexplored. Genre theorists sometimes seem almost to conspire to ignore historical variation. In 1978, A. W. Levi could still write that "the forms of literary presentation—the genres—are for the analyst somewhat like the Platonic ideas, beyond time and change, permanent archetypes of literary possibility." Michael Riffaterre is far from ignoring stylistic change, but avoids the problem of mutability in genre by his very questionable assumption that "code changes are mostly of a semantic nature."[21] And Todorov, although he sees the error of naïve synchronicity, distinguishes between "theoretical" and "historical" genres in a way that drives a fatal wedge between real literature and the purely speculative constructs of genre.[22] It is time that genre theory acknowledged the historical mutability of the genres themselves, and dealt much more freely with temporal concepts.

Claudio Guillén holds out the promise of just such a "primarily historical" view.[23] From time to time he reminds us that genres change, and he signally enlarges our understanding of at least one generic development, picaresque, by tracing its formation stage by stage. However, his theoretical statements continue to treat genres as fixed forms with a single state. "The genre Z," we are told, "should not be so comprehensive that it could not be said of a particular work, in the singular: this is *a* Z." This is suspiciously like saying that the description should be limited to defining characteristics. The present difficulty, however, is that Guillén's genre has one form only; so that Z is simply the general expression for all works in the set, or, if W is a work, in generic tradition, $Z = \{W\}$. To take account of diachronic change, a more recursive expression would be called for, such as $z_n + w_{n+1} \rightarrow z_{n+1}$. (That is, a genre at stage n is the type of works representing it then; any new work w_{n+1} using its coding rules tends to produce a modified form of the type.) Even this is simplistic; assuming as it does a linear sequence, whereas generic traditions are usually much more complex. But it may serve to bring out the point that statements about a genre are statements about the genre at a particular stage—about Z_n, not Z. Concerning a genre of unspecified date, or within very wide chronological limits, correspondingly little can be said. There is a good deal to say about Attic tragedy, Elizabethan tragedy, perhaps even modern tragedy, but not much that makes sense about all tragedy. Without some historical localization, discussion of genre tends toward the vacuous.

The best hope of escaping the dilemma seems to lie in a view of genre hinted at by several critics, notably Rosalie Colie. According to this view, we should allow for considerable diachronic variation, without necessarily, however, grouping different stages closely together. (Medieval romance is not the same genre with Victorian romance, or a medieval letter with a Victorian miscellany letter.) Nor, on the other hand, should apparent discontinuities panic us into abandoning tradition. Colie writes: "Though there are generic conventions . . . they are also metastable. They change over time, in conjunction with their context of systems. At the time of writing, an author's generic concept is in one sense historical, in that he looks back at models to imitate and to outdo. The work he writes may alter generic possibilities . . . almost beyond recognition."[24] If we take these words in full seriousness, we shall find them to have far-reaching implications.

The changes in genres go far beyond modification of this characteristic or that. In the course of time, whole repertoires of recognizable features alter. More than that: the very elements of literature, even the literary model itself, are subject to transmutation, so that the entire fabric of genre becomes involved in historical upheaval. When Aristotle described "the number and nature of the constituent elements" of literary genres, he may have set out an individual view. But the parts any other ancient might have used as categories or heads for a description would be just as alien, or as differently valued, in the eyes of a modern critic concerned with modern literature. Already Patrizi could see this. He too wrote about the parts of literature, but these were not the same parts as Aristotle had devised. The quantitative and qualitative parts, in Aristotelian theory scrupulously dissevered, he now merged. And at other points, too, he found the ancient analysis unsatisfactory. Thus, he not only denied that plot is the basis of unity, but even that it is a necessary element.[25] In our own age, we agree to take this for granted. But now the Renaissance literary model is obsolescent. Just as plot lacked its ancient force for Patrizi, so for us meter, once a necessary part of poetry ("che poesia non possa, ne farsi, ne esser senza verso"),[26] has come to seem less inevitable. It has a different function with us. We cannot disremember free verse, sprung rhythm, syllabics, prose poetry. In consequence, we far less readily think of genres as differentiated metrically. What expectation would the choice of heroic sestet excite in the modern reader? And the Spenserian stanza's generic links: do they not steadily weaken—whatever the fluctuations of poetic merit—as we move through Henry More, Shenstone, Thomson, Beattie, Wordsworth, Byron, and Keats, to Robert Bagg? Most stanza forms could now be freely exchanged without much loss of generic aptness. The model has changed: what challenges attention with us is the mere use of a stanza of any sort, rather than the traditional associations of its particular rhyme scheme. In much the same way, the system of style heights and related figures of rhetoric has been largely dismantled. The loftiest supernal verities may now be written about in the simplest low style, without giving any impression of *tour de force.* So too with other elements. Fundamentals that Aristotle took for granted—such as that poems consist of a linear succession of ordered parts—have almost all been displaced or modified.

Alterations in the elements must have wide repercussions through genres and groups of genres. It is not just a matter of the immediate changes entailed by the elemental form itself. There are more thoroughgoing and ramifying consequential trains of changes. Genre's whole texture, for example, must have felt the different tensions between verse and prose, when the typographic tradition replaced the chirographic, and memory began to atrophy. The earlier tradition implied an oral literary model, on which a whole system of oral genres depended.[27] When that model was replaced, so was every genre bound up with it. And the extent of later changes was in some ways greater still. It is not exaggerated by George Watson, when he says that "anyone bent upon reviving the classical theory of kinds and the forms of analysis that have traditionally accompanied it . . . would in no sense find himself inheriting a critical system in full working order."[28]

Synchronic and Diachronic Description

Genre criticism has tended to split into two quite distinct and almost unrelated activities. One is abstract speculation about permanent genres. It excited many during the Renaissance and for a century after, but is now regarded as unreal—unless, of course, it is structuralist. The other activity is plodding chronicle history of individual genres that continually transform themselves without ever waiting long enough for generalization. One concentrates on fixity (if necessary, inventing it), the other on change (even if no general ideas emerge). In the abstract, the polarity is the irreducible one of synchronicity versus diachronicity.[29] But good criticism will avoid or combine these opposites. It is a matter of tact in deciding where a historical accommodation is required, or when the broad generic outline may be treated as unchanged.

At least since the Romantic movement, criticism has in principle been committed to this middle ground. Concerned as it has been with recovering the historical moment of the work, or interpreting the author's meaning, its implicit assumptions about genre have mixed the diachronic and synchronic approaches. From this point of view, New Criticism and structuralism must be counted as aberrations—or new departures. But does not the analogy between literature and language support a more sychronic view? After all, we likened genre earlier to an extended Saussurean *langue* of additional coding rules. And language can surely be studied synchronically. However, language requires diachronic study also. It, too, continually changes and yet always remains the same: a contradiction that linguistics has approached by taking a series of synchronic views, each limited to its virtual present. Would it be open to genre criticism to do the same?

Here again, we come up against the limits of the analogy with language. Generic conventions differ from linguistic rules fundamentally. First, a literary work may willfully depart from its conventional *langue* in a comprehensive way, as no ordinary speech act departs from the grammatical system of a natural language. It is the height of literary creativity, indeed, to subsume or challenge tradition through such departures. But in language, such extensive grammatical innovation (except in special areas such as technical coinage) would have little success. Second, and *per contra,* writers are free to return to earlier conventional forms as no speaker of a natural language can. All literature is available, at least in some degree, as material for generic creation: quite remote atavisms, even, may find a response by virtue of the capacity of literature (the species' memory) to recapitulate old experience. Natural languages are not like this, however. One might hope for some success by reintroducing Gilgamesh epic conventions in a modern poem, but not by using Anglo-Norman to order a meal.

A famous analogy of Saussure's compares languages and chess games;

and this can be used to justify a purely synchronic approach to genre. In chess the position changes continually; but the stage arrived at on any move can be described accurately without reference to previous moves. The situation is similar, it is argued, with language and with literature: their states, too, can be described singly. Illuminating as the analogy is, it has a significant flaw. For a position in chess is not adequately described without specifying who has the move. And this introduces a diachronic element. To determine who has the move (as retrospective chess problemists will know) may involve opening up, with great difficulty, many previous stages. And if the stages of a chess game are severally unintelligible, this is truer still with genre. Its past states are so persistently active that a purely synchronic method would be unthinkable. We need to know many stages of the game, since any move is liable to answer another far in the past. This is one of the considerations that count against any linear conception of literary history, such as that of the Russian formalists, who tended to think of literature as a series of advances.

Moreover, the identification of genre is curiously retroactive. Usually "it is when, in the course of time and the progress of critical practice, it becomes apparent that a certain recognizable kind of critique fits a certain work better than other incompatible kinds" that we identify its genre. Then "we say that a work *is* a performance of the kind that criticism takes it to be and thus in the end establishes it as being."[30] Sparshott here makes genre too absolutely *ex post facto*. To me it seems more continuously operative throughout the life of the work, however uncertainly and secretly and mutably. Its explicit identifications—plural, not singular as Sparshott supposes—are themselves provisional, leading on to later revisions. Just as an interpretation reads generic features back into the work, and into earlier interpretations, so it in its turn is embedded in later criticism. The successive states of a generic conception are schemes each of which contains its predecessors. Again, change is not limited to accretion of revised criticisms, but can extend to large regroupings among several genres. One thinks of Chapelain's surprising relation of the *Adone* to seemingly heterogeneous poems by Musaeus and Claudian, or of Gordon Braden's recent connection of Marlowe's long misunderstood *Hero and Leander* with a close-knit group of Continental imitations of Musaeus.[31] These interpretations of genre are in part reconstructions, in part mappings of the literary landscape for the first time. Both might be assimilated, one may conjecture, to some later map showing Renaissance aspirations toward a new kind of un-Homeric epic, in which narrative action would be replaced by various forms of poetic digression—a kind subsuming the epyllion, yet not necessarily (as used to be thought) directly Ovidian in inspiration.

All this does not mean that we should turn from analysis to source criticism. It may mean, indeed, that for many purposes the most practical measure is to treat the development of genres as a succession of notional states to be analyzed synchronically—to study, say, "1600 English tragedy." This is to appropriate an important contribution of the Russian formalists, particularly Jurij Tynjanov, who explored the idea of literature as a series of structures examinable by arbitrary section. Thinking of a genre as a series of stills is at least better than ignoring its movement altogether. But if we follow this plan, we must beware: it will tend to conceal the less regular ways in which genre really alters.

Two particular cross-sections of a genre's time-worm mainly interest critics. These are: (1) the original generic state when the work in question was written; and (2) the state in the critic's own time. Intentionalists may be concerned to reconstruct 1; but every critic inevitably relates the work to 2, the genre he knows. From this we come to assume, in our inveterate egocentricity, that our own generic identifications obtain universally, so that we can safely treat this epicede as a short lyric, or that romance as a novel. We treat genres, in effect, as if they had only a single state. This confusion of 1 and 2 blurs much criticism. It might sometimes be avoided by giving the *radix* of observation; indicating at least whether the original genre or the present state is meant ("sixteenth-century epigram"; "nineteenth-century romance"). That would not get in the way of synchronic description, once historical adjustment had been made.

Occasionally, other generic states are of interest. These include the state at publication (perhaps long after the time of writing); at the time when reputation grew, or was modified; and when its interpretation significantly developed. Thus, Spenserian critics need to know something about the generic conceptions in the neoclassical age of Thomas Warton, for whom interlaced romance did not exist as a respectable genre. Warton thought that *The Faerie Queen*'s polyphonic narrative occasioned "infinite perplexity to the reader": Spenser would have found a better model in Tasso than in Ariosto.[32] Theoretically, every critical contribution brings about a new generic state. But to try to operate a system with so many fine gradations would in practice put an end to critical discourse altogether. We should always be acquiring, never using, generic information. A less rigorous method must suffice, using such terms as "medieval comedy," "Elizabethan comedy," and "Restoration comedy." On the other hand, some current terms are too unrestricted in period to have much value. We need finer discrimination than "the novel" represents, even if it brings us uncomfortably close to the limits of knowledge.

Evidence for Genre

For earlier states of genres we are not circularly dependent on previous criticism with its own circularities and confusions. The outmoded genres "defined" by older criticism are still widely used. But fortunately there are other ways to arrive at generic ideas. Evidence for previous states of genres is in fact more plentiful than may be supposed. It can be drawn from a variety of sources, not all much explored: (1) authorial statements, specially valuable so far as conscious genre is concerned; (2) contemporary practice (for example, in *imitatio*): elusive evidence, since the second-rate reduce genre to recipe whereas the great may transcend its local forms; (3) early readers' comments, perhaps reflecting groupings now obsolete, such as Pope's extraordinary connection of Davenant with Donne;[33] and (4) indirect constructive inference. So much of genre's operation is unconscious that this last source often provides the most information.

The last point calls for expansion. Constructive inference, which may work from literature or criticism or other evidence, can be very indirect indeed. For example, it may draw conclusions from the form of statements made about other genres not directly in question. Or it may deduce something from the existence of contradictory views. In his *Life of Pope,* Johnson says that "an epitaph . . . implies no particular character of writing, but may be composed in verse or prose. It is indeed commonly panegyrical, because we are seldom distinguished with a stone but by our friends; but it has no rule to restrain or modify it, except this, that it ought not to be longer than common beholders may be expected to have leisure and patience to peruse."[34] Almost immediately, however, he rescinds this freedom. In practice, it seems, an epitaph must include the name of the deceased but not the information that he died; it must not mix Latin and English; it must not introduce mythology; and it should not praise what is common to "every man who is wise and good."[35] Even without bringing in *An Essay on Epitaphs,* we can see a discrepancy. Yet it is highly improbable that Johnson was confused on these points, or in process of learning about them for the first time. The discrepancy therefore allows us to infer that the rules he applies in the judicial passages had an implicit rather than a fully conscious existence, even for so educated a reader as Johnson. They surfaced only when he was obliged to deal with a specific case (for example deficient particularity of praise) or when he was studying the rules in question in a learnedly systematic way, as in the *Essay on Epitaphs.* When Wordsworth considered the same kind, he made a similar point about particularity of circumstance: "The reader ought to know who and what the man was whom he is called to think of with interest."[36] For him, it was a matter of explaining the "laws" of the epitaph as a "species of composition." But for Johnson, the law about particularity was apparently an unwritten one, or one easily forgotten.

In a similar way, there are inferences to be drawn when Edward Thomas remarks, about *February Afternoon,* "You didn't realize that it was a sonnet I suspect."[37] We can infer not only that the poem was meant as a sonnet, but that Thomas regarded certain sonnet rules as optional, or at least mutable. There was a type of poem characterized by these rules, which would have been easily recognized by Eleanor Farjeon. And there was a distinct type, lacking these marks of the late nineteenth-century sonnet, which was not yet so familiar.

4. Historical Kinds and the Generic Repertoire

Many attempts to clarify literary genre founder in the confusion of treating all generic types as belonging to the same category. If there is only one range of generic types, the critic faces an impossible task in distributing works among them. As he well knows, most works combine many types. This is a different problem from the one presented by generic change; but the two are linked, as later chapters will argue. First we have to distinguish the various sorts of generic types.

Categories

Literary works can always be grouped in different ways. Thus, Tom Stoppard's *Rosencranz and Guildenstern Are Dead* might represent several sorts of genre. Like *Waiting for Godot*, it could be taken as a modern morality. At the same time, like Gilbert and Sullivan's *Rosencranz and Guildenstern*, it could be taken as an epicyclic work extending the fictive world of *Hamlet*. It is a serious comedy, but it has also been called an absurdist drama. And in much the same way *The Winter's Tale* has been treated as comedy, tragicomedy, near-tragedy, and romance. Part is pastoral; although, even in this, Autolycus embodies the contrasting values of what is variously termed "Hesiodic" (Rosenmeyer) and rogue or "boisterous pastoral" (Taylor).[1] Again, we recognize a structural type, in which analogous actions (the Hermione plot and the Perdita plot) reflect upon one another. Finally, in the sheep-shearing scene, *The Winter's Tale* has masque "elements," as we say.

True, the genres identified vary with the purpose and the knowledge of the speaker. A hurried ticket agent may be content with "comedy"; a critic may have time for agonizing about minuter distinctions. Moreover, generic types vary in their definition: we do not distinguish much where we are not well informed. And some types may be inherently indistinct and prone to overlap. But much the commonest—and least understood—reason for "overlapping" of genres is their belonging to different categories. A morality is simply not in the same range of genre as an epicyclic work or an absurdist drama. And no progress can be made without differentiating at least a few of these categories. We shall attempt to distinguish the following: *kind* or historical genre, *subgenre, mode,* and *constructional type.* Thus, *The Winter's Tale* is a tragicomedy in kind, with parts that are pastoral or romantic in mode. But it is not a romance in kind. Without distinguishing some such categories of genre, criticism must sink into incoherent confusion. For analytic convenience we can distinguish the categories in terms of the features making up the generic repertoire. Only kind and subgenre ever use anything like a complete range of features.

The Generic Repertoire

The repertoire is the whole range of potential points of resemblance that a genre may exhibit. Although the process whereby we identify genre is obscure, retrospective analysis can arrive at many characteristic features. Every genre has a unique repertoire, from which its representatives select characteristics. These distinguishing features, it is worth noting, may be either formal or substantive. As Austin Warren says, generic grouping should be based "upon both outer form (specific metre or structure) and . . . upon inner form (attitude, tone, purpose—more crudely, subject and audience)."[2] And Guillén cautions against the vagueness that comes from concentrating exclusively on external features, or on internal ones such as "the 'essence' of tragedy, or the 'ideas' of the Russian novel."[3] The best of the older theorists, in fact, always kept external and internal forms together in discussing the historical kinds. Thus, Aristotle's tragedy is constituted by realizations of certain elements (*merē*): namely, story (*mythos*); character (*ēthē*); dialogue (*lexis*); characters' thought (*dianoia*); spectacle (*opsis*); and song, the lyrical element (*melopoiia*).[4] And the best modern criticism concurs. We still think of Attic tragedy as characterized by both substantive and formal features. The genre is identified not only by the presence of *epeisodia* and *stasima,* of certain metrical patterns and certain devices (for example, *stichomythia*), but also of a serious plot with reversals and discoveries, a noble protagonist and emotions of high intensity, occasioned by a conflict of values. *A fortiori* with later tragedy and with other historical kinds. All have characteristic internal forms. It would be wrong to defend genre by arguing that it does not restrict contents. Indeed, that line of thought may have encouraged the notion of genre as a merely formal encumbrance.

Not all categories of genre combine internal and external characteristics, however. As the broad term "genre" is used in this book, it includes not only the historical kinds but also the more or less unstructured modes, on the one hand, as well as purely formal constructional types on the other. These categories can be distinguished by introducing the idea of generic repertoire. In subgenre we find the same external characteristics with the corresponding kind, together with additional specification of content. It adds an obligatory part-repertoire of substantive rules, optional in the kind (to which it is related, therefore, almost as a subclass). Mode, by contrast, is a selection or abstraction from kind. It has few if any external rules, but evokes a historical kind through samples of its internal repertoire. Compared with historical genre, then, the subgenre category adds features, whereas the mode subtracts them. *Amoretti* 64, for example, is amatory in mode, Elizabethan sonnet in kind, of the blazon subgenre. Again, what may be called "constructional types" are purely formal. They occur in works of many different kinds—as does the widely distributed catalogue type, used in the same sonnet. And the composition of sonnets to form the sequence *Amoretti* exemplifies another constructional type, the collection.

We have now to look at the generic categories in a little more detail.

Kind

As I use the term, "kind" is equivalent to "historical genre," or the unhappily named "fixed genre." This partly agrees with recent critical usage.[5] But to use the current general term is not to accept its meaning altogether, or the whole nomenclature of individual kinds. Some terms in frequent use, such as "pastoral," really belong in an entirely different category. Nevertheless, there is a substantial basis of agreement about many historical kinds. Until recently, they received more attention than genres of other categories. Menander and other ancient rhetoricians described many kinds (*eidē*) quite minutely,[6] and Greek descriptions were often accepted by Latin writers and critics. But the latter also developed a sense of their own definite, though changing, customs. Horace may not refer to genre when he writes of his satires as trespassing *ultra legem,*[7] but he is certainly aware of a kind that Lucilius originated: "Cum est Lucilius ausus / primus in hunc operis componere carmina morem" (*Satires* 2.1.62–63). Renaissance criticism often returns, similarly, to a kind's historical originator. It reflects consciousness of tradition, whether represented by an authority (Aristotle) or a paradigmatic author (Horace, Petrarch). Sometimes in the Middle Ages and often from the sixteenth century on, kinds are traditionally named, often with the same labels used in ancient criticism. It is worth noting that the names of kinds (from which most other generic terms take their origin) are invariably nouns. A proposition of the form "This work is a *Z*" (to use Guillén's formula) normally identifies a historical genre.

Kinds may in this way give the impression of being fixed, definite things, located in history, whose description is a fairly routine matter. As we shall see, there is something in the idea of definiteness. But describing even a familiar kind is no simple matter. We may think we know what a sonnet is, until we look into the Elizabethan sonnet and are faced with quatorzain stanzas, fourteen-line epigrams, sixteen-line sonnets, and "sonnet sequences" mixing sonnets with complaints or Anacreontic odes. Besides such historical changes within individual kinds, there are wider changes in the literary model to be allowed for, with their repercussions on the significance and even categorization of generic features. Strictly speaking, discussion of a generic repertoire takes for granted a previous exploration of the range of constituent features and of their interrelation ("stratification") during the active life of the kind. A theory of possible constituents should be worked out for the period in question. This is no easy undertaking, when forms change so radically and rapidly. Even Roman Ingarden's circumspect organon *Das literarische Kunstwerk: Eine Untersuchung aus dem Grenzgebiet der Ontologie, Logik und Literaturwissenschaft* (1931) failed to take account of the radio play, with its new bearing on the theory of side-text.

Moreover, the survey of the repertoire needs to cover as many literary constituents as possible. In spite of its title, Ingarden's formidable work deals mainly with the stratification common to all discourse: it is by no means comprehensive from a literary point of view. An adequate inventory would have to take historical variations into account, and would include not only the linguistic features commonly considered (presentational mode, rhetoric, lexis, and so on), but also superstructural features more or less confined to literary discourse (closure, metrical forms, rhyme vocabularies, topics, and so on). All features are subject to changes of

function. Rhyme in Pope's literary world has a different content from
rhyme in Chaucer's world, and this would have to be allowed for in
treating the generic function of rhyme in satire. Similarly, the twelve-line
form of many Caroline epitaphs and elegies may have had a generic force,
rather than the number symbolism that would have been felt in their
Elizabethan predecessors. Almost any feature, it seems, can become
genre-linked and belong more or less regularly to a kind's repertoire. This
applies equally to what used to be called content, as opposed to form.
Images, motifs, and topics in the stratum of represented objects all form
part of a repertoire. And, conversely, a work's genre can affect its constituents' stratification. Thus, graphemes may have quite different functions
in concrete poems and in elegies, and images of the seasons are significant at different levels in georgics, haiku, and Romantic odes. The existence of such possibilities makes one think that reducing literary kinds to
very broad "discourse types" must be a mistake.

The generic repertoire, as usually described, may be typified by Guillén's list of the features of picaresque. Guillén specifies eight characteristics: the *pícaro,* a distinctive character-type seen in clearly defined situations such as orphanhood; the pseudoautobiographical form, implying
an ironic double perspective; the narrator's prejudiced view; his tendency
to generalize from exemplary experience, so that the form is "closed"
ideologically; the stress on problems of earning and livelihood; the observation of many different social groups; the *pícaro's* movement "horizon-
tally through space and vertically through society"; and the loosely epi-
sodic narrative structure using recurrent motifs, circular patterns,
incremental processes, and embedded subnarrations. Naturally, this bald
summary does little justice to Guillén's sensitive treatment. Nevertheless,
it may serve to bring out limitations of method. Thus, the synchronic
approach must ignore differences between early picaresque (*Lazarillo*)
and modern symbolic picaresque (*Felix Krull*).[8] Again, analysis is abandoned whenever a feature proves to be less than universally distributed:
the *pícaro* is "not always the servant of many masters" and "The place of
satire . . . is not quite secure in the picaresque." At such points one is
bound to feel that a family resemblance theory would have encouraged
more far-reaching exploration. For example, in many early picaresque
novels, the *pícaro's* versatile servant role, with its opportunity for altruis-
tic identification, is a highly significant feature. Nor does Guillén's
method allow him to say anything about picaresque's tenuous *mise-en-
scène,* the thinness of almost all its characters, or the *pícaro's* own insecure

identity. Pursuing the chimera of universal characteristics results, that is, in a much abbreviated inventory of the repertoire. Finally, the merging of kind and mode means that picaresque is treated as a subclass of novel, whereas in fact it began as a separate kind, with its own external structure. Nevertheless, Guillén has made an invaluable survey of the picaresque repertoire. It has the right kind of variety, ranging as it does over substantive and formal elements.

The question naturally arises whether we have to think of such a generic repertoire as listing only "field marks" or special genre-linked features (which would thus be quite distinct from the far greater number of "ordinary" features). Or are the kinds complete organizations? And are all constituents whatsoever ordered generically? Many literary features of all sorts (topical allusions, puns, half-rhymes) appear in several kinds— although not usually in very many, or at random. A few, such as structure, occur in all. However, a great many features must be articulated generically, at least in the broad sense of being suitable, for the kinds to have any existence. And certain features seem to be more closely genre-linked (amoebean dialogue in eclogue, Hymen in epithalamium). Spenser's lines

> Hymen is awake,
> And long since ready forth his mask to move,
> With his bright tede that flames with many a flake
> *(Epithalamion* 25-27)

have alliteration, common in some Elizabethan poetic genres; inversions, consonant with an elevated style height; and the tede, or pine-torch, epithalamic in a much more special way. Unless we connect the torch with the *kēroi* (tapers) of epithalamium, the passage would hardly be intelligible. And we should certainly miss the beautiful development of the convention later, in the "thousand torches flaming bright" in the heavens, with its suggestion that the spiritual qualities symbolized by the *kēroi* lead up to stellification. This is a brief example. But it is easy to see that if such generic indicators are commonly missed, the kind as a whole must be misunderstood.

Within this nuclear family of generic indicators, we may further distinguish local features, such as *incipits* or closure types, and more dispersed features, such as emotional tonality or scale. These latter may be elusive, but they exert a pervasive influence on other constituents. Most elusive of all are "absent features," that is, features normally excluded from a kind (puns, for example, from neoclassical epic and from Victorian hymns). In fact, it may well be that the majority of generic features operate unconsciously, until, perhaps, some gross infringement of rule draws them to our attention. To understand the kinds, therefore, we have to take into account a very wide range of features.

It may help to glance at the variety of features that have been generically organized; mentioning a few of the commonest, some familiar to criticism, and others that have been passed over. The arrangement is informal, since we are not in a position to say what structured sequence or system (if any) generic features form during recognition.[9]

1. Most kinds have a distinctive *representational aspect,* such as narrative, dramatic, discursive. They may have several. Thus, English Renaissance tragedy, although predominantly dramatic, often has subsidiary lyric or narrative sections (songs, *nuntius* speeches). In the English kind, the lyric elements are usually motivated, or at least occasioned by the action; unlike ancient tragedy, in which independent choruses occupy relatively fixed formal positions. Similarly, eighteenth-century English georgic may mingle descriptive, expository, and lyric aspects. And an Elizabethan sonnet sequence such as *Astrophil and Stella* is primarily lyric (as C. S. Lewis said, "It is not a way of telling a story"), and secondarily narrative and dramatic. Renaissance critics could regard the eclogue, with its dialogue, as a dramatic form: "The Poet devised the Eclogue long after the other dramatic poems."[10] However, Renaissance eclogue differs from the ancient type in freer use of lyric and narrative.

2. Every kind is characterized by an *external structure.* This point gains force from the comparative definiteness of the feature. True, the term structure is sometimes applied to rather doubtful internal patterns (including some whose existence is not so brilliantly elusive as to achieve incontestability), but that is not so here. I mean "structure" simply in the ostensible, obvious sense: the linear sequence of parts. Structures of this crude order can usually be demonstrated, so that factual disagreement about them is rare. We may dispute the significance, but hardly the fact, of such a sequence as *poetic induction / antimasque / masque / epilogue.* This gives kind a certain palpability, by comparison with mode, which is not characterized by external structure.

The idea of external structure entails a few theoretical complications. For instance, structure can be "external" in different ways: whether by physical division into chapters, stanzas, and the like, or by conventional organization of the contents. Moreover, structures that seem external to

us may once have had communicative or "internal" value—as with numerological patterns. But for the present purpose there is no need to go
into such questions. In practice, the criterion of structure is not usually
hard to apply. Attic tragedy has manifestly some such structure as *prologue / choral song / episode / choral song . . . / exode,* whereas neoclassical
tragedy has a five-act structure. Aristotle may hint at the demonstrability
of external structure when he speaks of the "members into which tragedy
is quantitatively divided,"[11] in a passage that greatly influenced Patrizi
and other Renaissance theorists. If each kind had a characteristic structure that was peculiar to it alone, this would almost suffice to distinguish
it. So Renaissance masque—one of the kinds that have a unique structure—is very readily identified.

But external structure is seldom so exclusive. (Division into chapters,
for example, occurs with many kinds.) Then we may look for a more
distinctive structure in minuter details, or at a slightly different level of
stratification. And we may find it—perhaps in stanza forms (the ro-
mance-six; the strophe), in rhetorical divisions (the parts of a classical
oration; the *invocatio, principium, initium* of epic), or in the sections of
narrative (episodes in epic; interlaced segments in medieval romance).
With very short forms, the external structure may reside in word division
or grammatical pattern, as when a Renaissance *impresa* or emblem motto
comprises a single word group. (William Drummond's *Short Discourse
upon Impresas* even argues that the best *impresa* or "word" should be "only
of two words, as *gang warily;* or it is good of one only, as *semper.* The farther it is from two, it is the more imperfect.") And graffiti have elaborately structured sound patterns. With larger kinds, division into numbered external parts may be generically distinctive. Thus, Renaissance
brief epics and biblical epics are commonly divided into four or six or
seven books, whereas classical epics are divided into twelve or twenty-
four books—either in accordance with ancient precedents or with number symbolisms (the hexaemeric six; the encyclopedic twenty-four). In
earlier literature, numerological structure regularly contributed to generic differentiation: triumphal poems usually had symmetrical structures
with a central emphasis; epithalamia were divided by temporal or nuptial
numbers.[12]

3. In ancient criticism, *metrical structure* was especially genre-linked.
Indeed, meters were so rigorously connected with particular kinds as to
provide a basis of classification. Quintilian and others probably regarded
pastoral as "heroic" because it used the hexameter line. But since then,

profound historical changes have loosened the old connections that may once have existed between meters and kinds. From early times, in fact, critics seem to have felt this tendency: Aristotle writes of iambics as formerly used for invective, but extended to comedy.[13] Some think of the form as promptly "becoming neutralized and abdicating its role as a generic label."[14] This may be something of an overstatement, but it is true that over a longer period—partly through expressive modifications, partly as a result of domination by single forms (the Augustan couplet; Romantic and Victorian blank verse)—metrical structure has lost most of its generic implication. Even meters that used to be limited to a few kinds are now available for many, if not all. Nevertheless, triple rhythms are still confined to a fairly narrow range of kinds—as polysyllabic rhymes are, to satire and light verse (*Hudibras;* Byron; Lehrer).[15] And many conventions, not all of them well understood, still link certain stanzaic and metrical forms with single kinds. Everyone knows a ballad's or a nursery rhyme's rhythm, even modified by a de la Mare or a Causley. Haiku, limerick, clerihew, and many other short forms have each a unique metrical structure. In one or two exceptional cases, meter is actually more closely genre-linked now than in former times. Common Meter is mainly associated with the Christian hymn, whereas the ancient hymn lacked a metrical form.[16]

4. As every kind has a formal structure, so it must have a *size*. This corollary of the doctrine of quantitative parts is by no means trivial. Indeed, size counts as a critical factor from a generic point of view. Here literary and linguistic organizations diverge. There are no linguistic constraints on the length of an utterance, whereas genre often determines length precisely (sonnet; computistic verse) and always exerts constraints on it. From Callimachus on (*Epigrammata* 13), writers have expressed keen awareness of this. Wordsworth twice voiced his sense of the sonnet's restricted scale: finding it compatible with variety and solace, lavishing on it images of possibility ("hermit's cell," "key").[17] But with a few honorable exceptions such as Paul Zumthor, critics have shown little appreciation of the point. Aristotle merely speaks of tragedy's action as "of a certain magnitude" ("mēden echon megethos"), the length being fixed by the limits of the competitive occasion and of the audience's ability to grasp the work as a whole. His Renaissance exponents went into the dimensions somewhat more closely. In fact, Renaissance treatments of most kinds touch on size. Chapelain, a little later, still sees the length of the *Adone* as raising serious problems of kind. But modern theorists

tend to speak rather dismissively of wordage limits for novel, novella, and short story.[18] The question is not an idle one: differences of size have many repercussions on the nature of the reading experience.

Kinds may be considered short, medium, or long. Variation of reading habits counts against much finer graduation, although in particular instances it may be useful: Puttenham distinguishes elegy from epigram by size. Short kinds include many stanzaically defined forms (strambotta; sestina), most songs (madrigal; blues), odes, elegies, many ill-defined "lyric" kinds (confessional poem; imagist poem), various epigraphic kinds (epitaph; motto), sayings (proverb; aphorism; maxim; modern epigram), literary riddles (acrostics; charades—as we know from *Emma,* "such things in general cannot be too short"), prose forms of a few paragraphs (prose poem; character), short narratives (parable; "short short story"). More than one of a short kind can be read or performed on a single occasion. Hence, they may aim at effects of variety or contrast with other items in a series.

Medium works can also be completed at a sitting, but not more than two or three at most would usually be attempted. Existing independently, they tend to have a more comprehensive, balanced content. Post-Renaissance dramatic and oratorical kinds (sermon; declamation) are mostly of medium length. So are the short story, fairy tale, brief epic, essay, and tract. Medium verse kinds include eclogue, descriptive sketch, verse satire. Poe may have overstressed the single sitting as a threshold. But we can agree that extension of the reading experience beyond it has many formal implications.

Works in long kinds normally require more than one sitting. They are regularly divided, indeed, into parts of no more than medium length that reflect the duration of notional reading sessions. Discontinuities between the parts have a profound effect on the total impression. In epic, romance, novelistic kinds, biography, journal—all kinds of long narratives—a sense of time's lapse is vital. A reader is to feel that he has not only visited but inhabited the fictive world. All long kinds, whether narrative or not, share certain features. Among these the transition is notable: external and internal divisions lend themselves to exploitation, by way of closure, lead-in, suspense, *entrelacement,* or other narrative or expository effects.

A specific magnitude, then, is a *sine qua non* of every kind. Each falls into one of the ranges of size mentioned above. Anomalies have a way of proving this rule. For example, the immensely long *Satire of the Three Es-*

tates is closely related to medieval morality, and in any case was performed in special circumstances: Renaissance critics were actually much exercised about the stamina of audiences, which they put at three hours or so. Again, several kinds straddle the division between short and medium (epistle; ballad; fabliau; fable). But these terms may cover more than one kind, to say nothing of mixtures. This is certainly true of epic (brief; classical), on both sides of the border between medium and long. Similarly with satire. There is at first some plausibility in Gilbert Highet's idea that its protean diversity, so baffling to genre theorists, implies a specially free, metamorphic, passe-partout form. But satire turns out not to be a kind, but a whole group of genres, well characterized by Highet himself, such as monologue, parodic satire, and narrative satire. In parodic satire, any literary (or nonliterary) type can be parodied, including forms of various length, from hymn to dictionary and scholarly edition (Bierce's *Devil's Dictionary;* Pope's *Dunciad*). However, this is obviously a mixed genre (and as such will be considered in a later chapter). None of the unmixed satiric kinds has a comparably elastic size. And with Menippean or narrative satires there seems to be a fairly strict limit, about the length of *Gulliver's Travels.* Longer satires seem to work against the generic grain. A brilliant success in this direction might constitute a new kind; as it is, we must call *The Apes of God* and *Giles Goatboy* generically inept, as well as too long.

It follows that a genre not characterized by any definite size is not a kind, in the present sense.

5. Closely related to size is *scale.* Scale, when combined with other features, may serve as rather a sensitive generic indicator. In a first reading of *Cranford,* for example, the abrupt dispatch of Captain Brown may be one of the places where we begin to identify the kind. If promising characters go down at this rate, we feel, the book is more likely to be a composite of sketches than, say, a Richardsonian novel. Similarly, picaresque's frequent changes of setting establish a scale that is enough to rule out several features characteristic of other kinds of narrative.

6. We have inherited a strong suspicion of the idea that *subject* may be limited generically. It has become a dogma that no subject is poetic or unpoetic. But if subject is properly understood, there really are unpoetic subjects.

In ancient and again in neoclassical literature, a firm decorum related subjects with kinds and so with external forms. Time and again, Horace and other critics said, or implied, as much: "In what measure [that is, hexameter] the exploits of kings and captains and the sorrows of war may be written, Homer has shown" (*Ars Poetica* 73-74); "A theme for comedy refuses to be set forth in verses of tragedy; so the feast of Thyestes scorns to be told in everyday tones that almost suit the comic stage" (ll. 89-91). In the Middle Ages, the little secular genre theory that existed stressed subject more than form, as in the *rota Vergiliana*. Renaissance critics resumed the ancient assumption: "Toute sorte de Poesie a l'argument propre à song subject," says Ronsard.[19] Indeed, "matters heroical and pastoral" (Sidney) were distinguished so sharply that they could be consciously mingled.[20] Nevertheless, Rosalie Colie is right to draw special attention to the great Scaliger's constant use of "matter as the definer of kind."[21] The assured comprehensivenes with which he assigns a whole range of topics to each kind—always it is "harum materia multiplex"—certainly astonishes. It leads Rosenmeyer to smile at the "divisionary ardour" with which Scaliger "merrily scramble[s] formal and substantive criteria." But most critics of that time would have accepted the scrambling in principle, even if they themselves lacked versatility and learning to perform it as powerfully as Scaliger.

More recently, decorum of subject has been obscured through the mutability of kinds. The skeptic can say, "It is now clear that no such line is to be easily drawn, or is perhaps to be drawn at all."[22] George Watson refers to the old error of supposing that only great men could have tragic fates—Ibsen has shown us that tragedy is not about kings. But we should not conclude from changes in tragedy's matter that it has none. Tragedy is not a "treatment" that might be applied to any subject. The problem of subject is too often approached via tragedy, a kind that happens to offer special difficulties in this regard. Even so, we can say that some subjects are inherently so somber that any but a grave, tragic presentation of them would be inconceivable in good literature.

Decorum of subject is also misunderstood because "subject" has changed in meaning. Of course many actions can be treated indifferently as comedy or tragedy—so long as "action" is left vague enough, or defined selectively. But subjects need to be allowed their ordinary specificity of associated actions and topics. The broad situation of bedroom farce could doubtless be treated with tragic solemnity—but then the subject, in its full sense, would be different. With some short kinds, subject is generally agreed to be constant. Epitaphs are normally about the deeds and qualities of a particular deceased person and their claim on our attention; funeral elegies are about the thoughts and feelings of those who mourn; proverbs are about common shared experiences.

It is a half-truth that literature has been liberated from decorum of subject. Certain individual constraints on subject have undoubtedly relaxed. However, their place has simply been taken by others, although these remain unformulated. Anti-intentionalism has concealed this, by confusing subject with intention. So Valéry (or Robert Creeley) will deny writing about a subject. Then, if ever, is the time to suspect an intentional fallacy. He may have intended, only, not to have a subject. But in any case, writing about "no subject" itself implies a choice of genre. There is a subtype of process poem characterized by ostensible avoidance of subject and by concealed preference for a very narrow range of topics indeed, mostly trivia or rudimentary universal experiences. A characteristic subject is, in a word, the unmarked form. If there is no appropriate matter, or very various matter, this itself becomes a characteristic peculiarity—as with 1630 epigram or epistle. Without pretending that every kind has a precise range of subjects all its own, we can claim the obverse: that no kind is indifferent to subject.

7. Closely related are the *values* inherent in all kinds. These have been among the themes of several fine studies, such as Rosenmeyer's *Green Cabinet,* with its account of the epicurean values in certain pastoral kinds. A kind's values tend to elude brief treatment, but they are nonetheless highly characteristic. They operate in very different ways. Thus, proverbs impart a relatively unformulated wisdom. But the values of epic and romance constitute definite systems: one thinks of the rank-ordered virtues of classical and of Christian epic, contrasted in *Paradise Lost;* or the chivalric codes of medieval romance; or the partly pre-Christian values of Norse saga.[23] In such kinds, much of the meaning may lie in a modification of the value-system.

Elusive though generic values may be to the theorist bent on formulation, they seem accessible enough to the reader. We soon begin to recognize the moral world of the sagas. Such intuitions take us some way. But a kind's values are not quite to be identified with the values of the moral "world" it portrays. The vernacular homeliness of 1580 eclogue; the intimacy of Augustan satiric verse epistle; the professional precision of 1970 thriller—all these communicate values that figure little in the life they represent. For the values of a literary kind are often deeply hidden. Satire may seem chaotic or nihilistic, but in reality it is more often traditional, if not conservative. Its positive values are so implicit, are offered with such elaborate obliquity of surprise and such sudden dénouement, that in order to communicate themselves they must be venerably familiar. (Postmodern underground satire proves the rule: it is addressed to true believers who already share the satirist's views.) A distinctive value of satire is its strangely secure candor—as if confident that truth exposed is better than truth colored or made bearable.

8. Each kind has an emotional coloration, which may be called *mood*— almost in the sense of Milton's "That strain I heard was of a higher mood," where he raises *Lycidas* in generic pitch. Mood plays a specially vital part in gothic romance, where it often colors character, atmosphere, and natural description in an unmistakable way. But even when mood has been a conscious preoccupation of the writer, it remains notoriously ineffable to the critic. Some of the theorists ridiculed for their fatuous hypostatizations ("the tragic spirit"; "the essence of comedy") may have had this feature in mind. However that may be, mood seems undoubtedly to belong among the features of kind. Sometimes, it can be associated with local indicators of genre—a point to which we shall return in a later chapter.

9. Many kinds used to have a characteristic *occasion,* at least initially. In these occasional kinds (epithalamium; epicede; genethliacon), relations with ritual and custom were particularly intimate and rich—as Scaliger was fond of demonstrating. Puttenham jocosely refused to call songs performed at supper epithalamies, since the kind's first part had properly to coincide with the bedding, whereas the second covered the bride's inexpert "shrieking and outcry." But occasion has been a feature of other kinds too. Attic tragedy was partly determined by festival requirements; and several of Shakespeare's plays have a large festal element. In *Twelfth Night,* much in the action and the characters would once have been recognized as appropriate to the Twelfth Night festivities.[24]

Some kinds depend heavily on the original occasion. Occasion and setting controlled so many of the motifs, images, and ideas of masque that the form survives only in a ghostly way without them. With such forms, information may have to be supplied by annotation, or by addition of a title. An epigraph that explained itself on stone must in print be entitled: "Written over a Study" or "Epitaph. On Sir William Trumbull."

Changes in the social function of literature have made occasion less important. But it still operates: some contemporary poetic kinds are calculated to answer requirements of the poetry reading.

10. Occasion, in its imaginary, attenuated form, coalesces with the stylistic feature *attitude,* which is often characteristic in the short poetic kinds.[25] Ancient lyrical forms, for example, often seem to imply actual interpersonal relations; and these may remain associated with equivalent

later kinds. Thus, the *propemptikon* or valediction of equal to equal, characterized by affection, may reflect the relation of fellow pupils at rhetoric school.[26] And Donne's "A Valediction: Forbidding Mourning" adopts a similarly intimate stance (not unmixed, though, with the didactic attitude of the superior-to-inferior *propemptikon*). In the same way, the poem of patronage presupposes the special attitude, deferential yet advisory, of poet to patron. And even the contemporary confessional poem has its distinctive attitude. This is not, as one might expect, spontaneously intimate. It is more deliberately staged—almost like the attitude of one in the act of adding to a public personality or "image." Thus, confessional poems convey gratuitous information that would be out of place in an "overheard" meditation by Yeats or Eliot. Lowell will tell us the names of his summer cottage's "owners, Miss Barnard and Mrs. Curtis," or remark: "Our cookbook is bound like Whitman's *Leaves of Grass*— / gold title on green." The confessional attitude here contrasts with that of the verse epistle, whose intimate direct address limits informativeness.

11. Narrative kinds may have a distinctive *mise-en-scène*. This is a highly developed feature with romance, science fiction, the gothic short story, and the psychological novel. With certain types of verisimilar novel, however, setting may be insignificant.[27] Similarly in poetry: the 1915–18 war poem has an elaborately conventional realistic *mise-en-scène,* whereas the pastoral eclogue, through all historical periods, is with few exceptions set in country lacking any detailed realization whatsoever.

12. *Character* is the focus of much existing genre theory. This usually involves much fine-drawn moral analysis, since character is the personal form of such values. In epic, the generic protagonist has gone through a long course of development, but has always had a strategic moral significance. Spenser sketched its generic context when he related his Arthur to previous examples of "a good governor and a virtuous man": Homer's, Virgil's, Ariosto's, and Tasso's "dissevered ... parts in two persons."[28] In his own multiple heroes he plays on this convention by many differentiations, as when he traps the reader into accepting various respectably heroic forms of pride (the Redcross Knight's spiritual pride; Guyon's aristocratic disdain). And Milton, similarly, experts readers to recognize his Satan as hero of the pagan epic that *Paradise Lost* as a whole is not. In other kinds, too, character has long been treated as genre-linked. Aristotle says that the tragic protagonist should be "a man not preeminently virtuous and just," whose misfortunes are brought on "not by vice and depravity but by some error of judgment" (*Poetics* 1453a). The Aristotelian requirement that the tragic hero should be a "man of note" is altered

in the Renaissance, so that the stress falls on rank rather than prosperity. Rank becomes a means of distinguishing tragic and comic characters—a convention from which Shakespeare effectively departs. Later still, character, in the sense of personality, is a main focus of genre criticism. In debating whether *Pepita Jiménez* is a "religious novel," Patmore discusses it almost exclusively in terms of character. Today Bradleian character analysis is officially out of favor. But we still smuggle something very like it into criticism of novels, where many words are spent determining whether a narrator is "reliable" or not (or some fine shade, as with *The Good Soldier,* in between). Only we are not used to thinking of this as related to historical kind.

Of the relatively small number of literary character types, criticism has mostly confined itself to one: the hero—or, since his "decline," the antihero.[29] Other types, with the partial exception of the Fool, have received little extended attention.[30] This has obscured the association of several kinds with distinctive characters, who may nevertheless be vital to their generic communication. As Rosenmeyer has shown, much of the effect of the Theocritean and Virgilian pastoral eclogues has to do with shadings of the shepherd character. The ancient shepherds are youthful and simple, unlearned and innocent. The same is largely true of Elizabethan eclogue (Sidney; Drayton; Browne); except that a few shepherds have learned from the Petrarchan tradition to be relatively experienced. Still, the pastoral cast includes no character remotely like the pedant of comedy: indeed, it properly excludes even the georgic types, who are given to didacticism and necessarily better supplied with precise information. Even without formulating such differences, we are unlikely to miss them. The lines and limits of pastoral character are still recognizable in complex mixtures, as when Shakespeare's Perdita becomes involved in debate with Polixenes. From a similar point of view, the *engagé* intellectuals in Spenser's *Shepherd's Calendar,* if not without Continental precedent, constitute a striking enough instance of generic mixture.

In addition to character types, there are also types of character. Character scale may be genre-linked. So picaresque has "thin" characters, whereas the verisimilar novel commonly has more or less solid ones. And *Commedia dell'Arte* comedy is distinguished by quasi-permanent characters, who belong as much to the performer's world as to the fictional.

13. Neoclassical theorists early discovered that the action of a kind may have a characteristic structure. So "entanglement" or *entrelacement* and multiplicity of episodes typefied romance. In this it contrasted with epic. Chapelain pronounces that "unity of action, among the general rules that

every epic poem must observe, is in especial the principal one without which the poem is not [an epic] poem but a romance."[31] Romances consequently lack perfection, since "they pile adventure upon adventure, and include fights, love-affairs, disasters and other things, of which one well treated would make a laudable effect, whereas together they destroy each other." He failed to see how a reader could be moved by an action that did not give a "continuous" impression.[32] Some Renaissance critics valued *entrelacement* differently, but they would not have disagreed about its being a distinguishing feature of romance.

Discontinuous action also characterizes several modern kinds, such as the mosaic novel (Dos Passos' *Manhattan Transfer;* Doctorow's *Ragtime*) and the "work-in-progress' novel. Much of the latter's action is concerned with the writing of a book—sometimes the novel itself—or some other artistic enterprise that symbolizes the literary one (Sterne's *Tristram Shandy;* Lessing's *Golden Notebook;* Nabokov's *Pale Fire*). The discontinuous action of the kind is pretty regularly reflected in an external division into very short sections.

In a somewhat different way, actions may be related to moral patterns. So Northrop Frye has described the action of Elizabethan comedy as characterized by the pattern of entering, responding to, and leaving a "green world." There are several other comic structures, however, such as that of illusion and enlightenment (*Much Ado; Twelfth Night*). Kinds seldom have a single, defining action.

14. Every kind has its range of appropriate *style:* indeed, some have their being mainly through rhetorical organization. Their rhetorical selections follow in part from the subject matter of the genre. Medieval critics linked the three ancient style heights with Virgil's three paradigmatic works, and hence with other matters and kinds of equivalent dignity. And they specified figures appropriate to these "styles" in some detail—for example, Geoffrey de Vinsauf's *ornatus difficilis,* consisting of ten high-style tropes.[33] This seems a mechanical system; but the adjustment of style came to be governed, in the Renaissance, by a subtle decorum, which went far beyond mere distribution of kinds among styles:[34]

High	*Middle*	*Low*
epic	georgic	pastoral eclogue
tragedy	romantic comedy	satiric comedy
hymn	elegy	verse epistle
etc.	etc.	etc.

Rosemond Tuve and other scholars have explored the criterion of decorum in terms of subject constraint. But it might also be considered as part of the organization of the genres themselves.

We may distinguish at least two ways whereby style matches genre. First, certain kinds and groups of kinds may have their own lexical range. Within the literary diction of the period, individual kinds often have special preferences, both positive and negative. The latter have sometimes been absolute, as with Cowley's unquestioning assumption that "*spouse* is not an heroical word,"[35] or Elijah Fenton's similar feeling about *cow-heel* (which in Pope's Homer has to become "That sinewy fragment ... / Where to the pastern-bone, by nerves combined, / The well-horned foot indissolubly joined").[36] But a kind's congenial words are just as specific. Aureate diction was right for late medieval encomium. Tudor love elegy liked sighs to be "smoky." And around 1595 "sweet" had a special generic force in the amatory epigram and epigram-sonnet. But the classically inspired epigram boasted its capacity to admit all styles and subjects. And literature has increasingly come to rely on such kinds as are capable of a broad stylistic range.

More subtly, style can match kind by varying the proportions between rhetorical figures. Besides the three style-height proportions, Renaissance and neoclassical critics again recognized others of a specific nature. Some figures (such as hyperbole) were prominent in encomiastic kinds, some in devotional elegy (paradox, meiosis), some in pastoral kinds (anaphora), some in Augustan georgic or loco-descriptive poems (periphrasis); although there was never a tidy system distributing the figures among kinds exhaustively.[37] Such conventions allowed for countless special effects, when the expected rhetorical preferences were carried unusually far, perhaps, or mixed with those of another kind, or dropped altogether. The intimate effect of *Astrophil and Stella,* for example, partly comes from its diction, which falls below the level its psychomachic personifications lead us to expect, as the antilover sinks to epigram. Such mixture became increasingly common in the early seventeenth century and again in the nineteenth—a matter we will return to in Chapter 10.

During the nineteenth century, radical and exciting innovations in style unhappily coincided with a decline in rhetoric teaching. The idea became settled that generic rules oppress free creativity. Simultaneously, the rise of the novelistic kinds further obscured style's relation to genre. For in several kinds of novel, words have relatively little formal value.[38] This does not mean that style has lost its generic function. (To see that, one has only to review the violent imagery and nervous anaphora of the contemporary protest poem: the asyndeton and anacoluthon of the confessional lyric; or the rhetorical bravura of the work-in-progress novel.) Only it is less well understood. This miscomprehension shows in books on stylistics that contrive to ignore genre altogether. It also appears in many false generic identifications—reviewers treated John Fuller's *Epistles to Several Persons* as light verse, for example, missing the satiric epistle's use of informal style for serious matter.

Constrasts of the generic and the actual style are still among the most prominent of poetic effects. To take a famous instance, much of the éclat of John Ashbery's *Self-Portrait in a Convex Mirror* has to do with his beginning with the epigram-derived style and matter of the poem-about-a-painting—its suave easiness of connoisseurship, authoritatively laconic, endlessly knowing ("As Parmigianino did it, the right hand / Bigger than the head"), exhaustively descriptive—but then cutting in with "sawtoothed fragments" of life itself, the uncharted, whose exploration calls for a more tentative, so to speak elegiac approach (and is in fact accorded it in suitably abstract or hesitant passages, as in "supposition of promises"), but which meld imperceptibly with renewed art-historical mannerisms, so that the reader may easily have the illusion of authoritative statement extending to the larger questions of the longer poem.

15. Besides the traditional genre-linked constituents, there are others more recently distinguished, such as the reader's *task*. Frank Kermode has developed the idea of a hermeneutic task in the reading of a detective story. Requiring as it does the elucidation of a problem—often posed at the outset—it involves "interplay between narrative and hermeneutic processes." This peculiar double task makes the detective story exceptional among the novelistic kinds: "although all have hermeneutic content, only the detective story makes it preeminent."[39] But in another way the concept can be generalized. Many kinds (and by no means all of them narrative ones) entail characteristic tasks. Indeed, one of the pleasures of reading is that hermeneutic activity differs with kind. This kind will entice the reader into labyrinths of moral analysis; that kind will require exquisite discriminations between events which actually "occurred" in the author's fiction and those that are merely fictions of a narrator. Often the reader will be called on to discover an arcane structural scheme: no easy task with numerologically patterned medieval and Renaissance poems. Interlaced romance, again, involves the task of correlating widely separate episodes.

In every case, communication depends on the task's completion. Children who cannot apply proverbs to their own experience will not appreciate them.

The above are some initial letters of a kind's typical repertoire. But what I want to insist on here is that almost any feature, however minor, however elusive, may become genre-linked. Thus, particular sorts of exordium, closure, inset (digression; play within a play), symmetry, and other structural forms may be characteristic; and so may representational manners (naturalistic; surrealistic), besides qualities harder to categorize, such as the encyclopedic comprehensiveness of epic or anatomy. Any relatively infrequent or noticeable feature may be regarded for a time as generic.

Only for a time, perhaps. Always the features distinguished are liable to change with the interests of writers and critics. So literary form undergoes continual recategorization, as new parts of literature, and new ways of dividing the old, are introduced. Add to these the possibilities opened up through obsolescence of generic rules, and the kinds may well seem inexhaustible.

However, generic repertoires are not endlessly renewable. Every characteristic feature, as a means of communiction, must be recognizable, and this limits the relevant possibilities at any particular time. Even the figures of rhetoric do not exceed a hundred or two—and some of these are too common to have much generic potential. Far from dealing with an infinite set of features, then, we may find that a few striking traits effectively characterize a genre.

There is a view that the kinds have undergone so many variations and historical changes as to be indeterminate. Or, if they have any consistency, they fail to include most works of any great literary interest. This view is wrong. The kinds, however elusive, objectively exist. Their boundaries may not be hard-edged, but they can nonetheless exclude. This is shown by the fact that features are often characteristic through their absence. Thus, Renaissance pastoral eclogue excludes plot and philosophical content; the Regency novel of manners excludes politics and violent action. And in identifying genre, we can often be sure that at least the work does not belong to this or that particular kind. The skeptical view reflects the obvious need for a revised genre theory applicable to modern literature. But with older literature, too, there are many problems of identification. A work may not resemble any previously labeled kind, or it may seem to realize more than one. These are problems we shall return to, in connection with nomenclature and generic mixture. In principle, however, the normal case remains membership of a determinate though temporary kind. The kinds are subject to change; but that does not destroy their coherence, any more than that of other institutions.

Are the kinds organizations, or only assemblages of features? This is a question we shall not be in a position to approach until we know more about how they are recognized, and how they interact in generic systems. We can only say that a kind is a type of literary work of a definite size, marked by a complex of substantive and formal features that always include a distinctive (though not usually unique) external structure. Some kinds are recognizable by every competent reader. But the means of recognition remain obscure.

5. Generic Names

Of all the generic repertoire, single words seem to be the simplest feature to study. And of all sorts of word, it is almost inevitably names that we choose for separate treatment. Not only have names great evocative power and hence a special place in literature, but they seem to have a specifically generic function.

Characteristic Names

Many kinds and groups of kinds have characteristic personal names, or forms of name, that are recognizable by a competent reader. (Others, such as 1600 elegy, tend to exclude personal names altogether.) This was noticed in early treatments of genre, such as John of Garland's *Poetria,* where the Wheel of Virgil sets out Hector and Ajax as heroic or high-style names; Triptolemus and Coelius as georgic; and Tityrus and Meliboeus as pastoral.[1]

The names of satire are particularly conspicuous and have received a good deal of attention.[2] Highet, who examines the use of denigratory names by Morier, Gogol, and others, goes so far as to say that "distorted or ridiculous names are always a sure sign of satire."[3] As we shall see, this is slightly overstated. Nevertheless, it is easy to think of other examples to put beside Gogol's Hlopov ("Bedbug") and Lyapkin-Tyapkin ("Bungle-Steal"). Joseph Heller's satirical novel *Catch-22,* for example, has many such ridiculous names or nonnames: Mudd ("his name was Mudd"), Major Major Major Major, Scheisskopf, and Chief Halfoat.

Just as there are several types of satire, so there are several types of satiric name. In the satiric comedy of the Restoration, names are often explicitly meaningful, communicating moral estimates of their owners, as Petulant and Fainall. Distinctive though they are in period flavor, such names would be hard to distinguish from the type names of comedy. Grotesque names are more distinctive. Highet finds a clumsy variant of these peculiarly Germanic: The *Letters of Obscure Men* offers such instances as Mammotrectus Buntemantellus and Bartholomaeus Kuckuk. But many instances in English satiric drama of the Restoration lumber to mind, such as Chrononhotonthologos. And grotesque names certainly come in Dickens' satirical passages, as Highet notes. So we have Tippins and Podsnap in *Our Mutual Friend,* in the episode of the Veneerings' dinner; and, to add confirming instances, Pumblechook and Wopsle in *Great Expectations.* Dickens had a predilection for the grotesque, however, that extended beyond satiric contexts: he could even use the moderately grotesque name Traddles in affectionate comedy.

Another sort of satiric name, common in formal satires, is classical, either drawn direct from the paradigmatic Horace or Martial, or taken, as by them, from historical analogies. Hence Sporus (from Suetonius) and Atossa.

In satiric epigram, names are necessarily short. Jonson has Guilty, Poet-Ape, Woo-all, Beast; and Herrick has Cuff, Strut, Prig, Luggs, Gubbs, Greedy. There is a high proportion of type names in Latinate epigram, not only moral types but also the blanks of legal fiction: "Nokes went, he thought, to Styles's wife to bed."[4] Satiric names were not supposed to refer to individuals.

By contrast, the closely related epitaph form avoids type names. Names in epitaphs are generally either real names, or (to adopt Robert Louis Stevenson's term) obviously "punnable." Thus, we have "So died John So"; "Here lies John Knott"; the epitaph to John Sand ending "Sand I was, and now am dust";[5] that to Isaac Meek, inevitably ending "I have inherited the earth";[6] and many others. One might almost formulate the rule that epitaph names are real, punnable, or easily rhymed (as in "Here be the ashes of Jacob Todd, / Sexton now in the land of Nod").[7]

Amatory female names, particularly those of Renaissance literature, tend to be serious and euphonious. In love epigrams they often follow classical precedent, drawing on ancient poetry but not particularly on mythology. Herrick has Julia, Silvia, Perilla, Sappho, Electra, Myrrha, Corinna, Oenone; all of which occur in Ovid, Martial, or Propertius.[8] (The Latin model ultimately accounts for their ending in *-a*.) By contrast, the names of Elizabethan sonnet mistresses—mostly used in the titles of sequences—often come from mythology: for example, Pandora, Delia, Parthenope, Diana, Zepheria, Cynthia, Chloris, Aurora. Alternatively, they refer rather abstractly to the heavens, or to exalted moral qualities, or simply to beauty: Idea, Coelia, Caelica, Stella, Castara, Fidessa, and—in Scotland—Bellisa. There is a marked preference for names that have occurred previously in literature. So we have Barnfield's Cynthia from Propertius, Raleigh, and others; Barnes' Parthenope from Pontano; Tofte's Laura from Petrarch; and Daniel's Delia from Virgil, Scève, and others. In this context, Spenser's use of the ordinary English name Elizabeth in *Amoretti* is a very remarkable departure from convention.

Renaissance romance names are broadly similar, but tend to be more polysyllabic. The overlap between amatory and pastoral names (Delia, Phillis, Amintas) should be no surprise, love being such a large part of the content of pastoral.

Pastoral Names

It is perhaps in pastoral that the generic function of names comes out most clearly of all. There are quite enough of them for the system governing their use to become amply displayed. For we find, rather counterintuitively, that hundreds of personal names have been used in pastoral. (Sannazaro, who was almost as much quarried for names as Virgil, had loads to offer.) But certain of them, names such as Chromis, come out clear favorites. As the table shows, so close-knit is the pastoral web of imitation that a few dozen names appear in the works of many poets, from corner to corner of the genre.

To suppose that some pastoral names merely occur oftener than others would be to miss much of their significance. Actually they appear in individual works according to a distinct pattern. What we may call the "nuclear" pastoral names seem to be used to set the generic mood, or even as signals that it is being resorted to temporarily, within another kind. And in a mixed or included genre the names are quite likely to be all nuclear—as with the pastoral element of Marvell's *Damon the Mower*. All pastoralists use some nuclear names: these do much, indeed, to evoke the pastoral world for both writer and reader. They indicate pastoral unambiguously. What other genre, from Theocritus' *Idylls* 4 to Noel Coward's *Hay Fever*, does Corydon suggest?[9]

In addition to these "conventional" names, an eclogue will contain others that tune a special note or represent some individual contribution. These may be names that indicate a subgenre: a Theocritean precedent is

DISTRIBUTION OF COMMON PASTORAL NAMES

Aegon	Th	V	Sa	—	—	—	Mi	P
Alexis	—	V	Sa	—	Sp	—	—	P
Amaryllis	Th	V	Sa	—	Sp	—	Mi	P
Amyntas	Th	V	Sa	—	Sp	—	Mi	—
Chromis	Th	V	Sa	—	—	—	—	—
Corydon	Th	V	Sa	Si	Sp	—	—	—
Damon	—	V	Sa	—	Sp	Ma	Mi	P
Damoetas	Th	V	Sa	Si	—	—	Mi	—
Daphnis	Th	V	Sa	—	—	Ma	Mi	P
Doris	—	V	Sa	—	Sp	—	—	P
Galatea	Th	V	Sa	—	Sp	—	—	—
Lycidas	—	V	Sa	—	—	—	Mi	P
Meliboeus	—	V	Sa	—	Sp	—	—	—
Menalcas	Th	V	Sa	Si	Sp	Ma	Mi	—
Thestylis	Th	V	—	—	Sp	Ma	Mi	—
Thyrsis	Th	V	Sa	—	—	Ma	Mi	P
Tityrus	Th	V	Sa	—	Sp	—	Mi	—

Note: Th = Theocritus; V = Virgil; Sa = Sannazaro; Si = Sidney; Sp = Spenser; Ma = Marvell; Mi = Milton; P = Pope. Translations are excluded from consideration.

Polyphemus, the Cyclops in *Idylls* 6 and 11, who introduces slightly indecorous hints of an extrapastoral world.[10] William Diaper's *Nereides or Sea-Eclogues* (1712) has a typical if unusually large cast. It shows his keen sense of decorum in selecting names appropriate to the marine subgenre. Proteus (*Sea-Eclogues* 8) was mentioned in Theocritus' *Idylls* 8.52 as having herded seals; and the sea-nymph Galatea is ultimately from the same source. (The ancient eclogue was not divided into marine and pastoral subgenres.) Besides the "nuclear" names, such as Lycon and Chromis, in the tradition of Theocritus and Sannazaro, Diaper introduces many others, apt in various ways, from classical mythology. (Melanthus, for example, was one of the Tyrrhenian pirates, transformed into a dolphin in *Metamorphoses* 3.) But some of his most convincingly marine-pastoral names are invented, either from appropriate common nouns, such as Murex, a species of shellfish, or from history or prose literature (Hippias, "horseman," from Plato; Muraena, after the Roman family—or the fish *murena*).[11] Such inventions call for more than tact and ingenuity. The sense of an ideal marine variant of the pastoral world guides Diaper in enlarging it independently. His determined freedom may be gauged by the fact that he takes over only four of Homer's easily available Nereid names.[12] Other ecloguists worked in a not dissimilar way, using their "free" names to touch a particular tonality of pastoral.

Pastoral names were also organized quite differently, as *Schlüsselnamen* or key names. As everyone knows, at least from the time of Virgil personal allusions were introduced into pastoral. Either for satiric purposes or to exploit the impersonal genre's potential for subtly veiled communication, the pastoral names might be made to refer to real people. A "nuclear" paradigm was Tityrus, Virgil's own persona. On that model, other poets' aliases were added, such as Marot's and Spenser's Colin and Drayton's Rowland. From the medieval application of Tityrus as a pastor's or bishop's name there grew a tradition of satiric key names. Thus, Petrarch has Pamphilus (Saint Peter) attacking Mitio (Pope Clement VI),[13] while Boccaccio has Daphnis and Florida for the Emperor and the City of Florence. Elizabethan pastoral developed a special form of rebus, based on actual names but preserving the generic flavor, perhaps combined with additional wit—as *Philisides* (from *Philip Sidney,* but also hinting at "Lover of the Heavens"); *Algrind* (Archbishop *Grindal*); *Roffyn* (John Young, Bishop of Rochester or *Roffensis*). The early culmination of this tradition came in Spenser's giant double eclogue *Colin Clout's Come Home Again,* where pastoral names are found for dozens of once identifiable people, many of them writers.[14] The tradition of key names persisted in Augustan pastoral. Thus, Pope assumes the name of Alexis (suggesting Alexander), so that the transmission of a pastoral pipe from Colin Clout to Alexis in Summer 39-44 asserts his claim to be the successor of Spenser.

So far we have considered pastoral names as forming a single tradition. When we compare individual sets of eclogues, a very different picture emerges (see table).

In what may be called the Virgilian tradition, represented here by Petrarch, Googe, and especially by Pope, speakers' names are partly "nuclear," partly innovatory.[15] (Googe's *Eclogues* 7, echoing Virgil's and Petrarch's *Eclogues* 10, approaches the periphery of the kind, as its woodland names, Selvagia and Silvanus—the latter from the *Georgics*—lead us to expect. It introduces feminist and antifeminist satire, and such unpastoral cynicism as "tush / It's riches makes a man.") By contrast, Spenser's *Shepherd's Calendar,* although it mentions Pan, Tityrus, and so forth in passing, has not a single "nuclear" name among its speakers.

This striking departure from the common or classical pattern reflects the different generic direction of Spenser's work, which leaves the politi-

SPEAKERS IN ECLOGUES

Theocritus	Acrotime, Aeschinas, Amycus, Asphalion, Battus, Bucaeus, Comatas, Corydon, Daphnis, Gorgo, Lacon, Menalcas, Milon, Morson, Polydeuces, Praxinoa, Thyonichus, Thyrsis
Virgil	Alphesiboeus, Corydon, Damoetas, Damon, Lycidas, Meliboeus, Menalcas, Moeris, Mopsus, Palaemon, Thyrsis, Tityrus
Petrarch	Amyclas, Apitius, Daphne, Epy, Festinus, Fulgida, Fusca, Gallus, Ganymedes, Idaeus, Martius, Mitio, Monicus, Multivolus, Niobe, Pamphilus, Philogeus, Phytias, Socrates, Stupeus, Sylvanus, Sylvius, Theophilus, Tyrrhenus, Volucer
Sannazaro	Celadon, Chromis, Dorylas, Iolas, Lycidas, Lycon, Mopsus, Mycon, Thelgon
Googe	Amintas, Coridon, Cornix, Dametas, Daphnes, Egon, Faustus, Felix, Menalcas, Mopsus, Palemon, Selvagia, Silvanus
Spenser	Colin Clout, Cuddie, Diggon Davie, Hobbinol, Morrel, Palinode, Perigot, Piers, Thenot, Thomalin, Willye
Drayton	Batte, Borril, Gorbo, Motto, Perkin, Rowland, Winken
Philips	Albino, Angelot, Argol, Colinet, Cuddy, Geron, Hobbinol, Lanquet, Lobbin, Mico, Palin
Gay	Bowzybeus, Bumkinet, Cloddipole, Cuddy, Grubbinol, Hobnelia, Lobbin Clout, Marian, Sparabella
Pope	Aegon, Alexis, Damon, Daphne, Daphnis, Delia, Doris, Hylas, Lycidas, Strephon, Thyrsis

cal eclogue of Petrarch, Mantuanus, and others for an even more vernacular type. *The Shepherd's Calendar* was so influential that it in turn became a paradigm. It was the model for a type of semirealistic eclogue that was not necessarily political or satirical. To this "native" type, which originated with Marot and Skelton, and which claimed some classical authorization in Theocritus, *The Shepherd's Garland* belongs. None of Drayton's names is nuclear except Batte (Theocritus' Battos, also a lover), unless Gorbo is vaguely reminiscent of Gorgo. And each has a decidedly Colin Cloutish quality—although Drayton was careful not to share names with Spenser. But Shirley and Cotton did not have the same inhibition. And Ambrose Philips was slavishly Spenserian (when he was not Sidneian, as in his use of Geron and Lanquet). Even his Lobbin, though not a speaker in *The Shepherd's Calendar,* is Spenser's pastoral name for Leicester.

The Shepherd's Week, burlesquing these native pastorals of Philips, fastens surely on the names. Remorselessly Gay doubles their Spenserianism, or distorts them just enough to release bumpkin possibilities: Lobbin Clout and Lubberkin, Grubbinol and Bowzybeus. Gay's realistic eclogues were skirmishes in a pastoral war that does not concern us here. It is enough to notice that a point at issue was the provenance of names. Posing as the author of Tickell's *Guardian* essays in praise of Philips' pastorals, Pope writes:

> Mr. Pope hath fallen into the same error with Virgil. His clowns do not converse in all the simplicity proper to the country: his names are borrowed from Theocritus and Virgil, which are improper to the scene of his pastorals. He introduces Daphnis, Alexis and Thyrsis on British plains, as Virgil had done before him on the Mantuan; whereas Philips, who hath the strictest regard to propriety, makes choice of names peculiar to the country, and more agreeable to a reader of delicacy; such as Hobbinol, Lobbin, Cuddy, and Colin Clout.[16]

This has nothing to do with strictness in applying rules. All the combatants were in favor of regularity. Indeed, Drayton, Tickell, and Pope (in *A Discourse on Pastoral Poetry*) set out rules for pastoral formally. Nor is Pope's position here exactly one of an Ancient versus Moderns. It has more to do with opposition between the "rationalistic" theory of pastoral, based on Fontanelle, and the "neoclassic" theory of Rapin (and of Pope and Gay). For the latter, in the main, pastoral was an ideal reality, and Virgilian; whereas Tickell and Philips, with their rationalistic or psychological approach, saw the main pastoral tradition as coming from Theocritus and Spenser. (Paradoxically, following Theocritus meant avoiding his pastoral names.)[17] Yet Pope admired Spenser's pastorals and adopted important features from them. And he could be said to have more Theocritean echoes, at least, than Philips. Pope seems to have been drawn to the idea of a golden-age pastoral that would be exclusively poetical: *pastoral* pastoral, so to speak. With this in view, his pastorals—and it is significant that he calls them that, rather than eclogues—use mainly nuclear names, and only names in the right poetic lineage. For example, Strephon was familiar from Sidney's *Arcadia,* while Hylas comes in Theocritus, Virgil, Spenser, and Milton, although not as a specially pastoral name. This nuclearity accords with Pope's generalized, modally abstract form of pastoral.

Given such close organization of pastoral names, it was possible to finesse on expectation in various subtle ways. Earlier, I mentioned *Damon the Mower,* a pastoral lyric in which the mower bears a nuclear name. His world was cruelly destroyed "When Juliana came, and She / What I do to the Grass, does to my Thoughts and Me." *Juliana* may just possibly glance at Julia, the name of the love elegy mistresses of Johannes Secundus and Robert Herrick. But the main effect is that of an ordinary, plausible, unpastoral name: a name from the terrible unforeseen quotidian world by whose representative Damon is, a little comically, *bouleversé.* This is not to say that the name Juliana is out of place in pastoral, but that her sort of name and Damon's sort could not be interchanged without loss to Marvell's poem.

Names in Narrative

In the narrative kinds, also, names have a generic function. But their associational systems are too complicated for a brief treatment here. We can only glance at one or two broad aspects.

The tale, even when in the third person, may have characters who are not named at all; which accords well with its interior perspective. The fairy tale, however, may use conspicuously odd or exotic or meaningful names (Rumplestiltskin, Rapunzel, Keren-Happuch, Dummling). Such names are flavorful, but not particularly communicative. In medieval romance, names are more powerfully evocative of a special fictive province. Here again, we find unambiguous "nuclear" names of high associative value, such as those used by Milton to epitomize the world of romance: "Knights of Logres, or of Lyonesse, / Lancelot or Pelleas, or Pellenore." Romance names have received much attention; and critics have noticed that they may be deployed in characteristic ways. The best example one could choose is the device of delayed naming. So Chrétien delays identifying Perceval in the *Conte del graal,* in a way that greatly increases the name's prominence and weight.[18] And Spenser often uses the device, as when he avoids naming the Red Cross Knight until well into the second canto of *The Faerie Queen.* In sharp contrast are the conventions of the verisimilar novel, where the protagonist's name is given in full on the first occasion of use.[19] Other genres supply names in yet other ways—pastoral, for instance, without introduction, intimately from the beginning.[20]

The "fantastic high-sounding names" of the romances (as an eighteenth-century critic called them) continued into the period of the early novel. To some extent they even continued into the novels themselves (Pamela, Tristram). From the time of Deloney, however, novelists commonly gave their characters names "such as, though they sometimes bore some reference to the character, had a more modern termination."[21] More particularly, Ian Watt has argued that since Defoe complete and realistic names have been a generic characteristic of the novel, or at least a feature of "formal realism": "The early novelists . . . made an extremely significant break with tradition, and named their characters in such a way as to suggest that they were to be regarded as particular individuals in the contemporary environment."[22] Watt connects this with new ideas about individual consciousness and identity, and with the particularizing of character. Proper names, unlike universals, refer to a single individual. In previous literature, names did not imply fully individual entities, since the historical or fantastic names preferred would tend to activate a literary rather than a quotidian mental set. The type names of comedy, again, as Aristotle noticed, did not refer to single individuals.[23] Only with the novel, in fact, is fictional identity fully individualized.

This view carries much conviction. The introduction of characters with both given names and surnames—with all that these entail—was a change of profound significance. However, Watt's theory needs qualification, which he himself partly supplied in a previous article.[24] For one thing, the change was less clear-cut and more gradual than he argues in *The Rise of the Novel*. Earlier prose fiction, and even verse romance, was sometimes capable of preferring ordinary names to "characteristic" or literary names. If Lazarillo de Tormes is a slightly doubtful instance, many in Deloney are not (Thomas Cole, William Somers). And Lindsay's romance hero is circumstantially William Meldrum, "Laird of Cleische and Bynnis." Watt has to allow many exceptions. In a sense this is so even with his main examples. Thus, Defoe displays "onomastic nonchalance":[25] his names "though realistic, . . . are rarely the true, full, permanent names, ratified by baptism and legal record, to which we are accustomed" and which "symbolize the individual's stable social role."[26] Defoe's incomplete names reflect actual practice in the seventeenth century, when members of the lower classes seldom used surnames. They also conform to conventions of the literature of roguery, reticence about names being there good form. Besides, many of Defoe's names could be taken as characteristic—such as Moll, a criminal type name.[27] Yet many will feel that he already wrote novels and in some sense practiced formal realism.

Richardson consistently supplies both names, so that his novels seem to offer stronger instances. Yet *Grandison* gives a "suggestion of grandeur"; Pamela has obvious romance associations; and Clarissa is a mock-romantic name for "nymphs of the town."[28] Fielding uses many type names, in "departure from the usual treatment of these matters in the novel."[29] His full names are realistic enough (indeed, they may have been drawn from the list of subscribers to a book Fielding owned), yet they seem aimed at maximum generality or neutrality.[30] By the time he came to *Amelia*, Fielding, according to Watt, "realised" his onomastic irregularity: there he confines to minor characters his "neoclassical preference for type names." Smollett and Sterne offer further exceptions. All this is not to deny that ordinary contemporary names became "established as part of the tradition of the form." But James' criticism of the Trollopean "characteristic" name Quiverful should not make us forget other parts of the tradition, such as the one Dickens cultivated.

In any case, the distinction between proper names and type names is untenable on a hard-and-fast basis. Many have fallen into John Stuart Mill's error of supposing that real proper names are necessarily meaningless and distinguishable from "characteristic" or significant names.[31] But in fact the type names and literary names of fiction used often to be given in real life, and sometimes are still. Generic names for servants, for example, were imposed in place of the "real" name of the incumbent. And Camden lists many "meaningful" Christian names, such as Remedium Amoris, Reformation, Earth, Dust, Ashes, Tribulation, The Lord is Near, Discipline, Thankful, Praise-God.[32] The development of fictional names was not from common noun to proper noun, but from one coexistence of common and proper to another.

Camden was well aware that romances might set a fashion in naming, so that romantic and other literary names became common in ordinary life. (Spenser's son was christened Sylvanus.) And coincidence, too, must be allowed room. From whatever cause, we find that many names that seem obviously fictional turn out to have been available in fact. This is true even of *The Faerie Queen:* in real life Scudamore, Amyas, and Amidas (to say nothing of Una and Duessa) were all familiar enough. Spenser seems to exercise his wit in devising names that combine romance association or type meaning with ordinary possibility. His is a world of everyday magic, of gentlemen knights. Some Spenserian names are intricately ambiguous in this way. So Calepine not only groups phonetically with contrasting Calidore, but also suggests a Greek derivation (*chalepos* or *chalepaino*). At the same time, it is a real name (*Calepinus*) and hence groups with Aladine (from Aldus Manutius) and other names alluding to famous Humanists.[33]

There are further complications. We have to allow for Elizabethan fondness for "explaining" names (Camden even finds a pun in Perceval: *per se valens*), for rebuses, and for romantic nicknames or code names (Constable was "Sconsolato"). In the seventeenth century, moreover, it was a convention of polite courtship to use love names drawn from the romances for women, both in conversation and in intrigues. And novel heroines, as Watt notes, were usually given such names, which were highly valued—"a name that glides through half a dozen tender syllables, as Elisamonda, Clidamira, Deidamira, that runs upon vowels off the tongue."[34] For these and similar reasons, it is often hard to distinguish ordinary and literary names in the period of the early novel. A distinction was no doubt felt, but it would be felt differently.

Who is to know, then, whether it is not subtle formal realism for Richardson to name Pamela after the heroine of a romance much read by the godfearing?[35] In any event, the name Pamela Andrews, like Clarissa Harlowe, suggests a tension between romantic possibility and realistic setting. Such a complexity is supposed to characterize novelistic names, after Richardson (especially) realizes their potentialities. Certainly the allusive complexity is there, although even early readers cannot all have jumped to connect Clarissa with *Huon of Bordeaux* or the seduced unfortunate in *Night Thoughts*. But the genre of *Clarissa* is such that we may doubt whether there is much more in the name itself than a suggestion of romantic purity and goodness. For in the verisimilar novel, as distinct from the romance, names are relatively empty: they wait to be filled, to be given content by the unfolding character and experience of their bearers. The decisive contribution of Richardson is not so much complex suggestion as a consistently sustained specificity and contingency in naming. The names may be suggestive or vacant.

Above all, we need to qualify the idea that in the onomastics of the novel only the central figures matter. If the central figures have ordinary contemporary names, according to Watt, type names of minor characters are of no account. That cannot be right. All character names are of significance as possible indicators of genre. Not that including a few "nonordinary" names necessarily represents a failure to achieve formal realism. For a single novel will often combine elements of several genres. The principal character may be treated with his circle in the manner of a fictional biography, say, and be named accordingly, whereas the names of a subplot or subsidiary episode may reflect a change to the comic or satiric mode. Type names, indeed, are among the indicators that signal such shifts.

The common use of initials for names (Mr. B. in Pamela; Lord M. in *Clarissa;* Lord L. in *Sir Charles Grandison*) seems at first to count against a rule of full names. But the practice seems to have had its English origin in such works as Gascoigne's scandalous *Adventures of Master F.J.* (1573), where its purpose was precisely to hint at real names that might have filled the lacunas. There was a tradition against publishing the names of gentry; and Watt is surely right in thinking that Defoe and Richardson introduced the initial device to create "the suggestive and saleable aura of a true scandal of high life."[36] In subsequent periods, incomplete names and dates were often used to suggest scandal, or merely that the author was personally involved in the events narrated.[37] Even Austen, who normally gives full names, may use incomplete ones for a local purpose; as when she suppresses the name of "the ——shire militia" that the scandalous Wickham belonged to. Later, the device became characteristic of the tale (for example the incomplete date in the opening paragraph of *Treasure Island*) and of fiction scandalous in one way or another (*Die Marquise von O; Histoire d'O*).

Kafka started a new alphabet of initials. His K. is generally taken to refer to his own name, in the tradition we have just traced. But he subsequently became the paradigm of a new tradition. Since Kafka, a prominent initial name has come to indicate a nonprobable or experimental novel. The unnamed protagonist need not be identified with the author. Nevertheless, the historical origin of the device in that identification is clear enough. The initial name can also seem to decline to arrive at a formed and final intention. Hence, in all probability, its frequent use in the work-in-progress novel: Pynchon's *V* (1961); Berger's *G* (1972); Figes' *B* (1972); Sollers' *H* (1973).[38] Gaddis' *J.R.* is an instructive borderline case. It is in the main too verisimilar to call for an incompletely named character in the title; yet the fiction is damaged, and the narrative method even mildly innovative. Accordingly, the name is not a single initial but a pair; it might be a real-life nickname, or (in the United States) a given name, or a play on "Jr." and no name at all.

Watt's account of fictional names provides on the whole a sound foundation for generic description. Ordinary names (when we know which these are) are dependable enough characteristics of the verisimilar novel. But the names in novels become more interesting when we consider not only their naturalistic decorum but their function as local indicators of mode change. In *Tom Jones,* Thwackum, Square, and Blifil work best if we consider them as indications of a shift to satire, rather than as aberrations.

6. Generic Signals

Certain constituents appear to have a special value in communicating genre. As we have seen, almost any feature can function as part of a generic repertoire. But some are so immediately indicative, particularly during the early phases of approach, that they seem to have to do with recognition specifically. Of these indicators we shall discuss three: allusions, titles, and opening topics. The generic markers that cluster at the beginning of a work have a strategic role in guiding the reader. They help to establish, as soon as possible, an appropriate mental "set" that allows the work's generic codes to be read. One might call them the key words of the code, although they may serve this purpose at an unconscious level, or at least beneath the level of attention.

Generic Allusion

Apart from explicit labeling, the most direct form of indication is reference to previous writers or representatives of the genre. Thus, a longer work will gesture, as it were by denotation, toward the grouping it takes its departure from. Such generic references often come in the exordium, as a variant of the so-called modesty topos,[1] or *captatio benevolentiae*—as when Stephen Hawes humbly tells Henry VII that *The Passetyme of Pleasure* has been "compyled ... To folowe the trace / and all the parfytenesse / Of my mayster Lydgate" (ll. 47–48). This is taken (no doubt rightly) as an expression of humility. But it may also serve to draw attention to the work's congeners, Lydgate's *Pilgrimage of the Life of Man* and *Temple of Glass*—and hence to the pilgrimage and love-vision genres. Lydgate himself, in turn, followed Chaucer, the "Floure of Poetes" of *The Siege of Thebes* Prologue 39–57. This Prologue is surely one of the most elaborate generic allusions ever made. By a complex framing device characteristic of gothic mannerism, Lydgate presents his poem as a contribution to the tale-telling of the Canterbury pilgrims. Chaucer's own generic hints are more elusive, but can also be more communicative. In *The Book of the Duchess,* the narrator falls asleep over Ovid's tale of Ceyx and Alcyone, to dream of waking in a room painted with scenes "of al the Romaunce of the Rose." Taken in context, these allusions prepare the reader not merely for a work of consolation but specifically for an allegory of consolation.[2] The device of sleeping over an appropriate book was a convention of love vision, or became so after Chaucer.

In later and more allusive authors, references of this sort can be very oblique, yet at the same time highly organized so as to provide bearings that fix the work's generic point of departure in a discriminating way. A summational classic of mixed genre, such as *Paradise Lost,* will have a high concentration of generic allusions. Many of these tend to constellate closely in the exordium. Thus, the opening words "Of man's" momentarily recall the Homeric *andra* or Virgilian *Arma virumque,* and so the epic of antiquity: an association immediately modified by "till one greater man / Restore us." The double hero rather suggests Tasso, or Spenser. And the allusions to Exodus, Deuteronomy, and Saint John's gospel that follow—

> Sing heavenly Muse, that on the secret top
> Of Oreb, or of Sinai, didst inspire
> That shepherd, who first taught the chosen seed,
> In the beginning how the heavens and earth
> Rose out of chaos: or if Sion hill
> Delight thee more, and Siloa's brook that flowed
> Fast by the oracle of God; I thence
> Invoke thy aid to my adventurous song
>
> (1.6–13)

—establish a generic context that would be more in accord with biblical epic. "Dove-like sat'st brooding on the vast abyss" specifically echoes Sylvester's Du Bartas. And the biblical mountains confront the classical "Aonian mount" in the manner of the Christian or "heavenly Muse." Again, where Milton writes of his

> adventurous song,
> That with no middle flight intends to soar
> Above the Aonian mount, while it pursues
> Things unattempted yet in prose or rhyme
>
> (1.13–16)

he is treating a conventional exordium topic—what Curtius labels "I bring things never said before." But the passage is so close to "Cosa non detta mai in prose nè in rima" as to allude specifically to Ariosto. In such ways, a full generic context is established, so that when the inset pagan epic begins with the Virgilian *initium* "say first what cause" (1. 28), no fit audience is likely to take the formula quite at its face value.

Prose fiction makes frequent and sometimes elaborate use of generic allusion. Fielding set an early example, with prefaces that amount to essays in genre theory. Later, however, when the novelistic form was more familiar and easy to recognize, generic allusions tended to be more specific. They would often refer to a mode transforming the basic kind. Thus, Austen's *Northanger Abbey* has many references to Gothic romances—*The Italian* and *Udolpho* and *The Monk*[3]—although these are well worked into the story. Rather surprisingly, *The Turn of the Screw* does not rely only on implicit indicators of gothic (wild weather; a castellar *mise-en-scène*) but introduces an explicit mention of *Udolpho* and a conspicuous allusion to *Jane Eyre*.[4] Perhaps the need arises from the generic delicacy of the tale: its gothic must reflect the sensibility of the governess, yet at the same time serve James as the *point d'appui* for a further interiorized form exploring the motives of supernatural experience. A difficult or innovative or generically complex work may have to secure its generic context with many allusions. Joyce and Nabokov depend on them so heavily that books have been devoted to this one constituent in their work.[5] Or another example: when John le Carré made something of a new departure from espionage thrillers in *The Honourable Schoolboy,* he signaled this by references to Conrad and others who have used popular vehicles for the "Eastern novel."[6] The writer in effect is saying, "If you feel uncertain how to take this book, try taking it with those others."

But how is a reader to know which allusions function generically? *Northanger Abbey* has references to the Reverend Thomas Moss and Gay's *Fables,* as well as to gothic romances. How can signals of genre be told apart from "ordinary" allusions, which will often enough refer to kindred works in any case? Questions of authorial intention need not concern us: no doubt many generic allusions are unconscious. As to the question of function, it can sometimes be settled where allusions are made prominent by repetition, say, or gratuitousness. So de la Mare's story *A Nose* has two very noticeable allusions to fairy tale: "just like the wicked godmother in the old stories" and—this time in a catalogue of historical characters, with Cyrano de Bergerac—"Long-Nose in the fairy tale."[7] But many other instances remain ambiguous, so that the convention cannot be used as a mechanical proof of genre. When Hawthorne names the Pyncheon cock Chaunticleer, is he alluding to *The Nun's Priest's Tale* merely as a beast fable? Or does he mean to relate *The House of the Seven Gables* specifically to a subgenre of philosophical fables about fate and predestination? The daguerreotypist's interpretation of the "feathered riddle" supports the latter view.[8]

In contemporary literature, generic allusion steers toward a more covert manner. So Robert Nye's Falstaff will drop the name of John Boccaccio—who wrote "a poem in 50 chapters, entitled the amorous vision"—possibly to avoid too bald an allusion to the more relevant *Decameron* (arranged, like *Falstaff,* in 100 ordered sections). Similar ambages circumbend *Pale Fire.* Kinbote's dependably inept citation of Housman's *Shropshire Lad* is in effect Nabokov's own allusion to Housman's Manilius Preface, just as the *Essay on Man* analogue covers another more apt in the *Dunciad.*[9] Both underlying allusions are to works that turn the apparatus of scholarship against dunces. Here and in many other instances one sense almost a compulsion to name works claiming philosophical priority—even when, as with modernist or avant-garde writers, there is most eagerness to be independent and new.[10]

In some periods, preliminary allusion is not much used. Instead, adumbration of the generic context is removed from the work itself and developed in a proem or prefatory epistle (an example is "The Proem to the Courteous Reader" before Gay's *Shepherd's Week*) in a way that seems more explicit. But this preference is related to period style in the framing of literary space. We cannot assume that it corresponds to a new degree of consciousness of genre.

Allusions are often used as indicators of temporary changes in mode. For this they are economically effective. And the most highly developed and subtlest allusions, from the seventeenth to the nineteenth century, were to classical authors (together with one modern, Milton). The Augustan georgic, with its burlesque and descriptive offshoots, would be hard to imagine without the Virgilian echoes that signal changes in style height and articulate its various parts. Its genre effects are sometimes remarkably delicate. Even in a minor work such as James Grainger's *Sugar-Cane,* the stylistic elevation varies exquisitely. Thus, the largely heroic Second Book begins with directions for how to deal with marauding monkeys, using a distanced epic mode to elevate the subject in the Virgilian manner: "faithful dogs, / Of nose sagacious, on their footsteps wait" (2.50–51). The Miltonic "of nose sagacious" dignifies the dogs, as John Chalker remarks, with an almost mock-heroic suggestion that obviates oversolemnity. But the specific allusion to Milton's Death—"His nostril wide into the murky air, / Sagacious of his quarry from so far" (10.280–281), a passage itself based on the *Georgics*—also has a grim edge. These dogs will really kill. Grainger has used heroic allusion to achieve a finely poised tone. The *Aeneid* was equally indispensable as an epic paradigm for allusion to the heroic, both in mixed kinds and in mock epic. And in satire, similarly, Horace and Juvenal offered generic archetypes.

It would be an exaggeration to say that the old genres depended on classical allusion. But it is certainly true that the decline of classical education had far-reaching effects on many genres. When the ancient canon became less familiar it was not replaced by any modern canon comparable in authority. Consequently, generic allusion has become more restricted and less delicate. And indirectly the impact on the understanding of earlier literature has been profound.

Titles

Titles have received little critical attention.[11] This is unfortunate, in view of their importance in modern literature, where, as Wayne Booth says, "they are often the only explicit commentary the reader is given." But it is partly understandable, since the form is a comparatively recent one. Medieval titling was commonly by incipit or opening phrase. In any case, authorial responsibility for titling began in effect with print. Before that, "titles" were given by commentators, editors, or scribes—*Incipit Liber Boecii de Consolacione Philosophie*. Titles begining with *de* at first implied a *tractatus* or discursive treatise. But from Montaigne onward, the form was appropriated by the essay. In the vernacular, short titles of this type (*Of Studies; Of Resolution*) introduce most of the informal essays of Bacon, Felltham, and others. Thus, the titling convention of the essay inherits that of its generic antecedents.

Within any historical period, titling conventions differ from genre to genre. This comes out clearly in the dramatic kinds. As Levin notes, classical tragedies, and to a lesser extent Renaissance English tragedies, take their protagonist's name, often with a distinguishing epithet (*Oedipus Coloneus; Othello*). Aristophanic comedies, however, are named after a chorus or collective group (*Acharnians; Knights*), and the New Comedy uses names of character types (*Miles Gloriosus; The Provoked Wife*). Comedies, which tend to generalize, may also have titles based on such generalizing forms as proverb and idiom (*The Way of the World*).[12]

In prose fiction, the pretense of factuality at first dominated titling. Fictional narratives were presented as Memoirs or Adventures or Histories.[13] So we have *The History of Tom Jones, a Foundling*. Such a strenuous titular profession of factuality is now more indicative of pornography—for example, *The Authentic Confessions of Harriet Marwood*. But something like it occurs, in a less assertive way, in the use of personal names. A full personal name in the title of a narrative still indicates either a biography or a fictional biography—that is, a verisimilar novel. (Contrast between paired kinds sharing formal characteristics is a phenomenon we shall return to.) Note, however, that so far as fictional narratives are concerned, this is true only of men's names. For the heroine of a novel, the given name alone may suffice, by titling convention (*Evelina; Emma; Shirley*).[14] Watt sees in this a suggestion that the novel heroine is not regarded as a complete social being, until marriage has endowed her with a surname.[15] But there may also be a formal explanation. Just as novelistic forms could assimilate other conventions of romance, instead of replacing them, so with titling.

The novel, that baggy monster, is sometimes thought of as having ingested the romance altogether, so far as external shape goes. But in the nineteenth century we can still detect something of a distinction between their titling conventions. With some exceptions and apparent exceptions, full personal names are preferred for verisimilar novels, place names for romances (*David Copperfield;* but *Wuthering Heights*). This may have something to do with the special function of *mise-en-scène* in romance: the House of the Seven Gables is more than merely a setting. Other fiction whose mimesis falls short of novelistic realization, such as Peacock's, may also have place-name titles. Among apparent exceptions to the rule we should notice the novel *Middlemarch*—in which, however, a community, rather than an individual protagonist, is the focus of interest. Henry James, who often seeks to fuse romance and novelistic features, naturally has titles of both types. Real exceptions include titles within a *roman fleuve* (*Barchester Towers*), and a few separate novels (*Mansfield Park*). *Jane Eyre* is a romantic novel, and apparently its novel element is enough to carry the full-name title. The incomplete personal name, on the other hand, is more generally available. It can convey a romantic or a political suggestion—or both at once, as in *Coningsby*.

Titles with "and" linking two abstract nouns indicate novels of moral analysis. As Levin has suggested, the "and" is often equivalent to "contra": it promises a dialectical trial of strength between the abstractions, and perhaps also their eventual transformation (*Sense and Sensibility; Pride and Prejudice; North and South; War and Peace*).

In modern prose fiction we meet a variety of forms of title. Fashion plays a great part, as in the early twentieth-century vogue for echoic titling. All novelistic kinds used quotations as titles—mostly drawn from Shakespeare or Milton or the Bible, especially Ecclesiastes (*The Golden Bowl; The Sun Also Rises*).[16] Certain forms of title continue to indicate genre, but the indication is often very oblique or ironic. For example, titles of verisimilar novels seem to avoid an initial preposition, so that when they do have one, as in *Under Western Eyes,* a suggestion of space, even of exotic adventure, may be communicated—though nothing so obvious or even conscious as the travel-book form *Across* [+ *large natural feature*]. Steven Kellman notes that novels of ideas often have an apparently irrelevant or riddling title (*Under the Net; Cat's Cradle*). And fiction titles ending in numbers, we may add, tend to give an even more specific indication of genre. They announce a satiric dystopia. In *1984, 1985, Fahrenheit 451, Limbo '90, Slaughterhouse-Five,* and *334,* the dystopia lies in the future: these are all works that make some use of a science fiction vehicle.[17] But in several, the satiric mode is also very prominent, so that it may not be wrong to draw *Catch-22* and *The Crying of Lot 49* into the same grouping.[18] The bases of the convention are many: partly the Orwellian paradigm; partly number's suggestion of depersonalization; partly its "scientific" association; partly its hint at the provisionality of social forms.

In long poetic kinds, the form of titling and even the nomenclature of parts is largely determined by genre. As Levin has noted, epics may be named after a single hero (*Odyssey; Aeneid*). But with multiple heroes "the focus may shift to place: the *Iliad,* the *Pharsalia,* the *Lusiads.*" Later examples abound (*Gerusalemme Liberata; Paradise Lost*). Behind this shifting of focus, as the instance of the *Argonautica* suggests, lies the desire for a title that is fittingly unified. The convention, therefore, belongs to classical epic. In the more polyphonic medieval romance, by contrast, titles with "and" are common enough (*Floris and Blauncheflur; Ywain and Gawain*); so, too, in the Renaissance erotic epyllion (*Hero and Leander; Endimion and Phoebe*). "Qualified" titles of Renaissance and baroque epics (*Orlando Furioso; Gerusalemme Liberata*) mainly indicate heroic romance or romantic epic. But *Paradise Lost* recalls a titling convention of tragedy (compare *Adamo Caduto*), and may suggest a tragic transformation. Conversely, love tragedies may have titles with "and," on the romance pattern: *Romeo and Juliet; Antonio and Mellida.*

On the model of *Iliad* (that is, "Trojan," some such noun as "poem" being understood), many titles have been formed with an -*iad* suffix. At first these regularly announced an epic: *Lusiad, Franciade, Columbiad, Olympiad, Epigoniad, ?Athenaid.* But the consequent opportunity for parody and mock epic was too good to miss. Pope's *Dunciad* is the leader of a large group, including Churchill's *Rosciad,* Whitehead's *Gymnasiad,* Spence's *Charliad,* Cambridge's *Scribbleriad,* Smart's *Hilliad,* Chatterton's *Consuliad,* and Wolcot's *Lousiad* (to say nothing of Roy Campbell's *Georgiad*). On the same Homeric analogy, Musaeus' Hero being "Sēstias" ("from Sestos"), Chapman used the term "sestiads" for the parts into which he divided Marlowe's and his *Hero and Leander.*[19] But Renaissance writers were so fond of extending, misusing, and inventing generic language in a quasi-technical way that "sestiads" came to be used for the parts of any long poem similarly divided, as in Sheppard's *Times Displayed in Six Sestiads.* A similar malleability shows in Drayton's use of the fashionably heroic or pseudoheroic termination for the title of an ode—"A Skeltoniad."

Less obscurely, the ordinary nomenclature of parts works as a presentational device. In the Renaissance, "books" indicates epic, "cantos" romance or romantic epic. Spenser, then, in combining both terms in *The Faerie Queen,* prepared his readers for generic mixture. Other part terms are still more obvious: "turn" and "counterturn" can only divide an ode. But part nomenclature has also been used to impart subtler intimations. Pope's division of the *Essay on Man* into epistles rather than books is a case in point. It disarms any inappropriate expectations of systematic treatment, by suggesting a Horatian mode of "informal miscellaneous discourse."[20] Yet Pope's work is not exactly in the same kind with any of Horace's: he uses the part term to suggest the broader affiliation of the epistolary plain style.

Titling of short poems began with print. At first (as in *Tottel's Miscellany*) the titles were editorial summaries, perhaps serving merely to avoid headless slabs of print. They pick up phrases from the poem, or identify its kind. So Surrey's "Love, that liveth" is crudely dubbed *Complaint of a Lover Rebuked.* And Gascoigne entitles one of his poems *Farewell with a mischief, written by a lover being disdainfully abjected by a dame of high call-*

*ing, Who had chosen (in his place) a play fellow of baser condition: and there-
fore he determined to step a side, and before his departure giveth her this farewell
in verse.* Donne's influential titles, some of them his own, are, at their
best, of another order—crisp and informative, focusing the genre. *La Co-
rona,* for example, directs attention both to an Italian form of linked
sonnets and to a particular method of devotion.

It is thought that Jacobean titling conventions (from which modern
titling derives) took their origin from the Renaissance emblem. The emblem "motto" ("word") might be a tag or phrase or abstraction—corresponding to distinct types of short-poem title. Moreover, the relation between the elements of an emblem could be oblique and riddling, with
title, motto subtitle, picture and verse "explanation" all illustrating the
idea independently. This obliquity seems to have been transferred to literature by George Herbert, the first English poet to make full use of witty
titling. His titles may refer to an emblematic image (*The Altar; The
Church-Floor*) that is part of the Temple; or they may be texts (Ephesians
4.30: *Grieve Not the Holy Spirit, &c.*), in the divine emblem tradition; or
they may offer subtle tangential interpretation, introducing perhaps a
new aspect—even an image—not easily to be found in the poem itself
(*The Pulley*). As a framing device, the title naturally interested mannerist
poets. But Herbert's expressive titles also anticipate a modernist form—
the title so communicative as to be part of the poem, or at least an independent route to its meaning (*In a Station of the Metro; Her Monument,
the Image Cut Thereon*). In one-line and one-word poems, the title may in
a sense change places with the poem itself, as in Ian Hamilton Finlay's
One Long Arm of the World's Oldest Windmill. Such oblique, expressive, or
"essential" titles have an incidental generic implication. Originally they
were confined, in the main, to epigram and love elegy. And they still
tend to indicate the descendants of these genres.

Developing suggestions of Nelson Goodman's, John Hollander approaches titles as statements of intention. (It may be significant, in this
connection, that they are often added after composition.) Titling, like
the equally conventional device of avoiding a title, has a presentational
function. Indeed, as the example of found poems shows, appropriate
naming of any group of words is enough in itself to present it as a
poem—if not to make it interesting as one. But the presentational function may also be performed by external structures, such as meter. A
glance at the typographic design suffices to distinguish a major ode from
a familiar epistle. During periods of metrical stability, Hollander argues,

there is no need to title "pindaric ode" or "sonnet." This part of the argument carries at best very partial conviction: plain generic labels seem common enough in all periods. But we may agree that "when modern poems are extremely short and in addition seem generically inventive, the role of the title increases in importance."[21] Taking the White Knight's parody of Wordsworth as paradigm, Hollander distinguishes four Victorian conventions of short-poem titling: by subject (*The Leech-Gatherer*), by theme (*Resolution and Independence*), by internal quotation (first line, refrain line, or key phrase), and by symbolic suggestion (the "essential" title: *Haddocks' Eyes*).

To order the variety of titling conventions, Hollander proposes a typology based on degree of informativeness. On this axis they would range from "redundant" titles merely identifying the kind (*Song*), through fuller generic descriptions or announcements of occasion (*An Horatian Ode upon Cromwell's Return from Ireland*), ostensible topics (*Upon Appleton House*), subjects of meditation, and explanatory quotations or allusions—sometimes as difficult as the poem, like *Mariana in the Moated Grange*—to the cryptic or deliberately obscure (Wallace Stevens' *Jouga* and *Word with José Rodríguez-Feo*).[22] And we might add the type *To X.*, combining topical and generic information (circa 1630 epigram of praise or disparaise), as Herrick's *To Julia* and *To His Honoured Kinsman, Sir Richard Stone*. Many sorts of titles could be ranged along this axis. But others elude such grading because their informativeness is highly variable. Topical titles become cryptic, for example, with the passage of time. In any case, informativeness is only one of the possible axes. Titles might also be ranged, as Hollander acknowledges, according to their conventionality or shock value. As always, the axis we choose must depend on our purpose. And for many purposes the best arrangement is still by genre. Titles play a not inconsiderable part, in fact, in establishing the mental "set" with which we approach not only short poems, but any literary work. This is particularly true of the extended or analytic title. From the late sixteenth to the eighteenth century, titles quite commonly occupied the whole of the title page. They performed the function of the modern publisher's blurb, and might contain a description, summary, or table of contents. The title of Defoe's *Colonel Jack* illustrates a few of the possibilities: *The history / and remarkable life of / the truly honourable / Col. Jacque / commonly called Col. Jack / who was / Born a Gentleman, put Prentice to a / Pick-Pocket, was Six and Twenty Years a Thief, / and then Kidnapped to Virginia. / Came back a Merchant, married four Wives, and / five of them proved* Whores; *went into / the* Wars, *behaved bravely, got Preferment, / was made Colonel of a Regiment, / came over, and fled with the* Chevalier, / *and is now abroad completing a / Life of Wonders, / and resolves to die a General.* Within the capacious limits of such titles there was room for many indications of genre. Some of these were more or less explicit ("history and remarkable life")—but others were quite the reverse, as when key words came to acquire a quasi-conventional force: "The fortunes and misfortunes of the Famous *Moll Flanders* . . ."; "Roxana the fortunate mistress or, a History of the Life and Vast Variety of Fortunes . . ." As readers of fiction became more sophisticated, the analytic title fell into disuse, except for comic purposes. But one element of it, the subtitle, has continued to indicate genre. In Romantic and Victorian poetry, this was sometimes used rather exquisitely or disingenuously, to suggest unobvious generic ingredients. So Coleridge subtitles one poem *A Poem Which Affects Not to be Poetry* and another *Conversational* (later *Conversation*), while Clough disguises his mock-georgic *Bothie* as *A long-Vacation Pastoral*—adding, however, an epigraph from Virgil's *Georgics*.

Opening Formulas and Topics

The reader comes to the beginning of the work already partly attuned by the title. The opening words and topics are particularly influential, then, in preparing his expectations of genre in a more discriminating way.

Until the introduction of printing, an *incipit* often performed the presentational function of a title. This it might do either in explicit terms or by a formulaic phrase. So a poem beginning "Hail . . . !" is likely to be a carol or Marian hymn. Many such programmatic formulas are found also in later periods.

Longer works of the Middle Ages were often elaborately framed. From Alberic onward, rhetoricians gave a great deal of attention to the various ways of beginning a narrative.[23] They came to distinguish between narratives that opened in "natural" order and in "artificial" order—the latter abandoning chronological sequence and plunging *in medias res*. Unless the "natural" sequence was already well shaped, they preferred the "artificial" order as more elegant. Many different ways of generating it were listed.[24] Thus, it might be prefaced by a proverb, generalization, or prologue, indicating the theme. This device has shown remarkable staying power. We see it still used (although no longer quite to state the theme) in many novels of moral analysis: "It is a truth universally acknowledged, that a single man in possession of a good fortune, must be in want of a wife"; "All happy families are like one another: each unhappy family is unhappy in its own way."[25]

The extensive medieval treatments of *ordo artificialis* might be seen as attempts to develop a poetics of *entrelacement*. However, much of the resulting theory—such as the analyses of "direct" and "subtle" openings based on the *Ad Herennium* (1.4–7)—had applications far beyond polyphonic narrative. The rhetoricians seem rather to be grappling with the fundamental difficulty of presentation. The elaborate frames and devious subtle prologues of many medieval works give the same impression. These are not merely "results" (as Atkins suggests) of rhetorical doctrine, but address themselves practically to the formidable presentational problems of the period. For it was an age when literary genres were largely unconscious and implicit—when even history and story were imperfectly distinguished.[26] Significantly, perhaps, the *Ad Herennium* prescribed the subtle opening for causes "of the discreditable kind" (*turpe causae genus*); fiction was always somewhat discreditable in the Middle Ages. The prologues intervene between the work and its audience, establishing, with difficulty and only gradually, an appropriate mood for the particular genre to follow.

Renaissance accounts of genre confirm this impression. Minturno clearly expects every kind to have introductory generic indicators. In epic, the *propositio* sets a height: "Virgil combined the lofty and dignified styles in his proposition 'arma virumque cano,' and what follows is comparable." He considers several other examples, including the renewed or medial proposition, and comments that "if the proposition is virtually the poet's proem, it is . . . highly appropriate to move the reader's expectation and make him attentive at that point" (*Discorsi* 4).[27] In *L'Arte Poetica*, Minturno also considers the liminal conventions of many other kinds. The problem case of satire, which seems to lack any proem, is particularly interesting: "The opening is sudden and unexpected; since the satirist, driven by indignation and scorn, starts biting suddenly." But in actuality this results from art: it is all part of the satiric style of simplicity, lightness, brevity of sentiment, colloquial roughness of censure.[28]

These problems are not of local and historical interest only. Similar presentational conventions continue to be used in subsequent periods, and are perhaps a universal necessity. Even our sayings are prefaced by opening formulas (*"Like they say, if you're not cheating you're not trying"; "As the saying goes . . ."*). And fairy tales begin with forms ("Once upon a time . . ."; "There was once . . ."; ". . . there lived . . .") that we learn to recognize instantly under the heaviest of disguises.

In eighteenth-century georgics and georgic-influenced descriptive poems, it is a special "Virgilian" way of proposing the subject that is distinctive. One variant states the useful subject (or ostensible subject) summarily:

> Through Winter Streets to steer your Course aright,
> How to walk clean by day, and safe by Night,
> How jostling Crowds, with Prudence, to decline,
> When to assert the Wall, and when resign,
> I sing . . .
>
> (John Gay *Trivia* [1716] 1.1–5)

> The care of sheep, the labours of the loom,
> And arts of trade, I sing.
>
> (John Dyer *The Fleece* [1757] 1.1–2)

The formula resembles the epic *propositio* enough to activate the contrast that recurs throughout georgic. In *Trivia,* where the mock-heroic element is more prominent, the delay of "I sing" is correspondingly longer. Often, the opening will refer to georgic's varied and digressive, apparently wandering, movement:

> My muse shall rove through flow'ry meads and plains,
> And deck with Rural Sports her native strains,
> And the same road ambitiously pursue,
> Frequented by the Mantuan swain, and you.
>
> (John Gay *Rural Sports* [1713] 1.27–30)

> See! Winter comes, to rule the varied Year,
> Sullen, and sad; with all his rising Train,
> Vapours, and clouds, and storms: be these my theme,
> These, that exalt the soul to solemn thought,
> And heavenly musing.
>
> (James Thomson *Winter. A Poem* [1726] 1–5)

> The Chase, I sing, hounds, and their various breed,
> And no less various use . . .
>
> (William Somerville *The Chase* [1735] 1.1–2)

In other instances, such as *Windsor-Forest,* georgic's multiple interests and political dimensions are indicated more implicitly: "Thy forests, Windsor! and thy green retreats, / At once the monarch's and the muse's seats."[29]

Finesse on opening formulas offers a means of signaling genre that is both economical and precise. The epitaph's convention is as brief an example as can be chosen. In a recent anthology of epigrams and epitaphs, seventy-two of the latter begin "Here lie(s) . . ."[30] The opening "Here I lie . . ." is permissible in serious autoepitaphs. But otherwise the minutest departure from the formula "Here lies X.," once it is begun, is sufficient to initiate a generic modulation. This will usually be into the lower, uninverted style of the satiric or comic mode:

> Here X. lies dead, but God's forgiving,
> And shows compassion to the living.
>
> (Grigson 530)

> Here Delia's buried at fourscore:
> When young, a lewd, rapacious whore . . .
>
> (Grigson 294)

Or another example: Arbuthnot's pungent epitaph on Chartres, beginning "Here continueth to rot . . ." (Grigson 235). The epitaphs on living friends in Goldsmith's *Retaliation,* among the finest achievements in this genre, regularly use the satiric variant "Here X. (lies)": "here Cumberland lies . . . ," "Here Hickey reclines . . . ," "here Reynolds is laid . . ." Elsewhere, the departure from formula may indicate a serious epitaphic epigram on an unnamed deceased, as in Herrick's *Upon a Maid,* beginning "Here she lies (in Bed of Spice) . . ." Perhaps the greatest achievement along this line is de la Mare's epitaph for John Virgin, which derives some of its disturbing strangeness from the transposition of nameless addressee and faceless deceased:

> If thou, Stranger, be John Virgin, then the
> Corse withinunder is nameless, for the Sea
>   so disfigured thy Face, none could tell
>   whether thou were John Virgin or no:
>   Ay, and whatever name I bore
>   I thank the Lord I be
>   Six foot in English earth, and not
>   Six fathom in the sea.
>
> (*Ding Dong Bell* [1924] 21)

The poetic logic implies that, in either event, John Virgin still lives.

With longer works, the topics of introduction signify more, although they may be too familiar or unobtrusive to reach conscious attention. A beast fable, for example, will open with an early ascription of human moral qualities to an animal.[31] Of course, conventional topics of the exordium may appear in ostentatiously novel guises. Thus, the Induction to *The Malcontent,* in spite of the ultramodern mannerism with which Marston makes the players discuss the play and its lack of a prologue, is actually itself an ancient type of expository prologue, presenting information and suggesting an appropriate critical stance. Curtius has identified several opening topics: "I bring things never said before"; dedication or consecration; the duty to impart knowledge; the duty to shun idleness.[32] To these might be added, as we have seen, mention of congeners. Or there is the early metaphorical indication of a work's formal shape, as in descriptions of poets falling asleep before medieval dream visions;[33] epitomizing emblems opening books of *The Faerie Queen;* and the Roman Thames analogy in *The Heart of Darkness.* These prepare for a moral allegory.

Renaissance theorists gave close attention to the rhetorical "parts" of an epic fiction that came before the narrative itself—such as the *principium,* or indication of the action's scope; the *invocatio;* the *exordium,* setting the opening scene; and the *ianua narrandi* or opening of the action itself. This highly conventionalized epic introduction allows for subtly communicative variation. Thus, returning to our *Paradise Lost* example, we are struck by Milton's decisively original version of the classical *principium.* Colie remarks that the generic phrases "imply each other ... 'Arma virumque' implies 'cano,' and we must await Milton's 'I sing' at the end of the long complicated clause with which *Paradise Lost* begins." To put this in another way, "one greater man" irrupts into the midst of the ancient formula, extending and enlarging it. When "sing" comes, it is part already of the *invocatio:* "Sing heavenly Muse." As for the invocation, it is made to echo a famous liturgical passage, the Golden Sequence. Milton's opening thus serves as consecration, at the same time as it contains and deprecates the inferior subjects (and exordium topics) of pagan epic. The inset pagan epic that follows the *ianua narrandi* at lines 83–84 ("Satan ... Breaking the horrid silence thus began") is in this way prepared for. It can be distanced without much obvious recourse to burlesque, so that the reader's judgment receives a severer test than would otherwise have been possible.

In Romantic poetry, where the proemial conventions seem to be strikingly absent, they are often present, but in a deeply implicit form. *The Prelude,* itself conceived by Wordsworth as the "exordium" of a supreme poem, apparently jettisons generic grammar when it breaks into the direct apprehension of sensations in the very first lines:

> O there is blessing in this gentle breeze
> That blows from the green fields and from the clouds
> And from the sky: it beats against my cheek,
> And seems half-conscious of the joy it gives.
> O welcome Messenger!

This preamble was written separately, long before *The Prelude*. But once included it serves, surely, as an *invocatio*. Like the Neoplatonic Zephyrus, this "gentle breeze" is the quickening breath of the divine spirit. That Wordsworth had an invocation in mind seems plain from the canceled correction of lines 29–32, beginning "ye airy spirits." In the Miltonic manner he offers the spirits options as to how they may direct his course—and by implication that of his poem. It is a generic indication: the work to follow will be of high seriousness and epic scale. But how thoroughly altered in mode! If "O welcome Messenger!" is near to invocation, the opening "O," not at all vocative, suggests rather the expressive exclamation of lyric—"Oh there is blessing . . ."

The heroic novel drops the conventions of the epic exordium almost entirely, but has its own opening topics nonetheless. One of the commonest of these (in several literatures) is landscape description, often with political content. This impressive description is likely to run to at least a paragraph, as in *The Pioneers,* and may in effect occupy the whole opening chapter, as in *Nostromo.* Until the larger context has been provided by this means, the main characters are not introduced. In such ways, indicators of genre (here, the genre concerned with subjects of large national or political scope) can be communicated implicitly, by purely novelistic methods. It is not stated in words, but shown in the fictional world presented.

In approaching modern novels, we must expect still more implicit and assimilated generic indicators. Indeed, novels are supposed to have none. The shibboleth is that every novel makes a new start, furnishes its own context. But even where this seems truest, even in modernist novels, appearances deceive. Kermode instances *La Peste,* whose opening chapter, with its generalizing account of ordinary Oran, he compares to "one of Scott's leisurely overtures."[34] The "real" opening follows: "When leaving his surgery on the morning of 16 April, Dr. Bernard Rieux felt something soft under his foot"—which makes "no great departure from the famous norm of an opening sentence 'The Marquise went out at five o'clock.' " Of course, Camus put the descriptive introduction to original use, making it suggest a moral import in the plague, far beyond the public health emergency. But it also serves to establish the novelistic vehicle of his symbolic and composite work. To this end, he elaborately deploys generic conventions of the verisimilar novel, such as the opening chronographia. Only he gives a hint of something outside those conventions, in his use of a suppressed date: "The unusual events described in this chronicle occurred in 19——, at Oran."

Another topic of the novel exordium is establishment of the protagonist's identity. This tends to be a rather implausible business, particularly in first-person narration. By a generally accepted convention (and one that attracts little notice), the protagonist's name is given in full on the first occasion of use. In modern verisimilar novels this is often in the very first sentence—"Anne Linton drove north to Lichfield through the morning." Paul Scott finesses on the convention in *Staying On,* which opens with the naming of a character already dead, who nevertheless has a central place in the novel: "When Tusker Smalley died of a massive coronary at approximately 9:30 A.M. . . ."[35]

The convention, indeed, is hard to avoid. Even a postmodernist writer bent on upsetting ideas of the stable identity of characters will be caught up in it. John Barth does not escape it by opening *The End of the Road* with the memorable nonassertion "In a sense, I am Jacob Horner." In real life, people seldom begin a story by saying who they are in quite this round fashion. Barth's opening not only announces a literary work, but a first-person narration of a particular, nonrealistic variety—a genre that several of Melville's stories belong to. Whether or not Barth alludes to the riddling half-information "Call me Ishmael," Horner's terminal immobility is certainly related to that of the protagonist in *Bartleby the Scrivener*—another story that opens with a self-introduction.[36] Barth uses the conventions of his vehicle, the verisimilar novel; but with a difference.

Many novels described as unconventional in fact have the proemial indicators of the genre, if in a disguised or subverted form. On the other hand, when departure from novelistic conventions goes far enough—in the direction, say, of open form—the outcome may be a new kind. Postmodernist writers who consistently avoid the traditional conventions in effect set up new subgenres with new conventions. For example, there is a postmodernist short-story type that characteristically introduces forms drawn from nonliterary kinds. These may become absurd merely through being transferred to fictional situations, or they may be made so by "incorrect" use. Thus, the questionnaire form, a favorite for this purpose, is "misused" for narrative in Donald Barthelme's *Explanation* ("Q: He has struck me," and so forth).[37] The point of this new convention lies in the scope it gives for discontinuity—as indeed Barthelme makes explicit:

Q: Are you bored with the question-and-answer form?
A: I am bored with it but I realize that it permits many valuable omissions . . .[38]

He finds similar advantages in the travel-book form (*Paraguay*), automatic writing (*Bone Bubbles*), and the "scientific" report in discontinuous numbered sentences (*The Glass Mountain*). In all these instances, nonrealism and surface illogicality are indicated at the outset—or after only a single misleadingly logical paragraph in *Paraguay*. The opening of *The Explanation* is "Q: Do you believe that this machine could be helpful in changing the government?" And *Kierkegaard Unfair to Schlegel* opens with an answer to a question we are not given. Such devices serve as unobtrusive *rites d'entrée*. They establish a "set," or program for processing the generically coded work that follows. Dialogues beginning like this are clearly not to be read in the same way as those of a real questionnaire or interview.

However anarchic experimental writing may seem, it by no means presents a simulacrum of complete disorder. Any literary order at all constitutes in effect a frame, by distinguishing the work from the world beyond, which is not ordered in that way. And this is no less true, just because a writer intends the opposite. We may expect, then, to find indicators of genre in the opening of any work long enough to need them.

It has been possible to give only the merest suggestion of the variety of generic indicators. Allusions, titles, proemial formulas, and topics—these are only a very few of the possibilities. But the instances we have looked at may at least suggest how, in principle, genre can be signaled at the very threshold of the work.

7. Mode and Subgenre

Previous chapters developed ideas of generic repertoire and indicators. Using these conceptions, we may be able to carry further the distinction between different sorts of genre. Until now, we have bracketed kind, mode, and subgenre together as "genres," dealing in similarities rather than differences. But from now on we shall treat them separately. The historical kind was described in terms of the generic repertoire, and in any case is a familiar critical quantity. As we saw, kinds may be characterized by any of the elements of the generic repertoire; but invariably these include certain features, such as size and external form. Modes, however, involve a more elusive generic idea, and one that invites exploration. Mode's relation to kind is particularly unclear—perhaps because of many extended uses of the term "mode," the easiest of all terminological recourses.[1]

Mode

Terminology gives a point of departure. Although genre terms are notoriously inconsistent, they exhibit at least one regularity. The terms for kinds, perhaps in keeping with their obvious external embodiment, can always be put in noun form ("epigram"; "epic"), whereas modal terms tend to be adjectival. But the adjectival use of generic terms is a little complicated. Consider the expressions "comedy," "comic play," "comic." "Comic play" is nearly equivalent to "comedy." But "comic" is applied to kinds other than comedy, as when *Emma* is called a "comic novel." Then we mean that *Emma* is by kind a novel, by mode comic. In the same way, Fielding invited his readers to treat *Tom Jones* as a comic epic not meaning that it is a comedy (it has few dramatic features), but that it is modally comic. The terms for modes are obviously applied more widely. And at first it seems that they must therefore be vague. However,

they can be used exactly enough so long as the limits of their repertorial
implication are kept in mind. In particular, modal terms never imply a
complete external form. Modes have always an incomplete repertoire, a
selection only of the corresponding kind's features, and one from which
overall external structure is absent. Thus, to call Sidney's *Arcadia* pastoral
conveys no information about its external form. Indeed, no pastoral form
in that sense now exists: pastoral works may be songs, eclogues, plays,
elegies—or Heliodorian epics.[2] The *Arcadia* has inset eclogues, a form
often pastoral, just as *As You Like It* has inset pastoral songs; but local
structures do not affect the argument. Similarly, a modal term implies
nothing about size, so that there is no oddity in speaking of sonnets of
Tasso's as heroic. In short, when a modal term is linked with the name of
a kind, it refers to a combined genre, in which the overall form is determined by the kind alone. There is seldom room, except by a special *tour
de force,* for two external forms in a single work.

An apparent exception to this occurs when we speak, perfectly legitimately, of the heroic (epic) form of *Paradise Lost* or *The Rape of the Lock.*
Here, surely, the adjectival term is coupled with external form? But in
such cases the adjective is merely a grammatical transformation of the
noun, and refers to the kind, not the mode. Conversely, the phrase "a pastoral" implies the existence of a pastoral kind only grammatically: critically it is shorthand for "a pastoral elegy," "a pastoral eclogue," and the
like. And when Phineas Fletcher's *Sicelides* is titled "A Piscatory," this is
short for "A Piscatory Play." With unmixed genres, instructively, adjectival terms are never used together with the noun denoting the corresponding kind. Thus, we feel "heroic epic" to be pleonastic. Normally, a
modal term will imply that some of the nonstructural features of a kind
are extended to modify another kind.

Modal extension can be either local or comprehensive. Locally, modes
may amount to no more than fugitive admixtures, tinges of generic
color. All the same, they are more than vague intimations of "mood." As
we have seen, a mode announces itself by distinct signals, even if these
are abbreviated, unobtrusive, or below the threshold of modern attention. The signals may be of a wide variety: a characteristic motif, perhaps;
a formula; a rhetorical proportion or quality. Epic excursions within a
georgic poem are typical of local modulation, which some critics prefer
to treat in terms of inclusion. Such generic mixtures can be extremely
delicate, as Rosalie Colie's interpretations of Shakespeare have helped us
to see. Alternatively, the modulation may pervade much or all of the
work. Then the latter may be said to belong as a whole to two genres, a

kind and a mode. This possibility was early recognized—by Chapelain, for example, who argued in 1623 that the *Adone,* although epic in external structure, really represents a new genre: Marino "would tell you that he does not present the poem as heroic or tragic or comic, the term epic alone being suitable to it, although the poem has some admixture of all the other three."[3] Combination of genres, whether in hybrid kinds or modal transformations, forms the topic of a later chapter. Here I wish only to draw attention to the structurally dependent status of mode vis-à-vis kind. Only confusion can result from the current treatment of modal forms as if they were separate entities capable of existing on their own. This has led to much inventing of new "modes" that have no relation to any antecedent kind.[4] It is seductively easy to construct such speculative hypostases. But they are unlikely to prove any more useful than the old misty synchronic abstractions—"the lyric," "the comic," or whatever.

In principle, any kind might be extended as a mode. But in practice not all have been. Short kinds have seldom generated familiar modes, although nonce-terms such as "hymnlike" may suggest incomplete movements in that direction. One obstacle may be the difficulty of assimilating closed stanzaic forms such as the sonnet and *strambotta.* However, a few short kinds have generated well-established modes, with corresponding adjectival terms applied to style (aphoristic; proverbial). Most of these can be seen in terms of local inclusion, merely. But a few have had a broader and more organic function, notably encomiastic and elegiac.[5] And epigram's modal extension to a wide range of other kinds is a main theme of the seventeenth century. The epistolary modulation is another striking instance. Not only the seventeenth-century verse epistle, but also certain types of plain style ode exemplify it. Such features as intimacy of address and epistolary rhetoric become pervasive in poetic addresses.

Of the longer kinds, many have had corresponding modes, such as epic (heroic), tragic, comic, historical, romance, biographical, and picaresque. And some nonliterary—or no longer literary—kinds are usually recognized as having generated literary modes (topographical; mythological; apocalyptic). This makes it remarkable that several important literary kinds, notably georgic, essay, and novel, are not supposed to have corresponding modes. Can it be that these modal options have never been taken up? By no means. We see modal extensions of georgic not only in Hesiodic transformations of pastoral eclogue (Spenser's and Clare's *Shepherd's Calendars*) and of the pastoral play (*As You Like It*), but also in a poem of natural description such as Thomson's *Seasons.* Essayistic poems are common enough to suggest an emergent mode. And something modally novelistic can be seen in *The Ring and the Book,* which enters "unnecessary" detail of a sort usually omitted from narrative poems, but regular in naturalistic novels.

Not all modes, in fact, have been named or even recognized. Yet their distribution may be wide. Rosalie Colie draws attention to Herbert's and Marvell's modal extension of elements of the emblem form: she speaks of "the comfortable interaction of one poetic kind, understood in its specialness, the emblem, upon another, more open kind, the devotional lyric. These may stand as examples of genres fronting on one another, sharing their specialness in a common mode."[6] None of the poems she discusses retains the external form of the emblem (picture, motto, explanation). Their emblematic quality depends rather on imagery, on the deployment of an emblem-book furniture of seemingly dead metaphors: watches, books, vials, wings, tortoises, and the rest. But the emblematic modulation is not solely a matter of imagery. Colie mentions immediacy, precision, symbolic secrecy, the riddling relation of title to poem, the problem-solving hermeneutic task. And one might add minute description, as in Donne's *Valediction: Forbidding Mourning,* with its naming of the parts of its emblematic compasses. The emblematic mode has in fact quite an extensive generic repertoire. In *Triumphal Forms* I discussed another neglected mode common in the Renaissance, the triumphal. And futher instances could be multiplied. One that has shown remarkable persistence is the metamorphic, an extension from Ovid's *Metamorphoses.* It is frequent in the Elizabethan epyllion, and appears locally in *The Faerie Queen* (the first conclusion of Book III; the tale of Faunus and Molanna in VII) and in *Polyolbion.* Keats and Shelley often use it. And more recently extensions to science fiction have been attempted, as in Ursula Le Guin's *Lathe of Heaven.* Similarly, the gothic romance (*The Old English Baron*) yielded a gothic mode that outlasted it and was applied to kinds as diverse as the maritime adventure (*The Narrative of Arthur Gordon Pym*), the psychological novel (*Titus Groan*), the crime novel (*Edwin Drood*), the short story, the film script, and various science fiction subgenres (already foreshadowed in Mary Shelley's *Frankenstein*).

Some modes—notably pastoral and satire—cannot be referred with certainty to antecedent kinds. But reflection will show that this difficulty is due merely to their venerability and success. Thus, pastoral has been associated with many external forms. But in antiquity it was primarily the mode corresponding to the bucolic. Virgil's *Eclogues* are pastoral: that is, they are concerned with shepherds rather than with those engaged in other occupations (piscatory; horticultural).[7] And pastoral remained the main mode for eclogue, even after Sannazaro's popularization of the piscatory variant. This was partly understood in the Renaissance: Guarini speaks of pastoral drama as a genre that began with eclogue, but at last was developed at full length.[8] Subsequently it was further extended in combination with other dramatic kinds, so that Colie can describe pastoral as *"the* mixed dramatic genre."[9] It is true that pastoral elegy is also an ancient form. But even if it were shown to be earlier than the idyll, that would not undermine the present argument. For it was Theocritus' paradigmatic *Idylls* and Virgil's *Eclogues* that assembled the pastoral repertoire, so far as later writers were concerned.

Satire is the most problematic mode to the taxonomist, since it appears never to have corresponded to any one kind. It can take almost any external form, and has clearly been doing so for a very long time. Since the Middle Ages there have been satiric sermons. And in the same way satire can parody travel book (*Gulliver's Travels*), epic (*The Rape of the Lock*), diary (*A Diary of the Great War*, by S. Pepys, Jr.), index (William King), and dictionary (Ambrose Bierce).[10] However, Gilbert Highet's anatomy of the satiric genre helps us to see that this protean diversity is no real exception to what has been said about the relation of modes to kinds. Whether or not satire's origins lie in improvised dramatic forms, there can be no doubt that fixed satiric kinds existed in antiquity. Among these were the programmatic or formal satire (Horace) and the parodic satire (*The Battle of Frogs and Mice*). The term "satire" had nothing to do with "satyr"—although this was not understood in the Renaissance—but was probably drawn from cookery, and meant "mixture" (compare Juvenal's *farrago*). Diversity of form is paradoxically the "fixed" form of satire. It may use other kinds as vehicles. But even in parody, satire has its own modal repertoire. We have only to contrast satiric with nonsatiric parodies—such as Elizabethan "spiritual parodies" of popular songs; purely formal parodies; or postmodernist deconstructions (Barthelme's Balzac, for example)—to see that satire means more than parodistic imitation.[11] A radical moral stance is perhaps the most striking feature of the satiric repertoire. But one might also mention an oblique, ironic tone that often disguises the genre, sometimes the satirist himself, and always his extremity. The elision of proemial topics has already been noticed, and satire also keeps formulas of transition to a minimum.

To add to the taxonomic complexity of satire, there is the possibility of modal combination with other genres, in a way that does not empty them by parody. Thus, Joseph Heller's *Catch-22* is satiric but also a novel, and some of Edwin Morgan's *Instamatics* combine satire with imagist lyric. The *Dunciad* is an interestingly complicated example: although it has much vehicular satire (mock epic), some passages seem closer to mixture than to travesty. One can understand the talk of satiric epic or heroic satire: the conclusion of the Fourth Book is certainly serious and powerful. But its genre seems to be apocalyptic rather than heroic satire.

It is modes rather than kinds, and a relatively small number of them, that have dominated recent literary theory. These few familiar modes—comic, tragic, romance—are treated in a strictly synchronic way. Even now that we have given up defining imaginary hypostatizations such as the comic spirit, we still tend to describe the modes in isolation, quite apart from their parent kinds. This is understandable, of course. It is precisely by being less historically circumscribed that modes seem to hold the key to a coherent ordering of literature. External forms rapidly change. And kinds have also been linked to social institutions, along with which they have become obsolete—or, as we say, "outmoded." The modes, however, appear to be distillations, from these relatively evanescent forms, of the permanently valuable features. Thus, they have achieved independence of contingent embodiments and may continue to all ages, incorporated in almost any external form, long after the antecedent kind has passed away. Or so it seems. But sober thought will discover that even modes are subject to mutability and become obsolete when the values they enshrine, or the emotions they evoke, grow alien. The heroic mode, arguably, has passed in this way, not only because of changed attitudes to war, but because of the altered status of individuals. Certainly it is no longer much used, except occasionally in the historical or political novel. Moreover, a mode's character may itself undergo radical transformation. The medieval romance mode is not really the same with that of nineteenth-century romantic genres, and to proceed as if it were obscures more than it reveals of literature's continuities.[12] This is not to deny that mode has a vital function in literary history. Modal transformations, indeed, will be a theme of later chapters. But we can only make sense of mode and its relation to kind in developmental terms.

Subgenre

Most historical kinds may be divided, at least in principle, into subtypes. Thus, odes are Anacreontic or major, epithalamic (nuptial) or genethliac (birthday), according to subject and occasion. Such groups have a relatively simple logical relation: their features are more or less disjunct subsets of the sets of features characterizing kinds. In all probability it was this obvious inclusion of subgenres within a kind that gave rise to the misconception of genres as classes, discussed in Chapter 3.

Division of kinds into subgenres normally goes by subject matter or motifs. In fact, they are formed in just the opposite way from that which produces modes: subgenres have the common features of the kind—external forms and all—and, over and above these, add special substantive features. A piscatory or a sea eclogue is just as much an eclogue as a pastoral one, but it adds a new range of topics relating to fishermen rather than shepherds.

Introducing the category subgenre helps to resolve the old problem of whether genre is governed by subject or form. Rosalie Colie's finely poised discussion of *Il Cortegiano* shows the difficulty of deciding. Should we treat it as an *institutio* of education, cast in dialogue form (in which case Roda-Roda is right, and subject governs)?[13] Or should we treat it as a dialogue, determined by the form—the play of ideas, the abstraction, the dominant voice carrying the burden of instruction, and so forth? Thinking in terms of subgenres, however, we can see clearly enough that *Il Cortegiano* is a Renaissance dialogue, a kind intended to teach without being so comprehensive or systematic as an *institutio* (in spite of the appearances to the contrary in titles as arduous as Bryskett's *Discourse of civil life; containing the ethic part of moral philosophy*). Further, Castiglione's is neither a scientific dialogue nor, quite, a philosophical one; but rather the civil subgenre, to which Bembo's *Gli Asolani,* in its different way, also belongs. Colie's label "urban pastoral dialogue" is apt, for pastoral is also present, if only locally, as a modal coloration affecting the presentation of locality and the *paragone* of art and nature. In short, subject in itself does not determine the kind, which is dialogue. It does, however, determine the subgenre.

If subgenres are made by distinguishing additional genre-linked motifs or topics, it follows that we can carry the division and subdivision of kinds even further by specifying more and more minutely. For example, the Elizabethan love sonnet, itself a subgenre, might easily be divided into secondary subsubgenres, and even tertiary ones. Distinguishable types would include (a) liminal sonnets; (b) psychomachies; (c) symptomatologies of love; (d) *blasons;* (e) *baisers;* (f) narratives of exploits of Cupid; (g) sonnets on the beloved's absence; (h) complaints of unkindness; and (i) renunciations of love—all of them with respectable Petrarchan, Petrarchist, or French genealogies.[14] And specification could go further still. To take one possibility: the *blason* or catalogue of the beloved's features was sometimes developed on a large scale, a whole sonnet being devoted to a single item. Sonnets on eyes were so highly conventionalized as to have something of the status of a tertiary subgenre, with its own characteristic topics (color; wounding effect), *concetti* (eyes as suns or stars; pupils as babies), and classic models (Petrarch's *Non d'atra* and *Le stelle il cielo;* Tasso's *Spettacolo gli occhi*).[15]

There naturally arises the question of how far subdivision should be taken. For we need not regard the absence of literary terms for the subgenres as setting a limit. We need not confine ourselves to recognizing only those forms that our predecessors happened to name. However, subdivision beyond a certain stage becomes unwieldy, if only because it leads to as many subgenres as poems—to Hirsch's intrinsic genres, in fact. Such a division would merely duplicate the work of criticism, more cumbrously.

We can reasonably subdivide as far as evidence of schemata entertained by the writers themselves warrants. Thus, the popularity of Ioannes Secundus' *Basia* entitles us to treat the *baiser* sonnet as a subgenre. Second, we may have to regroup in accordance with our own generic schemata. Beyond this point, the decision is an exquisite one. Yet it affects criticism at every turn. If a tertiary division—however informal—was once recognizable, this has a bearing on our assessment of *imitatio*. It indicates a particular level of activity in the genre concerned. For example, the existence of a sixteenth-century anthology of blazons points to a high degree of consciousness.[16] And the pattern of imitation is consonant with three fairly well-defined subsubgenres, drawing imagery from jewels, flowers, and architecture respectively. Knowing this must affect our appreciation of such variations of the genre as *Amoretti* 64 (using flower blazon for wordplay), *Amoretti* 9 (allegorizing the jewel blazon), and *Astrophil and Stella* 9 (combining jewel and architectural blazons). Such poems take their point of departure from the second-order subgenre, so that naïve criticism treating them simply as blazons (the extrinsic genre) is likely to miss their subtlety. Getting to know old literature is very largely a matter of learning the subgenres.

Subgenres, then, seem akin to genres in Francis Cairns' sense: the ancient rhetorical *dispositio* rules. Indeed, the motifs of vernacular subgenres are often drawn, more or less directly, from the conventional topics of classical literature. It would not be hard to trace the descent of the "symptoms of love" type.[17] And it is tempting to identify Renaissance valediction with the *propemptikon* extensively analyzed by Cairns, which shares the same "primary elements": someone departing, someone bidding farewell, a relation of affection, and so forth. However, the *propemptikon*—unlike the valediction—was not a subgenre of elegy, but rather a rhetorical type: a family of topics and formulas. As such, it could combine with several external forms. Like many of the ancient rhetorical genres, it could be used in different formal kinds. Yet the rhetorical genres by no means resembled modes. We have to think of a distinct ancient literary model, in which composition was more rigorously determined by rhetorical conventions, from the overall *dispositio* down to the fine detail of appropriate figures. Not even neoclassical literature allowed rhetoric quite that status. Rhetorical types have less independence in the vernacular literatures. Nevertheless, the motifs defining subgenres often occur, perhaps with quite different functions, in other kinds altogether. We get some idea of the range of kinds in which the *blason* figured from D. B. Wilson's *Descriptive Poetry in France from Blason to Baroque*. Almost all the sonnet subgenres mentioned above could be matched by epigram subgenres based on the same motifs and topics. Herrick's Julia epigrams, for example, offer a full range of blazon motifs. Such substantive features seem to be easily transferred to neighboring kinds.

Subgenres also threaten to defy subdivision in that they are extremely volatile. To determine the features of a subgenre is to trace a diachronic process of imitation, variation, innovation—in fact, to verge on source study. At the level of subgenre, innovation is life. Here, simple resemblance hardly produces a literary work: at the very least there is elegant variation. And from time to time quite fresh subgenres will be invented, enlarging the kind in new directions altogether. It may be the conventionality of subgenres that strikes the beginner. But in reality they are the common means of renewal.

In modern poetry, the collapse of many kinds into "lyric" has given subgenre an enlarged function. Most short poems of our time belong to well-defined subgenres. But these modern subgenres are so numerous that, being mostly unlabeled, they are unrecognized in the main, and hard to describe. A few can be designated briefly, however: the confessional poem; the satirical last will and testament (originating from Villon and repopularized by Adrian Henri); the epigram on a historical personage (Robert Lowell's *History* offers many examples); the message from a symbolic country (Auden; Dunn); and the sinister catechism (de la Mare; Muir; Auden; Causley).

Another example is the poem about a work of art, which I shall select for fuller treatment. Literature about works of art has a long history, in which several strands can be traced: ecphrastic description of art objects or sacred images, in the manner of Philostratus, Achilles Tatius, Longus, and the Greek Anthology; allegorical description stemming from the *Tablet* of Cebes; the emblematic tradition; the *ut pictura poesis* doctrine; the practice of Renaissance poets such as Colonna and Spenser; and above all the epigram tradition descending from Marino's *Galeria*.[18] There was a seventeenth-century satirical subgenre of directions to painters. And Browning made crucial contributions, of narrative gloss and interior monologue. Nevertheless, the modern subgenre has primarily developed from a single influential poem, Auden's *Musée des Beaux Arts* (1939). This paradigmatic work already set most of the subgenre's characteristic features: its casual meditation; its topics (suffering, life's pattern, belief); its simultaneity of different "worlds" or narratives, with unimportant events stealing the show; its knowingness about art; and its choice of artist. (Auden's imagery is from three paintings of Brueghel's: *The Fall of Icarus, The Numbering at Bethlehem,* and *The Massacre of the Innocents.*) Randall Jarrell's *Old and the New Masters* (1965) is almost an answer poem, continuing but deflecting the meditation: "About suffering, about adoration, the old masters / Disagree" (compare Auden's "About suffering they were never wrong"), although with reference to different painters.

But a preference for relatively few painters, and a narrow range of their work at that, is a striking feature of the subgenre. A favorite is Brueghel. In a bibliography compiled by Eugene Huddleston and Douglas Noverr, nearly 12 per cent of the American poems on paintings listed refer to works by Brueghel. Perhaps it is that he offers images of broad human interest. They are also very familiar images—an important factor, to judge from their use as visual shorthand in poems of other genres ("And here from my high window Brueghel's winter / Locks the canal below").[19] And something is due to the influence of relatively early Brueghel poems other than Auden's, particularly Baudelaire's *Aveugles* and Merrill's *Dancing, Joyously Dancing.* Brueghel's prominence in the painting subgenre after 1962 is also to be linked to the impact of William Carlos Williams' popular if slightly disappointing *Pictures from Brueghel.* This volume suggested something of the possible variety of the subgenre, while fixing attention more firmly still on ten of Brueghel's paintings. Very few of Brueghel's other paintings have subsequently been chosen as literary subjects. Williams was interested enough in visual art to have valued Brueghel for his own sake. But the familiar images were also particularly well suited to imagist or objectivist poetry; and a poem-about-Brueghel subtype developed, with these qualities. One thinks of John Berryman's *Winter Landscape,* Howard Nemerov's *Hope and Brueghel: The Triumph of Time* and *The World as Brueghel Imagined it,* Joseph Langland's *Hunters in the Snow,* and John Taylor's *Brueghel's Farmers.*

More recently, it is Brueghel's tough realism that has been focused on, as in Tadeusz Rozewicz's *Didactic Tale* (on *The Fall of Icarus*), Tomas Tranströmer's ominous *After the Attack* (on *The Corn Harvest*), and Norman Dubie's *Land of Cockaigne: 1568* with its violent yoking of many Brueghel images. Other preferred artists include Vermeer (Nemerov's *Vermeer;* James Greene's *Art of Nature*); Botticelli (Gregory Corso's *Botticelli's "Spring";* Elizabeth Jennings' *Spring* (*Tribute to Botticelli's "Primavera"*); medieval miniaturists such as the Limbourg brothers (Samuel Menashe's *Sheep Meadow;* Marianne Moore's *Leonardo da Vinci's*); Rembrandt; Henri Rousseau; Monet; van Gogh; Whistler; and Picasso. There are also preferred subjects, independent of the choice of artist. Among these, Saint Jerome is prominent. Randall Jarrell's *Jerome* (1958) arose, as we know, from meditation on various Saint Jeromes by Dürer. But Jarrell was also familiar with Carpaccio's, Titian's, El Greco's, and other Saint Jeromes. Marianne Moore's *Leonardo da Vinci's* refers to Leonardo's *Saint Jerome.* And John Smith is content to mention "paintings" of "Saint Jerome and the Lion."[20]

The choice of pictures, indeed the introduction of visual art, is correlated with themes and topics. Images of Saint Jerome and his lion belong in meditations on achieving tranquillity through mental discipline. But his intellectual character is strongly marked—an iconography of the saint would in large part amount to a history of representation of the scholar in his study—so that his image also suits the subgenre's self-conscious preoccupation with artistic composition itself. Art's recasting may be set in antithesis to an immediately sensuous world: "The painter's vision is not a lens, / it trembles to caress the light"; "Brueghel the painter / concerned with it all has chosen ..."; "and the mind the resourceful mind / that governed the whole";

> The living quality of
> the man's mind
> stands out
> and its covert assertions
> for art, art, art![21]

Against all this intellectuality, the great painter's images are felt to epitomize experience. They accurately convey solidity ("it remained a wheat
field") and a reminder of experience enjoyed, or at least felt—an elegiac
reminder, since pictures outlive their subjects:

> Pray for the grace of accuracy
> Vermeer gave to the sun's illumination
> stealing like the tide across a map
> to his girl solid with yearning.
>
> (Robert Lowell *Epilogue*)

The Dutch masters seem best for this sort of solidity—and above all
Brueghel, the first great descriptive artist.[22] His paintings can easily be
taken as transcriptions of life's contingent arbitrariness, whereby the incidental may at any time become the point. This casual adventitiousness
is a well-established convention of the subgenre. It goes back to the "tor-
turer's horse" in Auden; and it is prominent, in different ways, in Williams' *Peasant Wedding* and the Taylor example.[23] Old pictures, often
with religious subjects, may also be chosen for the opportunity they give
of introducing, so to speak without prejudice, an older world picture.
There can be advantages, then, in primitive quaintness "maybe illustrating a fable" (W. S. Graham *The Found Picture*),[24] although the dangers
of *simplesse* or crudity are extreme (as witness Colin Kirkwood's *Storie di
Cristo: 14th-Century Paintings by Paolo da Venezia*). Or the paintings may
represent (in several senses) an old way of life, which the distanced poet
is able to anatomize: gently, as in Ruth Fainlight's *All Those Victorian
Paintings,* or terribly, as in Norman Dubie's *Land of Cockaigne: 1568.*[25]

Poems about pictures, then, constitute a true subgenre of the modern
genre that has succeeded epigram. They are not alike only in drawing
images from visual art. They are characterized, as a subgenre, by a constellation or family of features: by topics such as those described above,
and by rhetoric of a particular ecphrastic variety. The family traits may be
recognizable, indeed, even when no particular art object is specified—in
George Szirtes' *Baroque* for example: "See the lovely River Daugh-
ters / Twisting upward from the surge, . . ."[26] Perhaps there is no need to
insist further on the subgenre's institutional existence. It so happens that
a poetry magazine has held a competition for "poems about a painting."
However, my point is that this subgenre is not unlike others of our time
in its rapid development of topics and its exploiting of their possibilities
in combination, variation, and originality.

The familial coherence of the picture poem subgenre comes out clearly in comparison with a near connection, the poem about a photograph. That subgenre has a distinct range of topics. It tends to present nostalgic reverie; or meditation on personal origins (Charles Causley's *Wedding Portrait*); or more or less committed political comment (Michael Shayer's *These Are Faces;* Denise Levertov's *Photo Torn from the Times*).[27] Mixture of the two subgenres is possible, but then something different from both may result. W. S. Graham transforms the photograph poem in *Ten Shots of Mister Simpson:*[28] he renders the introspective reach to the very edge of making—a feature of his work—by the generic departure of taking the taking of the shots itself into focus. The outcome is not quite like a picture poem about art and nature. Nevertheless, the *imitatio* of Stevens and Williams is an important element. And significantly painting creeps in, in Shot 6: "A narrow Kiev light makes an ikon."

Kinds of Novel

Turning to prose, we find the status of subgenres similarly enhanced. Just as "lyric" has assimilated other short poetic kinds, making them all subgenres of lyric, so "the novel" has assimilated other kinds of prose fiction. A genre so comprehensive can have but a weak unitary force. Indeed the novel has largely ceased to function as a kind in the ordinary way. Its minimal specification has even been stated as "an extended piece of prose fiction"—a specification in which external form appears, but only as "extended" and "prose."[29] Within this enormous field, the novel in a stronger sense—the verisimilar novel of Austen and Thackeray, which many would consider the central tradition—is now only one of several equipollent forms.

Anyone discussing types of novel does well to acknowledge the comprehensive achievement of Northrop Frye. Based as it is on wide and considered reading, it suggests foundations of a theory of genres that may still in part be built on. However, some divergences should be mentioned. To begin with, Frye's typology is one of prose genres, not of novel genres. For he considers the formal differences between fiction and nonfiction relatively superficial—as also those between the narrative, didactic, and other presentational modes. With this I have not felt able to agree. The difference between fictional and nonfictional contracts with the reader seems to me fundamental.

Frye's four "strands," or formal ingredients, of prose are romance, confession, novel (in the strong sense), and "anatomy." The last is a formal type embracing the forms of Menippean or narrative satire, as well as of systematic nonfictional works such as *The Anatomy of Melancholy* and *Anatomy of Criticism*. It aroused initial interest, but has proved a source of difficulty and is too lacking in unitary force to be of lasting value without qualification. Menippean satire and systematic treatise are very different genres. Professor Frye may have combined them in a single category merely with a view to clarifying his symmetrical scheme based on the polarities introvert-extravert and intellectual-nonintellectual. Thus, novel is extravert, romance introvert, both nonintellectual. (Pure states of the four ingredients rarely occur, of course: forms of literary works result from their mixture in various proportions.) The scheme has attractive simplicity, and leads to groupings with heuristic value.

But there are difficulties. First, Frye takes no account of which element in a combination predominates or determines the external form. Yet it is surely not a matter of indifference whether one is dealing with a contractual kind or with a purely modal and perhaps debatable admixture. Second, Frye's polarities seem less formally determinate than others that might therefore be thought preferable, such as explicit–implicit, or opaque–transparent. Third, the synchronic method of *Anatomy of Criticism* tends to conflate very different genres. Thus, Frye uses "Menippean satire" for the forms of the ancient satiric prose kinds—narrative satire, utopia, and the encyclopedic farrago of *The Deipnosophists*—as well as for dialogue or colloquy, a form not necessarily satiric. Since the encyclopedic tradition led via Macrobius' *Saturnalia* and Martianus Capella's *De Nuptiis* to Burton's *Anatomy of Melancholy,* the term "anatomy" is taken to cover the Menippean satiric forms as well, which are consequently discovered in Burton, Walton, and (merged with novel) in Sterne's *Tristram Shandy* and in Peacock.[30] So many forms are united in the "anatomy" that it threatens to prove a baggier monster than the novel. There is no need to confine the term to its rather restricted sixteenth-century meaning—a nonsatiric systematic form much given to minute division.[31] But if the anatomy has any coherence at all, it is hard to see how this could be consonant with exploratory dialectic: Burton's *Anatomy* really has little to do formally with Walton's or Plato's dialogues. Even if there were room for another use of "anatomy" to refer to a large-scale grouping of works ordered by ideas, it could only be as one of a somewhat larger number of categories. Frye's scheme finds no place for such distinctive forms as picaresque, which is clearly not "central novel," but is not always very easy to construe as confession, romance, or anatomy, either. It seems necessary, finally, to make more concession to change in the genres and their groupings.

We probably do best to retain the broader concept "novel." It is too deeply in the grain of criticism to be removed without endangering continuity. And the novel is still a kind, even if one badly in need of subdivision. The idea that it alone of all forms is ageneric—has no repertoire of characteristic features—carries at best very partial conviction. True, there have been attempts to subdivide, such as Alan Friedman's dichotomy, on the basis of closed and open moral structures, in *The Turn of the Novel*. But progress has been slow, because of the reluctance to think in terms of subject matter. So Malcolm Bradbury: "The novel is not a traditional literary genre, like tragedy or comedy, but a general, varied, categorically distinctive form like poetry and drama . . . There is no one kind of matter [novels] contain or effect they produce."[32] At least this view reflects a sense of the wide range of novel types. And indeed the range is extraordinary. For the novel has ramifying roots in earlier fiction and nonfiction: epic, romance, picaresque, biography, history, journal, letter, exemplary tale, novella, to name only the most obvious. These filiations have persisted in the developed novel, giving rise in some instances to distinct subgenres. But the subgenres have only very gradually been acknowledged by critical thought, partly because of excessive emphasis on purely formal or rhetorical aspects.

The most influential division of the novel has been a dichotomy or bipolar analysis into *roman* and *récit*. Since Roman Fernandez's *Messages* (1926), this division has commonly been regarded as fundamental: it is the starting point of a great deal of criticism, particularly of the French novel. Yet although it is sometimes a useful analytic instrument, it is not a fundamental division, generically.

Indeed, such a division could hardly have arisen from study of the novel in English. For consider: surely it is in the work of Richardson and his followers, if anywhere, that we must expect the *roman* with characters whose existence is a *position absolue*. Yet Richardson's epistolary novels do not recount life at the time when it occurred (the characteristic of *roman*), but through documents subsequently written, in which the events "have taken place" (as in *récit*). The novel of Fielding and Edgeworth, on the other hand, had roots in allegorical tradition, while its authorial intrusions and interpolated essays never allow us to forget the telling in the tale. Yet it generally has no fictional teller. *Roman* or *récit?* In the nineteenth century, it is true, the epistolary complication disappeared. But allegorical and polyphonic and damaged narrative acquired growing significance. To the elusive novel of Thackeray or Meredith or James, let alone Dickens, the categories of *roman* and *récit* apply at best intermittently and remotely. One must be clear. It is not that these novelists mix the two divisions, as the half-Continental Conrad does when he inserts *récits* within his *romans*. It is that the division does not usefully apply at all. Dickens' characters are among the most memorable and brilliant in our literature. But their existence is not at all a position we are allowed to take for granted. They engage in significant coincidences; they change names and identities; they are even liable to vanish by spontaneous combustion. In fact, their existence is subordinated to their meaning. As for the mimesis of Thackeray and his successors, it is continually presented as subsequent construction—but not merely by a narrator: not as *récit*. In our tradition it is less decisive whether a narrator tells the story. With us, it is the novelist who constructs and arranges the past—even when, as in *Henry Esmond,* he has to use a strange third/first-person narration to do so, and even when the characters include historical personages.

A more fundamental division would be between a type in which the action's reality is unquestioned, and a type in which its fictionality is insisted on by the use of such features as multiple narration, rearrangement of chronological sequence, improbabilities, deliberate inconsistences, or the mixing of elements with different fictive status. In the first type, the novelist should either be absent altogether or unimportant: Trollope's intrusions have been considered blemishes. In the second type, the type of *Vanity Fair* or *The Egoist,* the novelist is triumphantly present, performing everything in appropriately brilliant style. Meredith offers many reminders that his characters are made up ("as you perceive, they live": "she was one of the creatures who are written about").

A slightly different dichotomy, but again one that is not purely formal, can be drawn from the remarks of James, Stevenson, and other nineteenth-century critics. I mean the division into novel and romance: the first of these realistic and detailed like its nonfictional formal models; the second more poetic, less minute, freer. External society and character were realized in the former, in the latter deep emotional experience. But we now distinguish other subgenres besides the romance and the verisimilar or "central" novel. There is the picaresque novel, the multiplot novel, the stream-of-consciousness novel or novel of lyrical impressionism, the antinovel, the faction or documentary novel, the historical novel.[33] These are all distinct subgenres of "novel" in its weak sense. Bradbury is right, in fact, to say that there is no one kind of matter in the novel; there are several. Thus, the picaresque repertoire mentioned in Chapter 4 differs from that of the verisimilar novel not only in matter but in form and proportion. Picaresque is not at all given to settled "solidity of specification."[34] Indeed, it has little time for irrelevance of any sort, having to cover far more ground in terms of *mises-en-scène,* sets of characters, and episodes. Some novel variants are best regarded as mixed genres, arising from modal transformation. But those mentioned seem to be true subgenres. And there are others, waiting to be named. As Virginia Woolf put it, "That cannibal, the novel, which has devoured so many forms of art will by then [in ten or fifteen years' time] have devoured even more. We shall be forced to invent new names for the different books which masquerade under this one heading."[35]

The central novel has been divided into a great many subgenres, by specifying additional subject matter. Setting is so decisive (even when not directly realized through description) that it often provides the basis of typology. So we have the factory novel, the school novel, the rustic novel, the city novel, the university novel, the provincial novel (and now the "regional novel"), the Indian novel, and the like.[36] Obviously overlapping with this typology is another, partly distinct, based on plot or mythos. Hence the adventure novel, abolition novel, war novel, crime novel, espionage novel, political novel, novel of faith and doubt, *Frauenroman, Familienroman* or domestic novel, nature novel, *Bildungsroman.*[37] All of these types (and there are no doubt others, recognized and unrecognized) have some degree of generic coherence. They differ not merely with respect to the one defining feature (crime; war), but a constellation of characteristic features. The proportions will vary: different constituents carry emphasis, or the same constituents sustain distinct functions. The Victorian factory novel realizes working-class characters seriously in a way not attempted in other subgenres of the time. But we should not go to it for verbal wit—any more than we should expect vernacular naturalism in the novel of faith and doubt. Ethical contents, again, have different functions in the crime novel and the domestic novel. But the extreme instance of altered proportions is perhaps the historical novel. Its setting, moral codes, mundane particulars—its whole world—has not only to be realized but also, as it were, *taught,* so that its most ordinary operations must be combined with exposition or compromised with stereotypes.

Many studies have been devoted to subgenres of the verisimilar novel—enough to show that such mainly substantive groupings have unitary coherence. The question almost becomes whether we are dealing with subgenres or kinds, for the external form may be partly differentiated. Certain subgenres display a marked tendency to become kinds—if indeed they have not been so all along. The surrealist novel exemplifies the former possibility. Early instances had much of the outward appearance of the central novel. But a subgenre that began with exploring special psychological provinces within the world of the verisimilar novel has now developed into a largely separate kind. This is marked formally by such features as extreme narrative discontinuity, unity depending instead on a metaphysic of universal connectedness (contrast the work of Claude Simon, say, with Dylan Thomas' *Map of Love*).

The other possibility, subgenres as unrecognized kinds, may be seen in the novel about writing, the work-in-progress, the *poioumenon,* or (as Steven Kellman calls it) the self-begetting novel. Writing easily seems a special "matter" within the verisimilar novel (in which writers have always been common enough as points of reference). Surely this is simply a subgenre (with its own topics, naturally, such as the difficulty of writing)? That is probably true of such a novel as *David Copperfield.* But the true work-in-progress novel from the very beginning exhibited strongly marked formal characteristics, so that in part at least it must rather be a distinct kind. As a good example of the problems of novel typology, it warrants more detailed treatment.

In the *poioumenon* or work-in-progress novel, at least one narrator or character is engaged in writing, whether a novel (*At Swim-Two-Birds*), biography (*Sartor Resartus*), autobiography (*Tristram Shandy*), notebook or other considerable work (*The Golden Notebook*). There are likely to be inset texts, or prominent accounts of books and papers (Teufelsdröckh's *Die Kleider* and autobiographical materials; Slawkenbergius' *De Nasis*). And there may also be an additional, symbolic work-in-progress (Toby's fortifications; coining in *Les Faux Monnayeurs*). In peripheral examples, this is the main representation of the creative process (daguerreotyping in *The House of the Seven Gables;* scientific research in Banville's *Doctor Copernicus;* Lily Briscoe's painting in *To the Lighthouse*). The inset works of art remind us that what we are reading is itself a work of fiction, and provide occasions for treating a principal theme of the genre: the relation of art to life. The form of reality to be found in fiction may be suggested by works of art within works of art (Butor, Huxley, Lessing), or by the reflexive relation of different *poioumena* by the same writer (Beckett, Durrell). Above all, the imaginary work being composed within the story continually gives opportunities for self-reference. Sometimes it mingles in an illusionistic way with the containing story. Then questions arise (as we see in the cases of Proust and Joyce) as to whether the work being written in the story is precisely the *poioumenon* itself. For characters of the main story may occur also as characters of secondary stories generated within it, which bear a "Quaker Oats box" relation to each other.

The frequent references to the process of composition make another feature almost inevitable: self-conscious highlighting of the style. Various styles are possible, but usually a self-deprecating irony stands out (*Sartor;* Rheticus' narrative in *Doctor Copernicus*), or extreme digressiveness (Beckett's trilogy; Nye's *Falstaff*), or both (*Tristram Shandy*).

Whether or not digressive, a *poioumenon*'s narrative is almost always discontinuous. In spite (it may be) of the narrator's ceaseless garrulity, fresh starts nevertheless perpetually have to be made. These return the reader to the fictive act, and may indeed mime the difficulty of the creative process. So Tristram will write "I begin the chapter over again"; and the narrator of *Molloy* "This should all be rewritten in the pluperfect."[38] Externally, the discontinuity is often reflected by division into very short chapters: *Tristram Shandy* has some of only a paragraph, to say nothing of those that are blank; and *Falstaff* has a numerological division into 100 chapterlets. (The reviewer who criticized chapter length in *Falstaff* was in effect criticizing Nye's choice of genre.) Or the *poioumenon* may have recourse to what Gray calls "serial" form: breaking the narrative up into many short sections. The Alexandria Quartet has an "elaborate machinery of diaries, notebooks . . . 'Consequential Data,' and 'Workpoints' . . . exposed structures . . . to remind us that we are once again in the laboratory of the novel."[39] And Stuart Evans' *Caves of Alienation* is a sheaf of brief documents, radio scripts, criticisms, and extracts from a novel. Multiple narration, whether through alternative versions or plural narrators (sometimes composing in competition with one another), is often central to the effect. Not infrequently, too, editorial presentation adds to the regression of embeddings (*Sartor; Pale Fire*).

Both digression and multiplicity perhaps express the malformed or divided personality of the writer-protagonist. Thus, Tristram's digressions, like his use of Slawkenbergius, stem from an incapacity to come to the point. Carlyle's editor is divided between his own skeptical nature and half-belief in the apocalypse of Teufelsdröckh (who has himself suffered a breakdown). Nye's Falstaff is in his forgetful near-dotage, besides having his memoir split between scribes with minds of their own. The writer in Busch's *Mutual Friend* is ill.[40] And Beckett's writer-derelicts are grotesquely reduced to the barely human. But we need to be cautious about psychological interpretation of generic forms—even about Freudian ones such as Kellman's. Not all novelists have the same motives for writing self-begetting novels. And besides, such a feature as multiple narration is an obviously appropriate form, in that a work in process has many potential fulfillments. However, we may agree that the genre is concerned with formation of new selves, a process symbolized by the literary creative process portrayed. The great work is to bring integrated identity out of a chaos of possibilities.[41] As a heuristic, tentative enterprise, open to great vagueness, the *poioumenon* shows a natural tendency to compensate by using very definite structural schemes. But we should not imagine that such schemes—Carlyle's stages of history and half-zodiac, Hawthorne's Seven Ages of Man, Beckett's mathematics and catechisms, Nye's calendar—represent the actual systems of the authors. They are armatures only, scaffolding for the bridge over chaos. Carlyle may not choose the labels for the paper bags of Teufelsdröckh's autobiographical materials quite at random (they are the darker, winter signs), but the astrological scheme is hardly presented as a part of his thought: "What matters whether such stuff be of this sort or that. . . ?"[42] No doubt Frye has these schematic divisions in mind when he calls *Sartor* an anatomy. But there is a vital difference between structure that functions as a direct expression of ideas, and structure merely used as a provisional and subsidiary device—in this case, to render the writer's division of the daunting void of the unwritten.

The work-in-progress genre has a long and full tradition in German literature (beginning with the *Künstlerromanen*) and especially in French, where it enjoys a far more central place in fiction than in English (Butor can even regard it as the privileged form of fiction). The earlier development is summed up in Proust, who provides the paradigmatic model for a modern phase represented by Gide, Mauriac, Butor, and Beckett. Kellman intelligibly sees the self-begetting novel as central to the *nouveau roman*. In English literature, the tradition is less familiar to modernists. Those of Henry James' tales that could be seen as embodying the *poioumenon* form only a small proportion, and in Joyce's omnigeneric *Ulysses* it has a relatively subsidiary place. The English form is not wholly derivative from French, however. Even before Sterne, there was a native tradition, beginning with anticipatory hints in Chaucer's dream visions, in mannerist reflexive poetry, and in plays-within-plays. Like all genres, the *poioumenon* has very considerably changed with time. The earlier examples were closer to satire: Sterne took over devices from Rabelais, and Carlyle's ironies are sometimes satiric quite as much as self-protective. But *Sartor* is also essayistic, going back for its local constructive paradigms to the heuristic form of gathering perfected by Montaigne. It has many passages concerned with its own writing, much like the authorial chapters of Fielding's *Tom Jones* or Cumberland's *Henry*. And Carlyle himself describes it as "put together in the fashion of a kind of Didactic Novel; but indeed properly *like* nothing yet extant." George Levine, G. B. Tennyson, and others make a persuasive case of considering *Sartor* as novelistic (for example, in its exploitation of point of view).[43] Indeed, by virtue of its escape from the straitjacket of naturalism, it has much influenced the modern antinovel. An equally important legacy, however, has been a certain skeptical seriousness about fiction, a sense of the writer's duty to deal with a whole cosmos (not omitting its human creator), to place things in the largest context: "Drawing-room is simply a section of Infinite-Space . . ."[44] It is such an "apprehension of the absolute condition of present things"[45] that has made it difficult for some twentieth-century writers to accept the conventions of the verisimilar novel. For this and kindred reasons, many have turned to the *poioumenon*.[46] In the modern period, however, the genre is more homogenously unified. Essayistic components are now comprehended within the fiction, and the tone (with a few exceptions, such as *Point Counter Point*) has moved away from satire. Whether the genre is to be viewed as kind or subgenre will depend on one's typology of the novel. Those who regard the novel as a very broad category, like poetry, may be sure that the *poioumenon* is a kind. But those to whom the novel is more of a genre may think of the *poioumenon* rather as a subgenre—although one in process of separate development, and probably emerging as a kind. It is being extended modally in mixture with other genres, such as the gothic novel (Carolyn Slaughter's *Story of the Weasel*) and the historical novel (*G; Falstaff; Doctor Copernicus*). And there is even a mock *poioumenon*, Barthelme's *Snow White*.

Other Types

The system of generic categories is complicated by the existence of several other quasi-generic groupings. These include mythic types (quest; divine retribution), types involving dependence on an antecedent (parody; pastiche), purely formal constructive types (catalogue; anatomy), and the collective productions of "schools" or movements (Metaphysical; Romantic; Georgian). They must be mentioned only to be dismissed.

Properly speaking, mythic types are not literary groupings at all: they occur indifferently in other media and even arts. They have no special basis in literature. This is not to say that critics should avoid speaking about them: Northrop Frye—to mention only one great instance—has shown us how interesting and illuminating their application to criticism can be. But they have little to do with genre.

In the second category come types of treatment of an "original" or paradigm. The latter may be a classic or famous work, as in pastiche, cento, or *imitatio;* or else a work to be rejected or ridiculed, as in parody, burlesque, or the answer poem.[47] There is no doubt that the ectypes in this category (say, imitations of Horace's Fifth Ode) form a very tightly knit group, sharing resemblances to one another through the original. But that is just it: their relation is not entirely a generic one, because it is too close.

Rather more like genre is the epicyclic or elaborative type: groups of works that exploit the fictive world of some great or popular predecessor (*Orlando Innamorato; Orlando Furioso*). It is an important type, for it includes such masterpieces as *Paradise Lost.* And it is a numerous type, for there are hundreds of *Robinson Crusoes* and *Gullivers;* scores of elaborations of the *Hamlet* world; many *Alices;* and, now, *Huck Finns* and *Jane Eyres.*[48] Sometimes the focus is a paradigmatic character rather than a work (Verdi's and Nye's Falstaffs).[49] Where the new work is a sequel to the original (or a "prequel," like Denis Judd's *Adventures of Long John Silver*), it is common to show specific points of departure from it—moments at which the reader can imagine himself looking, if you will, from the ectypic world through its door into the paradigm. And it is usual for relatively minor characters of the original to become major characters in the elaboration: Claudius or Horatio is the hero of the epicyclic *Hamlet,* not the prince. In spite of those approaches to "rules," however, the type is not quite a genre. Elaborations of an original have the latter as their context, rather than each other. Their relations are radial, not circumferential.

Turning to constructional types, we come to a vast although neglected subject, which asks at least a volume to itself. Every literary craftsman knows their importance in composition, and every reader—usually without knowing it—depends heavily on them in his responses. Nevertheless, it seems at first easier to set this category aside. Constructional types such as theme and variation, sequence, catalogue, inset, and frame are purely formal devices, which can be used with any matter.[50] Surely they are ingredients only in genre? Certainly each is compatible with many genres—as Queneau's *Exercises* show many times over, so far as the variation form goes.

However, it is not quite so simple. How are we to regard forms such as genealogy, which are not exclusively formal? Constructional types also shade off into metrical forms and technopaegnia: into figure, concrete, and conceptual poetry. Ring composition, a very common type, may have substantive value, and in the hands of an Edward Thomas can become the basis of a Georgian lyric subgenre. In fact, whereas in long works the constructional type is an ingredient only, in short poems it may almost by itself make a subgenre. Thus, the cumulative pattern of *The House That Jack Built* constitutes a type of (usually political) modern epigram. And conflation of matrixes, a deconstructive device only in *Ulysses,* is the whole basis of a certain lyric subgenre. Edwin Morgan has given us many examples. Or there is Donald Justice's *Orpheus Opens His Morning Mail,* which combines inventory of letters with events in the Orpheus narrative.[51] Such overlapping of the constructional and subgenre categories need not trouble the post-Wittgensteinian theorist.

Finally, there is the category of *oeuvre* and collective *oeuvre.* School productions may have a repertoire of features extensive and coherent enough to suggest genre; yet they exhibit them independently of the historical kinds. The Metaphysical poets wrote in many different kinds; yet their poems may bear a closer resemblance to one another than that between, say, the love elegies of different schools—or even between poems by the same writer. The resemblance is close enough to have prompted Earl Miner's special use of "mode"—as in "Metaphysical mode" and "Cavalier mode."[52] This is not the same term as in "pastoral mode" although, as we shall see, a formal mode (*videlicet* extension of epigram) contributes in no small way to the Metaphysical style. Individual *oeuvre* interacts particularly closely with genre. This grouping is currently unfashionable; its integrity, even, has been challenged, by Michel Foucault.[53] But at least there can be little doubt of its effectiveness as a quasi-generic type. An *oeuvre* operates almost as a self-created subgenre within the institutional genre. It forms an idiolectal variant of the latter. Thus, the work of Dickens, although various, has a characteristic personal repertoire, not only of diction and style (*zeugma; allegoria*) but also of story type, character, symbol, *mise-en-scène*. Certain pleasures in the elaborate description of urban settings of advanced delapidation and rococo ugliness; certain confusions of animate and inanimate; certain preferred sources of imagery (theater; food): all these taken together can be thought of as Dickensian, rather than characteristic of any one novel of Dickens'. Hence discussions of the Dickens world, the Dickens theater, the Dickensian city. The idiolectal rules of *oeuvre* supplement those of genre in assisting the reader to respond, so that they play a particularly important part in the case of difficult or innovative writers (or writers with a cult reputation). Those familiar with the private meaning of frontiers in Auden's early work are better placed to interpret individual poems of that phase. Similarly the Lob character type is a convention in Edward Thomas' *oeuvre*. When we interpret an individual poem, whatever the anti-intentionalists say, we should be as ready to go into questions of *oeuvre* as of subgenre.

8. Generic Labels

One of the chief obstacles to a historical theory of genre is instability of terms. Not only do generic labels change with time, but also (and this is far more confusing) the same labels come to be used in different ways. Some of the difficulty now felt with traditional genre theory—alike in identifying kinds and in applying the recognitions critically—arises from such confusion of terms. Not that we should for a moment dream of a single authoritative set of terms. It is neither possible nor even desirable to arrive at a very high degree of precision in using generic terms. The overlapping and mutability of genres means that an "imprecise" terminology is more efficient. Since there is no end to the genre distinctions that might be made, there is no point in making more of them than the critical end in view requires.[1] This conceded, problems of labeling remain that should not be ignored. It is unsatisfactory, to say the least, when dictionaries of literary terms treat genre labels as univocal. And there has been too little discussion of the terminology of genre.[2]

Sources of Confusion

Confusion of terms begins with the earliest naming of a genre, sometimes with the originating writer himself. Writers often mislabel their works, deliberately or ignorantly, modestly or for an ulterior literary purpose—as in Chaucer's description of *The Tale of Melibee* ("a litel thyng in prose . . . this tretys lyte / After the which this murye tale I write"). The label for a new genre is almost necessarily the result of retrospection to antecedent forms, so that although it may be interesting genetically, it is unlikely in the long run to prove satisfactory. Fielding called *Tom Jones* a comic epic in prose. And others similarly have drawn terms from earlier related genres. In the 1726 Preface to *Winter,* Thomson mentions the brief epic Job, "that noble and ancient poem . . . crowned with a description of the grand works of nature," as well as Virgil's *Georgics*. Yet brief epic is not so much the genre as the generic material, or point of departure, for Thomson's descriptive poem. To begin with, new genre almost *ipso facto* lacks an agreed label. As Bacon noted with respect to the essay, "The word is late, but the thing is ancient. For Seneca's Epistles to Lucilius; if one mark them well, are but Essays,—That is dispersed Meditations, though conveyed in the form of Epistles."[3] The novelty may remain unlabeled; identification of a new grouping is difficult, and sometimes too difficult. But even if a label is attached at once, confusion soon sets in. Thus, the term Bacon introduces, "essay," may not have been meant by Montaigne as a generic term, but simply as an apt title.

Spenser's importation of a Pléiade titling convention offers a similar instance. By calling his 1595 volume *Amoretti and Epithalamion*, he relates his work to such French collections as Ronsard's *Amours* and Du Bellay's *Regrets*. As Rosalie Colie has noticed, the Pléiade exploited "metaphorical thematics" in their titling style.[4] (Beside the *Gaietez* and *Soupirs* one might put Ioannes Secundus' influential *Basia* epigrams.) However, Spenser's term *amoretti* ("wooings; flirtations") was taken up by Drayton in a changed sense. His predecessor's volume contains Anacreontic odes, as well as the major ode *Epithalamion:* an apparently hybrid grouping that in actuality reflects the doctrine of the sonnet as *melos,* song, or minor ode.[5] Nevertheless there is a distinct shift from Spenser's usage, when Drayton gives one of his 1619 Odes the title *An Amouret Anacreontick.* It is a stanzaic ode, titled on the same principle as Barnaby Barnes' *Carmen Anacreontium.*

Metaphorical labels have often proved conveniently loose. Such are the medieval semigeneric figurative titles satirized by Rabelais.[6] *Malleus, speculum,* and *fioretti,* like the Renaissance "anatomy," raise expectations of a specific kind; but they are vague, formally, by comparison with the classical genre terms. That is not to say that metaphors cannot die into dependable labels. Something like that happened with certain species of poetic garland: "The crowns of poets are not made only of myrtle and laurel, but also of vineleaves for fescennine verses, ivy for bacchanals, olive for sacrifices and laws, poplar, elm, and wheat for agriculture, cypress for funerals, and innumerable other kinds of leaves for other occasions."[7] And similarly *entremet* (side dish) has become a specific kind of interlude.[8] Cookery (or taste) provided many such metaphors. So Scaliger used the culinary terms *mel, sal, fel,* and *acetum* to distinguish four subgenres of epigram, following a tradition that went back in part to Horace and continued without much change until the nineteenth century.[9] *Mel* had an obvious fitness to sweet feeling; and so with sharp *acetum*. But even here, there are obvious possibilities of confusion in the case of *fel* and *acetum*. And what is *sal* to some, may seem sharp and abusive to others. Originally *satura* was also a term for mixed food such as salad—hence, a medley. And Juvenal referred to his satires by the rougher name *farrago* (mash for cattle). The postclassical confusion with satyrs' roughness, registered in the spelling *satira* (*satyra*), dominated both theory and practice in the Renaissance. But in the eighteenth century the culinary metaphor returned: the satirist Wolcot (Peter Pindar) writes of "the Variety of Entertainment in his pretty poetical Oleo"—that is, olio or hodgepodge.[10] And the filiation continued as late as Washington Irving and his coauthors, who used the title *Salmagundi* for their satirical papers in prose and verse. It is perhaps significant that this, the stablest of generic metaphors, should denote the loosest, most polymorphous, and least constricting of the kinds.

Even with simple literal descriptive terms confusion may arise, from such trivial sources as perfunctory labeling. During periods with little critical interest in genre, or when generic questions are settled by classical fiat, the labels tend to be automatic and umbrellalike (fifteenth-century "treatise"; twentieth-century "lyric"). But the most carefully devised generic terms can become inconsistent or obfuscated too—and for more interesting reasons. These have to do with regional and temporal variations.

Regional Variations

Genres have circumscribed existences culturally. Individual works may sometimes partly elude locality; genres never. *Magister Ludi* intrigues a few British readers, but the kind that *Das Glasperlenspiel* embodies finds little acceptance with us. We tend to regard novels of ideas as symptoms of eccentricity or aborted naturalism. Similarly, the French until recently had no science fiction: Jules Verne was a splendid, and in any case only a partial, exception. More often, however, regional differentiation is less complete than this, consisting rather in distinctive variants of roughly equivalent genres. Thus, the Western haiku is distinct in several ways from the Japanese; it lacks, for example, any convention of season words. Such distinctions affect not only the content of generic terms but also their boundaries and consequently the grouping of literary works. A familiar example is the British term "detective story" and the American "mystery," which are not at all the same. The latter merges easily into the thriller of Hammett, Chandler, or Macdonald, whereas the former remains sharply distinct. Neither the thrillers of Fleming nor the entertainments of Greene could possibly be taken for detective stories. In such a state of affairs, translations, imitations, and other interchanges between literatures obviously must be powerful agents for generic change, not to say enlargement of critical terminology.

But there can never be anything like exact equivalence between the generic terms of different literatures. A useful analogy is with the structure of color terms, whose boundaries also are situated differently in each language. As has often been observed, there is no one-to-one correspondence between the color terms of individual languages.[11] This does not mean that the color (or genre) terms give form to material otherwise amorphous. Rather should we think of them as belonging integrally, like all words, to the culture of a particular society. Sapir's dictum applies *a fortiori* to genre: "The worlds in which different societies live are distinct worlds, not the same world with different labels attached." In different societies, different features are salient, in genre just as in everything else—only more so, since literary conventions are most intimately bound up with national culture. However, just as with color terms, some distinctions may be universal. Certain of the systems of genre terms in different literatures are to this extent isomorphic, that they share the categories of genre that I have called kind, mode, and subgenre. And some closely related societies (French, Italian, British) recognize roughly similar principal modes such as comic, tragic, pastoral.

Beyond that, nothing can be taken for granted. French *pastorale* is not even roughly equivalent to English *pastoral* in the sixteenth century, since the French distinguished the more developed *pastorale* (or *bergerie*) from the *églogue* (or *bucolique*) in a manner quite foreign to English literature.[12] The saga seems to have been as peculiar to Iceland as the *skaz* to Russia or *costumbrismo* to Spain. Such local genres are legion. Of course, a distinction between labels need not necessarily imply much difference in thought. Elizabethan English had no term exactly equivalent to *odelette*, the name of a form initiated by Ronsard: "odelet" or "small ode" was not idiomatic. But we had the form itself, and Drayton felt toward a label in his coinage "amouret."[13]

Direct transplantation of terms tends to be disastrous. The notorious case of Dryden's translation of Boileau's *Art Poétique* inspires dread. (A *rondeau* is not a "round," nor a *ballade* a "ballad.") Much less obvious are the different assumptions underlying roughly equivalent terms. Italians familiar with the *Commedia dell'Arte* must have meant *carattere* in a sense somewhat distinct from that of "character." Of course, there is enough overlap between national genre systems for translation to be within the bounds of possibility. But its difficulty perpetually reminds one of cultural differences. And sometimes these are profound. Consider the relation of *roman* and *récit,* on the one hand, and, on the other, novel, romance, fiction, narrative. Or think of the alien groupings of literature implied by such terms as *Kleinlitteratur* or *Triviallitteratur.*

Temporal Variations

Changes in genre with the passage of time engender far more confusion of terms. This danger is also more insidious, because invisible. The term "epigram," for example, has been used continuously since the sixteenth century, so that it is far from obvious how far it has changed in meaning and application, or how far the kind itself has altered. Tudor epigram is not to be equated, either as a label or a form, with modern epigram. We should hardly now apply the term to narrative poems like Jonson's *On the Famous Voyage.* Such changes are so pervasive and incalculable, translation across centuries so difficult, that one could wish genre terms carried a "radix" showing the relevant date. In that way it might be possible to avoid confusing "sixteenth-century epigram" with "twentieth-century epigram."

When a genre changes, its label may drop out of use but be retained for the old state of the genre, as happened with the love complaint. Or the label may be forgotten, along with its content. An interesting instance, not without bearing on contemporary poetry, is the term *silva* (*silvae, sylvae*). A *silva* was a collection of encomiastic odes, epigrams, and other short verse kinds. The individual *silvae* or "bits of raw material" were occasional pieces, rapid effusions on the model of Statius' *Silvae,* in a great variety of forms—especially epithalamium, genethliacon, valediction, consolation, encomiastic description, and other types of praise. Statius' contemporary Quintilian lacked sympathy with what was then a new vogue for deliberate roughness. He regarded it as a fault that certain writers "run over the material first with as rapid a pen as possible, extempore, following the inspiration of the moment: this they call *silva.*"[14] But the idea of the sketch or improvisation attracted Renaissance writers: Poliziano called his verse lectures of 1480–90 *Silvae*, perhaps with the same implication (roughness, miscellaneousness) as Jonson's title *Timber* was to have.[15] The influential Scaliger made *silva* a verse collection genre, fundamental to his approach to occasional poetry. And as if in response, poetical *silvae* burgeoned: Ronsard's *Bocages*, Jonson's *Forest* and *Underwood*, Phineas Fletcher's *Silva Poetica*, Herbert's Latin *Lucus*, Cowley's *Sylva, or, divers copies*, Herrick's *Hesperides*, and Dryden's *Silvae: or, the second Part of Poetical Miscellanies*. The impromptu character of the form was no longer counted a fault. Scaliger explained the ancient term as derived "either from the multifarious matter, from the crowd of things crammed in, or from their roughness [*ipsis rudimentis*]. For they used to pour out unpolished effusions and correct them afterwards."[16] However, Scaliger's subsequent rules for various kinds of individual *silvae* such as epithalamium make it clear that the "spontaneous" expression was to be formed from the outset by regular art.

In modified forms, the label *silva* has maintained a tenuous tradition: Coleridge's *Sibylline Leaves*, Leigh Hunt's *Foliage; or Poems Original and Translated*, Whitman's *Leaves of Grass*, Stevenson's *Underwoods*, Lowell's *Notebook*, and Edwin Morgan's *New Divan*.[17] But although the last two, at least, show a clear understanding of the form, this is not widespread among their readers. We tend to take for granted the idea of a collection of poems on various subjects and in different forms, without reflecting that such collections constitute a specific genre. It seems almost as if the genre were too dominant, too nonpareil, to have a name. But how far has the *silva* genre itself changed? Have its characteristic qualities quite altered? Or would our criticism of *silvae* be the better for focusing on their variety and their appearance of spontaneity?

Labels may also confuse because of changes within a genre. This may have been the case with satire: the ancient uncertainty between *satura* and *satira* (*satyra*) has been attributed to the existence of an earlier, dramatic form of satire. Within tragedy, similarly, the changes that brought the Attic to the English form (with its comic admixture, its violence on stage and its disunity) certainly confused classical critics. All the same, retaining the old label has seemed justified. Through all the changes (and in spite of medieval application of the term to narratives about the falls of princes) there is an impressive coherence in the modal grouping. So, too, with certain other kinds, such as the essay, which from being an unworked gathering later became a highly polished form only just recognizable as the same kind.

With the sonnet, however, the confusions are more numerous, and of a different sort. To begin with there is the enormous metrical diversity, even within the fourteen-line sonnet: from Petrarchan, Shakespearean, and other traditional types to Hopkins' long sonnets, Auden's playful variations and Lowell's open-form epigrams. Then there is the inner diversity that these forms cover: the sonnet as stanza in a long poem or a sonnet sequence; the heroic single sonnet of Tasso or Milton; the Elizabethan epigrammatic sonnet; and the Romantic lyrical sonnet. Even if we accept all these as sonnets, we may baulk at Gay's use of the label for his pastorals—a usage that goes back through the Elizabethan "songs and sonnets" to early Renaissance conventions whereby a sonnet was a short ode or canzone, or any short lyrical or amorous poem. Here the kind's boundaries have shifted considerably.

Perhaps most extreme of all is the change in nomenclature and grouping of comic works. Medieval comedy, as everyone knows, is liable to be not only nondramatic but unfunny. True, it shares a few features with ancient and Renaissance comic forms: colloquial style, a happy outcome, and the presentation of an *imago vitae*. Still, the use of the same term for the *Divina Commedia* and the *Comedy of Errors* is a little confusing, to say the least. And although we are not usually aware of it, similar changes of grouping are so widespread as to be almost universal. The nomenclature of elegy, epigram, and eclogue will serve to illustrate this point.

Elegy, Epigram, Eclogue, Romance

The classical elegy was a poem in elegiac distichs (alternating hexameters and pentameters). Originally implying a lamentation, the term was later used for hymns, epigrams, genethliaca, and other types. As Cairns notes, it belonged to a broader category of genre than hymn or genethliacon.[18] Yet it was not a blank, subject-free, purely formal genre. Even in its extensions it retained the character of passionate meditation. Scaliger interestingly suggests that the matter of love elegy is connected with that of funeral elegy by the lover's "death."[19] But Elizabethan and Jacobean critics, while they retained the ancient term, often distinguished "mourning elegies" and "anniversaries" (with the lamentation of funeral elegies omitted) from love elegies—although the latter might be "crying Elegies" (*Philaster* 3.2.65). Under the influence not only of classical epicedium but of Christian sermon—and perhaps of Petrarch's elegies in the *In Morte* section of the *Canzoniere*—conventional topics of epideictic rhetoric developed in the English funeral elegy. And eventually these became quite distinct from anything in classical elegy. Thus, the mourned person might be considered in connection with the ages of life, the gifts of the Spirit, regeneracy, sainthood, relation to Christ, or the cosmic identifications of encomiastic hyperbole.[20] Later still, Wellek and Warren recount, Gray's *Elegy* in quatrains decisively interrupted the tradition of elegy as a tender personal poem in couplets. And some of Shenstone's quatrain elegies departed even further from the ancient form, by offering generalized expression of entirely solitary sentiments. So far as love elegy was concerned, eighteenth-century criticism tended to discard the label. "Amorous verse" was referred to instead by such terms as "ode," "passion," "love song." In the nineteenth century, a still more diffuse elegiac tradition spread, of odes, monodies, and even ballads, on "love, transience, disillusionment, death, and kindred puzzling and challenging themes" (as Abbie Potts has it).[21] Now the metrical form was often a quatrain of alternating long and short lines. And what the elegists wrote were likely to be called "lyrics," or simply—as we come into the twentieth century—"poems." For Ruskin expressed a common view when he wrote that "lyric poetry is the expression by the poet of his own feelings"[22]—something we should no longer be inclined to accept. We still call old poems "lyrics," but apply the term less freely to new ones. The changes might be roughly summarized as in the table below.

The Renaissance epigram—and the epigram as Johnson still defined it—was "a short poem terminating in a point." In keeping with its suggested origin in epigraphy, a chief feature was terseness: the epigram might not be as short as a distich, but whatever its length it was not supposed to have room for rhetorical figures. Its style was plain. However, it had a great variety of subjects, from epitaphs and encomia to for-

ELEGIAC LABELS

16th–17th century	18th century	19th century	20th century
(Love) elegy, passion	Love song, ode, amorous verse, passion, etc.	Love poem, lyric	Love poem
(Mourning) elegy, anniversary, epicede, etc.	Elegy	Elegy, lyric	Elegy

tuitous events and anecdotal "narrations."[23] Indeed, Robertello's *De Epigrammate* (1548) developed the theory that epigram subgenres were particles, or modal applications, of other genres—epic, tragedy (as in epitaphs), comedy, satire, *silva*.[24] The epigram's characteristic structure lay in its witty closure, to which all that went before could be seen as leading, all of a sudden, up.[25]

Its style being usually spoken, plain, and rhetorically low, epigram was in contrast with lyric. Thus, Minturno sharply distinguished the sonnet from epigram by its lyrical "sung" canzone-like sound.[26] However, when Estienne's publication of the newly discovered *Anacreontea* (1554) and his edition of the Planudean Anthology (1556) revealed the possibilities for love epigrams, other theorists (Varchi, Pigna, Tasso) began to associate sonnet and epigram, rather than to contrast them.[27] The sonnet came to be thought of not only as part of a sequence but as a separate form—not unlike the *mel* or emotionally sweet epigram. Soon "sweet" became very much a sonneteers' word. In fact, the epigrammatic modulation that extended to elegy and other forms around 1590 was transforming the sonnet too. Sidney's spoken diction and sharp wit, Shakespeare's couplet closures, Herrick's fourteen-line love epigrams: these and many other instances show how far the blending went in this direction. Meanwhile, Jonson and others were using the epigram's plain style for every type of lyric, returning in this to a classical view (Pliny *Epistles* 4.14) that the two genres are indistinguishable.

But in the nineteenth century, renewed influence of Greek epigrams led to an even greater predominance of the sweet, unpointed, lyrical type. Now the taste for *mel* epigrams displaced all the other tastes distinguished by Scaliger—salty joking (*sal*), mordant satire (*acetum*), pungent malediction voiding gall (*fel*), and foul ugliness (*foetidas*). The development of the epigram took several directions, sometimes returning to its Greek roots, sometimes leading—as in Landor, Meredith, and Hardy—to personal revelation. At all events, however, it was the lyrical rather than the pointed form that came to constitute epigram—to such an extent that representatives of the genre could be labeled, without qualification, "lyrics." The term "epigram," on the other hand, was now reserved for poetry of the past, or else for pointed speeches such as the antithetical witty sayings of Oscar Wilde or his characters. Again, there has been a thoroughgoing change of labels, which may be very roughly summed up as shown in the table opposite.

The content of "eclogue" has also changed radically. Already the Vir-

EPIGRAM AND LYRIC LABELS

1550	1600	1900
Lyric (sonnet, etc.)	Sonnet, lyric	
		Lyric
———————		
Epigram	Epigram	
		———
		Epigram

gilian type was a departure from the Theocritean. Most would agree, for example, that in their artificial and so to speak ostentatious naïveté, Virgil's literary shepherds differ from those of Theocritus, who are oblivious to pastoral rules.[28] And surely all must find Theocritus' settings actually rural beside Virgil's more figurative ones. Nevertheless, the early grammarians used the same term "bucolics" for both the *Idylls* and the *Eclogues*. And in fact the differences proved almost negligible compared to the great departures of Renaissance ecloguists. For the latter often exchanged the mocking, detached tone of Theocritean pastoral for the polemical bitterness of ecclesiastical satire. In Petrarch or Mantuan or Spenser the allegory of pastoral eclogue could have an almost Orwellian starkness. Moreover, the Renaissance eclogue contained much material that would formerly have been regarded as georgic—a form in contrast to pastoral. Dialogues of youth and age; the calendar of seasonal labors; real hardships and suffering; political and military leadership: these and other extrapastoral topics were introduced without much suggestion of limits having been passed. Love, a destroyer of the ancient pastoral *otium*, became an ordinary subject of the Renaissance eclogue. True, consciousness that these were modern transformations was not quite lacking. Scaliger, for example, clearly enjoys naming the newest subgenres of eclogue. And Herrick seems to express a sharp sense of generic terminology in one of the liminal poems to *Hesperides,* where he pretends to advise his Muse to stay safely at home piping to the "private cottages":

> There with the Reed, thou mayst expresse
> The Shepherds Fleecie happinesse:
> And with thy *Eclogues* intermixe
> Some smooth, and harmlesse *Beucolicks.*
>
> (*To His Muse*)

The two labels correspond to alternative companions, the "handsome Shephardling" and the "Girl (that keeps the Neat)." Such discriminating distinctions were by no means universal, however. Even in the Augustan period, the strictly Virgilian "pastoral" (Walsh, Pope) coexisted uneasily with the looser and more bucolic "native" type of Philips and others—to say nothing of more obviously unpastoral extensions such as piscatory, nautical, viticultural, and even hunting eclogues.[29]

In the eighteenth century the form developed in ways that had a good deal to do with confusions about the term "eclogue." Such confusion was not new: in the Middle Ages, the satiric eclogue had been authorized by a false derivation of "eclogue" from *aig-* and *logos* ("goatish speech")—as is still seen in the Elizabethan spelling "aeglogue."[30] But by a later, seventeenth-century shift, the term came to be almost equivalent to "dialogue," so that in all probability "pastoral eclogue" would neither have been felt as tautologous nor as indicating contrast with (say) piscatory eclogue. R. F. Jones may well be right in saying that so many of the features specific to pastoral eclogue (song contest; cumulative simile; elegiac lament) were laid aside that it became an empty, omnipurpose form. If so, it is futile to try to construe *A Town Eclogue. 1710* (attributed to Swift) or Gay's *A Town Eclogue* or Lady Mary Wortley Montagu's *Six Town Eclogues* as burlesque pastorals. They are antipastorals, rather, or a new form altogether. For the town eclogue soon became an independent genre, in which "eclogue" provided only a rudimentary vehicle. This consists of not much more than a dialogue set within a scene whose description serves as a frame. Besides the satirical town eclogue, there are other subgenres, showing a wide range of contents: native eclogue (Gay, Ramsay), foreign eclogue (Collins, Chatterton), political eclogue (Jenyns, Mason), and war eclogue (Collins, Coleridge). Eclogue has come to mean, in effect, "a dramatic scene."

Other labels have undergone similar alterations. The changes cannot be ascribed, either, merely to the carelessness of critics, or to superficial circumstances. They reflect deep and pervasive changes in the grouping of literature itself. But the changes have in turn further affected the relations between works—their neighbors, their contexts, their meanings, their values, their status.

The confusions in labeling are not always easily disentangled. It is hard to know, for example, when conservative labels became anachronistic. Had this point been reached by "interlude" and "moral" (morality) in Shakespeare's time? An old label, which already carries a heavy legend, may be applied to an emergent genre in need of a name. Thus, "romance" was used for the early novel, and so was another ancient label, "history": "As this Sort of Writing was intended as a Contrast to those in which the Reader was even to suppose all the Characters ideal, and every Circumstance quite imaginary, 'twas thought necessary, to give it a greater Air of Truth, to entitle it *an History.*"[31] And "novel" itself was another old bottle for the new wine. An entire study might be devoted to this one group of labels and their multifarious implications. In the nineteenth century, "romance" was revived as a label for what I must crudely describe as the nonnaturalistic novel. (Romantic and Victorian writers were fond of returning to earlier labels for historical authentication of their generic novelties.) It would not be easy to say how much retrospection there was in the term "romance" as, say, Hawthorne used it, compared with Hurd or Scott—to say nothing of later turns of the screw by James and by Stevenson. And meanwhile, quite apart from retrospective labels, each individual kind is continually, inexorably changing, all the time adding further extensions, new transformations; so that the terminology, even when it remains outwardly the same, changes internally without our noticing. These changes of label have an almost irreversible entropy, in that earlier implications obstinately defy the imagination. How is one to unthink subsequent meanings and recover the first crudity of terms?

The number and sort of generic labels change widely with critical interests. So, in former periods when interest in rhetoric and in literary ceremonial was high, and when classical precedents were enthusiastically embraced, critics used separate labels for many subgenres now lumped together, such as funeral elegy, epicede, anniversary, epitaph: all of which are now elegy. We for our part have developed elaborate distinctions between shades of naturalism. And we have labels for a great many subgenres of novel according to *mise-en-scène,* besides such terms as "adventure," "fabulation," "fiction" ("a fiction"), "denatured novel," "lyrical novel," "antinovel," "faction," and the like.

For such reasons there are no exact one-to-one correspondences between the generic labels used in different historical periods. Even if all casual or erroneous labeling were cleared up (to say nothing of labels wittily misapplied, as in Cotton's *Valediction,* which is not really a valediction at all, but what used to be known as a complaint): if all the terms were ordered and brought into apparent correspondence, still there would be no true equivalence. Old labels can never be taken at face value;

they must always be approached with a due sense of their obscurity. The commonsense assumption that a sonnet is a sonnet will not withstand scrutiny for a moment. But this is not to say that partial translation of terms is beyond hope. Early generic terms can often be brought to bear in a way that improves, at least, our understanding of a work.

Genre Labels in the Middle Ages

Terminological discontinuity can be so extreme that entire genre systems break up or temporarily go out of use. So the modernist movement, committed to a myth of "breaking the forms," avoided genre labels altogether for a time—or else would invent playful new ones. And it is commonly agreed that medieval writers felt a supreme indifference toward the traditional genres: even got on pretty well without any genre theory at all. Their few generic terms are supposed to be casual and chaotic. Wimsatt and Brooks sum up the views of many when they write that "the medieval lack of interest in these classical genres [*scilicet* comedy and tragedy] and their norms is clear."[32] It is assumed that medieval writers had no sense of genre. And if that were true, reasons for it would not be far to seek. C. S. Lewis comments on the leveling antigeneric effect of argument from authority in the Middle Ages: "The poet is ranked with the scientist as authority for a purely scientific proposition. This astonishing failure or refusal to distinguish—in practice, though not always in theory—between books of different sorts must be borne in mind whenever we are trying to gauge the total effect of an ancient text on its medieval readers."[33] However, this may rather be a reflection of different categorization of realities. Perhaps it has as much to do with the limits of medieval science as of medieval rhetoric. And Lewis' remark that the medieval habit survived in Burton alerts us to further possibilities. After all, Burton was far from being indifferent to genre—was engaged, indeed, in a consciously ironic transformation of the anatomy form, which would later develop in the direction of the psychoanalytic treatise.

It seems obviously true that awareness of genre was in abeyance during the Middle Ages. Not that the classical terminology disappeared, of course. Grammar masters of the twelfth century dutifully mention the traditional kinds; Geoffrey de Vinsauf's thirteenth-century *Poetria Nova* takes them for granted. But many of the writers give little more than bare catalogues of terms, with perfunctory definitions much like the drastically reduced account of tragedy given by Chaucer's Monk, the starkness of which seems to Wimsatt and Brooks to mark the loss of all sense of what is appropriate to tragedy and comedy. All the genre terms are liable to be used in strange ways. Thus, John of Garland tells us that "a Realistic Fiction is a fictitious event that nevertheless could have happened, as is the case in comedies. And no invocation should be made in a comedy, except for an insoluble complication in the plot."[34] The division into fable, history, and realistic fiction is recognizably that of the *Rhetorica ad Herennium*. But John's arbitrary characterization of comedy is odd. And he continues:

> Furthermore, one kind of historical narrative is an epithalamium, which is a wedding poem. Another is an epicedium, which is a plain song apart from a burial, that is, one that is composed for someone not yet buried; whence Virgil of Caesar ... Another is an apotheosis, which is a poem that celebrates deification or the coming of a soul to glory. Another is a bucolic, which is about cowherding. Another is a georgic, which is about agriculture. Another is a lyric, which is about drinking and eating or feasting and love of the gods. Another is an epode, that is, "a line resembling a *clausula*," which celebrates horse racing. Another is the secular song.[35]

There follows a distinction between invective, which is intended to malign, and satire, in which evils are recited for the sake of reform. (The vagueness here may help to explain Bernard de Morval's calling his *De Contemptu Mundi* a satire.) Still in the same subdivision, apparently, "one kind of narrative [*hystoricum*] is tragedy, that is, a poem that begins in joy and is brought to an end in grief. Another is elegiac, which is a song of misery that contains or recites the sorrows of lovers. A species of elegy is amoebaean, which usually consists of a contrast between two characters, or a lovers' quarrel, as in Theodolus and in various places in the *Eclogues*. And note that every comedy is an elegy, but not vice versa." Chaotic though they seem, several of these strange observations can be made sense of. For one thing, "narrative" has to be read in the context of forensic rhetoric, where "dramatic" was as much a form of narration as, say, "exegetic."[36] It neither implies nor excludes narrative in the modern sense. Second, "epodon" originally referred to the shorter verse of a couplet, which indeed resembles a *clausula*. Third, every comedy (versified narrative) is an elegy in the sense of being in elegiac meter. However, even if John's remarks could all be shown meaningful in their own terms, they would not suggest much interest in the detail of classical genres.

Instead, his concern is a practical one, with kinds actually being written. Doubtless in consequence of this, he has a tendency to recategorize them—sometimes, it appears, in order to bring genre theory in line with Christian thinking. Like other medieval poets, John is eager to transform the classical genres. A simple but touching instance of this comes in his treatment of epitaph. Having defined it as "a poem inscribed over a dead body," he gives first a Virgilian instance (*Eclogues* 5.43–44), and then what is evidently an epitaph for himself. However, unlike Virgil's Daphnis, John is still living. His epigram transforms the pagan genre: he has stated the generic rule only to break it.

Such generic transformations make up so great a part of medieval and later literature that we shall return to them in another chapter. Here it may be enough to recall the transformations of epithalamium that began with Martianus Capella's enormously influential *De Nuptiis Philologiae et Mercurii*. Generic transformations and innovations became so frequent that we find Matthew of Vendome having to argue the advantages of old subjects and genres against new.[37]

With medieval writers, we have to cope with quite unfamiliar genre terms, or with classical terms used in an unfamiliar way. These make up an entire system that is strange. We cannot even take for granted the book-author unit, whose integrity nowadays only a Foucault questions. For the label "book" was applied to works of several hands, such as the *Morte d'Arthur*. In this striking but by no means atypical example, Malory is both more and less than a single imitative author using source material. We have rather to think of him, in C. S. Lewis' apt metaphor, as the last builder of a cathedral with work of many different periods. In the Middle Ages, the conceptions of originality, authority, and authorship were all different, and so, therefore, was that of book. Far form being a synonym for "work," "book" was in contrast with the shorter "ympne" and "thing," as well as with "chapter," *capitulum,* and the like.[38]

Adequate theoretical and general rhetorics would have cleared up many of these difficulties. But most medieval rhetorics were meant as practical manuals. And they were often so specialized as to relate to only one or two genres. On the one hand there were extended studies of the art-sermon giving elaborate *dispositio* plans; on the other there was no accepted term for "poem."[39] Consequently, in spite of there being some areas in highlight, many terms remain obscure, particularly semitechnical labels such as "treatise." But at least we can be fairly sure that during the Middle Ages new genre terms were introduced and used with some degree of consistency. Thus, the impersonal and direct general "complaint" was clearly distinguished from the ironic satire.[40] Other important new labels were "dream," "vision," and "pilgrimage" for dream visions or allegories of various types; "legend"; and "romance."[41]

Medieval genre terms are thus fraught with many problems. Even when the author himself attaches an explicit label, as Chaucer sometimes seems to do, his meaning may be in doubt. So in the *Canterbury Tales,* statements by Host or narrator that offer potentially valuable generic signposts have in the event given rise to very divergent views.[42] True, several critics have agreed that the tales of Fragment VII (Group B$_2$) exhibit some sort of generic complementarity. But whether this depends on alteration of "sentence" and "solace" (whatever exactly these terms mean), on parodic relations, or on antitype development remains far from clear.

The problems encountered are well illustrated by a crux at the end of *Troilus and Criseyde,* where Chaucer looks to the future: "Go, litel bok, go litel myn tragedye, / Ther God thy makere yet, er that he dye, / So sende myght to make in som comedye!" (V. 1786–88). Donald Howard argues that this must refer to the *Canterbury Tales,* since "comedy" in the passage is in contrast with "tragedy." Consequently, Chaucer "could not have meant *The Legend of Good Women,* for he would have called it, as he did, by the generic term legend . . . Its subject matter is far from comedy as Chaucer would have understood the term."[43] The current orthodoxy takes the medieval sense of "comedy" to be on the lines of Evanthius' definition, still in part followed by Dante (in the Letter to Can Grande) and many other medieval writers, according to which comedy differs from tragedy by beginning in turbulence and ending in tranquillity. So conceived, it is a suitable genre for Christian works, such as the *Divina Commedia,* and the *Canterbury Tales*—which can easily be seen as moving away from worldliness and passion toward blessedness, at least in its inner movement. But this conception of comedy provides no explanation of many critical passages. As we saw, John of Garland could write that "illa species narrationis que dicitur Argumentum est Comedia" ("the sort of narration termed Realistic Fiction is Comedy"). There can be no question of his limiting the proposition to fictions with happy endings: he uses "comedy" simply in the sense of "versified tale."[44] Further, even the contrast between comedy and tragedy may have a purely stylistic import. So in *De Vulgari Eloquentia* 2.4, the three styles that Dante distinguishes, of tragedy, comedy, and elegy, evidently correspond to the three styles by height—*illustris, mediocris,* and *humilis.*[45] Here again comedy is not to be thought of as a genre in Evanthius' sense. If we keep this possibility in mind, we may be less sure that the passage in *Troilus* cannot refer to *The Legend of Good Women.* The three uses of the term are not completely different words; indeed, it is the fact that they are different senses of 1400 "comedy" that gives rise to much of the confusion. Atkins speaks of medieval comedy as "a new narrative form, based on a misconception of ancient poetry." But the basis is rather more than that.

We may be inclined to think of medieval literature as a generic waste-land or labyrinth. There are signposts, but these only confuse matters further by their baffling ambiguities. They may be classical, or classical misunderstood, or classical reinterpreted, or vernacular equivalent, or vernacular oblivious, or vernacular artful and innovative. However, as the existence of fairly sophisticated epistolary rhetoric shows, all this is not to be put down to mere incapacity—still less to disregard for genre. We have to look for explanations of the disorder, first in the practical aims of the grammarians, and second in the difficulties that emergent forms present to the genre critic. No doubt these difficulties might have been overcome by more powerful intellects. But in that age the best minds were otherwise engaged: not in secular rhetoric, or even in *artes praedicandi,* but in Scriptural commentary.

And there, among exegetes of the book of books, we indeed find writers concerned with the deeper issues of literary theory.[46] Far removed from the vagueness of vernacular terms such as "book" is the subtlety of the commentators' distinctions between *compilatio (compilator)* and *collectio (collector).* Only the former, it seems, implied orderly arrangement of materials. A *collector* was not necessarily responsible for all the collected items—as David, *collector* of the Psalms, was not *auctor* of the whole collection. (Perhaps Chaucer's narrator pretends a similar status.) On the other hand, the Book of Wisdom and 2 Machabees were ordered *compilationes.* Commentaries on these books (such as Nicholas of Lyre's on 2 Machabees) have a theoretical bearing on the contemporary *compilatio* genres, to which Raban Maur's *De Universo,* Bartolemaeus Anglicus' *De Proprietatibus Rerum,* Vincent of Beauvais's *Speculum Maius,* and Lambertus Audomarensis' *Liber Floridus* belong.[47]

The need to delineate the authority of the Bible and its parts led to clarifications of the titles *auctor, commentator,* and *scriptor,* as well as *compilator.* There was much subtle discussion of the relationship between parts and whole in *ordinatio partium.* And, at a somewhat later date, the same interest in *formae tractandi* issued (as A. J. Minnis has shown) in careful identification of the genres of individual books of the Bible. The *Compendium Totius Biblie* of Pierre Auriol, for example, goes far beyond Saint Jerome's simple Biblical Poetics in this respect. Particularly interesting is the innovative naming of new, or newly labeled, modes. To mention one instance, fourteenth-century exegetes distinguished a mode they called "prophetic." They described this *modus vel forma prophetialis* in some detail. Thus, it should be popular, diversified with parables; its diction should be simple and familiar; and its narrative should be discontinuous.[48]

But the theoretical ideas of the medieval commentators, however great their interest, lie outside our present field. It is enough to notice the existence of a body of genre theory matching medieval literature in depth and sophistication. The confusing generic labels of the period are far from proving it a time innocent of genre.

New Terms

The instability of labeling and the confusion of the terms that we consequently inherit in our criticism have tempted some to reduce our terminology to a system. They have introduced new, clearly defined genre terms that may mean one thing precisely. This hope is not without precedent: the ancient rhetoricians multiplied terms just as freely. But it has been specially prevalent in the phase of genre theory beginning with Northrop Frye (who resuscitated or invented many terms, such as "alazon," "dianoia," "eiron," and "anatomy") and continuing with the structuralists. The hope is vain, since success in propagating new terms implies failure in maintaining their precision. They are univocal only until they are used. More seriously, a system using many new terms runs the risk of being internally self-consistent, without engaging in the main critical argument. Frye would have to lay aside his special uses of "mode," the structuralist his "text" and "discourse types" before their views could become fully assimilable. It seems best to retain current terms wherever possible, accepting or qualifying or rejecting the conceptions they entail, even though doing so may involve difficult explanations and troublesome controversies. In general, the tension between new and old ideas needs to be sustained by employing and turning the critical language in current use.

The practical reasons for retaining accepted terms are obvious. But there is also a theoretical consideration. Existing genre terms (at least those in wide use) derive great value from their correspondence to real groupings. It seems reasonable enough to suppose that a literary genre actually existed, if there is a label for it in our shared critical language. To put it no higher, authors will have written within an intellectual world that recognized the genre in question. However, it would be quite another matter to suppose that existing terms provide anything like a list of all the possible genres. Some remain unnamed through oversight; others are emerging through changes in literature.

How many terms do we need? Broadly speaking, two sorts of additions to genre terminology are worth considering. First, names may be needed for developing kinds and subgenres. Or genres previously unnamed may come to be recognized. Or new groupings altogether may emerge. In all these cases, terms may legitimately be invented. New kinds obviously call for new names, although new modes will not. Indeed, it is vital to relate each mode to its corresponding kind, since the continuity thus displayed is of significance. Second, the literary model itself may change, so that elements come to have a different value, and function in generic repertoires in a new way. (So, in the development of English poetry, syllable counting and stanza patterns gained meaning at one stage and at another lost it.) Accounts of such changes, it might be argued, should make do without new terms, because these obscure the very changes being traced.

To sum up: the criticism of every period yields some discriminating and many casual genre terms. And always the generic label needs to be distinguished from the genre itself. Both change, if not necessarily in step with one another. Nevertheless, deliverate innovations in terminology should be kept to a minimum, since they weaken continuity of understanding.

9. The Formation of Genres

It is time to look at genre's historical dimension. Until now we have discussed the main categories—kind, subgenre, and mode—as coexistent, without much reference to their development. They were related purely by class inclusion (subgenres of a kind) or by representative selection (mode's attenuated suggestion of the corresponding kind). Viewed diachronically, however, the categories turn out to have a developmental relation. Subgenres and modes are formed from kinds by a historical process that is fundamental to an understanding of literary forms. It is one of the laws of literature. To see how this may be, we have first to consider how kinds themselves are formed.

Primitive Origins

Of the origin of many genres we know nothing. The main kinds, including those with corresponding modes, mostly go back through Latin to Greek literature, where their beginnings are lost in pre-Homeric obscurity. More is known about the rise of the novel. But it, too, has an ancient history in its antecedents in epic, romance, and other forms—and besides, its status as a kind is problematic. So far as the classical kinds are concerned, the earliest examples extent presuppose others: "The genres are as old as organized societies."[1] Menander the Rhetor may have regarded Homer's works as prototypes, but historically considered they were probably not the first instances of the genres they represent. Similarly, "topical sophistications of a highly developed kind occur in the work of the early Greek lyric and iambic poets."[2] Already complex generic rules had been formed (even if these were more implicit and less tidy than rhetoricians were to suggest). In fact, the earliest phases of kinds seem often to have been ritualistic, if not actually part of the religious rites associated with common situations.

With English literature, origins are almost as inaccessible. *Deor* is already allusive in style, conventional and cryptic in diction. And *Beowulf,* too, is artfully formulaic. Generic origins, it seems, lie well behind an elaborate heritage of oral literary forms. From all this, it follows that discussion of ultimate origins can be no more than speculation. To get beyond speculation about how kinds are formed, we have to turn to their later stages, or to the origins of more recent kinds.[3]

Speculation about generic origins has partly taken the form of relating them to archetypes or *mythèmes,* psychological or anthropological types underlying social mythologies. Sometimes this carries conviction—as, for example, in Richmond Lattimore's analysis of story patterns in Greek tragedy. The patterns have ramifying formal implications: to mention only one instance, they explain the degree of free will possible in certain subtypes of Attic tragedy. Yet it is disconcerting how the story patterns out across genres, appearing not only in tragedy but in fairy tale and Shakespearean comedy—to say nothing of mythological and historical avatars.[4] By comparison, the conventional genres are made to appear superficial.

Much of Northrop Frye's typology, similarly, is based on story types, myths, or narrative motifs. These are so universal, and have such deep roots in the anthropological ground of human nature, that inevitably they seem more fundamental. However, referring literature to the deep structures of myth is not necessarily a fundamental thing to do. In literature, myths need not be specially significant, any more than deep structure in language is more profound than surface structure. This is not said to diminish the ultimate aims of Frye's genre criticism.[5] The present point is merely that an adequate account of generic formation would have to come to grips with specifically literary features. That is, it would have to account for what constitutes the genre as a literary form and not as something else. But Frye's archetypes are often discovered in aspects of a work that are quite minor from a literary standpoint. Belinda's Proserpina role, indeed, is only arguably present at all in Pope's poem, considered as a poem. Tracing anthropological origins is perfectly legitimate, but it is unlikely to tell us much about the genres Pope is using, so long as literary qualities are passed over. Apart from anything else, the original meaning of a story may have been forgotten so long ago that it has come to be used with a different value altogether and to have no significant relation to the archetype.

Without taking a narrow view of literature, we need to allow it its distinct form of existence. But archetypes, although they may be indirectly associated with genres, have no specially literary status. They appear just as much in other media, other fields of discourse, other arts; they are to be reckoned psychological rather than literary types. They may be consitutents of literary genres—but only if literary criteria of relevance judge them to be so. Myth criticism in effect reduces literary forms to unchanging nonliterary forms, as if that explained them.[6] For the thoroughgoing myth critic, genres have no origins: the whole concept of formation presupposes a more historical orientation. But from our present standpoint the origin of kinds is a real problem, to which their connections with mythic patterns, however interesting in themselves, offer no solution. Story types are not necessarily genre-linked. Nor need they have any literary interest or importance. It is only when myths make up a considerable part of a kind's repertoire (as with Attic tragedy) that the idea of primitive preexistences has explanatory power.

In this sense, the hypothesis that some kinds took their substance from earlier myths or stories has limited validity. The idea of story material's being transferred from other kinds, or from outside literature, is useful. Even so, it proves very difficult to refer generic origins to altogether external forms. For the transfers seem to have been part of a larger process of generic transformation that obeys literary laws.

A similar hypothesis is that literary genres took their origin from earlier nonliterary discourse types. One of the fullest developments of this idea is Andre Jolles' *Einfache Formen* (1930), which offers nine preliterary genres as the building blocks for more complex genres. These nine are supposed to correspond to basic speech situations. The "simple forms," however—saint's legend, legendary story, myth, riddle, proverb, (court) case, memoir, fairy tale, and joke—turn out themselves to be complex genres, many of them, in their own right, with their own developmental and in part literary history. Jolles' rather arbitrary selection of early genres provides no basis for a systematic account of origins.[7] Still, the notion of combining preexisting forms is useful, even if the building analogy is too simple. Only it needs to be carried further and seen as a continuous process, manifested as much by the so-called simple forms as by any others. Useful, too, is Jolles' idea of extraliterary or subliterary forms converted or "raised" to literary uses. Tzvetan Todorov perhaps exaggerates when he says that "from a structural point of view, each type of discourse usually referred to as literary has nonliterary relatives which resemble it more than do other types of literary discourse."[8] However, it is true that many kinds seem to have arisen partly from popular or subliterary forms. So we have the literary fabliau, the art ballad, the art song. Defoe's novels demonstrably depend on earlier criminal biography. And the erotic novel is inconceivable without centuries of subliterary pornography. (The use of syntax and prose rhythm to mime the sexual act, which Joyce put to great effect in Molly Bloom's soliloquy, was a feature of the genre as early as *Fanny Hill.*) In this perspective, literature appears as the small apex of a very large and very blunt pyramid. Many of its generic innovations could be described as elevations of the subliterary.[9]

Another hypothesis is that genres are functional in origin. This need not be a crudely reductive notion explaining literature in terms of practical "causes." Better expressed, it posits an original perlocutionary setting. So Francis Cairns writes that "every genre has a 'function,' which is often to convey a communication of a certain character."[10] This is certainly true of such genres as the *propemptikon* or farewell, and it probably applies also to some English kinds. We may distinguish (although the ancients did not) between two sorts of actual contexts: religious and secular. The *propemptikon* was used on secular occasions; whereas early tragedy had a ritual setting in sacred festivals such as the City Dionysia. Literary theorists have long been interested in functional origins of the second type. Scaliger, in particular, speculates about the anthropological or ritual background of individual conventions almost as a matter of routine. Thus, he relates each convention of epithalamium in turn to an ancient nuptial ceremony: on the *kēroi* he refers us to Plutarch; on the custom of making noise to hide the bride's cries, to Virgil and Catullus.[11] As we have seen, Puttenham passes this on with augmentation: "The songs were very loud and shrill, to the intent there might no noise be heard out of the bed chamber." Epithalamia such as Spenser's would hardly be functional in quite this immediate way. Still, *Prothalamion* was about an actual double spousal, for which it may have been commissioned, and which determined many of its features. And many far more recent epithalamia have served actual occasions, like Auden's for Giuseppe Antonio Borgese and Elisabeth Mann. In fact, those that do not have a real setting perhaps depend on the reader's generalized sense of epithalamic occasion, drawn from those that do.

However, many kinds have no discernible occasion or function. Perhaps we might think of "primitive" kinds as more functional than later ones. But, even among the former, there are large exceptions. Much of the interest of epics, as of novels, lies precisely in our sense of their nonfunctional, "unexplained" character. However, recent disclosures of the occasional element in Elizabethan drama make one hesitate before rejecting the theory of original occasion. Perhaps we can only say that the theory works better with some kinds (funeral elegy, epitaph, genethliacon) than with others (love elegy, epic, romance). We should be clear, too, about its limitations. When Renaissance theorists traced epigram's brevity to an original epigraphic function, this was far from being a full or adequate explanation. It does not exclude alternative possibilities, such as that epigrammatists composed briefly in order to simulate inscriptions, or that epigraphists imitated earlier brief forms.

Throughout, function is complicated by overdeterminations of expressive value. Features that may have had an original function easily become means of literary communication. So the epic invocation of the Muse may have begun as an actual prayer to a *daimon*. Later, it became a more or less perfunctory convention, until Milton revitalized it, perhaps even reactualized it, in the serious prayers that open *Paradise Lost* 1 and 3 and 7. Similarly with the epic catalogue, such as Homer's list of the Greek ships and champions. Originally, it may have been a social acknowledgment of the auditors and their kin, but its subsequent value has been formal and expressive. It serves the exposition by bringing in characters economically and giving a sense of scope. Or it glances at other legends, "matters" that are not to be treated, and so suggests a literary context for the work, perhaps also communicating the poet's ideas for other projects—as when Milton's catalogue of devils reflects interests he planned at one time to explore in separate works.[12] Or else it is ordered, like Homer's, as a structural pattern. Probably no literary catalogue is entirely devoid of such expressive values. Now it is true that lists of a practical character are among the earliest writings that have survived. But we are not entitled to assume that there were not even earlier oral and nonfunctional catalogues.

Monogenesis

By a theory almost diametrically opposed, the origins of genres are located in the achievements of individual writers. Each kind has a single inventor, in this theory, or at most two or three: epic goes back to Homer, tragedy to Aeschylus, the verisimilar novel to Fielding and Richardson, the historical novel to Scott, the open-form long poem to Pound and Williams. There is no need to exemplify a theory so widespread. Inventors of kinds have been honored since ancient times and continue to dominate much of our thinking about origins. However, when remote antiquity does not obscure the period of a kind's beginnings, they can always be shown to have preceded the inventor. Before Scott there were romances, and the regional novels of Maria Edgeworth; before Fielding, picaresque novels and Defoe; before Defoe, criminal biographies and Elizabethan novels. Pound and Williams were not the first to write long poems following the rhythms of ordinary speech, nor were Browning and Whitman. And Thomson, whom Johnson credited with the invention of a "new kind," could draw on a long tradition of descriptive and georgic poetry.[13] Moreover, in considering individual origins we have also to allow for the possibility of polygenesis. Comparative studies have steered toward the conclusion that original creativity is often doubled, even in other literatures with their own independent lines of development.[14] Here, too, we should not forget the Russian formalist case for considering literatures and their genres as systems. For the formalists and their successors, the individual innovation that composes disparate materials from different literatures to form a work of a new kind was seen strictly in terms of interaction between autonomous systems.

Still, whatever systems may be exerting pressure, it remains true that a single writer's creativity can play a decisive part in originating a new kind. Neoclassical epic and the heroic parts of English georgic depend in a special way on Milton's epics. And similarly *To Penshurst* began, in some sense, the country house poem. Because of its high value, that is to say, it had an almost paradigmatic function. This status is not a matter of formal value only, but of content and personal worth. Such a work becomes institutionalized and leads to change: it generates not only faithful imitations but original works that nevertheless relate to it rather than to its predecessors. Before *To Penshurst* there were less successfully experimental antecedents, such as the river encomia of Leland, Camden, Vallans, and no doubt others much dimmer. Had they been brilliant, a very different genre might have developed. As it is, estate poems by Carew, Waller, and Herrick, and more distantly Denham and Marvell, allude to Jonson and each other, but not to Jonson's largely occluded predecessors. He is the founder of a new line.

This must be qualified in one respect. All the poets mentioned, including Jonson, imitate classical and Continental authors. Like many literary inventors, Jonson is really in part the mediator of literature of a much earlier period. But imitation of *loci classici* should be distinguished from generic imitation. The former is centralized, so to say. It relates directly to a few ancient instances which provide passive and transgeneric models. But generic imitation, although it may often go back to a single admired work, also develops a life of its own. And it partakes more of active emulation. Whereas early representatives of a kind may (like Carew's *To My Friend G. N. from Wrest*) imitate the first master in an almost epigonic way, there is subsequently a good deal of cross-imitation (such as Marvell's, of Carew's compliment about statuary of living men). By this means the generic forms are rapidly enriched. Doubtless we can partly attribute this to competitive anxiety of influence—to the need to assimilate the values of a predecessor. (Fictional characters show this with particular clarity; their moral qualities are often accretions of those of earlier protagonists in the kind.) But there is also something nearer to cooperation—as if the kind were a group meditation. In the case of the country house poem, the group even had social coherence, sharing a direct interest in such topics as the house's proportions and unpretentiousness, the estate's microcosmic features and its resources, hospitality, and "good lordship," the lord's lineage, his piety, the tenants' loyalty, the poet's debt, and the like.[15]

The contributions of successors, in fact, are quite as decisive as that of the "originator." That is obvious from the fact that if the originator has no successors, his achievement can only be an isolated one, without any significance for genre. On the other hand, in literary coteries or schools, new kinds develop with comparative ease and rapidity. The Metaphysical elegy is a good example. Another might be the short, deceptively simple, oblique Georgian poem with resonant implications. Hardy (as in *Boys Then and Now*) is perhaps a paradigmatic inventor. But the kind became a favorite with the Georgian school, who carried it to exquisite extremes of obliquity. Many instances could be found in Edward Thomas, Andrew Young, and others. Sometimes such school activity is noticed by contemporaries. As early as 1854, Aytoun could write that "all our spasmodic poets introduce us to their heroes in their studies."[16] An extreme example of quick development in a school is the Elizabethan sonnet sequence. Its mushroom growth, subgenres and all, largely came within the 1590s. After the ultimate orginator Petrarch, the proximate originator Watson, and the paradigmatic Sidney, patterns of cross-imitation became far too complex for any stemma of borrowings or influences. In such cases critics understandably have been tempted to regard the entire work of the school as quasi-generic, and to construct such groupings as Earl Miner's "Metaphysical mode."

Assembly of the Repertoire

Voltaire wrote of the Italians as having "made out of pastoral a new genre for which they had no models."[17] But in literature there is no creation *ex nihilo*. On the basis of known examples, at least, all postmedieval genres have used older genres as components, and our knowledge allows us to say the same about many medieval genres. Either the new kind is a transformation of an existing one, or else it is assembled. Assembly, too, uses existing generic materials.[18] But these components may be small in scale and diverse in origin. Thus, the sonnet sequence assembled several generic and quasi-generic types, such as the individual sonnet, the *silva* of varied short poems, the *psychomachia,* the courtship patterns of romance and love allegory, and many others. And similarly the estate or country house poem, as Jonson assembled it, combined many earlier components, both general and specific: topographical encomium, descriptive poem, epigram, epistle, and such classical motifs as praise of hospitality, or the symbolic tree of family greatness (Caesar's; Sidney's).

Assembly of the repertoire of Renaissance comedy was on a larger scale. During the Middle Ages ancient comedy had become so faint a memory that it was not even known to be acted rather than recited. Nevertheless, comedy continued under the guise of miracle play, or various forms of courtly or popular entertainment (momerie, *ludi,* revels). Renaissance theorists now rejected the medieval genres as worthless,[19] but playwrights knew better, and took from them the generic substance for new kinds. All the subgenres—court, city, and country comedy—were composite in this way. Country comedy took over narrative patterns from the romance and the magical *ludi.* All three found intrigue plot types and characters in Plautus and Terence, or in the intermediate *Commedia dell'Arte.* Comic motifs abounded in academic drama and colloquies. And Plautus' *Amphitryon* even offered an example (contrary to Aristotle's precept) for linking double plots, serious and low in thematic relation. Once elements such as these were assembled by Lyly, the court allegory was in turn available for ironic transformations. It would require a separate book even to outline the assembly of the complex comic repertoire. But it should be plain already that Renaissance dramatists did not lack generic materials. Renaissance comedy certainly was a new kind. But it was not one created out of nothing by Lyly or Shakespeare or Jonson.

Literary kinds are not always made out of other kinds in the same literary family. From time to time exogamy brings more exotic generic material into the repertoire. The influence of foreign models may broaden the concept of a genre.[20] Or imitation of an unfamiliar classical source may be decisive—as often happened during the period rightly called "Renaissance." Then an impression of novelty may result, for the most conscious imitation is often apprehended as originality.

Material of a much earlier period has been of value in the assembly of many new kinds. One thinks of the contribution of Latin genres to English innovations from the sixteenth to the eighteenth century, of Greek in the nineteenth, and Renaissance in the twentieth. Surprisingly, however, borrowing between contemporary literatures does not seem able to produce a new assembly in the same way. It is as if each literature had its own law of development. Individual borrowings may take place across literary boundaries, but tend not to have any immediate effect on genre. So with the assembly of the English masque: although political allegory was common in Italian masques, it took a considerable time to enter the English form—and when it did, it came via the native pageant.[21]

Or assembly may draw on extraliterary genres—rather as innovations in law sometimes work by "legal transplant" of rules from one system to another. The English georgic, a kind with such wholly delightful exemplars as Gay's *Trivia* and *Rural Sports,* took much of its generic material from the didactic verse treatise or essay (Moffett's Italian-derived *Silkworms;* Dennys' *Secrets of Angling;* Heresbachius' *Four Books of Husbandry*).[22] Other poetic kinds of the seventeenth century made use of the form of the meditation. And many studies of the same period have traced the literary elevation of nonliterary or subliterary types: familiar epistle, commonplace book, book of devotions, colloquy, prolusion.[23] The essay assembled elements of the treatise, the colloquy, the adage, the exemplum or sententia collection, the encyclopedic gathering of authorities, and the Humanistic letter of informal instruction. The early autobiography combined courtesy book, chronicle, epistle, anecdote, exemplum, and essay. Some markedly extraneous genres have been utilized. Several genres have made use of nonliterary catalogue forms, such as the bill (Jonson *Epigrams* 73; Pound *Cantos*). And games have always been popular as structural devices: one thinks of Sidney's or Suckling's barley-break, Middleton's chess, Pope's ombre, Eliot's and Calvino's tarot. There are even concrete poetry subgenres that use algebraic forms such as matrix and permutation (Morgan's *Opening the Cage* and *The Computer's First Christmas Card*). In our own time, as I have mentioned already, another principle resource is the elevation of previously subliterary forms. From one point of view the experimental short story can often be seen as a serious, if not solemn, version of an earlier genre characterized by facetious freewheeling. Several of Barthelme's stories recall in this way the type represented by O. Henry's *Municipal Report*. Todorov's dictum that "a new genre is always a transformation of one or several old genres" is clearly right in its broad lines.[24] But it needs qualification: either we have to expand "genre" to include nonliterary forms, or else we must allow for extraliterary transplant as a separate means of innovation.

Todorov's thinking is influenced by the indispensable Russian formalist doctrine of "canonization" of nonliterary forms. While literature's innovatory thrust may draw strength from the past, it as often moves laterally and turns to popular culture for its devices. This gave rise to Shklovskij's law of the "canonization of the junior branch."[25] The historically minded Russian formalists were highly appreciive of innovation, and could be flexible in exploring it in unconventional ways: their work retains much interest, even for those who cannot quite accept the underlying progressivism of their belief that it is when art cannot advance that it requires deliverance by the noncanonized.

Subgenres go through a similar stage of assembly, except that the emphasis is on adding new matter than form. So the war eclogue adds a topic not previously in the eclogue repertoire (although an "extraneous subject" was always possible).[26] However, the additional matter need not be absolutely novel. The piscatory eclogue of Sannazaro and his successors—unquestionably a new subgenre—specialized and regularized possibilities already adumbrated by the pseudo-Theocritean *Idylls* 22. We might write the development as *Idyll* → *Eclogue* {pastoral; piscatory; ... }. That is to say, the earlier kind did not distinguish subtypes, but allowed a variety of topics from which they eventually emerged. Similarly with novelistic genres such as the factory novel: a complex of substantive features entailed by the special setting is added to the rules of the realistic or verisimilar novel.

It might be supposed that one could form further subgenres like this quite freely, simply by adding more special subjects. However, that is only the case where the addition is not in conflict with the kind's existing rules. For example, the repertoire of the verisimilar novel does not allow for explicit representation of sexual intercourse, so that introducing it cannot lead to a new subgenre. Instead, it tends toward another kind altogether, with different criteria of observational accuracy. In this respect, *Lady Chatterley's Lover* betrays a deficiency of generic tact: fine though it is in many ways, it fails to avoid frequent *gaucherie*. Another instance is the divergence of the detective story. The central novel does not positively exclude detection. *Bleak House,* indeed, anticipates many common features of the twentieth-century detective story (the detective's attendance at the victim's funeral; explanatory confessions; multiple dénouements). Nevertheless, the problem of detection is uncongenial to the verisimilar novel, which has quite different hermeneutic tasks. *Bleak House* could not be thought of as inaugurating a subgenre.

With kind and subgenre alike, the phase of assembly may of course be largely unconscious. The author perhaps thinks only of writing in a fresh way. It will often be his successors who first see the potential for genre and recognize, retrospectively, that assembly of a new form has taken place. Then the assembled repertoire will become a focus of critical activity, whether formal or informal. The new genre may even be labeled. And now the repertoire begins to be applied restrictively in response to a sharpening sense of what belongs to it. Edward Herbert's *Life* still has some of the features of the essay, but already we sense him to be selecting from the available material in a distinctively autobiographical way: "I shall therefore only tell some things alike strange of my self."[27] The context shows that more than decorum of subject is meant.

Whether or not it is meant to be innovative, the assembled form is apprehended as a new genre only from a subsequent perspective. This retrospective critical insight regroups individual works, and sees them now as belonging to the new genre, now anticipating it, now differing in kind. In the eighteenth century, novels might be grouped with romances, or be seen as forming a new kind conceived in contradistinction to the romance. The Dedication to *The History of Pompey the Little* (1751) can still speak of Marivaux and Fielding as having brought "romance-writing" to perfection. It is only our point of view that Fielding's novels represent the infancy rather than the perfection of their kind. This introduces a concept of the first importance for understanding literary development. The earliest phase of every kind is the late phase of another, viewed from a different historical standpoint. Naturally we find it difficult to imagine any other groupings but our own. Nevertheless, it is fundamental to the appreciation of genre to grasp this principle of continuous movement of regrouping. Literature changes, but it is the same thing.

Primary, Secondary, and Tertiary Stages

For more than a century, the main concept of generic development has rested on a distinction between degrees of literariness. Two stages of art have been analyzed, variously called primitive and artificial, simple and sophisticated, naïve and sentimental, primary and secondary. The idea of primary and secondary kinds seems first to have arisen in connection with epic, the paradigmatic form. The seminal work in this still Romantic tradition is without question Schiller's *Über naive und sentimentalische Dichtung* (1795–96). Schiller contrasted realistically "naïve" with "sentimental" or reflexive art—the art of the writer conscious of his separation from nature: "The thing that touches us in the ancient poets is nature; it is the truth of sense, it is a present and a living reality: modern poets touch us through the medium of ideas." This showed a way to value both stages of art, the one for superior truth to nature, the other for warmer valuation of nature. Yet Schiller also encouraged a simplistic tendency to idealize the ancients and to exaggerate their primeval remoteness. "The older critics divided Epic into Primitive and Artificial, which is unsatisfactory," writes C. S. Lewis, preferring a distinction between "primary" epic (Homer, *Beowulf*) and "secondary" (Virgil, Milton).[28] Primary epic is heroic, festal, oral, formulaic, public in delivery, and historical in subject; secondary epic is civilized, literary, private, stylistically elevated, and "sublime." There are firm grounds for such a distinction. *The Fall of the Nibelungs* obviously represents a different and "earlier" stage of epic than the *Aeneid*, even though it is later in date. And there can be no question of Virgil's local awareness and use of Homeric precedents.[29] Even the bipartite structural pattern of the *Aeneid*, which has often been described as an *Odyssey* followed by an *Iliad*, may take up a Homeric formal device of duplication.[30] In the *Saturnalia*, Macrobius traced Virgil's imitations of Homer in detail, opening a long debate as to the advantages of first and second comers. But medieval ideas of epic were Virgilian. And in the Renaissance, Scaliger's famous critique of Homer and Virgil, although it inaugurates comparative literature in the modern sense, aims throughout to demonstrate the superior art and sophistication of the Latin poet.[31] Still, it is significant that whereas Aristotle treated epic in contrast with tragedy, the great Renaissance theorist was able to make a somewhat more historical comparison, between two stages of epic.

Notice that "primary" by no means implies superior value. Certainly it was the secondary writer whom Scaliger preferred. His preference for Virgil was so complete, his sympathy with Homer so slight, that in effect his criteria were those of secondary epic. Its forms are the forms he finds the earlier poet failing to achieve. Thus, Homer's formulaic epithets are simply faulted for their lack of variety.[32] There can be no doubt that Scaliger's demonstrations had a powerful influence on neoclassical criticism. It was Virgilian epic that became established as the "correct" form—so firmly, in fact, that many critics envisaged no further development. With a rigidity comparable to fixism in biology, they considered secondary epic as invariable. Only after the primitive came to be revalued could critics see the primary and secondary phases in a more fully historical light, and take a more neutral view of imitation that overgoes its model. We are now better placed to understand that Homer has his own form of art. It is also more apparent, now, that improvement—or at least change—did not stop with Virgil. *Paradise Lost* includes the Virgilian type, together with several others (notably the hexaemeron of Book 7 and the Biblical epic of Books 11-12), embedding them within a more complex form. And *Paradise Regained* represents another type of "brief epic." There are obvious limits, then, to the dichotomy between primary and secondary epics. Nevertheless, it is useful as a broad initial division for convenience of description.

As such, it can be extended with equal validity to other kinds besides epic. Consider eclogue. Let us suppose that amoebean dialogue and other ingredients were at first separate forms, or differently associated. Only when they were more or less regularly assembled could they function as genre-linked features of pastoral. This phase of first assembly, the phase of Theocritus, may be seen as primary. In the secondary phase, a Virgil or Calpurnius or Sannazaro makes a deliberate generic contribution, with some sense of distance from Theocritus. The primary bucolic is, if you will, part of the secondary bucolic's content. The latter is almost like a sophisticated *imitatio*, varying the primary form's themes and motifs, perhaps adapting it to new purposes (Virgil's personal allusions; Calpurnius' and Drayton's encomiums), but retaining its main features, including its formal structure. Distinct subgenres are now developed, and perhaps new ones added. So in his *Arcadia* Sannazaro realizes the piscatorial potentialities of Theocritus' form; and Scaliger, as he boasts modestly in the *Poetices,* adds yet another subgenre, the agricultural or manorial *villica* eclogue.[33]

Primary and secondary phases are naturally relative to historical viewpoint. Every writer is secondary in relation to some generic model. Thus, there is no permanent distinction, whereby Theocritean idyll is fixed forever as primary pastoral (and with actual singing matches), whereas Virgil's shepherds lie about a fictive landscape in purely literary guise. Theocritus is sophisticated, too, and perhaps had models of his own. Then again, Spenser and Drayton and other English pastoralists could treat both Theocritus and Virgil as primary models, producing as a result two variant types of eclogue, the "native" and the "pure." The distinction of phases is after all concerned with the conventionality of individual generic forms. Every writer uses conventions; but in a kind's secondary stage, particular conventions are available that were unknown as such to the inventors of the primary form. The advantages are obvious: Virgil is able to finesse on forms that he can take for granted as recognizable. The corresponding disadvantage is literariness. But although on the whole a secondary kind will be less direct and functional, this difference need not appear in all aspects—still less in all exemplars. So Renaissance epithalamium could still form part of actual occasions, in spite of the fact that its conventions were well understood (thanks to the critics and the commentators on the Song of Songs).

Relative or not, the distinction of primary and secondary kinds remains valid. There is a real use in discriminating between such pairs of forms as folk ballad and art ballad, traditional proverb and Blakeian proverb, the picaresque of *Lazarillo* and that of Le Sage, the naïve tale of adventure and Stevenson's conscious reordering of its conventions.

Within the secondary phase itself, however, there are wide disparities—wider, in some ways, than between primary and secondary. A world of difference separates the forms of epic written by Virgil and by Milton, or the eighteenth-century art ballad (such as Tickell's *Colin and Lucy*) and the modified symbolic form of *The Ancient Mariner*.

To do justice to such disparities, we need to distinguish a tertiary stage. This is reached when a writer takes up a kind already secondary, and applies it in quite a new way. The tertiary form may be a symbolic reinterpretation of the secondary. Thus, *Lycidas* is tertiary pastoral elegy, because the dead shepherd not only disguises an individual but symbolizes a *pastor,* and because the values of pastoral elegy are made to stand for certain thoughts about death that Milton means his own poem to resist or transcend. Similarly, *Paradise Lost* is tertiary in that it treats Virgilian motifs antiheroically and reduces them to subsidiary functions within a form of larger import. By contrast, Milton's epic reflects Christian values, achieving heroism and satisfying divine wrath differently from any pagan epic.

Tertiary development seems often to interiorize the earlier kind. We might compare Frye's conception of Romantic "mythological epics in which the myths represent psychological or subjective states of mind."[34] Thus, *Paradise Lost,* like *The Faerie Queen,* has little wholly exterior action. And Golding's *Pincher Martin* (which begins as a tertiary version of Taffrail's *Pincher Martin*) may have none at all. Stevenson's *Dynamiter* and *Ebb-Tide* belong to a corresponding phase of the adventure story—the one as burlesque, the other as symbolic. Or consider the motif of mysterious ancestry. From a primary version in ancient and medieval romance we can trace a secondary version in eighteenth-century romance and even in *Emma* (unless its ironic use there verges on burlesque). But George Eliot uses Deronda's illegitimacy as a symbol: his search for identity clearly takes the motif into a tertiary stage.[35]

It is also characteristic of the tertiary phase that it should be informed by interpretation of generic features. The secondary kind may savor the primary kind aesthetically, and so in a sense "reinterpret" it. But the tertiary takes individual conventions as material for symbolic developments that presuppose allegorical, psychological, or other interpretations of them. Hence, the application of abstracted features in modal transformations of such a kind as the gothic novel. In assembling the repertoire of the early "tale of terror," Walpole, Radcliffe, and Lewis seem to have been drawn by simple fascination with the sublimities of terror. Their ruins, darknesses, labyrinthine passages, and apparatuses of fear—even such a marvel as the gigantic armor of Otranto—remain uninterpreted and sometimes even unexplained. Secondary gothic exploits the repertoire more comprehensively (Maturin) or develops it by minute explorations of special possibilities (Poe). There is much sophisticated relishing, but little interpretation. Already in Hawthorne, however, we sense a strong tendency toward parable. Possible symbolisms are always being hinted at—even if not always very distinct ones. In Hawthorne, birthmarks or diseases do not merely horrify: they also signify. Moreover, Stevenson and James can take the gothic repertoire as material to be put to ulterior purposes, or as an old mystery to be demythologized. In *The Turn of the Screw,* for example, gothic is interpreted in terms of abnormal psychology and used to explore paranoid delusion. In particular, it is only in the later applications that it shows much awareness of sociopolitical meaning. In gothic science fiction, however, the politics become overt. And Kafka's *In the Penal Settlement* finds a metaphysical or political sense in the gothic apparatus itself.

All three stages, we have to recall, interpenetrate chronologically. They may even coexist within a single work. Thus, Theocritus and Homer, who grasp form with sureness and sophistication, have from one point of view secondary qualities. And if Virgil's Neoplatonic allegorists are to be believed, the *Aeneid* passed beyond the secondary epic of his Latin predecessors to a symbolic tertiary form, in a single leap.[36]

The taxonomic problem largely disappears if we think in terms of continuous generic development. "Primary," "secondary," and "tertiary" then become relative to an observer interested in particular generic forms. The edge of the pattern depends on how much of it has been unrolled; the same work may inaugurate one genre and belong to the tertiary stage of another. A writer may be both sophisticated and naïve, depending on the point of reference. Horace Walpole assembled the gothic repertoire "naïvely": he probably included the gigantic helmet in *The Castle of Otranto* for no better conscious reason that that he was fascinated by a helmet in Piranesi's *Carceri*.[37] Yet from another point of view Walpole was a tertiary romance-writer, in that his work is retrospective to the first gothic age and reapplies an ancient imagery and *mise-en-scène* to transform existing prose kinds in a highly sophisticated way.

The Death of a Genre

Aristotle is sometimes smiled at for saying that tragedy reached its perfection in his time. But it is true that tragedy as he knew it was complete. What we still call Greek or Attic tragedy reached maturity with Sophocles and Euripides; and other kinds of tragedy, such as Senecan, English, French classical, heroic, and the kind that *Death of a Salesman* embodies, are not tragedies in Aristotle's sense. A coherent cycle of development, it might be argued, was complete in his time. One kind of tragedy had reached the end of its life. And without the Renaissance, tragedy would in some sense have continued to be dead. The Russian formalists were talking about one form of the death of genre when they elaborated their doctrine of "automatization." Victor Shklovskij, for example, traced an inevitable course of generic development, from the stage of "perceptibility," when every detail is freshly savored, to the stage of mere conventional recognition, when the form provokes only an automatic stock reaction.[38] But this simplifies by concentrating on a single cause of death:

banality. Moreover, it is purely in retrospect, if at all, that one can speak of inevitability. What if the genre had been varied or revivified or transformed?

Many kinds have been spoken of as "played out," exhausted, spent. And it may be that frequent imitation can use up formal possibilities, to the point that a kind no longer offers sufficient fresh variety to promise excellence. This cannot be what is meant, however, when critics speak of the novel as "dead." Fine novels continue to be written. All the same, reports of the genre's death continue to be issued. And they may not be greatly exaggerated. They may reflect a sense that the novel, and in particular the verisimilar novel, has reached a critical stage of development. This need not be put in negative terms—the terms, say, of *The Sea's Green Sameness,* in which John Updike imagines narrative as a carcass we have been feeding off too long. But there is no doubt that the novel is undergoing radical transformations, toward what are perhaps to be regarded as new avatars. The older "appropriate forms" of the novel can now be handled with so much consciousness of their conventions that they may have suffered the death of definition. From this point of view, the modernist novel appears as a stage of decreation, in which the essences of various novel genres were extracted. So-called antinovelists have discarded element after element, as if pursuing the minimum essential to the kind. Several have eliminated the coherent narrator. Beckett not only gets rid of story, but even of secure identity. And Capote (although this is less of a new departure) dispenses with fiction. The novel has never received the explicit genre prescriptions accorded to ancient kinds, but it has suffered extremely intensive formal analysis that implicitly prescribed elements such as narrator, hero, dialogue, episode, character. Now these elements are either being dropped or taken up exclusively, as if their proportions and relations must be radically altered.

As with biological organisms, the moment of death is hard to fix. Does a kind die upon dissolution of its parts? Or when it ceases to be used for new works? Or when it ceases to interest? Or when readers cease to appreciate its forms? Does a classic's survival—misinterpreted as *Gulliver's Travels* used to be, and perhaps still is—constitute the survival of its genre? Does pastoral elegy live with *Lycidas?*

To speak of a kind's dying is to imply a biological analogy that has been exploded, at least in its evolutionary form, by René Wellek: "French tragedies were not born with Jodelle but just were not written before him."[39] But the objection that "there are no fixed genres comparable to biological species which can serve as substrata of evolution . . . no transformation of one genre into another" beats down a straw opposition. Who now would wish to draw a Darwinian analogy? Biologists no longer regard species as "fixed" simply by genetic determinism.[40] And as for transformation of literary forms, it becomes obvious enough once one abandons Wellek's synchronic notion of genre as a set or class. True, a genre is not a species either. But the analogy of genre and species is a useful one, which helps to point up differences as well as similarities in the object spheres. Wellek's point that *Phèdre* "will strike us as young and fresh compared to the frigid Renaissance tragedies" is not *à propos*, since it is not works that are said to age or evolve, but their genre.[41] Nor will it do to invoke the author's freedom of choice in "reaching out into the past for models or stimuli." Only individual works reach out beyond temporal limitations, not the kind. By virtue of its institutional organizing of forms, the kind is subject to the historical laws that govern all such organizations. Like any other, it must evolve.[42]

Kinds, like biological species, have a relatively circumscribed existence both in space and in time. Cultural barriers set one sort of limit. And cultural changes set another. The use of the essay, for example, a kind expressing liberal interest at first, began with Humanism in the sixteenth century; and one of its forms, the miscellaneous familiar essay, ceased to be popular after the crisis of Humanism in the 1930s.[43] The hymn has been in abeyance since supernatural belief receded. And Renaissance eclogue could not survive urban development, any more than georgic could keep up with the information explosion. Such limitations apply in a pervasive way, even to apparently formal aspects. Sudden surprising turns of plot in the short story took for granted a universe of belief, within which *peripeteia*s could disclose mysteries or at least prompt bafflement at the "rumness of life." Kipling is a transitional instance: his stories still have plots, and the plots still take odd turns (as in *Without Benefit of Clergy*), but the metaphysical implication seems too explicit for the device to hold much potential for future development. Or another example: the numerological organization of the triumph. This has obviously been affected by changes in the function of the stanza. But it is no coincidence, either, that numerical composition declined in the eighteenth century, a period when universal harmony came to be imagined in subjective terms, and when kingship lost its cosmic endorsement.[44] One is tempted to say (in a paradox that would be only apparent) that the more formal the generic convention, the more it depends on social context.

The obsolescence of a kind is a literary event of great consequence. For it alters the balance of significant forms, so that not only the kind itself but also related genres become less accessible. Thus, the discontinuation of the allegorical morality play has made certain passages in Shakespeare's tragedies obscure. (Understanding of old literature depends on at least some knowledge of the relevant genres.) A kind is doomed altogether when the education of its fit audience ceases. However, this limitation conceals a hope. If the kind never was open to all men, its remaining open to a few may be enough to preserve it for some future renaissance.

Modal Transformation

A kind's last stage by no means ends in mere extinction. For it may have generated modal transformations of other kinds. Then, even after the adaptive possibilities of the "fixed" kind have been played out, its corresponding mode may remain lively. The mode, with its selection of constituents, is less dependent on external forms. It is as if the kind were limited by its structural carapace, so that it reached the end of its evolutionary possibilities. But its modal equivalent is more versatile, being able to enter into new commixtures and to continue in combination with kinds still evolving. Tragedy was very nearly extinct in the nineteenth century, but Hardy wrote some fine tragic novels. Epic went out with *Paradise Lost,* but *Absalom and Achitophel* is heroic satire, the *Dunciad* satiric mock epic, *Nostromo* a heroic novel. Mode is not only a looser genre collateral with the fixed kind, but also its successor. Its existence, as we have seen, presupposes an earlier kind of which it is the extension. The two are in diachronic relation: kind tends to mode, or $k \rightarrow m$. This relation is in keeping with the general tendency of literature away from ritually determined forms and syntagmatically prescribed genres, and toward looser and more flexible conventions.

The modal extensions may be ephemeral, or may lead to new genres distinct from their parent forms. The idea of such transformation is vital for literary history, since it offers the only means of tracing the continuities that underlie many changes. Generic transformations are so ubiquitous and multifarious as to demand a separate chapter. Here I shall only list a few transformations, to suggest their diachronic character and their role in literary history: (1) the transformation of romance by the heroic mode, to produce the heroic romance or "romantic epic" (*Orlando Furioso; The Faerie Queen*);[45] (2) the development of picaresque as a countergenre to escapist chivalric romance; (3) Fielding's assembly of the repertoire of the panoramic novel (*Tom Jones*) from a comic transformation of prose romance, together with picaresque, heroic, romantic-epic, and other elements;[46] (4) Scott's assembly of the repertoire of the historical novel (*Waverley*) by romantic and historical transformation of the regional novel; (5) the transformation of the period novel by modal extension from the existentialist novel of ideas, as in *The French Lieutenant's Woman* and *G.* Such relations make up a continuous genealogy of forms. These crude formulations obviously omit intermediate steps and finer shadings. Nothing is said about allegorization in (1) or about Defoe in (3). Moreover, they trace only one line of development out of many. Another, of equal importance, descends through the intimate novel of Richardson and its romance transformation into the Jamesian form. And some of the formulations may be problematic—especially where regrouping or change of labels has taken place. Thus, *Waverley* was at first received as a regional novel, but is now regarded as the paradigmatic "historical romance" or historical novel. The exact formulation will depend on critical standpoint. Nevertheless, some such liaison of genres is a main strand in literary history. In principle, genealogies could be constructed that related the earliest literature, through successive transformations, to the most recent. It is in this stemma of genres that literature's continuity lies, rather than in the old stemmata of individual influences.

Modal transformations commonly make such modest departures from the kind that we can reasonably speak of "slow, steady change on the analogy of animal growth"—or, at least, of animal evolution.[47] Variations must accumulate before readers are ready to respond to a generic innovation. There is a development of many stages between the chivalric romance and Le Sage's picaresque with romance inset, or between Stevenson's semipolitical *Prince Otto* and the modern novel of espionage. The continuity of known types is a condition for the new statement. Without the romance, Stevenson's antihero would have no point; without the gentleman-adventurer's club ethics, Buchan's sympathy with the enemy, and, in turn, Le Carré's reevaluation of the idea of enemy, would lack some of their literary force. *Natura non facit saltum.*

Literature may take occasional leaps of generic originality. But these are probably less common than the obscurity of precedents and the latency of groupings lead us to suppose. Originative writers often had experimental predecessors—even if these were forgotten subsequently. A *Finnegans Wake* may depart radically from existing forms; but then it is likely to remain unassimilated, until more dilute imitations provide the missing generic context *ex post facto*. For literature's true enjoyment must always partly depend on interweaving the strange with the pleasurably familiar.

Kinds, then, may generate modes and so contribute indirectly to new kinds. In such cases their death may go unnoticed. But their components disintegrate, so that works not informed by a strong sense of generic decorum are likely to be strewn with the detritus of old kinds (as John Whitfield says of Pulci and the epic). In general, old structural conventions disappear altogether. On the other hand, the contents of a discontinued kind may survive in various metamorphoses, as long as they retain human value. All the same, the kind itself will be dead—perhaps even forgotten.[48] Literary resurrectionists—writers or critics—may dig far down into the cultural past to bring back former kinds. But these are not revivified without modification. Reintroduced kinds are different from their first avatars—and different also from what they would be if works of their type "just were not written" for a while.

10. Transformations of Genre

The processes by which genres change are the same as those that produce most literary change. To describe them fully—or any one of them—would be far beyond our present scope. It is, after all, a main theme of most literary history and much criticism. However, the processes can at least be categorized. Those that stand out may be identified as: topical invention, combination, aggregation, change of scale, change of function, counterstatement, inclusion, selection, and generic mixture.[1] No doubt there are others; but these would be enough in themselves to cover the main changes known to literary history.

Topical Invention

Genres change when new topics are added to their repertoires. Sometimes the topics are entirely novel, as when the photograph was first introduced into the poem about a painting. Cervantes' modern windmill was similarly a *novum repertum* so far as romance was concerned, as Rosalie Colie remarks. More often, as we have seen, it is a matter of specialization: of devloping a topic already within the repertoire. Student life was a well-established minor topic of the novel (Thackeray; the *Bildungsroman*) long before the university novel subgenre. Such topical innovations seem to characterize most new literary movements. Perhaps this is because they involve a turning from interest in form to interest in matter. A striking instance is the anti-Petrarchan and anti-Ciceronian movement of the early seventeenth century, which led to prolific invention of new matter—and to pervasive generic change.

"Invented" topics may be transformed from other genres or literatures or even other media. In this way, topics of love and of individual sensibility invaded epic: the English minor ode continued to draw matter from

Ronsard and Anacreon and the Greek Anthology, and religious epigrams incorporated sacred iconography and emblem material. In the Middle Ages and the Renaissance, such exchanges between arts were very free, and offered a wealth of resources for generic construction. Thus, the satiric scheme of Seven Deadly Sins owed much to visual art, while Elizabethan comedy made extensive use of matter connected with games and festive rituals, such as the Yuletide customs of *Twelfth Night* or the pageant and masquerade of *Love's Labour's Lost*.[2]

Topical invention may also lie in a fresh approach to existing topics.[3] But this usually amounts to a modal transformation. When Sidney equips Cupid with a gun (*Astrophil and Stella* 20) he does more than add fresh aspects to a Petrarchan topic. He is in effect making a counterstatement, or producing an epigrammatic transformation of the sonnet.

Combination

Combination of repertoires is one of the most obvious means of generic change. As we saw in the last chapter, the repertoire of the river poem may have contributed to the country house poem. But it also combined with other repertoires, such as that of the georgic verse essay, to form the long topographical poem (*Polyolbion* 18; *The Wonders of the Peak* 332–401). And later Marvell combined the local descriptive and estate poems with the retirement poem of Saint-Amant and Sarbiewski, to produce a complex form adumbrating the eighteenth-century poem of retirement. Combination of repertoires plays some part in most new forms of any magnitude. It is most obvious at the assembly stage. So the Elizabethan masque combined mummery, masquerade, pageant, and entertainment: discrete kinds that were to some extent recognized as such and referred to by their separate names. Subsequently, however, a successful combination will come to be regarded as a single repertoire. We are no longer much aware which features of masque derive from which contributory kind.

Aggregation

A different additive process is aggregation, whereby several complete short works are grouped in an ordered collection—as the songs in a song cycle or the ballads in a ballad opera. The composite work may be united by framing and linking passages, sometimes of a very substantial character (*Confessio Amantis; The Canterbury Tales*). Such an aggregate is generically distinct both from its component parts and from unordered collections. Thus, Boccaccio's *Decameron* represents a different genre from that of the tales it orders, as well as from the *Cento Novelle Antiche* or the *Cent Nouvelles Nouvelles*.[4] Aggregation's transforming effect is obvious enough in the epistolary novel or the sequence of sketches.[5] But other aggregate genres also transcend their component repertoires. So the calendars of Spenser, Thomson, and Clare order according to season, and thus create an expectancy of variations and contrasts—which may be fulfilled or finessed. It was certainly a generic transformation when Thomas Watson and Sir Philip Sidney, writing under Continental influence, ordered their love poems in sequences.[6] The Elizabethan sonnet sequence has a complex repertoire of its own, which includes such features as liminal conventions, narrative patterns, literary-critical digressions, mood changes, and numerological structure. In addition to sonnets, it usually includes other metrical forms, either interspersed throughout or (more often) added at or near the end. So *Astrophil and Stella* introduces songs after Sonnet 63; *Amoretti* has Anacreontics and a major ode; and Daniel's and Shakespeare's sequences are followed by complaints.[7] Similarly, any arrangement of lyrics or epigrams *en suite* is liable to change their genre. In Stevens' *Thirteen Ways of Looking at a Blackbird,* for example, thirteen haiku-like momentary lyrics became in aggregate meditative and metaphysical. And sequences by Morgan and by Crichton Smith offer several other striking instances.

Change of Scale

During the ages of rhetoric, writers often planned the scale of *dispositio* at a very early stage.[8] In such circumstances, change of scale was a means of generic originality—something that ancient theorists partly recognized when they attempted to describe it.[9] We have to keep it in mind, therefore, in tracing relations between genres. Changes of scale may be by *macrologia* or *brachylogia*. *Macrologia* magnifies, as when the *Divina Commedia* enlarges the epic *nekuia,* or descent into hell, to form a third of the work. Shaw's stage directions exhibit *macrologia*. So do individual letters in epistolary novels, by comparison with nonliterary letters. By contrast, *brachylogia* or *syntomia* diminishes, as when Archibald MacLeish reduces the Horatian epistle to a short poem on poetry, in *Ars Poetica*. Of the two, *brachylogia* is formally more interesting. It is necessarily complex, since in condensing it must find ways to suggest the original features not explicitly present. *Brachylogia* should be considered together with selection, *macrologia* with topical invention.

Macrologia makes room for fuller development, and so for new topics. It may thus have a decisive role in generic change. But it can hardly by itself produce a new kind. John Ashbery's *Self-Portrait in a Convex Mirror* may seem an exception, as *macrologia* of the poem about a painting. But there is also a confessional modulation—to say nothing of combination with the mirror poem, and more broadly with the American long poem. Similarly, Walton's *Complete Angler* not only enlarges eclogue, but also, particularly in the instructive passages, works toward a georgic modulation. And Thomson's *Seasons* offer new topics as well as *macrologia* of georgic description.

In a comparable way, the seventeenth-century vogue for reduction of scale shows again and again that *brachylogia* too is bound up with modal transformation. When Herrick miniaturized form after form in *Hesperides,* or Browne's essays epitomized encyclopedias, or Marvell's *Nymph Complaining* summed up the minor idyll by condensing its main variants, all this was not only an expression of the idea of *multum in parvo.*[10] It was also (or from another point of view) part of the epigrammatic modulation that dominated much of the literature of that period.

Relatively slight changes of scale can have surprisingly wide repercussions. In novels, for example, lengthening the temporal scale beyond a single generation easily shifts the genre toward family chronicle or *roman fleuve.* And how much of the generic character of *Finnegans Wake* springs from the special role accorded to wordplay—or even from the proportions of a single device, the portmanteau word?

Similar to *brachylogia* is the device of omission. This is undoubtedly a source of innovation, as in "There was a young lady of Crew / Whose limericks stopped at line two."[11] In a less assertive and more usual form (reminiscent of elision in architecture) it is a regular means of literary change. By disposing of transitions, formulas and the like, it leads to more sophisticated and condensed treatments and so assists the formation of a genre's late stage.

Change of Function

In ancient literature, the most minute change of function was enough to alter genre—perhaps no more than varying the speaker or addressee. Horace departed from convention in his First Ode when he addressed a *propemptikon* to a nonhuman addressee, the ship of state.[12] Small as they seem, such variations had a cumulative effect in changing genres and eventually loosening them. In modern periods, change of function has tended to be more drastic. But something very like Horace's addressee-variation can be seen in seventeenth-century religious poetry, in the use of Petrarchist conventions. The human beloved was replaced by the divine lover, the School of Love by the School of the Heart. Even some of the best works in the divine poetry tradition, such as Herbert's *Parody* altered the functions of a secular genre so directly as to amount to spiritual parodies. However, the features of love elegy could also be reapplied in a subtle and elusive way, as Rosemary Freeman remarks (Herbert's *Dulness* and *Glance*).[13]

Milton shows great audacity in changing the functions of quite fundamental parts of epic. He has a particular penchant for telescoping venerable generic forms in surprising ways. Thus, in *Paradise Lost,* Raphael's visit occasions a conventional flashback to a great work, which takes the uanexpected form of creation itself. But simultaneously the episode is an inset and a georgic essay, leading into a dialogue on astronomy. The epic episode is being made to work in a very unusual way. The invocations, similarly, are changed into occasions for autobiographical digression (an innovation that we can almost think of Wordsworth as developing by *macrologia* in *The Prelude*). These instances are obviously deliberate. But function can also change gradually and unintentionally—in response, for example, to changes in the literary model, such as the reduction of the informational value of stanza forms. Gradual change of function is probably perpetual. By contrast, in some periods, notably the seventeenth and nineteenth centuries, there seems to have been an aesthetic preference for altering functions. We can see the same taste in visual art, in the displaced or subverted forms of mannerist and retrospective gothic architecture.

Counterstatement

Claudio Guillén describes the relation of *Don Quixote* to *Lazarillo de Tormes* and especially to Guzmán de Alfarache as that of "a diametrically opposed masterpiece, which itself was able to serve as seed for a 'counter-genre.'" Cervantes' work differs from earlier exemplars of the genre in several striking ways: for example, in rejecting fictional autobiography in favor of fictional history.[14] Such antithetic relations within a genre are common enough. But much is gained by extending the idea of counterstatement beyond the limits of a single genre. We may think of certain new genres or "antigenres" as antitheses to existing genres. Their repertoires are in contrast throughout. In smaller genres, this contrast may take the form of rhetorical inversion, whereby dispraise is modeled on inverted praise, malediction on valediction, and so forth.[15] This has proved a fertile source of generic invention, as many answer poems testify. And on a large scale, something very similar seems to take place. From this point of view, early picaresque is itself an antigenre to romance. It is perhaps particularly antithetic to pastoral romance, whose sensitive hero is fond of contemplating love in retired solitude, and traverses much emotional experience before the final reconcilation. By contrast, picaresque knows no reconciliation of any depth. The *pícaro* is a tough outsider, who learns only the worldly wisdom needed for social adjustment and satiric observation.[16] This contrast of values, motivation, and mimetic "height" is quite explicit in Cervantes when Don Quixote enacts the exchange of romantic fantasy for down-to-earth reality. There is an element of burlesque in *Don Quixote,* as there is in the antiromance parts of Nashe's *Unfortunate Traveller.* Burlesque exaggerates generic features to absurdity, or juxtaposes them with contraries. However, an antigenre, unlike a burlesque, is not directed against a particular original. Moreover, it has a life of its own that continues collaterally with the contrasting genre. So picaresque and romance proceed in parallel, and may even be interlaced together in the same work, as happens in *Gil Blas.*

Epic has generated several antigenres. One of the oldest is the epic with a recent action (Lucan's *Pharsalia;* Cowley's *Civil War*). The Christian "brief epic" (*Davideis; Paradise Regained*) was supposed to be modeled on the Book of Job, but is obviously an antigenre to classical epic. All the types of Biblical epic developed during the Divine Poetry movement answered the pagan epic repertoire feature by feature. To the national or legendary action of Virgilian epic, they opposed the redemptive history revealed in Scripture: to invocation of the pagan Muse, they opposed invocation of Urania, or the Holy Spirit—or prayer to God. Milton takes up all these possibilities with remarkable premeditation, allowing them to confront one another within his own epic. The first two books of *Paradise Lost* use conventions of Christian epic, such as a council of devils; yet they can also be regarded as beginning a pagan epic with Satan as its courageous stoic hero. Later books, less ambiguously, offer a series of Christian epics of various subgenres (hexaemeron in Book 7; Raphael's martial epic in 6; Bartasian epic in 11 and 12).[17] In the Christian parts, as I mentioned earlier, the virtues of Messiah and Adam and the loyal angels directly contrast with those of the pagan hero Satan. Milton, no less than Cervantes, has combined genre and antigenre in a single work.

Among other antigenres, the anti-Petrarchan sonnet should not be omitted. The contrast of sonnet and epigram is somewhat obscured for us by seventeenth-century and Victorian development of the sweet epigram. The Renaissance epigram was predominantly low, spoken, and satiric, whereas the Elizabethan sonnet, being a brief love elegy or small ode, was middle in style, sung, and "sugared."[18] Modern readers may therefore miss the bold counterstated character of certain epigramlike sonnets. This applies not only to spiritual sonnets (Constable, Alabaster, Herbert),[19] but to sonnets of unideal love (Sidney, Shakespeare, Barnes). The antigenre comes out particularly clearly where a subgenre such as the *blason* is given a burlesque treatment.[20] I shall return to this point in connection with epigrammatic transformation.

So far as pastoral counterstatements are concerned, we have already met the long-standing antithesis between "native" and "pure" forms. These are typified by Theocritus, Spenser, Drayton, and Ambrose Philips, on the one hand, and on the other by Virgil and Pope. An antigenre in some ways more radical began with Gay's *Shepherd's Week*. Its near-burlesque treated pastoral topics "realistically"—just as the delicate *Trivia* did with those of georgic. Later in the century, descriptive realism often took the form of counterstatement to pastoral and georgic.[21] In Crabbe, the opposition is partly explicit:

> Must sleepy bards the flattering dream prolong,
> Mechanic echoes of the Mantuan song?
> From Truth and Nature shall we widely stray,
> Where Virgil, not where Fancy, leads the way?[22]

But if he himself alters the echoes, he by no means silences them. Repeatedly his burden is, in effect, that "Auburn and Eden can no more be found."[23] In Hazlitt's words, he checkmates "Tityrus and Virgil at the game of pastoral cross-purposes."[24] For his disagreeable landscape is based on a subsoil of conventional topics of eclogue. Even the flower catalogue is there—only replaced with weeds: "Hardy and high, above the slender sheaf, / The slimy mallow waves her silky leaf"—"silky" implying the cost of aesthetic values to the poor. Crabbe takes up georgic and pastoral topics, it seems, only to subvert them. So he elegizes the rural sports

("Where are the swains ... Who struck with matchless force the bounding ball") or diverts them, with changed function, into the inappropriate occupation of a bad priest.[25] Dennis Burden makes an interesting suggestion: "It is as though the establishing of this sense of contrast ... was necessary to get Crabbe on the move, but once the poem was in motion then its drive was realism and not contrast."[26] But from a generic point of view Crabbe's realism is indistinguishable from the "serious burlesque" of a countergenre.[27] Unfortunately, it was a sort of realism largely preempted by the novel. Wordsworth was careful to give it a more subsidiary and muted part.

However that may be, there is no doubt about the novel's thrust for a realism that will look nonliterary. This, as much as any pursuit of "that advantage which novelty never fails to have with the public,"[28] has more than once led novelists to resort to antithetic repertoires. The fictional biography had scarcely been established before a countergenre to it was inaugurated in *Tristram Shandy.*[29] Plot, continuity, scale, authorial intrusion: these and other features of the novelistic repertoire were countered so decisively by Sterne that he achieved a paradigmatic form still being imitated and developed. And the work-in-progress is only one of several antigenres to the novel. So Mitford and Gaskell tried for a form without strong incident or narrative connection—for the impossibility (as Mr. Besant might have said) of "fiction without adventure." Henry James agreed that "the story is the thing" ("the story and the novel ... are the needle and thread"), but counted green spectacles as story, no less than adventures, molding every constituent to the specification of the narrator's reality. And E. M. Forster wished that the novel could be something different and less primitive than a story—wished to belong, in James' figure, to a guild of tailors who recommended the use of the thread without the needle.[30]

With modernism, more extreme antitheses begin. A good example of the consistent antinovel is Joyce's *Ulysses.* A. Walton Litz is surely right to argue that no verisimilar novel can satisfactorily be extracted from it (however brilliantly Goldberg tries), since its fulfilled intention is "to disintegrate the well-made 'novel' into its origins, and then to perform a prodigious act of reintegration." He also alleges that Joyce "denies the validity of genres."[31] Joyce certainly talks about "the diversity of prose fiction," and attempts to evade the conventions of the novel by comprehensive inclusion, as well as by the use of an extreme digressive *ordo artificialis.* Nevertheless, it remains the verisimilar novel, primarily, that

Ulysses negates. In spite of Eliot's and Litz's confidence that Joyce has gone beyond the novel ("which will no longer serve"), I feel less sure. Does not he only go beyond (or against) certain recent genres within the novel? "The novel," after all, continues to develop vigorously. And one of its vigorous genres is precisely the antinovel. *Ulysses,* in fact, raises no special problem for the genre critic, unless he has an unhistorical conception of fixed kinds. Litz's account of how to read *Ulysses*—by attending to the specific generic conventions introduced and negated—is excellent practical advice. The debatable point is the notion of *Ulysses'* unique modernity: "it resembles many other works of literature, but other works do not resemble it."[32] From our present standpoint *Ulysses* seems a paradigmatic work, which novels by Beckett, Barth, and Pynchon follow and to some degree resemble. Moreover, *Ulysses* itself may fairly be said to resemble the much earlier antinovel paradigm *Tristram Shandy*—as, for example, in its approach to temporal scale, its narrative discontinuities, and its use of associational transitions.

However, the encyclopedic *Ulysses* is more than an antigenre of the verisimilar novel. Purer embodiments of that genre are Gertrude Stein's *Making of Americans,* or Beckett's later novels, which consistently make antitheses to novelistic forms. Beckett manages this in two ways, principally. First, he progressively eliminates features of the repertoire altogether: event, *mise-en-scène,* dialogue, even paragraphing. Second, he includes forms with a humanistic or religious implication that is effectually "canceled" (as Kermode puts it). Thus, to quote another critic of Beckett:

> *Watt* . . . is in fact an "anti-novel" in the tradition of Cervantes, Furetière and of course Sterne, a novel which disdains "to tell a story about persons recognizable as human beings in recognizable situations," and which introduces such extraneous matter as digressive anecdotes, snatches of song, exhaustive lists of objects and of logical (and illogical) combinations of possibilities, with an addenda section to contain the rejectamenta from the rest of the book; moreover, it develops minor characters at the expense of major ones, and, finally, fails to show any real action, any progression to a *dénouement.*[33]

It must be said that, in general, counterstatement seems to express a somewhat crude and extreme attitude to literary tradition. The seriousness of a Beckett or the greatness of a Cervantes may make more of it. But even at its best it leads to *tours de force* more often than great works of literature.

*   *   *

So far we have been mainly concerned with single genres. We turn now to transformations where genres are combined or mixed.

Inclusion

By a process as ordinary as embedding in syntax, a literary work may enclose another within it. If the inset form then becomes conventionally linked with the matrix, a generic transformation has taken place. So *The Faerie Queen* contained inset triumphal pageants, tapestry poems, metamorphoses, all of which became features of romantic epic and its descendants.[34] Epic, followed in this by the novel, is particularly capacious: it can contain complete works even of medium size.[35] So *Paradise Lost* achieves an important effect by a transition from Christian epic and hexaemeron to tragedy—"I now must change / Those notes to tragic." The Books that follow introduce a remarkable number of the features of tragedy, including *hamartia, anangke, peripeteia, stichomythia,* and unity of time.[36] Elsewhere, the same poem has room for a hymn, a sonnet, and various other forms.[37]

Inclusion is found in all literary periods, in a wide variety of genres of all sizes. Eclogues early included inset songs or narratives. And they were themselves inset in the romances of Sannazaro and Sidney. In one type of epithalamium there is recursive inclusion, a nuptial song within a nuptial song (Catullus *Carmina* 64; Ariosto *Song for the Third Marriage of Lucrezia Borgia;* Spenser *Prothalamion;* Gertrude Stein *Prothalamion for Bobolink and His Louisa a Poem*). Similarly with epitaph: it may have had epigraphic origins, and often reverts to this supposed primitive form, by including an inset inscription. The inscription proposed for Daphnis' tomb, in the epicede (itself inset) in Virgil's Fifth Eclogue, is a paradigmatic instance.[38] Subsequently the device was used to good effect not only for epitaphs, as in *An Epitaph of Sir Thomas Gravener, Knight,*[39] but also for love poems, as in Herrick's *Cruel Maid,* where the lover anticipates his own burial ("And write thereon, *This, Reader, know, / Love killed this man.* No more but so"). Here, as often, it provides closure for an epigram.[40]

In ancient literature, inclusion seems to have been governed by more restrictive conventions. These might call for a transitional passage introducing the inset. Moreover, the inset and the matrical genres were likely to be closely akin—as when a triumph was included in a genethliacon.[41]

Even in Renaissance and later literature, some kinds have been more hospitable to inclusion than others. Loose forms such as satire, dialogue, and anatomy are particularly prone to inclusion, so that they sometimes present a very confusing appearance to the genre critic (Rabelais, Castiglione, Burton).[42] Drama's composite character, too, has tended to encourage inclusion. Fabliaux were included in miracle cycles. Masques were common in Renaissance comedy. And the masque- or play-within-a-play became genre-linked to revenge tragedy, as in *The Spanish Tragedy*—a convention doubled in the *tours de force* of doubly-inset modified entertainments spiked by revengers (*Hamlet: Women Beware Women*). Such inclusion may be announced rather explicitly: "This is some antemasque belike, my lord" explains Bianca.

The popularity of inclusion in the late Renaissance can perhaps be related to the mannerist vogue for framing devices. Many works were self-embedded, so to speak, in inductions, prologues, epilogues, and the like, with consequent effects of artistic distance. And recognition of genres inset—and sometimes interacting with their setting, like the sonnets in *Love's Labour's Lost*—surely ranks high among the pleasures of Renaissance literature. Think of the complex framing of the play-within-a-play in *Hamlet,* with its own "prologue," its inset passage inserted by Hamlet, and its three audiences observing one another. Francis Berry has devoted a book to insets in Shakespeare.[43] But we find them everywhere at the time. In poetry, it was a main endeavor of art to achieve novel effects of inclusion. So Cotton inserts among the natural *Wonders of the Peak* (and what a delight to come upon it) an artful description of Chatsworth that is nothing less than a complete country house poem.

Inclusion is a fertile source of generic transformation. Nevertheless, it can hardly in itself provide the basis for a theory of literary change. Often it is a limited phenomenon, without effect on the matrical genre.[44] *Henry VIII* contains an inset masque; it remains a tragical history play. Trollope includes an epigram in *The Prime Minister;* but the novel is not an epigrammatic novel. Inclusion need not effect any generic change. Change is only likely to occur if the inset form is structurally assimilated; or if its proportion to the matrical work is large; or if it is regularly linked to the matrical genre. In any case, a theory based on local inclusion of complete works could not possibly account for the enormous variety of generic mixtures. Many of these can have arisen only from diffuse modulations, in which the transforming agent is an incomplete repertoire. Such modulations are able to color whole works, and eventually to alter genres.

With generic mixture, there opens a much wider field of possibility: this is the point at which the theoretical interest of genre abruptly increases. It is like the transition in mathematics from natural to real numbers.

Generic Mixture

Cicero, Quintilian, and Horace all advised that the genres should be kept separate—"Each subject should retain / The place allotted it, with decent thews"[45]—and their English followers repeated the advice. It is a familiar idea, accordingly, that classical and neoclassical theorists have preferred pure unmixed genres, whereas in periods "inimical to tradition" their fusion has been "exalted."[46] However, this contrast seems to be in very incomplete correspondence to the facts. Generic mixture can be found in good classical authors,[47] while in neoclassical English literature, mixed kinds positively thrived (Fieldingesque novel; satiric epic). The mannerist phase of the Renaissance was hardly a period inimical to tradition, yet its theorists pursued ideas of generic mixture with passion, and its writers achieved some of mixture's subtlest effects. Recalling the comparative deficiency of generic theory in the Middle Ages, we may be more inclined to think of proclivity to mixture as passing through a sequence of stages: apparent generic chaos; reassertion of pure genres and revision of labels; and new mixtures, progressively more audacious. The ubiquitous mixtures of the Middle Ages received scarcely any contemporary acknowledgment. Indeed, even the labels—such as "L'Epitaphe en forme de Ballade"—are often modern. Renaissance Italian criticism offers some sharp resistance to generic mixture (especially in connection with pastoral drama and romantic epic). Pasquier appears to feel the inclusion of documents in a history as a difficult mixture. Later the mannerist and baroque theorists open up the debate on terms more favorable, for a time, to mixed forms. But then the mixtures become chaotic . . .

Minturno emerges as a chief proponent of mixture. His enthusiasm for it shapes the entire *L'Arte Poetica,* which regularly discusses both pure and mixed versions of kinds—so that, for example, "pure satire" is followed by comic and tragic satire. He is sometimes vague about what constitutes mixture, however. And when he seems to be talking about mixture (being read in this sense by modern critics), he may mean only inclusion, or mixture of verse forms, or of prose and verse.[48] Rosalie Colie represents Sidney as arguing for *genera mixta,* on the strength of a passage in *The Defence:* "Now in his parts, kind, or species (as you list to term them), it is to be noted that some poesies have coupled together two or three kinds, as the tragical and comical, whereupon is risen the tragi-comical. Some, in the manner, have mingled prose and verse, as Sannazaro and Boethius. Some have mingled matters heroical and pastoral. But that cometh all to one in this question, for, if severed they be good, the conjunction cannot be hurtful."[49] Sidney cannot have been averse to mixture, since his own *Arcadia* mingled heroical and pastoral. Nevertheless, this passage argues only that mixtures are as morally harmless as their component genres, whereas a later passage attacks "mongrel tragi-comedy" on aesthetic grounds. Evidence of Elizabethan critics favorable to mixture has to be found in such elusive unexplicit passages as Drayton's comparison of his own odes to Horace's, which were "of a mixed kind," neither Pindarically high nor amorously Anacreontic. Drayton draws attention particularly to *His Ballad of Agincourt,* which he refers to as an "Ode . . . or if thou wilt, Ballad."[50] But the tendency of the evidence, from about 1590, is unambiguous. Labels such as "hilaro-tragoedia satyropastoralis" and "tragical-comical-historical-pastoral" show a positive rage for mixture.[51] The archmannerist Nashe can hardly get on with *The Unfortunate Traveller,* for stopping off to notice the latest change of style height or genre. Thus, he follows *Paulo majora canamus* with a string of puns; remembers that "he must not place a volume in the precincts of a pamphlet"; feels "more than duncified twixt divinity and poetry"; discusses sermons and slips into one; or warns "Prepare your ears and your tears, for never till this thrust I any tragical matter upon you." His satire is mixed with burlesque epic, tragedy, royal entry description, marvel, lyric, "passion," panegyric, travel literature, *impresa,* proverb, epigram, and other embedded or mingled forms.[52]

In the subsequent period, there was some recoil from the idea of generic mixture to the ideal of pure genre. A neoclassicist such as Rapin repeated Servius' view that only ten of Theocritus' thirty idylls were pure pastorals. He questioned whether pastoral could decently bring in fishermen: piscatory eclogue was for him not a subgenre but an extraneous mixture.[53] But when we move on only a few decades, mixture has gone so far as to call for radical regrouping. Wordsworth's approach to genre is freshly analytic, although when he treats mixture it is with a view to classifying. He lists six modes or "moulds" or "classes," then adds: "Out of the three last [idyllium, didactic, and philosophical satire] has been constructed a composite order, of which Young's Night Thoughts, and Cowper's Task, are excellent examples."[54] This analytic and classificatory approach to mixture finds its logical conclusion in Northrop Frye's theory of genres. Frye treats fiction as bound together by four chief strands: novel, confession, anatomy, romance. Mixture is simply a matter of combining these, regardless of external structure. "The six possible combinations of these forms all exist." And: "More comprehensive fictional schemes usually employ at least three forms."[55] The analytic approach will classify and illuminate the most audacious mixture, but has yet to prove itself with the local or microgeneric effects with which, in practice, criticism is concerned.

Hybrids

The most obvious sort of generic mixture is the outright hybrid, where two or more complete repertoires are present in such proportions that no one of them dominates. The component genres of a hybrid will necessarily be of the same scale: they are indeed neighboring or contrasting kinds that have some external forms in common. Thus, *The Ring and the Book* is less "a drama turned inside out"[56] than an aggregate of poems, each being a hybrid between a narrative poem and a dramatic lyric.

Sonnet and epigram often gave rise to bicorporate forms during the Renaissance. In comparing the sonnet with neighboring genres such as epigram, canzone, and ode, some critics, such as Robortello, Lorenzo de' Medici, Pigna, Tasso, Du Bellay, and Sebillet, stressed the resemblances between sonnet and epigram (brevity, "point," amorous topics, metrical pattern). But others stressed the differences between the two.[57] Minturno, in particular, contrasts them sharply: the epigram is a "particella dell'Epica," varied in mode, whereas the sonnet is melic (lyric), allied to canzone and song.[58] Epigram requires neither beauty nor grace of composition ("ne vaghezza, ne leggiadria di compositione"), but rather sharpness of wit or of matter ("agutezza di motteggio"). The sonnet's topics and formulas are more like the canzone's; even when it treats the same subjects as epigram, its style is different. Minturno thinks of the epigram as very short and epigraphic (epigrams of more than four lines should strictly be called elegies). But many saw the two genres as sharing much the same external structure, and used the epigram label for poems quite as long as fourteen lines. Conversely they might use "sonnet" for epigram forms, such as the sixain and douzain.[59] As Rosalie Colie has observed, the rhyme scheme of the English sonnet form with its concluding couplet was particularly well adapted for mixture with the distich-based epigram. She traces the historical convergence of sonnet and epigram under the influence of the Planudean Anthology, which had given the concept of epigram a more amorous turn. Sweet (*mel*) topics were still associated with the sonnet, whereas satiric, comic, and bitter topics (*acetum, sal, fel*) were linked with epigram—as, explicitly, in Harington's *Comparison of the Sonnet and the Epigram* (1618).[60] But several Continental sonneteers, most strikingly Du Bellay in his public and satiric sequence *Les Regrets,* reversed this convention. Du Bellay's sonnets could equally be construed as a sequence of quatorzain epigrams.[61]

In English, both Sidney's and Shakespeare's sequences achieve some of their most individual effects through hybridity. *Astrophil and Stella* has several "sonnets" (such as 30, "Whether the Turkish new-moon minded be") in which only the final distich reverts to Stella and speaks of love— an exact misuse of the sonnet and epigram external forms. Astrophil's intermittent plain style looks forward to Shakespeare's sonnets, where the couplets "move into a poetry of statement remarkable precisely for its austerity and abstention from figure."[62] Colie's brilliant account of the interweaving of lyric and epigram styles in the *Sonnets* decisively answers modern criticism that found the couplet closures and nonsonnet elements weak. And she is able to reapply the common observation of a satiric quality far more effectively in the context of generic mixture. Those arguments need not be rehearsed here. The present point is that in Shakespeare's *Sonnets* we are dealing with outright hybridity, rather than with internal modulation. Thus, quintessentially *mel* sonnets confront straight epigrams (such as the douzain 126 and the tetrameter quatorzain 145), and epigram-sonnets of obvious double genre, such as 95 ("How sweet and lovely dost thou make the shame"), with its juxtaposition of *mel* and *acetum.*[63] It is not a matter of a middle term between sonnet and epigram but of a hybrid keeping them distinct, "playing off two generic styles against one another, sometimes in concert, sometimes in opposition."[64] There is much to be said for the idea of Shakespeare's sequence as a book of epigrams.[65]

Structurally, sonnet and epigram could easily be seen as close relatives. The sonnet had developed out of epigram, and shared with it an interlaced rhyme scheme option.[66] Sonnet-epigram hybrids were formed, broadly speaking, in two ways. Epigram topics and style could be introduced in sonnet form, or the structure could be divided externally between the two genres.

Antisonnets followed the first method. A paradigmatic instance is

Berni's burlesque *blason* in Petrarchan sonnet form, *Chiome d'argento fine, irte e attorte,* an analogue of Shakespeare's Sonnet 130. Sir John Davies' exquisitely funny "Gulling Sonnets"[67] can be enjoyed either as satiric parodies or as delicate mock sonnets. Sonnet 8, *My case is this,* carries the legal conceits of *Zepheria* (1594) *à outrance.* And Sonnet 6, *The Sacred Muse,* follows out a sartorial *blason* of love through such items as "points of pride" and "his Codpiece of conceit," to "socks of sullenness exceeding sweet"—an oxymoron juxtaposing generic terms normally in contrast, the sweetness of a *mel* sonnet and the foulness and *sal* of the dark sweaty socks.[68] Elsewhere Davies scatters a few satiric Shakespearean sonnets through a book of epigrams (such as number 39, *In Fuscum,* on a playgoing libertine). Similarly Drayton, who as usual makes it clear enough what he is about. In the liminal poem to *Idea,* he rejects the "passion" (amorous mode)[69] and the "ah-me's" of "whining sonnets," claiming the variety of a "true image of my Mind" "in all humours"— the variety, in fact, of a *silva* of epigrams. This claim is substantiated in such sonnet-epigrams as *Idea* 8, an antiblazon uglier and sourer than Shakespeare's. But ironically the only writer who names the form is the anonymous author of *Choice, Chance and Change* (1606), who calls one of his satiric sonnet-epigrams an "epigrammical sonnet."[70]

Where structural apportionment of the sonnet hybrid was preferred, the most obvious solution was lyric quatrains followed by an epigrammatic distich closure. An example of this type, common in Shakespeare, is Sonnet 84 with its sharp conclusion "You to your beauteous blessings add a curse, / Being fond on praise, which makes your praises worse." But pedants advocated various alternative positions for the epigrammatic "point." For example Sebillet thought it should come at the second and third, or sixth and seventh lines.[71] But we naturally find other, unprescribed possibilities. Drayton's Sonnet 61, "Since there's no help, Come let us kiss and part," is a particularly fine hybrid in discrete parts: an eight-line dramatic epigram in low style, followed by a sonnet sestet of middle-style personifications and conceits. Interestingly, Drummond found the mixture disproportionately epigrammatic. When he writes that Drayton "showeth well his mind, but not the Passion," he is surely alluding to the words of the liminal sonnet quoted above.[72]

Rosalie Colie, to whom we owe much of our appreciation of generic mixture,[73] has shown how it encountered objections on grounds not only of aesthetic but of social decorum. Ever since Cicero's rather stiff interpretation of Aristotle put mixture of styles beyond the pale, their segregation had been related to political order. This is well illustrated in Minturno's favorable discussion of *fabulae mixtae* in the *De Poeta.* Mixed plots are those in which *dissimiles personae* are represented—that is, different ranks. His examples are the *Odyssey,* with its mingling of good and bad, aristocrats and shepherds, and the paradigmatic *Amphitryon,* called tragicomedy because of its mixture of kings and gods with slaves. Such thinking lies behind Sidney's stricter and perhaps more patrician criticism of plays that

> thrust in the clown by head and shoulders to play a part in majestical matters with neither decency nor discretion, so as neither the admiration and commiseration, nor the right sportfulness, is by their mongrel tragicomedy obtained. I know Apuleius did somewhat so, but that is a thing recounted with space of time, not represented in one moment; and I know the ancients have one or two examples of tragi-comedies, as Plautus hath *Amphitryo;* but, if we mark them well, we shall find that they never, or very daintily, match hornpipes and funerals.[74]

Taught by the interpretations of Empson and Ricks and others, we are used to thinking of Elizabethan and Jacobean double plots in terms of thematic resemblances.[75] The doubling is a matter of theme and variations. But, in origin at least, it seems to have been a generic and social decorum that distributed characters between tragic and comic plots—as indeed it did later, under French influence, in Dryden's mixtures of heroic and comic. In Renaissance English drama, segregation of ranks was not particularly severe. Nevertheless, its presence gives a certain edge to *The Winter's Tale,* that hybrid play *par excellence.* In its pastoral tragicomic scenes Polixenes and Perdita mingle with the real rustics—indeed "very daintily"—under exquisitely inappropriate disguises. King Polixenes, bent on tragic purposes, wears a shepherd's clothes and argues in favor of mixture. Perdita, noble by nature but seeming rustic through the mask of her nurture, and disguised again for the sheepshearing feast, as a goddess, argues the reverse.[76] Sophisticated capitalization on the indecorum of generic mixture could hardly go further—unless it does in the same play, in the clown's *nuntius* speech, whose heaped disasters carry to absurdity the multiplicity of incidents objected to in romance. And this in the very scene that sutures the play's tragic and comical-romantic parts. Perhaps even the gap of time separating the parts makes a generic point: one thinks of Sidney's exoneration of Apuleius' mixture, on the ground that "that is a thing recounted with space of time."[77] The romance that follows, for all the shortcomings of an "old tale," can in Shakespeare's hands lead to a final scene as serious and moving as any in tragedy.

English tragicomedy is a form of great interest which calls for far more attention than it has received. Erich Auerbach interprets it as the happy result of backwardness: the influence of antiquity had not yet misled Elizabethan dramatists into a false separation of the styles.[78] This thesis underestimates the English form's art. Marston and Shakespeare exploited confrontation of the styles (as Auerbach's own examples partly show), in ways that would have been impossible if these had not previously been distinguished. Jacobean tragicomedy, however, is certainly a distinct variety, and one of great potential. A key work in its development is Marston's *Malcontent,* which was entered in the Stationers' Register as "The Malecontent Tragiecomedia"—a reflection, in George Hunter's view, "of Marston's programmatic attempt to reconstruct this genre in English."[79] Hunter relates *The Malcontent* to Guarini's much discussed *Il Pastor Fido.* But its theoretical authority lay in Horace's difficult passage on satyr drama, and in certain speculations of Minturno's (if possible more difficult), which took their departure from the same *locus classicus.*[80] This background is clear from Marston's own hints: the Dedication's mention of "asperam hanc . . . Thaliam" (harsh comedy, a Horatian term), and the Introduction's ironically inverted announcement: "Sly: '. . . this play is a bitter play?' Condell: 'Why, sir, 'tis neither satire nor moral, but the mean passage of a history.' " The play itself mingles genres in a most intricate and judicious way. For example, it uses equivocal constituents that could belong to either. *Sententiae* suit both tragedy and diatribe satire; the double persona allowed by Altofronto's disguise is a device of great generic flexibility; and several speeches have an ambiguous tone (the facile satiric exaggeration of Malevole's incitement of Piero at 1.3.123 could easily be spoken, and interpreted, as a Vindice-like passion pointing to a tragic outcome).

Cyrus Hoy may be right in thinking that irony provides strategic common ground between tragedy and comedy.[81] He prefers satiric tragicomedy, and regards the earlier phase as superior. Incongruity between professions and behavior was then extreme, both in tragedy and in satiric comedy. Remarkable impingements were practicable. Comedy could "throw the tragic action into high if grotesque relief by providing a burlesque commentary." But the experiment of tragicomic exploration of evil seems to have proved too painful, too unresolving. Or perhaps the mixed form provoked a counterdevelopment within the component kinds—in particular, toward darker and "purer" tragedy. At all events, the later phase of tragicomedy, represented by Beaumont and Fletcher, seems to pursue more refined, not to say *raffiné,* aesthetic ends. Mixture is now exploited for theatrical switches of sentiment—or so the orthodox view has it. Hoy argues that the weakness of Fletcherian tragicomedy "lies in the formal arbitrariness of the definition" governing their mixed plots. A serious issue is ruled out by the artful avoidance of death: "A tragi-comedy is not so called in respect of mirth and killing, but in respect it wants deaths, which is enough to make it no tragedy, yet brings some near it, which is enough to make it no comedy: which must be a representation of familiar people, with such kind of trouble as no life be questioned, so that a God is as lawful in this as in a tragedy, and mean people as in a comedy."[82] But this is to underestimate Fletcher, who did not intend his brief address "To the Reader" as a theoretical justification of his "pastoral tragi-comedy." He probably knew that Guarini's *Compendio della Poesia Tragicomica* (1601) had gone far behind the crude notion of reversal leading to a *lieto fine.* And he certainly knew that Shakespeare's plays and his own explored more subtly and pervasively mixed actions containing apparent or virtual deaths, of a sort hardly covered by the popular definition he offers.

In the twentieth century, dark tragicomedy has returned in the plays of Samuel Beckett. Although it has other generic affiliations as well, *Waiting for Godot* can be regarded as a form of tragicomedy. But the mixture is so extreme and reductive as to suggest an antigenre. Elements of tragedy (*anangke, stichomythia*) are unmistakably present, but in a debased or parodic form, while the comic component, much of it rudimentary clowning, reduces human dignity still further. Beckett (and he is not alone in this) seems resolved to avoid tragicomedy's supposedly optimistic evasions, and to outgo the darkest possibility of its primitive phase.[83]

Satire

It is interesting that Hoy should see tragedy and comedy as coming together in "satiric depiction of life," since in other combinations, too, satire catalyzes generic mixture.[84] Many satiric works can be looked on as hybrid. To see why this should be so, we have only to glance back into the history of satire. As Gilbert Highet describes it, the genre falls into three subtypes: diatribe or satiric monologue, parodic satire, and Menippean satire. Now the last two of these involve mixture perforce. Parodic satire has no structure of its own: it must of necessity have a host form to inhabit and subvert. For it is like a mordant, dissolving away constituents' normal functions until all serve the satiric purpose. Even when the host repertoire is exceptionally complete and functioning more or less normally, so that the very completeness gives pleasure, as in *The Rape of the Lock,* nonetheless each feature is exaggerated or pointed in an ironic way. It is the same with Menippean or narrative satires. They, too, require borrowed structures—such as the travel-book kind inhabited by Gulliver's Travels or the dystopic science fiction of *1984* or the novel of *Decline and Fall.* As Highet notes, the use of the realistic novel as vehicle is hard to bring off successfully. This may be because two fundamental rules of the verisimilar novel, probability and balanced vision, have to be abandoned. Moreover, the verisimilar novel, presupposing an ordered society, has values incompatible with those of certain satiric subgenres, particularly apocalyptic satire—as the unevenness of attempted mixtures shows (*The Day of the Locust; Catch-22*). Parodic and narrative types are both perhaps to be construed as mixtures with monologue satire.[85]

Diatribe satire had itself a tendency to mixture. The terms for formal satire in antiquity—*satura,* and Juvenal's *farrago*—were names of mixed foods, salad, and mash. They denoted a feature that strikes every reader of satire: its casual diversification, whether improvisatory scramble or easy freedom. As Oldham says, "rambling stuff / May pass in satire." This digressiveness seems unprescribed, even uncontrolled. It is as if the writer's animus is rising and passing formal bounds. And this is undoubtedly the intended impression, to judge from centuries of theory. But there may also be tactical calculation: varying the direction of attack leaves its object uncertain.

The many genres already noticed as inset in *The Unfortunate Traveller* are probably to be seen in this light (as are the frequent self-references, a feature of satiric *farrago*). It is exuberant extemporality, rather than failure to meet the requirements of the forms, that occasions the generic digressions. These include what has been called "irrelevant moral discourses":[86] Nashe's rapid transitions from genre to genre can trick the best of critics. The Earl of Surrey's tournament armor—"his helmet round proportioned like a gardiner's water-pot, from which seemed to issue forth small threads of water, like cittern strings"—has elicited the fine comment "The watering can punches a hole in the Arcadianism, but typically Nashe at once snatches a delicate simile from this world of everyday objects which restores the damage."[87] But Nashe is not being ambivalent here: only switching to lyric. He still writes satire: but satire now of overelaborate, whimsical, pretty Arcadianism. And he can do as well himself, in that genre.

No satirist is more self-conscious, or more communicative, about his art's farragolike character than Carlyle. The "editor" of *Sartor* comments on how Teufelsdröckh's book "too often distresses us like some mad banquet, wherein all courses had been confounded, and fish and flesh, soup and solid, oyster-sauce, lettuces, Rhine-wine and French mustard, were hurled into one huge tureen or trough." Or he disparages the "confused masses of Eulogy and Elegy." Or he explicitly speaks of "this farrago."[88] I mentioned earlier that *Sartor* combines features of autobiography, essay, and novel or *poioumenon*. Here I should add that the transitions between genres are abrupt and unpredictable in the manner of a satiric farrago. A brief editorial interpolation (that "with all this Descendentalism, he combines a Transcendentalism, no less superlative") is enough to allow Teufelsdröckh to turn from a diatribe against materialism to an exalted Transcendentalist sermon about the "sky-woven" universe "worthy of a god." It is a generic tradition that Joyce remembered when he described *Ulysses* as a "chaffering all including most farraginous chronicle."

11. Generic Modulation

Generic mixtures need not be full-blown hybrids. In fact, it is more usual for one of the genres to be only a modal abstraction with a token repertoire. We shall call such mixture "modulation." In modulation, the proportions of the modal ingredient may vary widely, which leads to correspondingly various effects, from overall tones to touches of local color. In this way, "the poetic convention of one style" or genre becomes quite literally "the poetic resource of all styles."[1] Modulation is so frequent that we might expect it progressively to loosen the genres altogether, mingling them into a single literary amalgam. But it has been practiced for thousands of years without any such result.[2] Perhaps this is because generic components have to be somewhat discrete in order to have an appreciable effect. Imperceptible mixtures would not always serve the writer's turn so well. As sometimes in cookery, effort may go into blending ingredients in such a way that they remain partly distinguishable. Another reason may be that literary tastes change with time, so that genres dominating one period with their modal extensions are actually avoided in others. For in modulation we have to do with one of the principal ways of expressing literary taste.

A process that gives rise to most of the interesting generic effects in literature will probably escape full treatment anywhere, and easily defies it here. I shall merely glance at a few historical movements of taste—widespread modulations that may suggest the scope of the idea.

Modulations of Allegory

Medieval literature can easily seem a generic chaos. As we have seen, even when familiar terms are used, the works they label (such as Petrarch's bucolics) have very little apparent continuity with the corresponding classical genres. Some of these anomalies arise from confusion on the part of the authors. But some are better understood as modal transformations. In this connection, a tendency of the first importance is the "crossing of the pagan and Christian canons" referred to by Curtius.[3] New contents were put into pagan external forms, for example saints' *vitae* into epic or romance. And genres occurring in the Bible—such as pastoral, or the epithalamium of the Song of Solomon—were identified by the exponents of Biblical Poetics, and especially valued.[4] Biblical pastoral topics were consequently transferred to the eclogue (Christian *pastor;* separation of sheep and goats). Fortunately the history of medieval pastoral and its multifarious transformations, from Sedulius and Paschasius Radbertus to Petrarch and Mantuanus and Spenser, is now relatively accessible.[5] Similarly with extensions of epithalamium: it is fairly well established that the epithalamic journey of the Song of Solomon, together with that of Claudian and Sidonius, contributed to the formation of the dream-vision genre. Meanwhile the symbolic marriage of Biblical epithalamium was combining with pastoral in another way, to transform the eclogue and the love song.[6] These developments were connected with another, perhaps more fundamental: the allegorical modulation.

Allegory had a remarkable vogue in late antiquity and in the Middle Ages.[7] This is possibly to be attributed to changes in psychology. However that may be, the vogue was certainly confirmed by the practice of interpreting the Bible allegorically. Not only the "really" allegorical parts, such as Galatians 4:22–31, but any part not otherwise edifying was interpreted in this way. And the same method could be applied to Virgil's and Ovid's poetry, which needed thorough allegoresis merely to be tolerable. Such interpretation easily generated modal transformations. For allegory is quite as conducive as satire to mixture of genres. It can use almost any external structure or "outside" allegorically, making it the husk or *sens* of an inner *matière*—and modifying it generically in the process. From the period of ancient allegoresis based on Homer or the Bible, and of independent allegories such as Prudentius' *Psychomachia,* an allegorical repertoire gradually assembled. It included such features as personification, abstraction, metaphorically doubled chains of discourse and of narrative, generated subcharacters, deletion of nonsignificant description, and several topics (journey, battle, monster, disease). Parts of this repertoire have subsequently been extended to many other kinds: not only to epic and romance, but to tale, novel, and various poetic forms. Northrop Frye distinguishes continuous and intermittent allegory, but concludes that "allegory is thus not the name of a form or a genre, but of a structural principle in fiction."[8] However, allegory is by no means limited to fiction. And its intermittent occurrences, when considered together with instances of the full repertoire elsewhere, seem quite intelligible as generic modulations. This may even be true of extended examples. Spenser refers to *The Faerie Queen* as "continued allegory," but it has the external structure of romantic epic. If this is a debatable case of modulation (in that the allegory may be thought prominent and pervasive enough to constitute a hybrid), Tasso's *Gerusalemme Liberata* is less so. Although unquestionably *epopea romanzesco,* it contains many hints at a personification allegory, to which indeed the preface draws attention.

Angus Fletcher and others have shown how features of the allegorical mode appear in a great variety of kinds of works, from the early beginnings, through parables of Hawthorne, to such modern poets as Yeats and Eliot. I shall only glance at two instances illustrating the extreme diversity of early applications.

Martianus Capella's *De Nuptiis Philologiae et Mercurii,* written in the early fifth century, became one of the most imitated works of the Middle Ages.[9] Its allegorical and epithalamic journey to heaven influenced countless writers, including Dante, Hawes, and Spenser. Yet a modern reader may be more puzzled than attracted by its strange form, combining sober exposition of the liberal arts with an allegorical frame in a deliberately faulty style. In words farouche and involved, erudite and lurid, the frame tells of Mercury's wish to wed. He consults Apollo, who advises marriage with the learned virgin Philologia. The *artes,* personified by seven handmaids, are presented by Mercury to Philologia as a dowry, thus symbolizing the union of eloquence and learning. The full aptness of this beautiful allegory is far from obvious. It is not just that Philology needs eloquence to explain to others what she knows. More subtly, the *artes* are also gifts of Mercury, as one might say *communicated* to her by him.

As the digressive style and the mixture of verse and prose makes clear, Martianus intends a Menippean satire or symposium, a genre in whose transmission he was a key figure.[10] Indeed, the work is supposed to be told to him by Satire. He describes Satire as "various" (*miscilla*); which may reflect, or even announce, the mixed genre. At any rate, there is no doubt about the extension of features from the allegorical repertoire to what is primarily a symposiac treatise. Not only are there abstractions (Discordia, Seditio) and psychological or moral personifications (Sophia,

Psyche, Phronesis) but also a story of an allegorical journey.[11] The result is almost a hybrid, with allegory even predominating in the first two books. Yet as a whole the *De Nuptiis* remains a treatise. And we do not at all think of the modulation as a sugar-coating of didacticism, but rather as a transposition of the work into a strangely remote realm of autonomous abstraction.

By contrast, traces of allegory in *The Assembly of Ladies* are faint, and sometimes uncertain. It is plainly a dream poem; although this has needlessly been questioned, because of the misconception that kinds are definable classes.[12] The dream-poem genre is heterogeneous enough to be embodied in some works that are not fully dream visions. Moreover, the kind is subject to allegorical modulation. Some dream visions, such as the *Roman de la Rose,* are manifestly allegorical; others (and this includes some of Chaucer's) are less obviously so. *The Assembly of Ladies* primarily belongs to the nonallegorical dream-poem genre, as its remarkably realistic opening at once makes clear. It was a common form. Allegory has been called the dominant form of the Middle Ages; but fifteenth-century literature, at least, exhibits a contrary tendency toward naturalistic realism. Pamela Gradon makes the point very clearly when she includes *The Assembly* with other poems of its time "which are not true allegories but narrative or lyrical poems which use allegorical devices as an ornamental feature. These might be called pseudo-allegories."[13] Many of its characters are personified abstractions (Loyalty, Perseverance, Attemperaunce), but their descriptions are unallegorical and directly realizable in ordinary life.

This mixture could be approached as simply a matter of judging how the proportions are balanced. "That delicate balance which we find in true allegories between the visually convincing and the intellectually significant has here tipped over into the purely naturalistic."[14] Such an approach leads to impatience with the "shallowness" of allegory reduced to "an ornamental feature" (Gradon), or with a "silly" or "a chilly and irrelevant addition" (Lewis).[15] If, however, we treat *The Assembly of Ladies* as a dream poem modulated by allegory, the modulation may seem a matter of purpose and decision rather than otiose survival. The purpose is to assist communication in a narrative that would otherwise have been obscure or deficient in meaning.[16] Why is the lady pale? and why is there so much stress throughout on haste and tardiness, on concern about being ahead or behind the rest of the fellowship?

I do not mean to make much of the obvious allegory, with its familiar abstracts—Discretion, Acquaintance, and the rest—although some of these are finely realized. There is subtlety in details such as the subordination of Acquaintance (purveyor of lodgings) to Discretion (chief purveyor). But this explicit allegory is too skeletal to be the source of the work's liveliness. More interesting are the delicate hints of allegory in passages that have been taken as directly realistic. In the frame narrative, the lady is one of several in a garden with a maze. When a knight or squire asks her purpose, she replies:

> To walke aboute the mase, in certeynte,
> As a womman that nothying rought.
> He asked me ageyn whom I sought
> And of my coloure why I was so pale.
> Forsoth, quod I, and therby lith a tale.[17]

The questions may seem separate and inconsequent. But considered allegorically, they have consecutive force. If the maze were a labyrinth of love it would make moral sense that some of the lady's fellows "for very wrath" overstep the rails. Then we should regard in a different light her wish to be in the maze and yet not to care. Her paleness, on that assumption, would be a sign that she is not one of those "that nothing rought." The tale she tells to explain her paleness is about a visit to the house of Loyalty, where all must wear blue—that is, be constant. Men are debarred because of "somewhat": a lack of constancy (l. 149) that is not to be named, at least in her friend's company. Attending to such hints, as the allegorical modulation invites us to do, we can respond to this brilliant and enchanting tale as an entirety. We see that the tale is not only introduced by the prologue, but discloses an intimate confidence with a reflexive import for the relations of the frame characters.

Allegory's extension to a wide variety of kinds was common during the Middle Ages, and has understandably given rise to its description as a "dominant form." But this may suggest an automatic recourse to allegory that is far from characteristic of fifteenth-century literature. Forms such as those of *The Assembly of Ladies* or *The Flower and the Leaf* represent special complications for a specific purpose.

Epigrammatic Modulations

The second historical movement to be noticed here is the broad extension of epigram, from the late sixteenth century to the early eighteenth. Epigrammatic modulation is inevitably a main theme, since it is so much discussed, both in contemporary and in modern criticism.[18] Perhaps because of epigram's special place in education, its extension could be self-conscious. It is possible to find the explicit statement "I wrote an epigrammical sonnet" in a work of 1606.[19] We have already seen something of epigrammatic mixture in connection with structural inclusion and hybrids. But the epigram also influenced many kinds by means of modulation—to such an extent that Boileau, followed by Soame and Dryden, could speak of it as overwhelming Parnassus:

> The *Epigram*, with little art composed,
> Is one good sentence in a Distich closed.
> These points, that by Italians first were prized,
> Our ancient Authors knew not, or despised:
> The vulgar, dazzled with their glaring light,
> To their false pleasures quickly they invite;
> But public favour so increased their pride,
> They overwhelmed Parnassus with their tide.
> The *Madrigal* at first was overcome,
> And the proud *Sonnet* fell by the same doom;
> With these grave *Tragedy* adorned her flights,
> And mournful *Elegy* her funeral rites:
> A hero never failed 'em on the stage,
> Without his point a lover durst not rage;
> The amorous shepherds took more care to prove
> True to their point, than faithful to their love.
> Each word, like *Janus,* had a double face:
> And prose, as well as verse allowed it place ...[20]

It is hardly an exaggeration, so far at least as the seventeenth century is concerned. The great epigrammatic transformation that took place then profoundly affected a large part of literature, and even altered the literary model in an irreversible way. By making for concision, it changed the usual scale, texture, and standard of finish. It made wit and ambiguity valuable. And it gave the couplet—as much the epigrammatic distich as the heroic couplet—its Augustan primacy. On some kinds, the effect was creative; on others, devasting. Apart from Milton's bid to establish a separate sonnet identity through high-style affiliation with epic or ode (which could in any case be seen equally well as an attempt at heroic epigram), the sonnet virtually disappeared between Drummond and Cowper or Bowles.[21]

Epigram was well adapted to a metamorphic destiny. As Renaissance theorists such as Minturno and Robortello explained, its diverse tones allowed it to resemble many larger forms. Epitaph could be seen as miniature tragedy, encomiastic epigram as miniature panegyric or ode. Even the historian and the epicist could give matter to the epigrammatist.[22] Modulation involving epigrams worked in two contrary ways: either it could assimilate features of other kinds, or it could contribute its own to them.

What may be called the "diastole" of epigram can be clearly discerned in Herrick's *Hesperides*. This greatest of English epigram sequences accommodates features of an astonishing variety of genres. As we have seen, the liminal poem departs from its model in Bastard's *Chrestoleros* by introducing the epic *propositio* "I sing."[23] Rosalie Colie's comment deserves to be quoted in full:

> Nothing could less satisfactorily fulfill the epic "I sing"; the brooks, blossoms, birds, bowers are the pastoral so radiant in Herrick's book, *Hesperides*. The May-poles and Hock-carts refer to celebrations in the rhythm of a georgic year; brides and bridegrooms appear in pro- and epithalamia; dews and rains in philosophical or scientific poetry; times trans-shifting in allegorical, historical, or metamorphic poetry; and "How Roses first came Red, and Lillies White" points not only to specific poems in the *Hesperides* but also to Herrick's distinguished exercise in diminution, reducing Ovidian metamorphic topics to epigram size. Groves are the numinous *loci* of supernatural presence; "the Court of Mab, and of the Fairie-King" (Oberon) diminishes Spenser's epic story to thumb-nail scale. With "I write of Hell; I sing (and ever shall) Of Heaven," we return to the epic promise of the first words, now translated into sacred story—and realize that Herrick has in fact given all that he promised in the secular *Hesperides* (that mixed garden) and in the sacred *Noble Numbers*.[24]

And we find diminished versions of other genres, too. Besides the georgic year, there is the amorous *fasti* or calendar (Herrick's mistresses partly associate with months, led by Julia-July and introduced by Anna Perenna). There is a blazon subsequence anatomizing Julia's parts. There are minute Anacreontic odes (one of them in monometers), and scaled-down encomiastic odes. There are sonnet-epigrams on amorous subjects, valedictions, hymns, dialogues, satiric advice to a painter, a country house poem, and a prospect poem. And there is a tiny eclogue that contrives to account for the absence of its own song section. Perhaps the often-referred-to "poetic liturgy" will even suggest to some the great work of epic.[25] Needless to say, all subgenres of epigram are represented, not omitting the fetid.[26] All this might simply be seen in terms of *silva* variety. However, as Herrick's title hints, his aim is higher, at a patterned garden of the Hesperides. Like Jupiter's philosophical garden of forms, this generic epitome assembles a complete world. Its miniaturization has a thematic purpose, revealed most obviously perhaps where the ordering of flowers or weeds invites us to think also of the world in terms of reprobation, election, and resurrection. From the present point of view, the miniaturization has a special interest, in that it often puts hybrid genre out of the question. The larger forms are represented only by token features, so that the effects must be put down to scale change and modulation. Thus, calendars will be suggested but never fully implemented. And if epic book divisions can be glimpsed in the secular and sacred parts (*Hesperides* and *Noble Numbers*), it would be stretching a point to claim that the external structure of epic is fully exploited. Moreover, several genres are sometimes suggested within a single short poem. Herrick's liminal epigram, which uses the formulas both of epic or ode ("I sing") and of epigram ("I write"), can be regarded as moving between Pindaric and Anacreontic: between the grand and the minute, the meltingly amorous, or the pastoral—much as Cowley's liminal poem to *The Mistress* begins high and then confesses his lyre to be "enfeebled" by love.[27] Some of the pleasure such poems give springs from their neat minimality. To adumbrate so many generic forms within so narrow limits!

The "systole" of epigram breathed its influence out over just as many kinds. Its effect was pervasive, yet worked in partly determinate ways. Thus, elegy, madrigal, and even epithalamium incorporated distinct parts of the epigram repertoire: plain diction, pointed *concetti* (especially in the closure), variety of topics, concision.[28] The conceited style has been connected (by Praz, Mazzeo, Williamson, and others) with contemporary theories of *argutezza* or wit.[29] But these theories themselves developed, as Praz makes clear, in relation to epigram: "As *arguzia* (wit), in the words of Sforza Pallavicino, was 'a marvellous observation condensed into a brief sentence,' it is easy to understand why the artistic form which best suited the mind of a seventeenth-century man should be the epigram."[30] The fact that Metaphysical style is from one point of view simply the style of epigram has strategic importance for the literary historian. It directs attention, for one thing, to sources of Metaphysical writing, especially in sacred epigram. But source criticism is not the only possible response. The influence of epigram can also be approached as generic modulation. Critically, indeed, this is indispensable; when Metaphysical poetry is treated in terms of "lyric" it often proves difficult or even disgusting.

It should be clear that the modulation meant is different from inclusion. Praz goes so far as to call Crashaw's *Weeper* "little more than a rosary of epigrams or madrigals clumsily linked together, without progression."[31] But the poem is not epigrammatic in mode just because it uses material from previous epigrams or because it includes subepigrams. Regarded as a whole also, it exhibits the qualities of sacred madrigal transformed by epigram: notably the compressed spoken diction, the low style, and the extraordinary range of vehicular topics (Golden Tagus, walking baths, voluntary mint, and so forth). Moreover, the last lines— "Crown'd Heads are toys. We go to meet / A worthy object, our lord's FEET"—offer more than the paradoxical "point" or *concetto* of the thirty-first stanza (feet worthier than heads). By alluding to the Magdalene's adoration and the occasion of the preceding tears, they make an epigrammatic closure for the whole poem.

Extension of epigram had if anything a more striking effect on elegy. Valedictions such as Donne's—beyond any question elegiac poems of feeling—were strewn liberally with epigrammatic features. These even include "points," which it would be easy to see as less than appropriate to sad occasions of parting, were they not so exalted by wit's apprehension of the secret marvels of love. In *A Valediction: Forbidding Mourning* the modulation continues throughout. It appears in the wide range of topics, some of them quotidian (*trepidatio* of the spheres; the goldbeater's craft; compasses; technological emblems), as well as in the intimately spoken register, with scraps of dramatic direct speech easily accommodated— "some of their sad friends do say, / The breath goes now, and some say, no . . ." And the familiar conceit of the compasses is from an epigram-madrigal by Guarini. Above all, the strands of discourse are overlaid and compressed so closely as to make a dense texture of ambiguities, in which individual words count ("breach," "firm"), just as in epigram. The pointed closure, easy to miss for a modern reader not expecting the modulation, depends on a witty ambiguity: "where I begun" can refer to the traveler's external return to his love, or to the eternal return that their *constantia* makes possible. Donne's epigrammatic transformations of love elegy were influential in fostering the spread of such modulations. It is significant that when Cleveland used similar *concetti* of love's compasses and circles in his conversational elegy-ode *To the State of Love,* he packed many "points" into a single stanza:

> My sight took pay, but (thank my charms)
> I now empale her in mine arms,
> (Love's Compasses) confining you,
> Good Angels, to a Circle too.
> Is not the Universe strait-lac't,
> When I can clasp it in the Waist?
> My amorous folds about thee hurled,
> With Drake I girdle in the world.
> I hoop the Firmament, and make
> This my embrace the Zodiac.
>> How would thy Centre take my Sense
>> When Admiration doth commence
>> At the extreme Circumference?[32]

The vogue of the strong line of wit was extreme enough to provoke a reaction. Already Dryden disliked extreme Clevelandism—although his own "St. Cecilia's music-book" could with reason be described by Landor as "interlined with epigrams." And Addison rejected Cowley's "mixt wit." Interestingly, he regarded it as an illegitimate extension of epigram: "The only Province . . . for this kind of Wit, is Epigram, or those little occasional Poems that in their own Nature are nothing else but a Tissue of Epigrams."[33] The modulation had gone far beyond occasional poems. Major works of the seventeenth and early eighteenth centuries can sometimes seem bound together by catenas of epigrams. This might be said of works as different as Denham's *Cooper's Hill* and Pope's *Essay on Man.* One obvious sign of this is the integrity of quotable distichs, which in some cases have actually been detached and printed separately.[34] Yet we are not dealing only with local inclusion: such works have the tone and feel of epigram throughout. It is their mode.

In prose, comparable developments can be observed. Many commonplace books and similar works consisted quite literally of series of epigrams: Bodenham's *Politeuphuia* (1597), for example, and Meres' *Palladis Tamia* (1598). Another extension of epigram can be seen in the paradox or "problem," a genre to which Donne gave new status. Then there is the "sentence" or aphorism, whose ramifying and strategic functions throughout Renaissance literature have still to be fully explored.[35] It assumes such prominence in Bacon that "in their first form of 1597 the

Essays ... consist essentially of detached aphorisms on particular topics."[36] Brian Vickers has had to defend the work against critics who see "a mere collection of apophthegms from his notebook"—against the expectation, in fact, that "Bacon should have produced a connected piece of writing in the discursive whimsical vein of the tradition from Montaigne to Charles Lamb." With the remarkable logical and rhetorical construction of the *Essays* we are not concerned here. It is enough to notice that in effect Bacon modulates the essay with features of epigram. Owen Feltham ("pithy ... short breathed, but sound") carries this process further. He sharpens the aphoristic quiddities of experience to points, pressing always for hyperbolic concision:

> Long poetry, some cannot be friends withal: and, indeed, it palls upon the reading. The wittiest Poets have been all short, and changing soon their subject: as Horace, Martial, Juvenal, Seneca and the two Comedians. Poetry should be rather like a Curanto, short and nimbly lofty; than a dull lesson of a day long. Nor can it be but deadish, if distended; for when it is right, it centres conceit, and takes but the spirit of things: and therefore foolish poesy, is of all writing the most ridiculous. When a Goose dances and a Fool versifies, there is sport alike. He is twice an Ass, that is a rhyming one.[37]

Here epigram modulation shows in the diction, the brisk rhythm of short word-groups, the surprising complex turns of thought, the "points," and the fondness for a certain unexpected brevity (as in "that is a rhyming one"). Later the epigrammatic essay was returned to poetry by Gay and Pope.

It would be a mistake to stress the constructive aspect, since the epigrammatic modulation seldom led to impressive results in that regard. Being a short kind, epigram had most to offer in the form of stylistic resources. When Sir Thomas Browne makes out that all men are cannibals, that "all this mass of flesh that we behold came in at our mouths; this frame we look upon hath been upon our trenchers. In brief, we have devoured ourselves, and yet do live and remain ourselves,"[38] the pungent brevity, the compressed repercussion, the surprising turns, are unmistakably epigrammatic. The modulation goes so far in *Christian Morals* as to make for obscurity. Continuous prose demands to be more easily read than is compatible with frequent points. But Browne partly obviates this difficulty by repetition—as very obviously in this passage: "As Charity covers, so Modesty preventeth, a multitude of sins; withholding from noon-day Vices and brazen-browed Iniquities, from sinning on the house top, and painting our follies with the rays of the Sun. Where this Virtue reigneth, though Vice may show its Head, it cannot be in its Glory: where shame of sin sets, look not for Virtue to arise; for when Modesty taketh Wing, Astraea goes soon after."[39] Stylistic modulation of this kind has much to do with the characteristic flavor of seventeenth-century prose.

More generally, the epigrammatic transformation can be seen as one of the processes whereby literature came to be more intimate and informal, and to deal with sentiments previously expressed only in Latin. (In the extension of the plain style it was epigram, rather than satire, epistle, or comedy, that provided the main transforming impulse.) Still more broadly considered, the transformation may be said to have brought about changes in the very scale of literature. Textures were closer knit, so that what may be called literary events came to be expected in a work more frequently. Epigrammatic modulation made for compression—a pressure that was not released for a century or more. With the subsequent history of the transformation, however, we are not concerned here.[40]

Georgic Modulation

In the eighteenth century, georgic succeeded epigram as the most creative mode. Virgil's *Georgics* had been translated before,[41] but it was Dryden's translation, accompanied by an essay of Addison's (1697), that proved decisive in establishing the form. Not content with mere definition ("A georgic, therefore, is some part of the science of husbandry put into a pleasing dress, and set off with all the beauties and embellishments of poetry"),[42] Addison drew attention very clearly to each main feature of the repertoire. Thus, georgic at times presents "plain and direct instructions" *in persona auctoris,* yet is sensuously rich, since it "addresses itself wholly to the imagination: it is altogether conversant among the fields and woods and has the most delightful part of nature for its province."[43] The precepts chosen are those "most capable of ornament" and that fit together most seamlessly, shading one into another, although there may also be remote (but thematic) digressions. Above all, the main instruction is to be indirect: "the poet often conceals the precept in a description." The style, which should avoid vulgarity, nevertheless uses all the resources of poetry: the beauties of Virgil's *Georgics* are more "exquisite" than those of the *Aeneid*—a point implying all the interplay of high and low, near-heroic and near-bucolic, that makes georgic so flexible a form. Such was the repertoire deployed, with varying success, in formal English georgics: John Philips' *Cider* (1708), Christopher Smart's *Hop-Garden* (1752); John Dyer's *Fleece* (1757), and James Grainger's *Sugar-Cane* (1764).[44] All these are full of what Northrop Frye calls "modal counterpoint."

More interesting than these "correct" georgics, from our point of view, are the looser developments of the Virgilian repertoire. Chalker distinguishes three main traditions of georgic transformation. The subtlest departure is in mock georgics such as Gay's *Rural Sports* and *Trivia*, where the interplay of high and humble is put to amusingly disproportionate uses. A comically elevated *propositio* ("When to assert the wall, and when resign") will be followed by the distanced boast "This work shall shine, and walkers bless my name." Such elusive tones led to others even more so—to the "inverted mock" of Somerville, for example.[45] A second tradition consists of enlarged development of the descriptive parts of georgic, as in Thomson's *Seasons*. Many georgic themes are carried over, particularly retirement, patriotic sentiment, and vision of the Golden Age. Pastoral and bucolic passages contrast with others of heroic exoticism:

> from all the Tract
> Of horrid Mountains which the shining Alps,
> And wavy Apennines, and Pyrenees
> Branch out stupendous into distant Lands,
> Cruel as Death, and hungry as the Grave![46]

The third transformation worked by extension of parts of the georgic repertoire to local descriptive poetry. Denham's *Cooper's Hill* (1642) differs from more local topographical or estate poems such as *To Penshurst* in the more discursive, ranging scope of its political meditations. The digression through topics of retirement, panegyric, religious conflict, trade, colonization, and hunting (with its political allegory) is clearly colored by georgic.[47] This modulation eventually issues in the visionary politics of *Windsor Forest*. Pope's poem is throughout permeated by georgic influences, which can be seen in so prominent a feature as the powerfully realized analogy of hunting and war.[48]

A good instance of georgic modulation in the local-descriptive kind is Charles Cotton's influential *Wonders of the Peak* (1681). Just where its description narrows in focus to the scale of a country house poem—in the account of Chatsworth—it also widens to take in exotic vistas: "the scorned Peak rivals proud Italy" (l. 1264); "His Royal Chariot left, it seems, behind; / Whose wheels and body moored up with a Chain, / Like Drake's old Hulk at Deptford, still remain" (ll. 1296–98). Even the birds nesting "like Caesar's Swiss, burn their old native nests" (l. 1307). Or one might notice how easily the landscape becomes political *paysage moralisé,* where Chatsworth is "the proud Regent of the British Isle," assailed by the "perpetual war" of frosts, while "native snow . . . elsewhere round a Tyranny maintains";[49] and the Third Wonder, Tydeswell, an army that "Marches amain with the confederate Force" (rain). There are also historical and narrative digressions. The Queen of Scots Pillar gives rise to an extended passage of political reflection and exclamation, in a partisan Stuart sense:

> Oh England! once who hadst the only fame
> Of being kind to all who hither came
> For refuge and protection; how couldst thou
> So strangely alter thy Good Nature now,
> Where there was so much excellence to move,
> Not only thy compassion, but thy love?
>
> (ll. 235–240)

With effortless ease Cotton finds appropriate places for these features, in a poem that remains local-descriptive externally. Nevertheless, the overall coloration is unmistakable; *The Wonders* is a distinctly national poem.

Cotton is a more significant figure in the development of georgic than has been allowed. Indeed, Durling and Cohen are undoubtedly right in putting the origins of English georgic earlier still. We can see the beginnings in didactic verse essays of the sixteenth century and even in the prologues of Gavin Douglas. From this point of view, Drayton's *Polyolbion,* a difficult work to identify generically, can be seen as an early extension of georgic to local poetry. James Turner rightly exculpates Drayton of the fault of ignoring labor (a common fault among seventeenth-century landscape poets). But, as Turner hints, this is in part the difference between what he calls "watertight genres." Drayton's attention to labor is partly due to *Polyolbion*'s pronouncedly georgic modulation. Georgic played a not inconsiderable part in revaluation of work during the Reformation, particularly through extension to pastoral, which began to introduce the seasons, and hence their occupations.

An even looser georgic tradition can be thought of, in which its characteristically precise observation[50] was extended still further, to any ecphrastic treatment of nature in exquisite words. This extension stemmed from Augustan formal georgics, whose exact descriptions were often occasions for *tours de force* whereby texture or sound was matched to sense—as in Dryden's "He hears the crackling Sound of Coral Woods" (*Virgil's Georgics* 4.521). But similar effects (conspicuous for example in Milton and in the much despised Blackmore)[51] began to be attempted wherever illustration from nature was connected with wider ideas. Christopher Smart, himself a georgic poet, filled *A Song to David* with such precisions as "The grass the polyanthus checks / And polished porphyry reflects / By the descending rill" (Stanza 52), and "Strong through the turbulent profound / Shoots xiphias to his aim" (Stanza 75)—with its vigorous movement and mimetic sibilants. In the century that followed, these resources were even extended to prose, through imitation of Milton, Cowper, and others. Thus, in the descriptive sketches of Mary Russell Mitford, the *mot juste* came to count in a new, unepigrammatic way. And the novel, too, underwent georgic modulation. Hardy's immensely influential *Tess of the d'Urbervilles,* for example, although primarily tragic, has substantial georgic sections, where seasonal description and dairying and other labors are the occasion of some very sensuously-worded passages. (Particularly striking is the elaborate description of dying pheasants, a topic of georgic, in Chapter 41.) In nature poetry the tradition was closer knit: Wordsworth's *Descriptive Sketches* even appeared with epigraphs from Virgil's *Georgics,* and contained echoes not only of the *Georgics* but of *Windsor Forest,* Thomson's *Seasons,* and Cowper's *Task.*[52] Clough's *Bothie* is a more complex mixture, invoking the Muses of epos and idyll and combining these forms (or mock forms) with verse novel and verse epistle. The georgic component shows in several ways (seasonal description; formal and informal tuition), but above all in very frequent syntactic mimesis. This is sometimes minute, as in the line "One great glory of broad gold pieces the aspen" (8.48), with its long vowels in unaccented positions giving a continuous insistence. More often it is a broad syntactic mimesis, as in the lines rendering the passage of time:

> Ten more days did Adam with Philip abide at the changehouse,
> Ten more nights they met, they walked with father and daughter.
> Ten more nights, and night by night more distant away were
> Philip and she; every night less heedful, by habit, the father.
>
> (6.83–86)

Apt description of this sort is not merely a local resource, but colors the whole, so that we have to think of modulation as the process involved, as well as inclusion.

Elegiac Modulations

We may not yet have the perspective to be sure whether the nineteenth century is the most prolific of all literary periods in experimentation with genre. But it certainly offers an embarrassment of riches from the present standpoint. The novel in particular underwent many modulations, as well as extending its own mode to other kinds. Elements of its repertoire (above all probable contingency) crop up everywhere. *The Ring and the Book* can be seen as a novelistic modulation of dramatic lyric;[53] Clough's *Bothie* as novel-georgic;[54] and Shaw's macrologic stage directions as a similar modulation of the dramatic side-text. Among these multifarious nineteenth-century modulations one stands out: the elegiac.

This may not be self-evident. We are more familiar with the idea of lyric as the dominant mode of nineteenth-century literature. Almost every genre, we know, became lyric then—in the sense that its conventions were modulated expressively, or that shaping matched form with content, or that (if nothing else) the style at least was stylish. So we speak of a novelistic genre that grew out of this tradition as "the lyric novel." But we are not accustomed to think of this lyric tendency as elegiac. Newer groupings of genres shut off that insight. Nevertheless, the term "lyric" itself recalls an elegiac modulation: namely, that of ode, a dominant form in the neoclassical period. In the nineteenth century, "lyric," by then a vogue word,[55] acquired the elegiac sense "expressive," so that Ruskin could define lyric poetry as "the expression by the poet of his own feelings." Abbie Potts hardly exaggerates when she writes of "the elegiac century." If it were objected (misapplying Austin Warren) that "Gray's 'Elegy,' written in the heroic quatrain, not in couplets, effectually destroys any continuation in English of elegy as any tender personal poem written in end-stopped couplets,"[56] one might reply that elegy has not changed any more than was to have been expected of a genre so long-lived. And the elegiac repertoire has shown continuity, as well as change. Indeed, the quatrain has perhaps outlived the elegiac kinds, to become a feature of one of its successors, the confessional poem about mortality—for example, John Ashbery's fine poem *Fear of Death*.

The repertoire of elegy may at first seem elusive. But Scaliger, Tomaso

Correa, and other Renaissance theorists describe it clearly enough, while Abbie Potts' recent account, from the Propertian paradigm, is in broad agreement.[57] The middle style of elegy is flowing, artless, sincere, unaffected (*candida*), tender, pure, neatly groomed, clear, and, so to speak, open (*ingenua*). An elegist will be concerned with feelings, not with finely considered ideas (*sentiis exquisitis*), or wit, or sententiousness, or song, so that he will express himself in a manner that goes straight forward (*prorsus*).[58] In diction, elegy has propriety and elegance, features that may set it off from epigram. Moreover, although it can be intimate and highly passionate, it also tends to be more formal and figurative, more "florid," or "higher"—as witness Young's *Night Thoughts* or Tennyson's *In Memoriam* or Auden's *In Memory of W. B. Yeats*. The topics Scaliger lists are mostly those of love elegy: praise, commemoration of love, "Querela, Expostulatio, Preces, Vota, Gratulatio, Exultatio, Furti narratio, Fletus . . ." But he includes stock-taking (*propriae vitae explicatio*), perhaps in acknowledgment of a central notion of elegy: self-discovery. Elegy's meditation typically leads to recognition (*anagnorosis*) of feeling, to revelations and illuminations.[59] Hence, its images of light; hence, too, its "perceptive vision." Epicede, the longer epitaph, and sometimes epistle were its Renaissance kinds.[60] In the nineteenth century, however, a distinction was felt between elegy proper and elegiac "meditation about death and personal loss, transience, and unfortunate love."[61] "Elegy" in the second sense often refers to what I should describe as modulated ode.[62]

The mood of elegy, in this sense, is plainly the mood of a great part of Romantic and of Victorian poetry. Wordsworth, for one, is almost continuously concerned with meditation on feelings and with approach to illumination (or recession from it). Few would dispute that he generally internalizes both his own experience and the literary forms he uses to express it.[63] And to do this he extends the repertoire of elegy, introducing *anagnorosis,* in particular, into kinds where it was far from usual. Extensions of elegy were by no means limited to the Romantic poets, or to such a Victorian as "the tender Hood." We find them introduced everywhere. Many of Browning's dramatic lyrics from this point of view appear as expressive *propriae vitae explicationes* of their narrators.[64] And even the hyperclassical Landor moved in the same direction.

The entire repertoire of elegy might almost be constructed from Landor's *Simonidea* (1806) alone. The volume contains a version of what has become an anthology piece, *Rose Aylmer:*

> Ah what avails the sceptred race,
>   Ah what the form divine!
> What every virtue, every grace!
>   Rose Aylmer, all were thine.
> Rose Aylmer, whom these wakeful eyes
>   May weep, but never see,
> A night of memories and of sighs
>   I consecrate to thee.[65]

The expressive repetitions, the praise, the clear and simple love complaint, the tears, the consecration, the "wakeful eyes" perceiving loss: all these are characteristic of elegy. There are no points or neat turns of wit, and none of the abbreviation of Latin epigram, which would scarcely have had room for the anaphoras "Ah what," "every," or "Rose Aylmer." So far as the length and metrical pattern go, however, *Rose Aylmer* could also be an epigram. Are we, then, to think of elegy as overlapping with the new, Greek-derived epigram?[66] Doubtless an elegiac taste found much that was congenial in the *mel* epigrams of the Greek Anthology (which enjoyed a renewed popularity during the Hellenic vogue). They were unpointed, and sometimes very lucid and tender. Nevertheless, elegy and epigram were normally distinct. This becomes evident if one compares, say, Callimachus' *Heraclitus* with William Cory's famous translation, in which six lines are expanded to eight to allow for expressive repetitions far from the spirit of epigram: "They told me, Heraclitus, they told me you were dead"; "bitter news to hear and bitter tears to shed."[67] Cory transposed his translation, in fact, into elegy—the dominant short kind of his own time.

If *Rose Aylmer* is almost pure elegy, certain other short poems of Landor's (in some ways more interesting) are noticeably mixed in genre. *The Poet's Legacy*,[68] for example, is surprising enough to stop on something of a point: "Enough in going is the thought / For once we acted as we ought." It is a highly compressed closure. Yet the same poem has *adnominationes* ("Wisdom ... wise"; "gone ... going") and other repetitions, muted and concealed but extraordinarily sustained, in the numerous pronouns ("we" once per line; "others"). The resonant self-discovery strongly suggests elegiac modulation. Similarly with the epigram *Our Youth Was Happy*,[69] which seems at first to have a pointed closure. For its resonance, particularly the suggestion that the mourned dead include earlier selves, turns out to be elegiac. The poem pursues a meditative self-discovery:

> Our youth was happy: why repine
> That, like the Year's, Life's days decline?
> 'Tis well to mingle with the mould
> When we ourselves alike are cold,
> And when the only tears we shed
> Are of the dying on the dead.

Another group of Landor's short poems varies epigram by introducing confessional emotion. In *Why Do I Praise a Peach,* the compression, the trimming of connective particles, the brilliant (though figurative) closure, above all the Hellenic alternation of long and short lines, imply *mel* epigram. Yet there is surely elegiac modulation in the self-questioning and self-discovery:

> Greece with calm eyes I see,
> Her pure white marbles have not blinded me,
> But breathe on me the love
> Of earthly things as bright as things above:
> There is (where is there not?)
> In her fair regions many a desert spot;
> Neither is Dircè clear,
> Nor is Ilissus full throughout the year.[70]

Earlier passages indicate that Landor is surveying here the waste parts of his own genius. A more obscurely revelatory epigram is *How Often, When Life's Summer Day,* which again has a figurative closure:

> In those pale olive grounds all voices cease,
> And from afar dust fills the paths of Greece.
> My slumber broken and my doublet torn,
> I find the Laurel also bears a thorn.[71]

There is enough of a point to allow recovery from the confession—and yet, oddly, to intensify it too. Landor can give even a very short (but quatrain!) epigram features of elegy:

> The scentless laurel a broad leaf displays,
> Few and by fewer gather'd are the bays;
> Yet these Apollo wore upon his brow ...
> The boughs are bare, the stem is twisted now.[72]

The hint at repetition, the inversions of word order, the doubtful figures: all are in agreement with the elegiac pathos.

The elegiac modulation of epigram was discovered by many later poets, notably Hardy and Yeats, and later J. V. Cunningham and Robert Lowell. Apart from this tradition, Yeats' short intense poems—such as the self-epitaph—would be unintelligible. Not that earlier epigram lacked the capacity to express feeling. Spontaneity of effect was after all an ideal of the epigram *silva*. Nevertheless the distinction between epigram and elegy remains of consequence for poetry and criticism. For rejection of Victorian poetic diction by the modernists has had the indirect effect of making the survival of elegiac poetry depend on epigram, which now provides its usual external form. Conversely, we increasingly take for granted the interiorization and "perceptive vision" of elegy, so that short poems of other genres may nonplus by their lack of these. Jonson's *Epitaph on S.P.* may seem damagingly "unexpressive," or his great Cary-Morison ode impersonal.

The nineteenth century saw many other elegiac transformations, in prose as well as poetry. The type of familiar essay written by Lamb or Hazlitt or Stevenson was incomparably more expressive—and more self-expressive—than that of Bacon or Feltham. An even more striking example is the elegiac strain in many novels. Here I am not only thinking of its "straightforward" and yet repetitive, delayed, and emotionally charged action, although that is indeed a prose equivalent to an analogous movement in elegy.[73] But several Victorian novels essay a more distinctively elegiac modulation. Among these, Meredith's *Egoist* is supreme. It has other modal admixtures—notably comic, satiric, and (in the "Great Book") *poioumenon*. And like almost any novel it has local inclusions, such as the "rough truth" epigrams of Chapter 36. By contrast with these included forms, the elegiac elements interact more pervasively and set the emotional tone for much of the novel. Its rhythm is profoundly influenced by the pace of its prolonged meditations of feeling, which have a true elegiac persistence. One thinks of Meredith's own complaints, or his search for "The Heart of the Egoist," or his discovery of the true nature of Clara Middleton's feelings (for which "nature may be consulted like an oracle"). The discovery is shown directly in "Clara's Meditations" throughout the night (Chapter 21), leading to her tearful perception that "dark dews are more meaningful than bright," and more dramatically in the intensely charged probing of her heart during the great conversation with Mrs. Mountstuart (Chapter 35). No novel renders the *doctae puellae* of elegy better than Meredith's masterpiece.

With these substantive features of elegy go others, of style and diction. The traditional signal words of elegy—"trembling," "pensive," and the rest[74]—appear frequently in *The Egoist,* most often in relation to Clara. More remarkably, there is an expressive shaping of style, even of syntax, as a vehicle of passion. Examples naturally tend to be large-scale, like the tremendous convoluted simile of the jury foreman (Chapter 32). But one brief instance is the comment on Sir Willoughby's unfeeling observation of Laetitia's figure "swimming to the house":

> So, as, for instance, beside a stream, when a flower on the surface extends its petals drowning to subside in the clear still water, we exercise our privilege to be absent in the charmed contemplation of a beautiful natural incident.
>   A smile of pleased abstraction melted on his features.
>
> (Chapter 34)

The "for instance," together with the tone of detachment, shows easy command over the image, implying it to be chosen casually from among a number of possibles. Meredith is miming—just as in the stylish "privilege to be absent"—Sir Willoughby's superiority. Laetitia's status is reduced to that of an object, a mere "natural incident." Here the purpose of the mime is comic, to ridicule Sir Willoughby; but the image itself is elegiac, a "beauteous" sad presentation of the sinking Laetitia.

Expressive lyricism is quite foreign to the earlier novel. But it becomes increasingly prominent as we move from Thackeray and Dickens (with whom it is for the most part local), through Meredith (who first grasped its possibilities fully) and James, to the "lyric novels" of Virginia Woolf. *To the Lighthouse* takes the modification about as far as is feasible without dissolving the form of the novel altogether.[75] This whole development can be seen as a generic transformation, in which elegiac or "lyric" modulation of the verisimilar novel is the main process.

Similar changes, we may believe, make up the formal *entraînement* of all historical developments of literary forms. In principle, it would be possible to trace chains of generic transformations—some of them naturally very complicated—connecting the newest kinds of literature with the oldest. In the examples mentioned, one or two such lines of connection have been adumbrated. Thus, in the seventeenth century, the didactic verse essay was influenced by ancient georgic to produce a new, English georgic form. Georgic modulation of the local descriptive poem, in turn, led to the poem of natural description. And it was modulated by elegy to produce the Romantic nature poem. Similar elegiac modulations of the reintroduced Hellenic epigram issued in the late Romantic and eventually the Georgian short lyric. Other kinds present similar patterns of change and regrouping. In short, the whole developing tissue of literature is made up of multifarious extensions and interactions of genre such as those we have glanced at.

12. Hierarchies of Genres and Canons of Literature

The literature we criticize is never the whole. At most we talk about sizable groups of the writers and works of the past. This limited field is the current literary canon. Some have argued that much the same is true of individual works: that an "elasticity" in the literary artifact permits us to attend now to small samples, now to larger traditions and groupings of which the work in its unitary sense forms a mere constituent. However that may be, few will dispute the elasticity of *literature*. The literary canon varies obviously—as well as unobviously—from age to age and reader to reader.

The Dame Mutability who produces these marvelous changes has often been identified with fashion. Isaac D'Israeli, an early proponent of this view, argues that "prose and verse have been regulated by the same caprice that cuts our coats and cocks our hats," and concludes that "different times, then, are regulated by different tastes. What makes a strong impression on the public at one time, ceases to interest it at another . . . and every age of modern literature might, perhaps, admit of a new classification, by dividing it into its periods of fashionable literature."[1] Fashion's claim to rule has much plausibility. A desire for novelty, which should not be undervalued, has much to do with pleasure in literary form. Nevertheless, taste is more than fashion, and should never be subordinated to trivial laws of circumstance. To recognize taste for what it is, we need to glimpse something of its involvement in multifarious processes that are many of them quite unconnected, apparently, with literature. Their variety is the subject of Kellett's challenging essay *The Whirligig of Taste,* and it is one that calls for extended study. Here we shall be concerned with only one determinant: genre.

One is struck by how many of D'Israeli's instances of displaced fashions are described in generic terms: "the brilliant era of epigrammatic points"; "another age was deluged by a million of sonnets"; "an age of epics"; "dream" (that is, dream vision); "satires"; "romance"; "trage-dies"; "comedies." In fact, changes in literary taste can often be referred to revaluation of genres that the canonical works represent.

Canons of Literature

The official literary canon is nevertheless usually spoken of as quite sta-ble, if not "totally coherent." And the idea of canon certainly implies a collection of works enjoying exclusive completeness (at least for a time). Yet the Biblical canon was arrived at only after many vicissitudes and over a period of many centuries. At each stage it was categorically fixed (although subject to varying emphases—conciliary, denominational, sec-tarian, individual). But when it enlarged or contracted, the new canon, too, was definitive. Moreover, canonical books of Scripture were not merely authentic but also authoritative. This normative sense has prompted a useful extension of the term to secular literature. So Curtius writes of "canon formation in literature [that] must always proceed to a selection of classics" and that embodies itself in lists of authors, curricula, histories of literature, and canons of taste.

The current canon sets limits to our understanding of literature, in several ways. The official canon is institutionalized through education, patronage, and journalism. But each individual has also his personal canon, of works he happens to know and value. These two groupings have no simple inclusive relation. Most of us fail to respond to some of-ficial classics; on the other hand, through superior judgment or through benefit of learning we may be able to go beyond the socially determined canon in ways that are not merely eccentric. Someone must be first to see merit in an experimental work, or to revalue a neglected one. Transla-tions from foreign and early indigenous literature play a considerable part in such changes (Wyatt's Petrarch; Dryden's Chaucer; Cary's Dante). And infusions of elements from popular art have also a vital influence. In this way the narrative ballad, after centuries of belonging to popular literature and of exclusion from the literary canon, attracted the impar-tial interest of Gray and received art treatment from Wordsworth and Coleridge.

The literary canon in the broadest sense comprises the entire written corpus, together with all surviving oral literature. But much of this po-tential canon remains in practice inaccessible for a variety of reasons, such as the rarity of its records, which may be sequestered in large libraries. Hence the more limited accessible canon. Accessible literature is very much narrower than the *New Cambridge Bibliography of English Literature* might suggest.[2]

Practical limitations work in several ways, which can be mutually confirming. Most direct are the limits to publication: Traherne (1637-1674) could hardly be canonical until his principal works were "discovered" (1896-1897) and printed (1903, 1908). And even for a good novelist with a readership as wide as Trollope's, the canonical works (in the present sense) are confined to those recently reprinted. Similarly, contingencies of manuscript transmission have shaped the medieval canon; paperback publication and anthologizing still limit the accessible canon for some social groups; warehousing costs put some great books out of print; and the bibliophilic canon influences in unexpected ways the literature available even to scholars.[3] Perhaps only two or three Thackeray novels are canonical in this sense. With the performing arts, accessibility is particularly restricted. Who can tell how many Jacobean plays may not be better than the very few that happen to have been put on in our time? Reviving neglected plays is so difficult and costly that even attempts at "reverse censorship" by state patronage have failed to counteract the narrowing of our competitive acting tradition to an impoverished repertoire of half a dozen genres and few score plays. In 1978 there were three London productions of *The Changeling.* As for restrictive censorship, that has at times drastically narrowed the literary canon, to the extent of suppressing entire contemporary genres, such as satire and the political novel.[4]

Inside the accessible canon systematic preferences have often been exercised, which amount to selective canons. The selective canons with most institutional force are formal curricula. Their influence has long been recognized: it is treated in such studies as R. R. Bolgar's *Classical Heritage and Its Beneficiaries.* But reaction to an official curriculum may take the form of an "alternative" curriculum, equally strict, but until recently less examined by literary historians.[5] And always there is a briefer, more rapidly changing, unseen curriculum, of passages that are familiar and interesting and available in the fullest sense. Such selections are all responsive in one way or another to the critical canon. We might expect this to be liberal and catholic. But it is surprisingly narrow. The literature most critics' work relates to is not that listed in bibliographies, but the far more limited areas of interest marked by repeated discussion in journals—particularly journals such as *Scrutiny,* which have acquired influence. From this canon, a great many considerable authors are excluded. For example, the first fifteen annual volumes of *Essays in Criticism* (1950–1965) contain no article on Vaughan or Traherne or Cotton or Diaper or Smart or Clare or de la Mare. In fact, the *New Cambridge Bibliography of English Literature* records no criticism on Cotton after 1938. Even within the canonical writers, moreover, critics agree to operate, in the main, on beaten tracks (*Piers Plowman, passus* 18; Spenser's Bower of Bliss; Dryden's Achitophel). The best passages, of course. The individual choices that follow after all these selections inevitably light on very few writers, although by quirks of personal taste they may extend to unfashionable outsiders such as de la Mare.

We may think it fortunate that literature's generic nature is such as to enable samples to stand for much larger groupings by incorporating their types. Even so, the force of the literary canon would be hard to exaggerate. Apart from its obvious effects of exclusion and limitation, it has a vital positive influence by virtue of its variety and proportions. Arrived at through the interaction of many generations of readers, it constitutes one of our most significant images of wholeness.

Of the many factors determining canon, genre is surely among the most decisive. Not only are certain genres regarded *prima facie* as more canonical than others, but individual works or passages may be valued more or less according to their generic height.

The Generic Hierarchy

Genres may have several mutual relations, such as inclusion, mixture (tragicomedy), antigenre inversion (romance and picaresque), and contrast (sonnet and epigram). Another is the hierarchical: relation with respect to "height." So classical critics regarded epic as higher than pastoral. When the two came into juxtaposition, as in a formal georgic, style height had to change accordingly. Nevertheless, height was more than a rhetorical dimension: its normative force is unmistakable. From the late sixteenth to the early eighteenth century, epic ruled as not only the highest but also the best of all genres. Webbe called it "that princely part of poetry"; Sidney, "the best and most accomplished kind of poetry"; Mulgrave, "the chief effort of human sense"; while Soames and Dryden, following Boileau, said that in epic "fiction must employ its utmost grace."[6] At the other extreme, love poetry, and short poems generally, were rated low. Defending poetry against "lightness and wantonness," Harington wrote that "of all kinds of poesy the heroical is least infected therewith." But he could not say the same for "the pastoral with the sonnet or epigram." Within a century, "sonneteer" was to become a term of disparagement for minor poets—as in Pope's "some starved Hackny sonneteer."[7] In the late seventeenth century, epigram came lowest of all: it was "the fag end of poetry."[8] Soames and Dryden criticized Tasso for including "points of epigram" in his *Gerusalemme Liberata,*

> which are not only below the dignity of heroic verse, but contrary to its nature: Virgil and Homer have not one of them. And those who are guilty of so boyish an ambition in so grave a subject are so far from being considered as heroic poets that they ought to be turned down from Homer to the *Anthologia,* from Virgil to Martial and Owen's Epigrams, and from Spenser to Flecknoe; that is, from the top to the bottom of all poetry.[9]

From such statements, Ralph Cohen has concluded that the hierarchy of genres "can be seen in terms of the inclusion of lower forms into higher—the epigram into satire, georgic, epic; the ode into epic; the sonnet into drama; the proverb into all preceptive forms."[10] And certainly the principle of inclusion was much discussed by Renaissance critics, as we have seen. Epic, the highest kind and a norm for the others, was said also to be the most comprehensive. So Scaliger writes:

> In every sphere some one thing is fitting and preeminent, which may serve as a standard for the others; so that all the rest may be referred to it. So in the whole of poetry the epic genre, in which the nature and life and actions of heroes are recounted, seems to be chief. According to its pattern the remaining parts of poetry are directed. Because these parts exist in variety, . . . we shall borrow higher universal laws from the majesty of epic, so that their contents may be accommodated, agreeably to the natures of the different forms of each.[11]

But claims of inclusion in epic might be no more than attempts to give other kinds authority by showing them to be latent in the normative and original kind. Even if inclusion in a stricter sense was meant, it would be hard to apply the principle to other comprehensive kinds, or to extend it universally to all short forms. A sonnet or two might be found in a comedy here and there, and some songs in tragedies. But no theory can have been based on instances so exceptional.

The Renaissance doctrine of inclusion is beset with complications that need to be disentangled. Cohen rightly traces the idea to *Poetics* 26, a discussion whether epic or tragedy is the higher form of imitation. The more comprehensive is the better. But Aristotle prefers tragedy (not epic) for a sort of comprehensiveness other than inclusion: namely, its use of additional elements of representation, spectacle, and music. He says nothing to imply that tragedy may contain inset epics. In Renaissance epic theory, however, it often seems that inset structures are being discussed; and occasionally this is so. After all, epic sometimes really contains inset forms. But even when inclusion seems most certainly the topic, confusion of terms may deceive. When Minturno calls epigram "particella dell'Epica Poesia," this has nothing to do with inclusion of epigrams in epics.[12] Here *epica* refers to one of three broad presentational modes. "How many parts, then, has poetry?—Broadly speaking, three: one is called *epica*, the second dramatic [*scenica*], the third melic or lyric, as you prefer."[13] Minturno's *parti*—that wonderfully omnipurpose term, without which Renaissance literary theory would have been impossible—here means something like "categories of representation," or "divisions according to presentational mode." Elsewhere, however, as in Sidney's *Defence*, "parts" can mean genres, whether kinds or modes: "parts, kinds, or species (as you list to term them)."[14] Italian theory may have been misunderstood through confusion of terms such as this. It would be quite intelligible, of course, if lofty encomiastic epigrams had been regarded as heroic in a modal sense. But what are we to think when Dryden (who knew as well as Herrick that *Cooper's Hill* was a prospective or a georgic poem) writes that "this sweetness of Mr. Waller's lyric poesy was afterwards followed in the epic by Sir John Denham, in his *Cooper's Hill*, a poem which, your lordship knows, for the majesty of the style is, and ever will be, the exact standard of good writing"?[15] The main sense of "epic" here is simply *genus mixtum*—that is, neither pure enarration nor dialogue, neither lyric nor drama.[16] But a secondary, modal sense no doubt colors the passage, as "majesty" suggests. Similarly, when Dryden speaks of "heroic poetry ... of which the satire is undoubtedly a species,"[17] the context in a discussion of *Georgics* 4 shows that he is referring to modal admixture. The Virgilian passage has a local heroic coloring— "here is the majesty of the heroic." There is no doubt that epic as a kind "includes" the satiric kind. Perhaps because "the terms 'kinds,' 'species,' 'forms,' and 'genres' are used interchangeably,"[18] classical genre theory can seem more self-contradictory than it really was.

Seeing a contradiction between the inclusive principle and "the distinctiveness of kinds," Cohen chooses to deny the latter.[19] Certainly it would be hard to draw up a specification of genres that all Renaissance and all Augustan critics would have subscribed to. But the theorist of mutable genres is not obliged to produce such a specification. Just because early genre critics were uncertain or confused in formulating concepts of mode (which first emerged in the Renaissance), this is no reason to doubt the existence of genres with distinctive generic repertoires. These repertoires might be understood in only the dimmest way, and yet function well enough for the genres themselves to be recognized. And when early critics bewilderingly include "species" inside species, we should perhaps, with hindsight, discern promising attempts to organize the kinds in relation to the principal modes.

Cohen has rightly drawn attention to the ordering of the modes by height, in an "interrelated" hierarchy. Here again, it would be hard to maintain that a single, all-embracing hierarchy ever existed. Nevertheless, many height relations would have been agreed upon. So observers of a rainbow can agree that "red" and "violet" (or colors like them) are opposites, even though they themselves divide the spectrum differently.

In early discussions of genre we need to distinguish between full systematic accounts and brief lists. Scaliger, Minturno, and others describe hundreds of kinds and subgenres, some of them known only to theorists. By contrast, they also at times list a few main genres. These are usually the genres that were susceptible to extension beyond their original external forms—the genres that gave rise to modes. Familiar, quickly recognized in reading, frequently mentioned in criticism, they were the most valued genres, and may be rank-ordered in part according to value. A typical example, with epic first, is Edward Phillips' 1675 list of the categories (or "kinds") "under one of which all the whole circuit of poetic design is one way or other included": epic, dramatic, lyric, elegiac, epoenetic, bucolic, epigram. The phrase "one way or other" reflects Phillips' sense of the heterogeneity of the traditional paradigm, in which "lyric," "epoenetic" (that is, epionic), and "elegiac" were metrical categories with little if any modal application.[20]

The brief paradigm of genres derived from ancient authorities, particularly Cicero, Horace, Quintilian, and the fourth-century grammarian Diomedes.[21] We can best understand it by comparing variant forms widely distributed through later criticism (see table).[22]

These are ordered by several principles of articulation. One, particularly clear in Diomedes' influential work, arranges the genres according

PARADIGM OF MAIN GENRES

Cicero	Tragic, comic, epic, melic, dithyrambic
Horace	Epic, elegiac, iambic, lyric, comic, tragic, ?satyric
Quintilian	Epic, pastoral, elegiac, satiric, iambic, lyric, comic, tragic
Diomedes	*Genus commune:* epic, lyric; *genus ennarativum:* preceptive, historical, didactic; *genus dramaticon:* tragic, comic, satyric, mimic
Sidney (1583)	Epic, lyric, tragic, comic, satiric, iambic, elegiac, pastoral
Harington (1591)	Epic, tragic, comic, satiric, elegiac, amatory (pastoral, sonnet, epigram)
Meres (1598)	Epic, lyric, tragic, comic, satiric, iambic, elegiac, pastoral, ?epigram
Phillips (1675)	Epic, dramatic, lyric, elegiac, epoenetic, bucolic, epigrammatic
Dryden's Boileau ([1674] 1683)	Epic, tragic, satiric, epigrammatic, lyric (ode), elegiac, pastoral

Note: For convenience of comparison, the original sequence (explicit or implied) is exactly reversed in some instances.

to presentational mode. On this Aristotelian plan, they are dramatic (the author not speaking directly); enarrative (the author alone speaking); or mixed (both author and characters speaking). Analytic as this is, the genres inside each presentational category could easily be rank-ordered by value (for example, *tragica, comica*). The Aristotelian scheme accounts for the sequence *tragic / comic / satiric* in Horace, Harington, and Meres. it explains Phillips' odd introduction of "dramatic." And it underlies tripartite divisions of literature in Milton and many other critics.[23]

By another principle, as we have seen, poetical genres were ordered according to their verse forms. This plan was adopted by Quintilian and by Horace, whose ostensible subject in *Ars Poetica* 73–98 is the suitability of verse forms for various subjects. It accounts for the "iambic" genre in Meres. By 1598, however, the metrical differentiation was largely obsolete: Meres' only examples are Harvey and Stanyhurst. Similarly, "lyric"—not to be confused with the modern term—might refer to genres using lyric verse forms, or music of a certain type. (It excluded elegiac poetry, written for the flute.) However, "lyric" might also imply the ancient value-ordering, whereby lyric poets were preferred to melic poets.[24] This high valuation of lyric persisted and reemerged strongly in the seventeenth century: Charles Cotton, in a verse epistle to Brome, apologizes that he is unable to manage an ode. "Elegiac" was almost as ambiguous, implying not only "mourning elegy" (Harington) and love elegy, but also elegiac verse. So Phillips' lyric, epoenetic, and elegiac may all be metrical categories.

The combination of different ordering principles made for flexibility and allowed a surprising amount of room for development. But in the long run, in spite of the ingenious conservatism of such as Meres, radical change was inevitable. When the long-standing paradigm was finally abandoned in the early eighteenth century, the result for genre has been called confusion. One historian has spoken of "collapse in all of the conventional literary structures." The exaggeration of this is plain from the passage that follows: "all of the smaller enclosed literary kinds began to disappear or undergo mutation into their most misshapen possibilities."[25] In fact, the sonnet had given way to epigram long before the eighteenth century. Every genre, indeed, had been undergoing mutation all along. Such change is not misshapen or monstrous, but normal.

The normality of generic change is such that we cannot expect to understand the variants of the modal paradigm, or of the systems that replaced it, in synchronic terms. They can only be grasped in the dynamic context of literary-historical development.

Changes in the Generic Hierarchy

The height to be assigned to pastoral has long been matter for debate. When it was given new status by Virgil, its place became quite problematic. Part of the difficulty shows when Diomedes treats *Eclogues* 1 and 9 as *genus dramaticon*—he regarded the others, presumably, as *genus commune,* the composite presentational category. But pastoral continued hard to value, since by metrical criteria it belonged with epic, whereas in the *rota Vergiliana* (despite its name a vertical hierarchy) it rated low. In the Renaissance and in the seventeenth century, pastoral claimed a place among the eight paradigmatic genres, as the lists of Sidney, Meres, Phillips, and Boileau illustrate. (Harington, too, includes pastoral with other "amatory" forms, in his six-genre paradigm.) Pastoral was then a high and serious kind, capable of veiled significance that could "include the whole considerations of wrong-doing and patience."[26] But, as Cohen remarks, its scope subsequently narrowed. And its status was correspondingly reduced, until Johnson's famous remarks showed it on the way out, the object of dispraise and distaste.[27]

Epigram's movement is still more striking. In the older lists, it makes no separate appearance, although satiric epigrams, such as those of Archilochus, would have come under iambics.[28] Harington, himself a practitioner, grants epigram a place in his lowest, amatory category: "the pastoral with the sonnet and epigram." Meres cannot keep it out. He lists and exemplifies the traditional "eight notable several kinds of poets," but feels obliged to add a paragraph on epigram, in indeterminate relation to the rest. Phillips compresses the dramatic genres into one, yet finds room nevertheless for epigram. And in Boileau and Dryden, epigram is up at fourth place. These promotions were no more than what was due, for the early seventeenth century saw a remarkable rise in the status of epigram. It dominated much of literature. Rosemond Tuve connects the increased number of short sixteenth-century poems other than songs with "the slow establishment of a reading rather than a listening public during a hundred years of printing."[29] And one might find another cause in the wide use of epigram composition in schools. Estienne had published the *Anacreontea* in 1554 and the Planudean Anthology in 1566. Partly under their influence the Neolatin epigram reached a height of finish and brilliance by the early seventeenth century, when the Greek Anthology's full wealth of epigrams became accessible through the copying of the Palatine manuscript and the publication of Grotius' Latin translation of the Planudean abridgment. This seems to have come at just the right juncture for maximum effect on vernacular poetry. Perhaps, too, the epigram's brevity and freedom of subject were ideally suited to a period of rapid change. At all events, it rapidly displaced other short forms. (Waller, Herrick, and other epigrammatists, had they lived a little earlier, would have written sonnets.) And the kinds not displaced were nevertheless proudly influenced by the epigram. As we saw in an earlier chapter, it transformed them modally, so that they emerged as new forms—such as the witty pointed love elegy that we know as Metaphysical lyric. Epigram also had much to do with the cultivation of effects of closure in end-stopped couplet verse. And it partly underlies the reformulation of ideas about the poetic process in terms of wit.

Such influence may have been the chief warrant for epigram's new place in the paradigm of genres. Boileau seems to imply as much in his disparaging comment (translated closely by Soames and Dryden) on "the epigram, with little art composed." He is critical of "points," and sees their popularity as threatening a dictatorial rule (one suspects that in his overall disposition he put epigram fourth of seven genres, in the central place, to underline its "sovereignty" formally):

> They overwhelmed Parnassus with their tide.
> The madrigal at first was overcome,
> And the proud sonnet fell by the same doom;
> With these grave tragedy adorned her flights,
> And mournful elegy her funeral rites:
>
> . . . . .
>
> Each word, like Janus, had a double face:
> And prose, as well as verse allowed it place . . .[30]

Disliking the newly elevated status of epigram, Boileau and his translators use a sort of recommendatory historiography in an attempt to restore what they see as right proportion: "affronted Reason," they hopefully pretend, at last excludes points from serious writing—"none should use 'em without shame, / Except a scattering in the epigram." It is a standard classicizing effort, trying to resist the transformation of genres by reaffirming their boundaries. The attempt, hindsight shows, was a temporary aberration of criticism; the transformations, far from overwhelming literature or presaging a "breakdown," were perfectly normal.

The same period saw other changes of generic status, including some that affected the modal paradigm considerably. Donne and others raised the amatory elegy to new heights. And by 1700, satire—which Castelvetro had denied even the name of poetry—had been promoted above the middle position it had held for a century (with brief fluctuations): Dryden, Pope, Swift, and others considered it fit for some of their most ambitious work. If the heroic transformation of satire in *Absalom and Achitophel* does not quite demonstrate this, the possibility of a satiric epic such as the *Dunciad* surely does. A little later, according to Joseph Warton, the satires of Ariosto were more read than *Orlando Furioso,* and Churchill was more in vogue than Gray.[31]

Another remarkable case is georgic. Estienne and Sidney could doubt its right to any poetic status at all: they compared didactic writers to "the meaner sort of painters," who "counterfeit only such faces as are set before them" and lack invention of their own. Yet by the early eighteenth century, critics were speaking of didactic poetry as "second to epic alone," if not its equal.[32] Dwight Durling and John Chalker have written instructive and delightful histories of the English formal georgic, which need not be detailed here. In any case, the changed valuation of georgic was part of a much broader development in didactic writing. Sidney referred to didactic writers generally: all "that deal with matters philosophical, either moral, as Tyrtaeus, Phocylides, Cato, or natural, as Lucretius ... or astronomical, as Manilius and Pontanus; or historical, as Lucan"— the sort of writer who "takes not the course of his own invention."[33] These categories, which cut across the boundaries of verse and prose, serve as a reminder that the paradigm itself had in effect become one of poetic modes. The Elizabethan defense of literature was primarily a defense of imaginative literature or "poesy." But the effect of Camden and of Raleigh was felt: and Bacon, Browne, and others developed the essay-like treatise with such success that they restored the literature of archeology, geography, and history to its earlier, Renaissance status.[34] Cotton's verses on Walton's *Lives* were not alone in conceding victory in the *paragone* to "History" (that is, biography). In the ensuing revaluation, georgic, essayistic, and other didactic poetry rose to the very highest level of estimation. Cotton, Denham, Dryden, and Pope all did some of their most serious work in such genres. By the late eighteenth century, however, the didactic genres were no longer quite on this height. In *An Essay on the Genius and Writings of Pope* (1756, 1782), Joseph Warton divided English poets into "four different classes or degrees": (1) "the sublime and pathetic"; (2) "such as possessed the true poetic genius in a more moderate degree, but who had noble talents for moral, ethical, and panegyrical poesy"; (3) men of wit, of elegant taste, and lively fancy in describing familiar life, though not the higher scenes of poetry"; and (4) mere versifiers—who nevertheless included such as Sandys and Fairfax. Having examined Pope's works at very considerable length, Warton judged that "the largest portion of them is of the didactic, moral, and satiric kinds, and consequently not of the most poetic species of poetry; ... his imagination was not his predominant talent." This may seem a ludicrously predictable conclusion, showing how limited evaluation by classifying is bound to be.[35] But Warton's not inestimable purpose was really to discover how much true poetry (imagination) there could be in the best didactic and satiric works of a writer he genuinely admired. And in the difficult task of assessing achievement of the recent past, he succeeds pretty well: Pope comes out "next to Milton and just above Dryden."[36] Johnson is supposed to have put Warton down decisively when he wrote: "To circumscribe poetry by a definition will only show the narrowness of the definer, though a definition which shall exclude Pope will not easily be made."[37] All the same, the slide in Pope's reputation continued. Besides, Johnson's own estimation of didactic writing seems very little higher than Warton's: "In a didactic poem novelty is to be expected only in the ornaments and illustrations." He admires the ornaments in the *Essay on Man,* but thinks metaphysical morality a subject matter "perhaps not very proper for poetry." As for the essay, he rates it lower than an essayist might be expected to—"an irregular indigested piece; not a regular and orderly composition."[38] This, after the publication of Hume's *Essays.*

The influential Hugh Blair took a similarly restrictive view of didactic writing in his *Lectures* (not published until 1783). Addison, he finds, offers numerous examples of "the highest, most correct, and ornamented degree of the simple manner." Nevertheless, although "the most perfect example in English," he lacks "strength and precision, which renders his manner, though perfectly suited to such essays as he writes in the Spectator, not altogether a proper model for any of the higher and more elaborate kinds of composition."[39] Didactic epistles, similarly, "seldom admit of much elevation." And didactic poetry in general, being unsupported by "high beauties of description and poetical language," has to please by spirited conciseness and sprightly wit, which "the higher species of poetry" seldom admit. Here heights of style and of value are very closely associated. Thus, Blair judges that "in the enthusiasm, the fire, the force and copiousness of poetic genius, Dryden, though a much less correct writer [than Pope], appears to have been superior to him."[40] Pope was less distinguished in "the more sublime parts of poetry."

The new value that Blair accorded to description will have been noticed. By the time of his 1815 *Preface,* Wordsworth was listing six modes "in the following order": narrative, dramatic, lyrical, idyllium, didactic, philosophical satire. The scheme reflects discernment of emerging forms. Whereas formal georgics fall in the didactic category, descriptive poetry has won a broad new genre, idyllium "descriptive chiefly either of the processes and appearances of external nature, as the Seasons of Thomson; or of characters, manners, and sentiments." Moreover, the "impassioned epistle" is now considered "a species of monodrama," as if in anticipation of the development of the dramatic lyric.

The many and complex transformations of genre in the nineteenth century do not lend themselves to brief treatment. Some large movements stand out, however, even for that period. Wordsworth included in his narrative mode "that dear production of our days, the metrical Novel," alluding perhaps to Crabbe or to Scott.[41] But he can hardly have foreseen how far novelistic forms would penetrate literature and criticism in the century to follow. During that period, of which we are now becoming historically conscious, the novel in its various kinds came to dominate the interests of critics and the expectations of readers. The novelistic mode worked its way, in fact, to the top of the generic hierarchy. It would be hard to construct a paradigm of genres for a literature so profusely inventive. But that is not because of uncertainty as to which modes were in the ascendant. Already the criteria of the naturalistic novel were generalized in value judgments. This is what gets Ruskin into difficulty with Dickens: he thought him admirable, yet "as a caricaturist . . . he put himself out of the pale of great authors."[42] But of the growing status of almost all the novelistic genres, no demonstration is needed here. Henry James could unpreposterously aver that "the Novel remains still, under the right persuasion, the most independent, most elastic, most prodigious of literary forms." And by 1975 Frank Kermode was able to treat novels as classics together with, if not quite in the same sense with, Virgil's *Aeneid*.[43]

Within the novel itself there are different strata. For example, a relatively firm distinction obtains between verisimilar novels on the one side and thrillers, westerns, and fantasy on the other. This may not be openly acknowledged as a hierarchical distinction. Nevertheless, many libraries and bookshops segregate the serious and unserious genres quite strictly. Science fiction was until recently sold together with pornography.

Available Genres

Generic change ramifies extensively in a way that holds deep implications for judicial criticism. It is not only a question of league tables within individual genres—of mere fluctuations in that "imaginary stock exchange" proscribed by Northrop Frye as a serious subject.[44] We have also to envisage movements on a larger scale, bringing changes in the interrelation of whole genres and in literature's distribution between them. These are changes that even an innovative paradigm such as Wordsworth's can do no more than hint at. In particular, we have to allow for the fact that the complete range of genres is never equally, let alone fully, available in any one period. Each age has a fairly small repertoire of genres that its readers and critics can respond to with enthusiasm. And the repertoire easily available to its writers is smaller still: the temporary canon is fixed for all but the greatest or strongest or most arcane writers. Each age makes new deletions from the repertoire. In a weak sense, all genres perhaps exist in all ages, shadowly embodied in bizarre and freak-ish exceptions. (A history of the future, the anonymous *Reign of George VI,* was published as early as 1790.) But the repertoire of active genres has always been small and subject to proportionately significant deletions and additions. In the early eighteenth century, for example, novel and georgic rose in the hierarchy and were extended, while epic was deleted. These crude generalizations no doubt need to be refined. One might wish to qualify the last of them by allowing for heroic transformations such as mock epic; for translations; for criticism of earlier epics; for Os-sian (which, however, has significantly to be given an imaginary genesis in the past); and perhaps for Johnson's unswerving glimpse of quality in Blackmore. But the observation stands, and could be taken with others like it to imply a system of genres such that any deletion has repercus-sions on neighboring genres. When epic declined (the argument might run) its functions passed to the georgic and novelistic genres, which cor-respondingly rose in status and grew in scope to occupy some of its fic-tive space. For example, the epic hero was succeeded by the hero of prose fiction or biography. And in our own age, in much the same way, a de-cline of the verisimilar novel might be seen as compensated for by a rise of biography (often semifictional biography), which supplies some of the demand for "solid" characters, left unsatisfied by fabulations and *poiou-mena.* A similar compensation might be argued for in the case of the now almost extinct familiar essay. Surely it is no coincidence that simultan-eously the critical essay has proliferated?[45] Some critics have been tempted to think of the generic system almost on a hydrostatic model— as if its total substance remained constant but subject to redistribution.

But there is no firm basis for such speculation. We do better to treat the movements of genres simply in terms of aesthetic choice. In this way, deletion of epic will be seen as having posed a problem for the adventur-ous writer. He would turn, perhaps, to the next highest genre, which in the case of poetry was likely to mean georgic. (In Virgilian georgic, in-deed, elevated heroic passages played a great part.) Later, description might be his best recourse. Or the serious writer could take up the rele-vant history with a great national action, the moral novel, or other prose forms whose summits were no longer overtopped by epic.[46] Montaigne, the "bold ignorant," explored the new subject of individual identity in an extracanonical genre of low or indeterminate status; but Carlyle, pursuing in *Sartor* a similar subject, was able to aim his essaylike papers at a far more sublime pitch, from the platforms of modal vehicles—treatise, biography, and epic (the great work; the *nekuia*).

Reputations

The generic repertoire influences the critical canon decisively, through its limitations and its order of values. The case of Scott *vis-à-vis* Austen is instructive—the anomaly that Scott enjoyed an international reputation while Austen remained virtually unknown. This can only in part be explained by *Waverley*'s appearing in 1814, when Scott was an established man of letters. It has also to be put down to the ease with which Scott's work was related to existing genres, especially the regional novel already made valuable by the work of Maria Edgeworth. Edgeworth's novels, which also enjoyed Continental fame, were frequently treated as the literary context of Scott's first romances. Scott himself was more anxious to draw attention to *Waverley*'s individual combination of romance and history. He multiplies allusions to heroic romance predecessors; introduces romantic poems and songs as quotations or as intrafictional events; follows what he calls an "ambagitory" narrative method; and continually emphasizes the romantic character of landscapes ("this narrow glen . . . seemed to open into the land of romance"). And almost as often he refers to "my history"; distinguishes between frivolous romance and the true romance of history; or recalls the historical perspective of "sixty years since." But in spite of all this, the possibly disingenuous postscript to *Waverley* acknowledges the precedent of Edgeworth's Irish tales in the most deferential terms; and it was in the context of the regional novel that Croker and others assessed Scott's new efforts. Hers was the norm: as her biographer puts it, "critics begin informally to draw up their rules during the period that Maria Edgeworth is writing, often directly stimulated by her tales."[47] This comparison favored Scott's loosely articulated fictions. He could offer just as abundant details of daily life, characters equally plausible as members of a real-life society, episodes no less coherent than hers. Austen's superiority in construction was less obvious. And inevitably her novels were associated with the domestic, feminine, "lower" elements in Edgeworth's *oeuvre*.

When a genre drops out of the repertoire, reputations may be severely affected. Take the case of brief epic, which is now not only inactive (like classical epic) but also unrepresented by critically available exemplars, at least in the vernacular. Except, that is, for *Paradise Regained.* Reception of this sole survivor is consequently embarrassed and uncertain. Our difficulty is not ignorance as to whether *Paradise Regained* surpasses other specimens of its kind. (Critics might be prepared to concede that—to grant that the others are poor specimens.) Rather is it a difficulty in appreciating where Milton's special efforts come. Is one of them the experimental development of an epic *stylus humilis?* When the poem appeared, opinion as to its success was (to Milton's impatience) divided. Edward Phillips relates that it was "generally censured [that is, judged by the generality] to be inferior to the other [*scilicet Paradise Lost*]", but that "it is thought by the most judicious to be little or nothing inferior to the other for style and decorum."[48] Significantly, it is on the style of *Paradise Regained* that the strongest recent attack has nevertheless fastened. A defense might be attempted against Wallace Robson's charge of stylistic colorlessness. Something could be made, for instance, of Milton's astonishing accumulation of alternatives, a feature condemned by Broadbent as failure in sensuous realization, but arguably miming the act of choice so as to draw the reader closer to Christ's predicament. But any such line of defense would have to count on much common ground of familiarity with the brief epic form. And this is no longer widely shared. Wilkes had to write an article to establish one of the genre's rudimentary conventions (the use of set positions). And Lewalski wrote a book merely to show that the genre itself existed.[49] It should surprise no one if *Paradise Regained* has the lowest reputation in the Milton canon.

Robert Herrick's reputation has suffered differently, from alteration rather than deletion of genres. When *Hesperides* appeared in 1648 it was probably well received. But subsequently the satiric mode displaced the epigrammatic and the lyric, and Herrick received less attention. He was anthologized, but only anonymously; so that he remained almost unknown to the eighteenth century. This break in tradition hardly fostered a true appreciation of *Hesperides.* When it was rediscovered in the century that followed, some of the epigram subgenres it used—especially the *foetidas* and *fel*—had become so obsolete as to be unintelligible and repugnant. Consequently Victorian readers overlooked the complex variety and balance whereby its different epigram types offset one another. Their overwhelming preference for *mel* epigrams led them to concentrate on a single element in the work. It was almost exclusively the flower poems and sweet love epigrams that they anthologized. On this foundation a towering reputation was raised: Swinburne called Herrick "the greatest song-writer . . . ever born of English race." As a lyricist, indeed ("the very note of lyric poetry"), he could put him above Jonson. But a claim so partially secured could not be sustained for long. T. S. Eliot seemed to be restoring sanity, almost, in "What is Minor Poetry?" when he preferred the Metaphysical Herbert, but made an interesting and apparently balanced plea for Herrick as a minor classic, worth reading *in extenso* for a "something" that is "more in the whole than in the parts." Nevertheless, Eliot could not or would not see a unity in *Hesperides:* he missed "a continuous conscious *purpose* about Herrick's poems." My point is not at the moment to fault his judgment, but to draw attention to the pressure of altered genres, which worked to limit Eliot's view of the range and stature of the heroic epigrammatist.

In distinguishing major and minor classics, Eliot insists that the same genres might offer examples of both—as indeed is the case (or so he argues) with Herbert and Herrick. But the view that genres are inherently major or minor has been more widely accepted, if not openly acknowledged. Dame Helen Gardner brings out stipulations about the difference between a major poet and one who is merely very good, in such a way as to make this view clear. She states implications about genre that are usually left comfortably latent: "The major poet's work must have bulk; he must attempt with success one or other of the greater poetic forms, which tests his gifts of invention and variation; he cannot claim the title on a handful of lyrics however exquisite."[50] This proposition would be hard to disagree with; yet it entails a hierarchy of genres, with lyrics low and "greater poetic forms" high. At the same time, the hierarchy is so far from being a rigid one as to leave many matters of rank unsettled. We are left to decide how large a handful of lyrics might bring majority (Herrick's 1,400?), whether lyric forms might combine to make major aggregate work (Martial's *Epigrams?* Lowell's *Notebook?*), whether "lyric" itself might not mean very different things in different periods, whether in fact a great poet need be a major poet.

Canons and Great Traditions

The considerations looked at in the previous section lead one to infer that generic changes help to shape canons of taste and hence of availability.[51] This can be brought out by comparing the Renaissance poetic canons of various critics and anthologists. Johnson's seventeenth-century lives were of Cowley, Denham, Milton, Butler, Rochester, Roscommon, Otway, Waller, Pomfret, Dorset, Stepney, John Philips, Walsh, and Dryden. His inclusion of Philips can readily be related to the recent promotion of georgic. And if that of Roscommon is at first surprising, we soon recall that Pope "celebrated him the only moral writer of King Charles' reign."[52] As for deletions, the fact that the Augustans had restricted the epigrammatic mode and rejected concettism accounts for the absence of some expected names.

Later changes in the canon may be exemplified from influential anthologies. Perhaps none has been more influential than Francis Turner Palgrave's *Golden Treasury*.[53] So many generations of young readers formed their ideas of poetry from this remarkable work that for long it counted as a literary institution. Its generic bias can be guessed at from the title: *The Golden Treasury of the Best Songs and Lyrical Poems in the English Language*. Omitting singletons and doubletons except where a very long text is chosen, the 1861 canon is Drummond (7), Dryden (2), Herrick (7), Jonson (3), Lovelace (3), Marvell (3), Milton (11), Shakespeare (32), Spenser (1). The second edition of 1891 adds Campion (10), Sidney (5), and Vaughan (3), while increasing the representation of Herrick (8), Marvell (5), and Shakespeare (34). Quiller-Couch's *Oxford Book of English Verse* (1915) is on a scale three times larger, but goes further back and forward, adds many minor singletons, and attempts interesting learned promotions such as William Browne (7) and Cartwright (4). Allowing for these differences of coverage, the chief changes are reduction in Campion (8) and increases in Carew (6), Donne (8), Dryden (5), Dunbar (4), Herbert (6), Herrick (no less than 29), Raleigh (5), Jonson (11), Surrey (3), King (3), Spenser (7). In John Hayward's conservative and popular *Penguin Book of English Verse*,[54] the alterations of Quiller-Couch's canon are surprisingly few. Proportionately, there are cuts only in Carew (2), Cowley (1), Milton (6), Sidney (3), and Spenser (3), with Dunbar and Greene disappearing altogether.

From the present viewpoint some of these changes are readily intelligible—so far as understanding in terms of genre can go. Particularly when individual items are considered, the selections by no means seem arbitrary expressions of taste, or effects merely of fashion's random movements. We notice, first, the declining value of song after a high point around the turn of the century. Much the same is true of all undramatic or impersonal lyric genres; hence, the rise and fall of Herrick, Cowley, Carew, and Wotton. Exceptionally, Campion's representation keeps up, perhaps because of an apparent imagism. Second, the dramatic lyric is increasingly favored—no surprise, in view of Browning's relation to modernism. So Wyatt's and Donne's representations grow; more of the Sidney items come from *Astrophil and Stella;* and Herbert, as we have seen, assumes major status. A corresponding revaluation of plain and spoken styles shows up both in the 1915 *Oxford Book* and in Hayward (bringing additions to Wyatt, Jonson, Dryden), even if neither goes to Yvor Winters' extreme in that direction. A third change elevates the genre that is significantly called "Metaphysical lyric" (additions to Donne, Herbert, Traherne, Vaughan). Finally, Cambridge critics and New Critics agree to prefer short forms: Milton, at some sort of apogee in 1915, is "dislodged"; Cartwright and Browne of Tavistock are ignored again; and Drayton and Fanshawe and Cowley are cut.

In Dame Helen Gardner's *New Oxford Book of English Verse 1250–1950* (1972), which allows of direct comparison with Quiller-Couch's *Oxford Book,* these tendencies continue, some of them very noticeably. Thus, Herrick's representation is halved, from 29 to 13; and Carew, Cowley, and Milton are all reduced. Campion is slightly increased; Jonson considerably so. And Donne, Herbert, and Vaughan all double their representation, at least, to reach what is surely the high point of the Metaphysical poem or epigrammatical elegy.[55]

The same movements naturally find reflection in the canons of formal criticism. They can be traced in the journals, in Ford Madox Ford's nevertheless splendidly individual *March of Literature* (1938), in the almost institutionalized symposium of Boris Ford's Pelican *Guide* (1954–1956), and in the relevant volume of the Sphere *History* (1970). In the *Guide,* essays on or dominated by a single writer presuppose a strikingly Metaphysical canon: Donne, Herbert, Marvell, and (clearly under the same colors) Cowley. The Sphere *History* carries the tendency further, compressing Jonson and the Cavalier lyricists into a single chapter. After thirty years the Sphere critics are still pretty well in step with Ford Madox Ford, for whom Donne was "supremely great" but Herrick "mere Herrick." But the latter now gets seven pages, while Surrey and Sidney also reappear. Moreover, the long forms begin to attract interest again: Spenser revives in his transatlantic Adonis-garden; Milton is undislodged; room is found for a chapter on the epyllion; and Drayton actually gets a few scattered mentions.

The canons of prose fiction operate more severely, not being so much qualified and moderated by anthology publication and oral performance.

In the prose canon, too, genre has a profound influence. But it is a less conscious one, since many prose genres are unlabeled. Saintsbury's *Short History of English Literature* (1898) lumps together verisimilar novels and historical, gothic, and other romances. All are "novels." Reade and Peacock are admitted to the category without question; and Stevenson is the last "great novelist" of the nineteenth century. In subsequent criticism, however, the canon of literary fiction has become restricted, effectually, to one genre: the naturalistic novel. This restriction, rather than any deficiency in Stevenson's work, accounts for his being scarcely mentioned in Ford's *Guide* and excluded altogether from the earlier editions of Lionel Stevenson's *Victorian Fiction: A Guide to Research* (1964). For similar reasons, Stevenson and Peacock receive only the briefest of notices in the Sphere *History,* and de la Mare none at all. Behind these pedagogical works lies original criticism, such as that of F. R. Leavis. His influential great tradition—Austen, Eliot, James, Conrad—has been objected to as particularly restrictive in the case of Dickens, whose one consistently serious work, according to the early Leavis, was *Hard Times.* But on its own terms this view was almost justified. Leavis was one of the few to apply the generic canon of his time with consciously sustained awareness. And even now there is little understanding that *The Great Tradition* sets up consistent limits of genre. Sterne's work-in-progress form, Scott's historical romance, Dickens' allegorical romance: all are demoted. It is a logical corollary of the apotheosis of the verisimilar novel.

Is our own generation, being more instructed in theory, free from such genre prejudice? It would be pleasant to think so. But the short story returns with us to favor, and so does romance (*Wuthering Heights,* scarcely mentioned by Saintsbury, is for Kermode a classic; the reputation of Meredith's elegiac romance rises). Another great tradition, that of Dickens and Joyce, has replaced the old. And beside this more recent canon—which includes Hawthorne, Melville, James, and Conrad (in new aspects), as well as Woolf and Beckett—we already glimpse further "alternative traditions" based on emergent or previously uncanonical genres: the dystopic fantasy (Pynchon, Vonnegut), the fabulation (Barth, Barthelme), the *poioumenon* (*The Golden Notebook*), the historical novel of ideas (*The French Lieutenant's Woman; G*). With older literature it is the same. Our most vigilant revaluations, even those that seem most inspired by moral rather than formal values, may turn out to spring from buried generic pressures. Perhaps individual revaluations only succeed when they are in accordance with laws of genre. One such law might be that of compensation, as in the alternating preference for long and short forms.[56] *Aurora Leigh* is currently being rediscovered not just because it is a good poem, or a good poem by a woman, but because it is a good *long* poem.

13. Systems of Genres

The hierarchic paradigm is only one of many systems of genres. Most have been constructed with the aim of arriving at a taxonomy of literature—as if literary genres were fixed classes that could be ordered permanently. Fallacious though they are, however, some of these systems should be looked at: they may embody useful principles. The insight of the Russian formalist Jurij Tynjanov remains true, that genres cannot be studied in isolation from an order of genres. It is only in the context of changing generic paradigms that a single genre's function can be grasped.

Organic Universals

Many of the systems depend on a formal distinction, said to be fundamental and universal, among three ways of representation. They are called—confusingly enough—lyric, dramatic, and narrative. These representational modes go back to Plato's division of literary discourse into authorial, figural, and mixed, according to whether the feigned speaker is poet, character, or both.[1] As developed by Aristotle, this division according to speaker underlies much ancient, Renaissance, and neoclassical theory.[2] It is still made, in effect, by Frye, although he divides the first "radical of representation" by introducing a less fundamental distinction between oral "epos" and written "fiction." Distinguishing written and oral literature as he does leads to interesting ideas. However, it remains true that the very same work may be read silently or performed. Frye's new radicals cannot be validated without emphasizing relatively subsidiary aspects of narrative—and without ignoring extensive tracts of early modern literature meant to be read aloud. Moreover, the radicals are loaded with a greater weight of generic content than as purely neutral elemental aspects they seem able to carry.[3]

The modern distribution of genres between the divisions lyric, dramatic, and narrative—a separate idea—has been attributed to Francisco Cascales (1617). But the dubious distinction probably goes back at least to Minturno.[4] Subsequently the "organic modes" acquired pseudo-generic characteristics. And then they progressively swallowed up the other genres, until it was only these large universals that were written on by genre theorists such as Staiger and Meyer.[5] The result was a bad one for literary theory. The confusion and vagueness inherent in "ideas" of "the Narrative" or "the Dramatic" or (worst of all) "the Lyric" were aggravated both by German hypostatization and British muddling.[6] And a tendency to speak of the representative modes as having contents and values—even in some cases as "seeing" the universe—affected Bovet, Guérard, Langer, Käte Hamburger, perhaps even Ingarden and Frye. This is by no means to say that such theorizing about generic world-views is totally empty: after all, we must suppose that genres offer distinctive possibilities of vision, and distinctive limitations. The line of thought led to some of the Romantic period's most interesting insights about the variety of aesthetic psychology. One thinks of Schiller's *Uber naive und sentimentalische Dichtung,* or Victor Hugo's three ages of mankind (primitive-lyric, ancient-epic, modern-dramatic). Such ideas are by no means so flimsy as bald summary tends to make them appear. In a work like Susanne Langer's *Feeling and Form,* intuitive speculations of great sensitivity are to be found. Yet the subjectivity of this branch of criticism is so extreme that even at its best it hardly provides a sound basis for theory to build on. And only the stringency of a Wellek could measure the full (or empty) vacuousness to which this "insoluble psychological cul-de-sac" has led, at its worst.[7] It issued in triads of the sort chronicled, perhaps rather too indulgently, by Guillén.[8] These ineffabilities were impenetrable enough to justify Croce's explosion, and had much to do with the end of classical genre theory. They all stem from a single misconception of the category of the representational "modes"—a misconception that finds classic authorization, rightly or wrongly, in Goethe. For the three radicals are elemental, not generic; building blocks, not archetypes.

Representational mode, in fact, is only one of many elements in a work or a genre. Moreover, it is usual for several representational modes to combine or alternate or mix within a single work. This obviously applies to eclogues (as Diomedes early recognized); to epistolary and therefore quasi-dramatic novels (as Goethe observed); to novels with passages in purely dramatic form; to choral *parabases* in Greek tragedy; to French tragedies with narrative exposition, dramatic action, and lyrical conclusion; and so forth.[9] Less obviously, there are elusive modes, such as contribute to "unreliable narration" and mixtures of the authorial and figural modes, as in indirect discourse, suppressed direct speech, or interior monologue.[10] (Think of the collaboration of Boots with the narrator in Dickens' *The Holly-Tree:* "Boots could assure me that it was better than a picter, and equal to a play, to see them babies.") And how is one to assign the speakers in novels by James or Faulkner or Bellow? It is sometimes said that the elusive narrative methods exploited by the novel have made the old categories inadequate. But this is not true if Plato's "mixed mode" is interpreted subtly enough. All the elusive effects merely realize new possibilities within the representational mode of narrative. The old categories remain indispensable as part of an *analytic* method. But as Viëtor already recognized, the universal representative modes have to be distinguished quite sharply from genres.[11] Use of a particular representational mode may imply certain entailments (the author as speaker, for example, tends to be freer with temporal sequence than a dramatic character would be). But these are not implications of a generic nature. Genres are types of whole works, whereas the universals never refer to more than one part of the repertoire. As Hernadi comments, the representational modes are "best applied in the study of what may be called the 'molecular structure' of discourse."

The universals' limitations from a taxonomic point of view are painfully clear. Their mixture is the rule rather than the exception, and in any case they describe only one aspect of representation. Moreover, the seductive simplicity of the triad encourages speculation toward a closed synthesis. Attempts have even been made, notably by Hirt, to derive one of the universals (diegesis, mimesis, mixture) from the others, in the hope of discovering a logical or chronological evolution from elements more fundamental still.[12] Such speculations are interesting, but too remote from the experience of literature to have much use in ordering the genres. In any case, they rely heavily on the concept of mimesis, which seems less fundamental now that literature's dependence on earlier literary material and conventions is better appreciated. We no longer think of it as in any direct way an imitation of life.

Analysis according to speaker dominated the ancient approach to the universals. But the frequent difficulty of determining the speaker (or point of view) in modern fiction has led theorists to alternative bases of analysis. Susanne Langer's brilliant Kantian speculations may be regarded as transitional; subsequent theory has built on the linguistic substrate in a more systematic, less metaphysical manner. The talk is of "discourse types," which are thought to be a matter of ordinary experience, or at least of ordinary linguistic analysis. Is not the difference between description and narration in a story fundamental?—as every schoolboy shows he knows, by the way he skips. In reality, analysis by discourse types shifts the basis altogether, to language function. But it appears to do no more than extend the representational modes by addition. Perhaps Aristotle never meant his scheme to be exhaustive, but only discussed three modes out of a larger number? In any event, Guillén is clear that the development of forms such as the essay has made a fourth universal necessary.[13] Scholes and Klaus agree, calling this fourth mode Essay, or thematic literature. Ernst Elster (1903), however, proposed five elements: narrative, dramatic, lyric, descriptive, meditative.[14] And many similar schemes have been developed, or in principle could be, on the basis of the various divisions of language function (such as Bühler's "representational," "expressive," and "conative").[15] Thus, there is literature of persuasion (conative), expression, description (topographic poetry; descriptive sketch) and exposition (Renaissance "anatomy"; philosophical essay). And an impersonal gnomic or epigraphic functional mode might be discerned in proverbs, *imprese,* and certain concrete poems.

But analysis of genre on the basis of language function will not do, either. Other aspects may be no less decisive—not only substantive aspects, but also formal ones not describable in terms of function. In some good verisimilar novels words may have no interest in themselves, but only as communicating information that sets out the story. That is to say, the language works in a "transparent" manner, signifying constituents on a different (narrative) level where the literary form is to be found. In such a genre alternative linguistic realizations might be substituted without difference to the work. Indeed, all narrative art is to some extent independent of linguistic considerations, and therefore not fully accessible via nineteenth-century concepts of autotelic language. In drama, again, words may be subsidiary, unintelligible, even absent altogether. It is of interest in this connection that Susanne Langer denies drama to be literature at all, treating it together with film as a separate *poesis,* independent of language.[16]

The Chicago critics, on the other hand, reacted to overemphasis on the language element in literature, to the extent of basing their approach on a rhetoric of motive. Hence, the distinction between mimetic and didactic motives became for them a fundamental one. But again the single criterion becomes in the end monistic and unconvincing. The contrast between speech as *lexis* and as *praxis,* for example, proves elusive in descriptive criticism, and utterly useless as a means of distinguishing genres.[17] We can see what Olson means when he calls the *Divina Commedia* didactic: the term describes its purpose. But we cannot agree that its representative mode is didactic, rather than narrative and mimetic. The Chicago critics' rhetorical monism, combined with their classifying approach, has proved infertile.

In short, the right application of the idea of elemental representative modes is in descriptive analysis. There, indeed, the modes are indispensable. In classifying the genres, however, the frequency of mixtures and of intermediate instances makes them much less useful. Growing awareness of this has led to many revisions of the Aristotelian system, which have moved the basis of analysis from speaker to language function, purpose, or some other single criterion. But still the genres seem to resist subdivision into any one set of "universals." Even what Austin Warren calls the "ultimates"—poetry, fiction, and drama—cannot reach this taxonomic goal. From Diomedes onward, every attempt to distribute the genres into such categories has run into insuperable difficulties.[18] The problem is not a modern one, to be solved by a modern scheme improving marginally on its predecessors (or merely standing them on their heads). It is not just that, say, "intermediate genres—such as the verse novel, the lyrical novel, the *poème en prose*"[19]—have recently developed. There have always been genres, like Menippean satire, that obviously eluded classification. And this helps us to see that all literature eludes classification, even by the categories most useful in its analysis.

Maps of Genres

Taxonomic arrangement of the genres has persisted, nevertheless—not only on the basis of the universals, but also on other lines. In particular, systems in the form of generic maps have been constructed. Some of these have historical interest, or even suggest principles by which genres might be at least partially ordered.

Several ancient and medieval systems have metrical differences as their main basis, although this may not always be obvious. Matthew of Vendome's *Ars Versificatoria* is a good example. The vision of four generic beings figured as waiting women (*pedissequas*) accompanying Philosophy seems quite mysterious. But in context the four genres—Tragedy, Satire, Comedy, Elegy—turn out to be largely metrical types, elegy, for example, being characterized by *inaequalitate pedum*. Other generic features, including topical ones, are also suggested, but only the metrical explanation accounts for the otherwise puzzling choice of these as the four "quae in metricis modulationibus dominantur."[20] Apparently Matthew is not offering a select paradigm, but something more like a sketch map of the whole literary field. It is also possible, however, that this obscure passage may anticipate certain Renaissance schemes that will modify the *rota Vergiliana* by ousting georgic. In that case, Tragedy–Comedy–Satire is already an alternative to Epic–Georgic–Pastoral, with the problematic lyric genres accommodated under Elegy.[21]

The *rota Vergiliana* or Wheel of Virgil itself, a scheme attributed to John of Garland, was one of the earliest maps, and its influence continued to be felt in the eighteenth century (see figure).

THE WHEEL OF VIRGIL
From Edmond Faral *Les Arts poétiques du 12ᵉ et du 13ᵉ siècle*
(Paris 1962) 87.

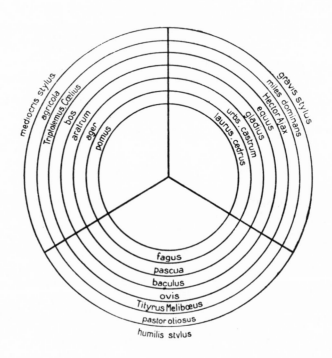

This memory diagram lists corresponding features of three modes: heroic, georgic, and pastoral. But it does so in such a way as to claim a comprehensive inclusion, or at least ordonnance, of the whole of literature—not to say its social and natural matrix. As has often been pointed out, the *rota* develops the Ciceronian system of three style heights, which indeed it refers to.[22] That system no longer inspires much enthusiasm now, after centuries of stylistic mixture—to say nothing of the virtual disappearance of one of the styles. It was once fertile and effective, however, and universally taken for granted. And it assisted the creation of much of our literature in ways that are only beginning to be appreciated. There was far more to the system of style heights, certainly, than any brief schematic statement such as that in the *Rhetorica ad Herennium* could possibly convey. Nevertheless, considered as a map, the *rota* itself must be condemned as misleading and confusing. It implies a quite false contiguity between heroic and pastoral. In fact, to make any sense at all it should be redrawn, as John of Garland himself redraws it, in columns. It is in effect a system based on a single axis or dimension: style height. Over the centuries this feature came to occupy a vital place in many genuine systems, so that such thinking about genre has tended to be influenced by social context.

The ambitious system of Thomas Hobbes obviously takes its starting point from the *rota,* although his "three Regions of mankind" are "Court, City and Country." These he correlates with three "sorts" or modes: heroic, "scommatic" (derisive), and pastoral. But then he combines the division by height with "manners of representation," narrative and dramatic. The resulting two-dimensional system is taken to yield "neither more nor less than six sorts of Poesy": "For the Heroic Poem narrative, such as is yours, is called an *Epic Poem.* The Heroic Poem Dramatic is *Tragedy.* The Scommatic Narrative is *Satire,* Dramatic is *Comedy.* The Pastoral Narrative is called simply *Pastoral,* anciently *Bucolic;* the same Dramatic, *Pastoral Comedy.*"[23] It is a remarkable anticipation of analytic genre theory, and has not received the attention it deserves. The modern approach is supposed to begin with Goethe, who related the genres to three *Naturformen* corresponding roughly to the representative modes epic, lyric, and drama. He allowed for mixture of these. But unfortunately he regarded them as more than elements. And by arranging the genres in a circle, he set the pattern for many subsequent spatial arrangements of a similarly vicious kind.[24]

Many recent systems of genres take their immediate point of departure from Frye's *Anatomy of Criticism*—intelligibly, in view of its underlying return (*pour mieux sauter*) to earlier tradition. Frye's various systems revive a medieval manner of arbitrary creative schematism. For example, he proposes a pattern of four broad *mythoi* or narrative categories ("romantic," "tragic," "comic," and "ironic" or satiric) with logical priority to the "ordinary" genres. The *mythoi* are based on myths of the natural cycle, so that he arranges them in a circle, like divisions of the day or the year. This scheme has been faulted for inconsistency: romance corresponds to spring in the 1951 version, summer in that of 1957, and the second half of the cycle in that of 1965.[25] But revision is perfectly in order. A more principled objection might be made to the scheme's incompleteness. If such "pregeneric" categories existed, they would surely be more numerous. Frye's can all be arranged (in another implied diagram) on the one vertical axis "innocence-experience." Thus, romance remains at the ideal end and satire at the realistic, while tragedy moves in one direction ("down") and comedy in the other. A good deal of literature, both heroic and verisimilar, could not usefully be distributed on such an axis.

More influential is Frye's series of five mimetic or "fictional modes": myth, romance, high mimetic, low mimetic, irony. (Here "romance" and "irony" bear still further meanings: each of Frye's schemes uses terms in senses proper to itself.) This series is based on the "hero's power to act" in relation to human society and the environment. In myth, for example, the divine hero is superior not only in degree but in kind, both to society and to nature:

1. myth (hero superior in kind to both)
2. romance (superior in degree to both)
3. high mimesis (superior in degree to society)
4. low mimesis (not superior)
5. irony (inferior).

Scholes criticizes this scheme for irregularity. It omits certain combinations of society and environment, in particular the "middle mimesis" that would correspond to naturalism. But Frye is more concerned here with historical insights than with pure theory. And what concerns us is whether any such scheme at all could in principle be used to map the fictional genres—so that, for example, "legend, folk-tale, *Märchen*, and their literary affiliates and derivatives"[26] would belong to the category "romance." We should remember that Frye drew up the scheme to clarify a historical thesis: that "European fiction, during the last fifteen centuries, has steadily moved its centre of gravity down the list."[27] As an observation about myth displacement and demythologizing, the thesis expresses a valuable insight. But as a scheme it posits fixed categories whose existence remains problematical. For one thing, the displacement of myth has altered all the other categories too (the measure of "superiority" itself is different, in pagan and in Christian societies). For another, the genres to be distributed have themselves changed, so that whereas medieval romance may belong to the eponymous fictional mode, Victorian romance by no means does. Frye's theory, although it appears dynamic, really presupposes a fixed, synchronic system as the stage on which its drama of displacement is enacted.[28] It is in that drama, with its exciting illuminations, that our interest really lies—not in the static scheme. Frye is historical in spite of his theory.

The constraining fixity of the scheme becomes obvious in connection with Frye's second thesis about the displacement of myth. He asks us to think of the fictional modes as *"mythoi* or plot-formulas progressively moving over towards the opposite pole of verisimilitude, and then, with irony, beginning to move back."[29] Scholes and Fletcher are almost certainly right in thinking that this and similar passages in *Anatomy* imply a cyclic progression. Here Frye's theory needs all the subtilizing that Angus Fletcher can give it, in such terms as "imaginative periodicity."[30] For the modern period obstinately seems far less the age of irony than does the period of Swift and Pope and Gay and Voltaire. And even if such discrepancies could be ironed out, there would remain a question whether the "lowest" category has any contiguity or continuity with the highest.

Frye's successors have mostly jettisoned his myth criticism, concentrating on the (less interesting) categorial element in his works. The improvement of his theory of fictional modes by Robert Scholes attempts something altogether simpler and more logical than *Anatomy*. Scholes' theory suffers from similar drawbacks, however, without offering so many compensating insights. Scholes abandons almost all of Frye's diachronic thesis, which he regards as of no taxonomic value. He substitutes a purely analytic spectrum of possibilities, according to whether the fictional world is "better than the world of experience, worse than it, or equal to it." In its simplest form we have:

satire | history | romance,

where "history" includes all presentation of actual events and real people (biography; autobiography), besides the fictional counterpart of this, presumably in neutrally verisimilar fiction.[31] When Scholes develops this triad, introducing intermediate instances and finer distinctions—in particular, between types of novel—he significantly feels a need to curve the space of the map. So it betrays its lack of an adequate number of dimensions (see figure).

MAP OF MODES

From Robert Scholes *Structuralism in Literature*
(New Haven and London 1974) 137.

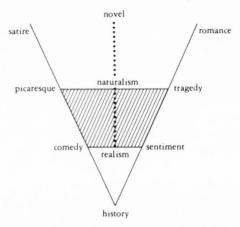

The novel occupies the angle, and "has tended to draw from both sides of the spectrum."[32] Particular objections come to mind. Surely it would be more in accordance with literary history to have picaresque facing romance, and comedy facing tragedy, thus representing contrasts that form the actual basis of a large number of mixed and hybrid works (Cervantes, Le Sage, Jacobean tragicomedy). But again we are more concerned with the underlying principles. The fundamental objection is to unhistorical hypostases so easily marshaled as to be remote from literature. They seem to exist solely in the interests of comprehensive symmetry; if they have no connections with each other, these must be created mythologically: "Sentiment is the darkest and most ordinary of the high worlds. It looks towards the chaos of satire, and it may see virtue perish without the grace of tragic ripeness."[33] What this seems to mean is that the cartographer is in difficulties: "Here be personified hypostases."

Benefiting from these and many other theories, Paul Hernadi's *Beyond Genre* offers a procedural survey of about sixty genre systems. Unfortunately his conception of historical genres is limited by the chimera of defining classification, and his modes are loosened (as it were, by reaction) into generality and vagueness.[34] Nevertheless, he contributes an ingenious system based on the axes thematic–dramatic and private–dual. These axes order four "congruent rhombs," areas of uncertain continuity designated lyric, dramatic, narrative, and "thematic." In each of the rhombs the same axes are supposed to be quadruply replicated (see figure).[35] The doubtfulness of the relation between the rhombs shows up as soon as we consider their convergences. At the center of the chart, for

MAP OF MODES
From Paul Hernadi *Beyond Genre*
(Ithaca and London 1972) 166.

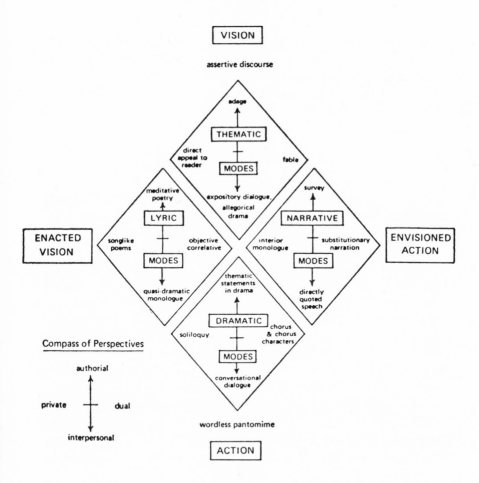

example, the "thematic modes" tend at their least authorial toward dialogue, whether expository (symposium) or allegorical (morality play). Meanwhile the "dramatic modes" tend from the other side—supposedly in convergence—toward "thematic statements in drama." But these tendencies are not toward the same form. Explicit thematic asides in naturalistic drama, say, are quite different from the implicit *significationes* of good allegorical drama. It would be more plausible to compare them with adage—the form indeed that such a thematic statement might well in practice assume. But adage is away at the far north of the chart. It seems that other dimensions (abstractness; explicitness) must be taken into account, if the designated forms are to be adequately represented on a chart. And this is only one difficulty of many. Hernadi's diagram takes account of some resemblances but ignores others.

Hernadi clearly senses the need for additional dimensions. For on the vertical axis (authorial-interpersonal) he has in effect superimposed another, quite distinct, which he calls "vision-action." The trouble with this is that action (as in a morality) need not be any less "authorial" than statements expressing vision. Perhaps as a gesture toward meeting that point, "allegorical drama" is oddly placed under the thematic modes, not the dramatic.

Against Maps

Some of the more recent genre maps are so complicated as to prompt questions about what they are meant to achieve. Are they meant as pedagogic aids to the beginner? Do they purport to describe an order that actually exists, in some interpersonal mental space?

It seems not to be generally understood that all that maps of genres can do is to order them roughly, without quantification, in relation to one or more axes, each indicating the presence, in greater or lesser degree, of a single quality or its opposite. In practice there is seldom any conscious attempt to introduce more than two axes. Even the clock diagram used by Graham Hough to develop Frye's ideas about allegory does not quite manage to smuggle a third axis in under the guise of a circumference (see figure).[36]

Each map is limited, therefore, to setting out resemblances purely on the basis of one or two qualities. In a notable understatement, Hernadi says, "We seem to need several systems of coordinates."[37] It is instructive to compare the methodology of pattern recognition, where the dimen-

MAP OF MODES
From Graham Hough *A Preface to "The Faerie Queen"*
(London 1962) 107.

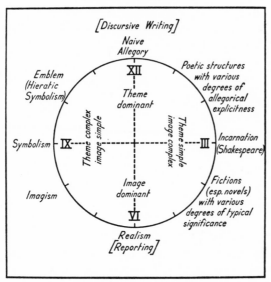

sionality of feature space tends to be a good deal larger—anything from twenty to two hundred dimensions. In fact, almost any salient quality or constituent of literature is a potential dimension. So are external facts such as temporal, geographical, or class distribution, although these have usually been neglected by generic cartographers.[38] Of course, not all axes are equally valuable. Similarities measured by mere numbers of shared predicates are meaningless: the variables have to be weighted. Possible axes include: authorial-interpersonal (as in Hernadi's scheme); private-communal (Hernadi); the "height" of the world imitated (Frye and Scholes); rhetorical height; ecomiastic-vituperative (Averroes); comedy-tragedy (Langer); thematic-nonthematic; psychological polarities, such as subjective-objective or introvert-extravert (as in Frye's scheme of "specific continuous forms");[39] rhetorical and stylistic spectra, such as opacity-transparency or metaphorical and metonymical (as in David Lodge's scheme).[40] As the last example sometimes shows, axial features that are superficial or narrowly distributed may have to have their corresponding terms so much "expanded" that they become unhelpful as ordering principles. Other features have a wide distribution and many implications. Thus, transparency of language is correlated with the use of a prose medium and with certain types (narrative; expository), just as opacity is correlated with lyric. We need to distinguish a similar factor: transparency–opacity of form. With some writing we are not made much aware of form, whether structural or stylistic. Such transparency, which suits works with a stress on instrumental values, correlates in twentieth-century fiction with the naturalistic pole, as against the schematic. The transparent–opaque axis sharply distinguishes the Jamesian novel from the Steinbeckian. And it sets most short stories (even verisimilar ones) apart from novels of the latter extreme. The factor of size may also have many partial correlates, if we may judge from the explorations of Paul Zumthor. Scale, hybridity, transparency–opacity of language—all these dimensions seem implied by that of size. (Short stories, for example, hardly ever display much generic mixture.) Moreover, ordering the genres on this basis leads to many suggestive analogies, such as that between short story and lyric at one extreme, novel and epic at the other.[41] At intermediate magnitudes generic mixture is frequent, both in poetry and prose. Thus, "compounding of narrative types" is commonest in the novella;[42] dramatic hybrids are arguably more frequent than pure kinds; and in poetry equal mixture forms the *raison d'être* of several middle-length genres, such as georgic. The selection of factors, then, is by no means random or unrestricted. Above all, it must depend on the purpose of the map. Where kinds are being ordered, for example, size may be a useful factor. Not so with modes. By selecting suitable factors, simple diagrams can be constructed to illustrate particular points about the relations of genres.

But the comprehensive map is a chimera. Simply from the multitude of potential axes, we can see how impossible it would be to make an adequate map on which all genres, let alone individual works, were assigned places. How would their relations be expressed in spatial terms? Topologically? Hologrammatically? And even if we could establish spatial coordinates, what would these tell us?[43] When Scholes makes the classical novel occupy a segment, in which "Dickens, Thackeray, Meredith, and Hardy tend more toward the edges and corners,"[44] he uses a dangerous metaphor. We should be clear why this is so. For one thing, the features of literature are too numerous for a map of corresponding dimensions to be useful. For another, no literary factors are privileged in the sense of belonging to a real order of nature.[45] We can establish that certain generic terms are distinct, but not that they have any natural order. (In this they resemble color words, and may be incompatible without being necessarily ordered.)[46] Indeed, it is hard to exaggerate how nominal the genres are. For example, there are in a sense as many of them as we care to count; they are types, rather than fixed categories with borders. Thus, third, they are unsuitable material for factor analysis, which is a classifying procedure. Fourth, even the notion that they are forms imposed on a multidimensional continuum simplifies, since no such "content substance" is ever presented to us for shaping. Tradition always gives us what is already formed, so that the features we order depart from earlier ones, and differ according to our own culture.[47] That is to say, the genres have an actual cultural history that denies them the innocent passivity of mere substance. They are no longer available for free arrangement, but have already entered into active intergeneric relations. These earlier interrelations cannot be ignored, for they were effective in changing literature itself. If genres are to be represented in feature space, therefore, a series of synchronic maps will be required, in order to do some justice to their changing relationships. No existing map, however, makes much of an attempt to take the diachronic existence of genres into account. Scholes' tokenism in this regard is characteristic. He represents complex changes in the novelistic forms by a single move in his sector diagram, whereby fiction is shown "going beyond naturalism."[48] He gives no hint that the lines of the diagram themselves are in flux.

And there are other objections. The idea of a map of literature may be taken to imply a comprehensiveness of view. We are entitled to assume that if time allowed, all literature could in principle be located on the white spaces of the map. But in practice, genre maps order only a few "major genres" or "pregeneric forms," without leaving, so to put it, ordered white spaces. Yet the nature of genres is such that any system ordering them, however partially, needs to be open and incomplete. Another objection is that cartographers of genre quite ignore the common phenomenon of generic mixture. How is a work to be mapped, if it has elements of several genres? Hernadi's diagrams probably imply that a work with elements of two genres is located on the border between the relevant generic areas. But then more complex mixtures involving several genres would be ruled out.

It is hard to avoid the conclusion that the whole enterprise of constructing genre maps is theoretically unsound. In mimicry of scientific procedure, it invents a spurious objectivity and permanence for entities that in reality are institutional and mutable. This conclusion brings a certain relief, for if literature could be mapped it would be a good deal less personal and interesting. Hernadi's recognition that observing the modes of discourse "depends on the critic's approach"[49] subverts his cartographic constructions, but is potentially more constructive than any of them.

One of the most interesting theories of genre is, perhaps significantly, a system that was never fully worked out. I mean that of Jurij Tynjanov, who anticipated the Prague School in the conception of literature as a completely coherent yet dynamic structure.[50] Tynjanov thought of literature as a complex system with its components—some of them, like the genres, distinct "orders" in themselves—continually interrelated in dynamic tension. The system is such that its components do not coexist, but struggle for preeminence. All "perceptible" literary phenomena, in fact, arise from preeminence of "dominants" in the individual work. And in the evolution of literature at large, the dominant quality or differentiation of genres or groups of genres similarly alters as a result of confrontations with neighboring cultural systems. One of Tynjanov's favorite examples is the hierarchy of genres, which he seems to have thought of as interacting directly with social conventions.

Much subsequent theory has taken Tynjanov's insights for granted. Certainly his ideas about the complexity and interrelatedness of literary groupings must be evident throughout the present study. For his work has the great virtue of combining diachronic and synchronic approaches, at least in principle. He had the historical imagination to appreciate something of the extent of literary change, yet also the audacity to envisage a coherent system in which every component exercised a constructive function. The idea of multiple orders is a powerful and subtle one, allowing (for example) for a certain autonomy in literary genres, without insulating them altogether from historical causation. Nevertheless, Tynjanov's approach, like that of the structuralisms that followed his lead, presents serious difficulties. One is his overemphasis on conflict: in formal aspects, at least, both generic groupings and individual works seem often to achieve their effects through concord rather than conflict. Also, the linguistic model, as we have seen, is inadequate. Finally, Tynjanov conceives the literary system much too tightly. The reality is less orderly and less impersonal: if "dominants" stand out it is because they are valued or preferred by people—who may fail to see some of the alternatives altogether. Far from there being complete "orders" exactly filling the structure of literature, we have to rest content with a human clutter (or creative *disorder*) of overlapping or only partial systems. Indeed, there is

no evidence that genres form systems at all, as distinct from loose groupings. Certainly there is no reason to think of deterministic generic systems, or to replace individual contribution by "creative necessity." The
most we can say is that genres exert pressures on the writer, or that the
current generic paradigm limits his choices. In short, Tynjanov's theory
of generic evolution is too Darwinian.

Intergeneric Relations

How then are the genres ordered? It seems truer to speak not of any spatial order, but of intergeneric relations of the sort discussed in previous
chapters. Insofar as there is any system, it consists, I believe, of these specific relations between genres. Several of the relations, as we have seen,
are diachronic ones. This is obvious in the relationship of composition,
when components combine to form a new kind. But it is no less true
with the relation between modes and parent kinds—the kinds from
which they take their origin. Such diachronic relations are fundamental
to the understanding of literature. Often a modulated form will be unintelligible generically unless by reference to an earlier, perhaps even obsolete, kind.

In any synchronic repertoire of genres, some have no particular mutual
relation. Others may be related by inclusion, modulation, or the ambivalent bond of antigenres. Besides these, there are the relations of similars
and dissimilars, of neighbors and contrasting pairs (tragedy, comedy).
Nothing very complex need be made of such relations. Thus, the resemblances between elegy and romance noticed by Patricia Parker, [51] such as
the suspension of closure and of meaning, stem from no mysterious "affinities"[52] but from readily intelligible common elements. Romance narratives often call for expressions of feeling and for meditation on its
changing significance, and these are functions of Latin elegy—hence,
many elegiac inclusions and modulations. But romance need not be elegiac: it can also be heroic. Just as simply, neighboring kinds are those
with most features in common, at least of those obvious in the period.
Commonly there will be only a single external difference (short story and
novella; novella and novel). This very proximity, however, can make the
relation of neighbors unstable. They may be so carefully distinguished by
critics that a contrast develops between them, as happened with Renaissance sonnet and epigram. At first merely distinguished from the sonnet
in the same way as the canzone, the epigram subsequently came to be felt

as an antigenre. In the same way, William Walsh described pastoral lyric by contrast with Latin elegy: "There ought to be the same difference between *pastorals* and elegies, as between the life of the country and the court; the latter should be smooth, clean, tender and passionate: the thoughts may be bold, more gay, and more elevated than in *pastoral.*"[53]

The concept of contrasting genres seems worth developing. We can distinguish three sorts of contrast.[54] (1) Some may be called complementary, in that presence of the one genre tends to imply absence of the other. So comic and tragic modes are rough complementaries. Most of Shakespeare's plays could be thought of as either the one or the other; even the histories of Elizabethan parlance being modally comic (*Henry IV*) or tragic (*Henry VIII*). The existence of tragicomedy does not disturb the complementarity: indeed, as we have seen, hybrid mixture precisely depends on the components' remaining unfused. Only momentarily do we laugh and cry at once. (2) Other contrasts are more like gradable antonyms in semantics: they lie toward opposite ends of some significant axis. So with epic and pastoral, respectively above and below an implicit height-norm, which as the modified *rota Vergiliana* recognizes is to be found in georgic, where the poet uses his own voice. Such systems of antonyms have established themselves as fertile generators of literary artifice. Georgic has its heroic digressions and its mock epic passages. And during the Renaissance, when pastoral was defined in contrast to epic, mixtures of the two allowed many effective juxtapositions. Such are the irruption of war into the pastoral world in Sidney's *Arcadia,* and Calidore's truancy in *The Faerie Queen.* So too with satiric epigram, which has long been in contrast with epic. D. J. Enright's epigrams on the Fall of Man gain much of their piquancy from the meeting of these generic immiscibles. Like the antonyms of semantics, those of genre are not absolute. Thus, the obsolescence of epic made georgic the high form in the eighteenth century. This counts against the feasibility of grading a series of mimetic heights, such as Frye's fictional modes. At any one time, at least, there seem to be only two antonyms and a norm. (3) A third sort of contrasts have a converse relation comparable with the semantic converseness of "buy" and "sell." These pairs of antigenres include romance and picaresque romance, novel and antinovel, sonnet and sonnet-epigram. Here the one antonym implies the presence of the other. The antinovel continually depends on evocations of the novelistic forms it avoids, so that if the novel were to become obsolete, so would it.

A genre's various contrasts are all subject to change. Thus, in the earlier Middle Ages, epic and romance were complementary forms of long narrative.[55] But by the nineteenth century that relationship had long dissolved: the romance and the verisimilar novel had become antonyms in respect of detailed naturalism. On the axis of fictionality, however, the verisimilar novel is an antonymic neighbor of the biography. Their similarities, down to such minutiae as an opening chronographia, are obvious enough; yet their difference has until recently been no less sharp. Only a slack biographer has allowed himself a novelist's omniscient or speculative invention of thoughts, let alone of actions. Johnson was not disparaging the novel when he warned off would-be biographers of Savage in these terms: "It must be expected they will supply from invention the want of intelligence, and that under the title of the Life of Savage they will publish only a novel filled with romantic adventures and imaginary amours." But now the contrast seems to be in process of change. For one thing, it itself is being used as material for creative play, in the *poioumenon,* as well as in the experimental novel, where fictive status is a frequent preoccupation. For another, nonfictional characters offer an easy means of supplying the new demand for "real" characters. At all events there was a late seventies vogue of fiction with historical characters, often writers or composers: for example, Maurice Edelman's *Disraeli Rising* (1975), James Aldridge's *One Last Glimpse* (1978, dealing with Fitzgerald and Hemingway), Beryl Bainbridge's *Young Adolf* (1978), Frederick Busch's *Mutual Friend* (1978), Ronald Harwood's *Cesar and Augusta* (1978), Keith Alldrit's *Elgar on the Journey to Hanley* (1979), and Andrew Sinclair's *Facts in the Case of E. A. Poe* (1979). And on the other side we find deliberately fictionalized biographies. Margaret Foster's *William Makepeace Thackeray: Memoirs of a Victorian Gentleman,* for example, is a very interesting attempt at biography by imagined autobiography. Here, however, the sense of tour de force, of incompatibles strenuously yoked, is still quite strong.

When the structure of contrasting genres changes, it can become very difficult to interpret works that depend on antonymic effects. During the English Renaissance, pastoral and georgic were almost complementaries. Pastoral was the ideally poetic genre, whereas georgic was conceived in such didactic terms that its qualifications as poetry were dubious.[56] In terms of height, the two differed without contrast. But pastoral's masking of the poet's voice, and its characteristic *mise-en-scène* and topics, were more sharply distinct. In its purest form, it was concerned with otium, with art (singing, narrative), with emotions ("a little quickness and passion, but that short and flowing"[57]), and parenthetically with the herding of sheep or goats. So far as direct realization went, it excluded strenuous work of all sorts, not least intellectual. Above all, its world was timeless, a golden stasis rounded off by the completion of a single unvarying day. With this in mind we can see Spenser's *Shepherd's Calendar* as boldly innovative, modulating the pastoral eclogue as it does into a very distant georgic key. He added matter of religion, following Petrarch's and Mantuanus' Neolatin precedents; extended the expression of strong feeling (almost direct through Colin, as well as disguised, through other personae);[58] and made the beautiful addition of a calendar, praised by Pope (not without reservations) for its comparison of life to the seasons, which "exposes to his readers a view of the great and little worlds, in their various changes and aspects."[59] In a similar direction, *As You Like It* ventures even further. It is beyond question a pastoral play. Yet it is also the most didactic in Shakespeare's *oeuvre:* its characters all seem bent on teaching one another, with various degrees of seriousness. What is more, much of this instruction is about time. Ganymede teaches Orlando punctuality—not to speak of lecturing on how "Time travels in divers paces with divers persons" (3.2.302). "There's no clock in the forest" (where men "fleet the time carelessly"), but Touchstone brings his dial with him and is able to instruct Jaques about "how the world wags . . . from hour to hour" (2.7.23–27). And Jaques in turn instructs Duke Senior about the Seven Ages of Man. These and other measures of time, notably the ages of the world and the seasons of the year, are frequently alluded to or sung about beyond any necessity of plot. It is a play that makes pastoral and georgic confront one another, in fact, with a generic effect sharper even than that pastoral modulation whereby it "hangs odes upon hawthorns and elegies on brambles" (3.2.352). Unfortunately, most of this effect, on which the understanding of the play depends, is now lost. Not only has the contrast between pastoral and georgic ceased to be felt, but the mere difference between them has become blurred and hard to recover.

Is any contrast of genres so extreme as to preclude mixture altogether? It seems not, although this is very nearly the case with complementary contrasts. They may be juxtaposed in hybrids, as we have seen, but only by segregating and diluting the component genres. A work can hardly be epigrammatic and lyric, spoken and sung, at the very same time. The anomalous case of Elizabethan satiric tragedy has to be understood in the light (or the obscurity) of a fallacious theory of satire that derived the term from "satyr." Generally the hybrid collapses into plain satire—as in Marston's *Malcontent,* where Malevole's satire continues throughout, regardless of his being in or out of disguise. With many other generic pairs, we are only entitled to say that the mixture seems never to have been attempted. We find heroic romance and heroic satire, but not heroic limerick, or clerihew, or essay. Sometimes this is as much because the uncombined pairs have nothing to do with each other, as because of any irreconcilable mutual repugnance of values. But there seems also to be a historical limitation whereby writers only mix genres that are simultaneously available. It may simply be that epic has no relation with forms that developed after its obsolescence as an unmixed kind. For a variety of reasons, in fact, contrasting kinds seem to be comparatively suitable candidates for mixture. Insofar as there are genre systems, in short, these are apparently governed as much by inherited contingencies of literature at particular times as by synchronic genre logic.

The inference of this chapter is that the aims of genre systems should be conceived less ambitiously. Certainly genres have very little taxonomic potential, since they lack the status of fixed categories. As for the mapping of genres, except for simple expository diagrams it is theoretically unsound. Not only do maps require many dimensions, but they fail to allow for diachronic variation. Any adequate system would have to refer to the real history of genres in their changing relations. Genres are better understood, I have argued, through a study of their mutual relations, which actually affect writers and readers in a way that is not possible with locations on a chart. These relations are partly diachronic or dynamic (formation, combination, mixture), partly static (similarities, contrasts). But even the synchronic contrasts are not absolute or fixed. In the course of literary history, they will soon have been replaced by others only roughly equivalent.

14. Genre in Interpretation

If genre is of little value in classification, what then is it good for? This book has set out the idea that it is a communication system, for the use of writers in writing, and readers and critics in reading and interpreting.[1] No writer needs to be persuaded of the value of genre. Studying it enables him to orient his composition to previous work. And, more creatively, it extends a positive challenge or "invitation to form."[2] Indeed, activity in genre theory has tended to precede or coincide with periods of great literature, and to arouse the interest of the best writers.

In reception, genre operates in at least three ways, corresponding to the logical phases of criticism—construction, interpretation, and evaluation.

Construction of the Original Work

The first phase of the critical act should be construction—that is, determining the features of the work intended. To use these terms obviously implies intentionalism, but need not, I hope, lapse into the intentionalist fallacy.[3] It is simply the realized intention that construction aims to recover—intention in the most inescapable sense. What signals, it asks, were originally sent? What vocabulary selections were originally made? What local meanings were originally conveyed? What rhymes and other rhetorical patterns and structures? What conventions? What innovations or variations? With earlier literature, in particular, this descriptive phase is lengthy, difficult, and unlikely to be completed. Yet it seems to me a *sine qua non*. The patterns, structures and meanings that it recovers have a privileged status unqualified by subsequent sound-changes, semantic changes, or changes in convention. The constructive phase is commonly omitted from accounts of interpretation, as if it could be taken for granted. But a literary work is never "given." In actual fact there are no words on the page, no conventions, no meanings.

The last point calls for expansion. In receiving a work, the reader has to construct every feature in its level, by interpreting signals at a lower level of organization. From ink marks we infer letters, phonemes, word-segments, and other constituents, according to a system of learned conventions. And if the conventions have not been learned, transmission may fail altogether, or the work may be misconstructed and consequently misconstrued. If we cannot read Elizabethan handwriting, or know insufficient medieval grammar, or have never met William Carlos Williams' line-break conventions, we may not get far enough to grasp what the features of a work are, let alone interpret them. Usually a reader only shares enough conventions with the writer to construct in part. Nevertheless, scholars and critics can do much to recover the original features more fully by cooperative effort. We are not to think of construction as merely subjective, in contrast to the objective physical data of ink marks. For as Charles Altieri rightly argues, it is not only empirically verifiable facts that are objective. The objectivity and determinacy of institutional facts are also to be affirmed: "Objectivity here depends not on the physical properties of things but on the procedures for reading which the members of a culture share by virtue simply of their education into that culture."[4] We need not follow Altieri, however, in trying to break down the pyramidal model of the artifact as encoded signs of ascending meaningfulness. True, the frusta of the pyramid often overlap. Adult readers scan several words at once and may be led by a couplet end-word to expect its rhyme. Such shortcuts are incompatible with a tidy, hierarchic pyramid: we have to allow for the fact that generic and other schemata of a higher level (and often erroneous ones) assist or interfere with interpretations of lower signals. But when he says that "most of us are far less clear about the physical materials constituting the sign than we are about the semantic content, if not the pragmatics, of the utterance," Altieri omits indispensable steps that must intervene, even if they are unconscious ones. Logically, and in difficult cases practically, the higher levels depend for objectivity on the lower. In any event, the critic is not obliged to rely solely on the opportunistic and unreliable shortcuts of the reader.

The critic needs to construct deliberately as well as to read frequently. In difficult instances he will try to work along as many confirmatory facets of the work's pyramid as possible. Thus, he may compare different manuscript and printed versions, adduce external as well as internal evidence, consult lexicographic and historical authorities. Iconographic elements offer a particularly useful redundancy, since in iconography language is transparent, and independent of the more complex semantic systems. And similarly recoverable features exist on every scale. Even so, it is not uncommon to find different critics arriving at different constructs, to such an extent that their subsequent disagreements come to an impasse. They are speaking, in effect, about different works.[5] We need procedures, then, for eliminating errors of construction. Yet critics have written far more about the "Principle of Plenitude"[6]—about generating as many meanings as possible—than about choosing which meanings are possible. The only limiting criterion that has proved to be of much use is appropriateness to context.

Construction of the original work is bounded, first, by a context of historical and biographical possibility and probability. Blake's "dark satanic mills" are probably not factories. Historical context is a reliable guide, up to a point. True, it is itself a construct based on probability, but of a different kind from those of literature, and arrived at by largely independent routes. Literary works may be exceptional documents. Nevertheless, there is no reason to join Wimsatt and Beardsley in allowing exeats from historical context ("the history of words *after* a poem is written may contribute meanings which if relevant to the original pattern should not be ruled out by a scruple about intention").[7] Unfortunately, however, historical possibility by itself is not an adequate guiding principle. Many disputes arise in connection with alternative meanings, none of which can be ruled out as historically impossible.

Another constraint is literary context. Here "context" itself has several senses. It can mean the drift of the work as a whole[8]—in practice a useful thing to keep in mind when constructing locally difficult passages. In theory, this sense is uncomfortably vague, and gives rise to an obvious hermeneutic circularity. How can we know the whole, until we have constructed the parts?[9] By another sense of the term, Beardsley applies literary context in a very specific way: "In assembling, or feeling out, the admissible connotations of words in a poem, we are guided by logical and physical possibilities."[10] This Principle of Congruence is so timeless in its generality that we forget to ask whose idea of a "fit" satisfies it. If a Yale formalist or a deconstructionist were construing Johnson's comment on Birch—"a pen is to Tom a torpedo"—would he be free to find congruence of shape between a fountain pen and a submarine missile? If, however, congruence is subject to diachronic criteria with regard to referents, why not also with regard to connotations? Or to notions of congruence? For example, the Four Elements were once considered a logical "place."

Literary context is perhaps best conceived in Husserl's terms, as a "horizon of meaning": "The interpreter's aim, then, is to posit the author's horizon and carefully exclude his own accidental associations."[11] Linguistic horizons of meaning set definite limits, although ones that seldom determine many uncertainties of implicit meaning; and horizons of literary meaning are again too wide. A more discriminating guide is the generic horizon. Genre can be a powerful instrument in construction, since its conventions organize most other constituents, in a subtly expressive way. "The genre provides a sense of the whole, a notion of typical meaning components."[12] It need hardly be said that the limiting genre is the state of the genre at the time when the work was written.

The value of the generic horizon is obvious from the difficulty that arises when it is missing. Francis Cairns notices a tendency to see merely faults of composition, where in actuality writers are exploiting an assumed familiarity with forgotten genres. Generic conventions now lost once allowed connections to remain implicit: "The logical incompleteness and apparent internal inconsistencies of many ancient writings are a consequence of their non-individual character, that is, their membership of genres."[13] And in this respect English literature is little different. The story of the Man of the Hill in *Tom Jones* seemed extraneous until it was construed in terms of the picaresque romance genre.[14] Defoe's novels are still hard to make sense of, until they are viewed against the horizon of the anterior genres, rather than that of the Victorian novel. The pleasure of Gay's *Trivia* fails to be communicated unless it is seen as mock georgic.[15] And *Lycidas* would be as unintelligible without any background of pastoral elegy, as *Paradise Regained* has proved to be, without brief epic. Guillén gives other examples.[16] But to exemplify is to mislead: criticism should always work within such generic horizons, not merely in particular instances.

The processes of generic recognition are in fact fundamental to the reading process. Often we may not be aware of this. But whenever we approach a work of an unfamiliar genre—new or old—our difficulties return us to fundamentals. No work, however avant-garde, is intelligible without some context of familiar types. To begin with, only a very broad generic affiliation may be available ("concrete poetry," "lyric"). But an identification so crude will hardly be adequate for the uptake of the literary communication. At times, it is true, we think that we are grasping an unfamiliar genre simultaneously with the work that first embodies it for us. But this is to oversimplify a complex event, in which the context of other genres, larger, neighboring or contrasting, guides our recognitions. Innovative works tend to be obscure precisely because their generic context is not yet obvious.

So far as older works are concerned, the hermeneutic act has long been understood to be bound up with identification of genre. Wilhelm Dilthey's classic article of 1900 sums up the central problem of exegesis like this: "The whole of a work is to be understood from the individual words and their connections with each other, and yet the full comprehension of the individual part already presupposes comprehension of the whole. This circle is then reduplicated in the relationship between the individual work itself and the spiritual tendencies of its creator, and it returns again in the relationship between the work and its literary genre."[17] The hermeneutic task has something been represented simplistically as one of comparison between works or parts of works, and especially between the parts and the whole. But it is at once a more elusive and a more institutional activity than this suggests. A few generic features, especially external ones, might be arrived at by comparison. But the genres themselves are known inwardly by a complex interaction of insights, experimental relations with literature, and relations with other critics—by a "familiarity" acquired through encounters, direct and indirect, with the generic family. In particular, we have to construct an impression of the anterior state of literature—of the genres from which the original work took its departure. For this we have to try to detach ourselves temporarily from modern assumptions. That is to say, we have to learn to unlearn our developed expectations as to what is noticeable, different, innovative in the genre. We have to adjust for a different range of alterity. And in doing so we are not at liberty to invent generic groupings as we like, but have to come to terms with the institutionally objective genres discovered by the methods of literary history. Our relations are with critics and writers as well as with works.[18]

Günther Müller, Karl Viëtor, and others have held that reconstruction of genre is caught up in a special version of the hermeneutic circle, with knowledge of individual works depending on knowledge of the genre, and vice versa.[19] Against this, however, Ralph Cohen observes that "statements about identification of generic features operate on a quite different level from those about poetic functions." For "concepts of forms . . . can be arrived at by comparison of classification systems and are not dependent upon interpretation within a work."[20] Their different degree of abstraction makes generic constructs independent, at least in part, from constructs of meaning and function. Genres have an institutional existence that transcends (or lacks) the privacy and fine shades of meaning of the individual work.

Reconstructing genre also, however, comes up against another hermeneutic problem, that of ineradicable knowledge. If genres had been immutable, they would have offered a relatively easy means of breaking the hermeneutic circle, as Cohen has explained. But as it is, we encounter a further obstacle. In order to reconstruct the original genre, we have to eliminate from consciousness its subsequent states. For the idea of a genre that informs a reader's understanding is normally the latest, most inclusive conception of it that he knows. And unless he can unknow this conception, it seems that he cannot recover meanings that relate to the genre's earlier, "innocent" states. Our familiarity with the post-Jamesian novel surely makes it impossible for us to grasp the original qualities of Thackeray, who may perhaps have been the first to assimilate style, tentatively, to point of view instead of to objective decorum. How can we now feel the relative audacity of his mimetic syntax? In the same way, how did Shakespeare's realistic departures from romance strike audiences to whom naturalism was unknown? Scholarship can mitigate but hardly remove such an obstacle. To have an earlier generic convention explained is to lose some of its effect; to learn from annotation that a feature was once innovative is not the same as recognizing its first strangeness.

Formidable as it can be, however, this obstacle is not in principle different from those met in constructing literary works that issue from another cultural context or are written in a foreign language. In all such cases we have to unlearn (that is, temporarily suspend) our own values and associations, and the rules of our own language or idiolect. These leaps of imagination, too, are unthinkable for those who take up certain extreme theoretical positions. From Sapir's view that one's world is unconsciously built on language habits a relativism can be developed that makes translation impossible. But this does not correspond to practical experience. "It may well be that we can never totally absorb or understand the 'world' of other languages, but it is clear enough that we can obtain a very fair understanding of them."[21] So it is with literary works that relate to earlier states of a genre: by mutually confirming paths we can approach close enough at least to arrive at a useful generic construct. The role of genre is a little like that of memory, when we try to reconstruct our infancy. We have to strip away false or suggested recollections and subsequent ideas. Nevertheless, our memory is a great help. The continuity of generic tradition gives a similar access: full of pitfalls, yet indispensable. The continuity of the tradition means that through genre something of an older world is still available, just as history can with care be reconstructed from our unconscious.[22]

Granted the horizon, it can still be objected that the same horizon encloses a great many possible works. As William Righter says, the statement that a work is a tragedy tells us something about it, but not nearly as much as we want to know.[23] However, a generic horizon is more than a single lax parameter. No one familiar with such studies as Monica McAlpine's Genre of "Troilus and Criseyde" or Ralph Cohen's Unfolding of the Seasons will suppose that identification of genre need be a perfunctory or external business. We have to distinguish between mere classification and the true system of genre, which is made up of conventions rather than abstractions.[24] Genre criticism is not indeed the whole of criticism. But in construction it makes an invaluable contribution, by locating the work's individuality vis-à-vis convention.

This point comes out clearly in the problematic construction of Shakespeare's Hamlet. Does Hamlet delay? As Morris Weitz's analysis shows, genre criticism has its usual decisive role.[25] It is because E. E. Stoll identifies the play as a revenge tragedy that he rejects Coleridge's construction, with its psychological account of Hamlet's delay. For Stoll, the delay is an epical convention that "makes the deed momentous when it comes at the end." Hamlet's self-reproaches are not conceived dramatically in terms of psychology. For Dover Wilson, however, this is "moonshine": the delay is part of a consistently realistic portrayal of psychological weakness. The dispute is not one that will be quickly settled in all its aspects.[26] But we can see that both parties misconceived the relation between timeless originality and generic convention. Stoll is wrong in supposing that the existence of a conventional "popular heroic revenger" prevented Shakespeare from varying this type by introducing procrastinatory traits. And Wilson is wrong to deny that Shakespeare's communication lies precisely in such departures. In other words, the revenger and malcontent types are not classes to which Hamlet belongs or does not belong. Shakespeare is free to question the values of the genre—but can only use its terms to do so. There is no temperamental irresolution in Hamlet except what decorum of character requires. Nevertheless, Hamlet's revenge is enmeshed in scruples exceptional in the genre and amounting to a comment on it. Without knowledge of revenge tragedy, then, Hamlet would be incomprehensible: no valid construction would be possible.

When a valid construction of any aspect of a work is arrived at, a number of elements normally fall into place. Sparshott perhaps means this when he writes of "a particular kind of criticism found effective."[27] The best readers find criticism effective when it is based on construction faithful to the original: only then will it really work. In principle, the critic aims at reconstructing every aspect in this way. But human deficiencies and limitations of knowledge are such that in practice construction very often remains incomplete. There are generally aspects of the work that entail questions without simple answers, at least for the time being—questions already involving the critic, therefore, in the phase of interpretation. Suppose that the question whether in Blake's time "dark satanic mills" could be factories were not settled. In that event, decisions on related aspects of construction might involve interpretation, and be affected by political views about the Industrial Revolution.

Some theorists go so far as to argue (in effect) that all construction is enmeshed in interpretation, because it is necessarily expressed in anachronistic language. In a sense, indeed, this is true—but only in one so weak that the practice of criticism remains unaffected. To those critical solipsists who argue on similar grounds that the concept of original meaning is vacuous, a short answer is possible: in that case their own meanings do not exist either.

Interpretation and Indeterminacy

Once the construction corresponds as far as possible to the intended original, criticism moves on to the phase of interpretation. This is the heart of criticism, as distinct from reading. Even if we had time machines or telepathy, so that literature's reconstruction was automatic, we should still need to interpret it in our own terms. How far is Hamlet's delay justifiable? We do not stop with the "then-meaning,"[28] that is to say, but go on to discuss the significance. Pure construction lacks all interest, particularly if the genre concerned has no live tradition of reading and imitation.

The second phase works in a manner almost opposite to that of the first. In its pedagogic analogies and critical persuasions, interpretation tends to enlarge and blur the forms that construction defined. It is diastole to the former systole. Thus, when we focus on Homer's original epos, clarity and magnification are incompatible: it "shines in the distance, if clearer and clearer, yet also smaller and smaller . . . It needs to be reinterpreted and artificially brought near us."[29] Presenting an old work entails inevitable falsification, since it has to be in part restructured. There is nothing mysterious in this. The structuralist mystique should be rejected; deconstruction is no more than a regrettable but unavoidable necessity. But it need not be irresponsible either, although its consequences are far-reaching and incalculable. For interpretation is bound to deal for the most part with what interests the critic or his audience—preferably both. It must speak more directly to their condition and their interests than the strict proportions of the work can justify. And the whole bias of readers' attention varies with time and place in ways that the author could not foresee. Devices, levels of organization, even whole genres lose interest—as happened with syntactic inversion, with strict pentameter prosody, and with brief epic. The critic must in part submit to this Demogorgon of change. If his interpretation were faithful to every proportion of the original, it would be of very little use. So he will have relatively little to say about the schematic rhetoric of Shakespeare's history plays or of *Paradise Lost,* since during the last two centuries interest in rhetorical schemes and in structural proportion has given way to interest in tropes and tonal effects. It is repugnant to admit that we cannot appreciate features of these great works. But this must often be so. When the literary model alters, the parts of literature that readers have competence for must alter too.

Most serious of all, the concept of meaning itself has undergone radical changes during the last millenium. Allegoresis will no longer work for us as it worked for Dante or even for Shakespeare. And medieval interpreters similarly felt that they could not possibly allow the constituents of the *Aeneid* or of the *Metamorphoses* to have their original functions. They restructured these pagan works in accordance with new moral concerns, treating epics as allegories and subjecting them to a thoroughgoing "accommodation." As Frank Kermode uses this term, it refers to "any method by which the old document may be induced to signify what it cannot be said to have expressly stated." Some medieval allegorical interpretations were perhaps intended as applications rather than meanings.[30] Nevertheless, it seems as if "the books we call classics possess intrinsic qualities that endure, but possess also an openness to accommodation which keeps them alive under endlessly varying dispositions."[31] The classic lives, if one may so put it, at the cost of losing itself. From this point of view it is only partially "above" history. After so many accommodations, what hope or desire is there of recovering anything like the intended meaning? Dilthey, in spite of his profound awareness of herme-

neutic problems, took for granted an unchanging "general human nature" that allowed communion across the ages. But consciousness, to say
nothing of methods of interpretation, seems to alter in accordance with
cultural changes.[32]

As I hinted earlier, medieval accommodation of the *Aeneid* can be seen
as a rather drastic recategorization. Some such process may be universal
in the case of literature that lasts. Not only does each genre change, but
the work may come to be identified with a different genre altogether.
Thus, in the Middle Ages, few ancient epics survived that the *Aeneid*
could have been grouped with. Regrouping always affects significance, although not always in so extreme a fashion. For grouping is implied in
every interpretation, even if only in a reviewer's gestures toward "avant-
garde fiction." In subsequent criticism, a complex work will call for
progressively tighter generic identifications. *The Crying of Lot 49*, for example, has been connected with Menippean satire, several of whose characteristics it shares (self-reference; inconclusiveness of closure).[33] But a new
grouping may have begun to emerge, which relates Pynchon to Vonnegut and to apocalyptic satire of a new kind marked by mosaic techniques
inherited from Nathanael West and Dos Passos. If so, *The Crying of Lot
49* will be interpreted in the light of *Gravity's Rainbow* and *Slaughterhouse-Five*, rather than *Giles Goat-Boy*. And its significance is bound to
alter in consequence of this new generic affiliation. In such ways genre
has always been a principle of evolutionary change—in contrast with natural evolution, in which it is the type that survives the exemplar.[34]

If their interpretation is so bound up with generic change, must we not
regard literary works as indeterminate? Many recent critics have thought
so, and by no means all of them farouche structuralists. We find Wolfgang Iser, for example, a careful and sensitive reader, positively delight-
ing in the concept of literary indeterminacy. To be sure, he is moderate
in practice. He finds indeterminacy primarily in modern literature, where
the sense is left "open"—and even there does not exclude the author
from some faint participation in meaning. Indeed, the reader's involvement may consist in "bringing out the author's own premeditated yet
unformulated intention of the text."[35] Nevertheless, the plurality of a
work's meaning is for Iser fundamental. It was Ingarden's "blind spot"
that he could not "accept the possibility that a work may be concretized
in different, equally valid, ways."[36] Other critics have more thoroughgoing views on indeterminacy. Frank Kermode not only speaks of "the intrinsic plurality of the text," but of "the completion of the text"—not

merely of its meaning—by the reader.[37] And much effort goes into finding or opening up "gaps" of indeterminacy, such as may allow reader participation.[38] These are more likely to be found among the narrative discontinuities of romances than in verisimilar novels. Hence, perhaps, the special attention paid to Hawthorne and Emily Brontë. Kermode rejoices that as time passes "the constraints of a period culture dissolve, generic presumptions which concealed gaps disappear, and we now see that the book [*Wuthering Heights*], as James thought novels should, truly 'glories in a gap,' a hermeneutic gap in which the reader's imagination must operate, so that he speaks continuously in the text."[39] But we may question whether generic presumptions disappear: they seem rather to change into others, their historical successors. And in any case it is hard to see reduced coherence as anything but loss to the literary work. Nevertheless, these ideas of indeterminacy should not be diagnosed as mere bad effects of Yale formalism; or as overextension of political iconoclasm (here inappropriately directed against legitimate authorial privilege); or as modernism slipping too far away from communication. They embody some insights, even if they are theoretically unsound.

For it must be said that E. D. Hirsch's powerful defense of the determinacy of literary meaning stands unanswered—indeed virtually unquestioned. *Validity in Interpretation* (1967) accords genre a central place in hermeneutics, being indeed based on the doctrine that all communicable meanings are types. Through arguments too detailed to rehearse here, it establishes criteria whereby some interpretations can be judged valid, others invalid. Few counterarguments have been offered: the theorists of indeterminacy have mostly chosen to avoid Hirsch's position altogether. An exception is Kermode's argument that literary works resemble legal texts in having indeterminate terms applicable in unforeseen circumstances. This is interesting but not entirely plausible. Kermode surely makes a mistake when he denies that literary "determinations" are more constrained than legal ones. Few legal texts are much determined in respect of emotional tone, for example, or of the other various "overdetermined" redundancies that give literary texts their lasting integrity.[40] Similarly Davis' argument that Hirsch is concerned with a "narrowly rhetorical concept of meaning" can carry at best but very partial conviction.[41] The indeterminists seem to be trapped in a false dichotomy of "thematic determinacy versus indeterminacy,"[42] and to have missed the subtlety of Hirsch's distinction between different sorts of meaning. In practice, the issue has been settled by the decisive fact that the only effective interpretations professing to be "open" turn out to be those that (like some of Kermode's) respect the author's original meaning. Criticism that does not respect authorial rights is invariably unsatisfactory.

Graham Hough's congenial approach to the matter seems at first to offer a possible *rapprochement,* through its recognition that both composition and reading have a large unconscious element. But he applies this insight in a rather disappointingly one-sided way. The work has "an infinite, or at least an undefined, capacity of meaning," since its formal organization "is a partly unconscious process; and the personal unconscious of the author is linked with the collective unconscious." The effect is unpredictability: "this vast ocean of possibilities is indeed canalized by the occasion and conscious intention of the individual work, but we cannot determine with certainty what will flow through the channel."[43] Against this it must be said that literary works not only canalize, but also integrate and communicate. The authorial unconscious has a far more active and creative role than Hough allows it.[44] That has still to be reconciled with the continued creativity of readers.

It may help to distinguish different sorts of indeterminacy. (1) First, there is the indeterminacy inherent in all language, in that words do not have fully determined meanings. This by no means precludes such agreement about their use as is necessary for communication to take place.[45] With literature, it is true, the lapse of time entails further lexical indeterminacies—rather as in Borges' story *Pierre Menard, Author of Don Quixote,* where the identical words of Cervantes have different meanings when rewritten in a later century. But as we have seen, conventional redundancies prolong the possibility of literary communication. In any case, the communication itself is determinate. (2) There is indeterminacy in Ingarden's sense, meaning places of indeterminacy, gaps in representation, especially of fictional objects. Such indeterminate, or rather undefined, contents are sometimes intended to be vague, inconsistent, or the like; sometimes they are so through deficiencies of imagination. Neither sort of gap calls for any addition by the reader beyond the intended original. The reader's part is like that of the recipient of lexical indeterminacies in category 1 above: namely, to take up the communication by applying appropriate knowledge of the codes governing the constituents concerned. Ingarden seems concerned actually to circumscribe the reader's discretion—as his sharp distinction between the work and its concretizations suggests. No doubt different readers supply different valid concretizations, such as colors of hair for characters with hair of unspecified color. But such contents are not among the types of the work itself, and are adequately covered by Hirsch's arguments against psychologism. Another type is (3) indeterminacy of total analysis. Literature's effects are often hard to define: perhaps, indeed, "the charm of art inheres in that which is indefinable."[46] But agreement about a literary work does not depend on exhaustive definition of its effects. (4) Last, there is indeterminacy of overall meaning. Only this sort of indeterminacy, with its corollary that works mean whatever we like, needs to be denied. But it is a generous error, insofar as it is motivated by a wish to encourage uninhibited approach to the classics. It arose, however, from various confusions about literary meaning: confusion between the meanings distinguished by Hirsch as "the meaning of a text (which does not change) and the meaning of a text to us today (which changes)";[47] between meaning and broader significance; and between meaning and thematic formulations. Interpretation properly concerns the whole form and content, not merely schematic formulations.[48] There need be no dispute about local indeterminacy, which does not interfere with communication of the work. As to the question of overall indeterminacy, it can be reduced to a single issue: namely, whether the original realized intention is in any way privileged. When so much is in flux, indeterminacy has all the attraction of a Gordian measure. But the stark alternatives of structuralist theory prove on examination to be illusory. Hermeneutics is not "the alternative to accommodation,"[49] but its preliminary accompaniment. And there is no real choice between "closed book" and "open text," authority and plurality, life (indeterminacy) and death (determinacy). In actual practice, the freedom to interpret is never unconditioned. The critic operates in an organic situation, in which scholarly reconstruction and interpretative criticism repeatedly complement one another. The fallacy committed both by indeterminists and by conservative philologists can be seen as a false opposition between two logical phases of interpretation.

Once the phase of construction is accorded logical priority, some authorial privilege has to be accepted. The "then-meaning" was this, and not that. But the restriction this puts on interpretation is less felt than the oriented experience of trying to arrive at the original work. Critics attentive to scholarship find themselves sharing many objective agreements. Such an orientation may be far from ensuring good interpretation, but it is a *sine qua non*. No responsible critic feels free to play the trival game of attaching interpretations at will, regardless of the original meaning. As we have seen, valid constuction depends upon identification of signals in terms of conventions shared with the author. And validity of interpretation similarly depends upon inclusion of the original meaning. The critic dare not be ignorant of it. Such a spectacular critical error as mistaking *Paradise Lost* for a simple classical epic with Satan as its hero is a sufficiently dreadful example. And there are others as bad. This is not to say that the interpreter can choose only between a single correct interpretation of a classic and many false ones. As Charles Altieri sees the issue, "determinacy in literary criticism is not certainty, nor is it thematic summary; rather it is the possibility of reaching public agreement that a given description of the texts both accounts for the features competent readers take as relevant and organizes them in a way that satisfies our expectations about the coherence of a kind of action implied by the particulars described."[50] To this we need to add that competent readers take the work's original meaning as an especially relevant piece of knowledge.

That knowledge is not always a simple matter. As I have mentioned, the original meaning may be different from the one intended and consciously expressed. Dodgson wrote about *The Hunting of the Snark:* "I didn't mean anything but nonsense . . . But since words mean more than we mean to express when we use them . . . whatever good meanings are in the book I am very glad to accept as the meaning of the book."[51] These unconscious meanings are not only a matter of the private feelings of authors who know themselves imperfectly—as in some of Housman's "ironies." The original work may also contain implications hidden at the time of writing. So a classic may actually in some sense have "meant," originally, what some interpreters imagine they prove the work's indeterminacy by adding. This is close to Altieri's point that the multiplicity of interpretations generated by a classic does not prove its "openness," but is "a function of the depth with which it renders actions and their possible significance."[52]

In all this coming to terms with original meanings, we must not forget what age we live in ourselves. It is a delusion to suppose that we could ever become contemporaries of the original readers. And even if we could, it would be treachery to ourselves.[53] It is right to bring one's own preoccupations to works of antiquity. In any case, part of the experience of an old work is precisely a sense of its distance, its alterity. For in interpretation—as distinct from construction—we do not suspend our sense of the present, but call up all the awareness we can muster of our place in history. Only then can we freely grasp, for what they are, the perennialities of a classic that has also been allowed to exist in its own freedom.

Here the function of genre is again vital. We have some chance of learning our historical place as readers if we attempt to interpret the original work not only in terms of its first generic affiliations, but also of the subsequent genre it generated. By considering old and new groupings, a generic approach can put the work in historical perspective without losing an authenticity worth having.

Perspective, however, is a treacherous concept. For perspectivistic criticism tends to elevate "authenticity" at the expense of correctness, thus leading to historical relativism. All depends on how the perspectives—authorial and modern—are related. They cannot be related by the impossible fusion that Gadamer imagines. Rather, we have to envisage something like the two perspectives of Hirsch's antihistoricist theory. On the one hand, we cannot stop having our own standpoint. On the other, "a text cannot be *interpreted* from a perspective different from the original author's. Meaning is understood from the perspective that lends existence to meaning ... Every act of interpretation involves therefore at least two perspectives, that of the author and that of the interpreter. The perspectives are not fused; they are entertained both at once."[54] And not only these two perspectives. For if we are not entirely obsessed with our own interpretation, we may occasionally be able to entertain the perspectives of other critics. Hirsch's theory might be developed in such a way as to allow for many points of view. Indeed, it entails some such development, if the critical community is not to be ignored. These plural perspectives, however, are not unstructured. To suppose that would be to embrace indeterminacy in another form, demoting the author's work to the status of one among a multitude of substitute inventions. How then are the perspectives structured? We might think of the historical succession of valid interpretations as resembling the skins of an onion. They become progressively more comprehensive and (in some respects at least) more enlightened, so that they indeed "accommodate" the original perspective, if not quite in a Kermodian sense. It is embedded in all the valid interpretations that are in turn embedded in their successors. However, interpretations that truly come to terms with the author's perspective are to be distinguished from those that merely notice it perfunctorily as a point of departure. Valid interpretation, that is to say, incorporates original meanings as significant parts of the new: the critical onion is not heartless. At the same time, we should not expect its skins to be concentric spheroids. Interpretations may interpenetrate each other, becoming less inclusive in one direction or broader in another.

They form, moreover, a generic grouping of their own. Each kind, each author, each considerable work, has its idiosyncratic subgenre of criticism. As in other genres, there is a complex tradition. Many of the interpretations will be accumulative, whether as classic statements or elegant variations; but others will be reactive or innovative.[55] To adopt Jean Starobinski's useful term, there are different interpretative gestures.[56] Starobinski is surely right to rehabilitate such nonspecialized but nonetheless effective gestures as selection, glossing, and allegoresis. And we may go further. The genre of a work's interpretations include some deficient in scholarship, critical method, accuracy, logic—but nevertheless valuable. Even the simplest reading (which lays no claim to be a critical contribution) belongs to the genre, in that it perforce inherits older critical ideas, at however many generational removes. Other members of the critical family are no doubt black sheep. Yet their creative wildness— their adventures in indeterminacy, it may be—can only impress themselves on us by taking departure from a previous firm line of interpretation, a determinacy that they imply, however negatively. In the economy of criticism, erroneous interpretation may be almost indispensable to critics in the main line.[57] Perhaps only the indeterminacies of Empson could have challenged Ricks' better interpretation of Milton. There is some plausibility in the view that a genre of interpretations has a structure. In this structure, criticism based on ideas of indeterminacy have place, and need not be rejected out of hand. But its place can at best be regarded as a very peripheral one. As with any genre, individual contributions have to take their places within a coherent tradition.

Critical genres are very closely interrelated with the generic states of literature itself. In fact, interpretations often contribute to new states of a genre—for example, by proposing new groupings. These new groupings correspond ideally to improved states of understanding: the later congeners throw light on their predecessors. Moreover, addition to a genre must be counted one of the more eloquent interpretative gestures. Thus, the literary together with the critical genre can be seen as a group composition, through which understanding collectively deepens. However, there are defections from this ideal. The grouping of a work can go badly wrong. For example, the grouping of Milton's epic with Blake's, eccentric to the main critical tradition, imposed comprehensive alterations as a price for continued admiration in an individualistic age. It turned out to be short-lived, although still interesting for the questions it raised about psychological contents. Similarly, Stanislavsky's production of *The Cherry*

Orchard as tragedy, although it brought out a real aspect of the play, led to a false grouping with inappropriate congeners, from which it has taken years to disentangle Chekhov's play. And *Hamlet* has not recovered yet from its grouping with novelistic psychologically motivated literature. It has become a difficult, even obfuscated, play.

A historical tradition flows from the original meaning and grouping down through the genre to the new interpretation and regrouping. The continuity of generic descent, without in any way precluding foolishness, orients wisdom about a work. Every critic worthy of the name senses this, and tries to assimilate earlier valid conceptions of the work as part of his own approach. If he has done this effectively, the classic is an open book to him.

Genre in Evaluation

During the third phase of criticism—evaluation—questions of genre are just as central. With the exception of the Chicago School, however, critics have been frightened off them by the specter of prescriptive genre. Concealed prescriptivism is therefore ubiquitous. Most critics subscribe to the ancient principle whereby major genres are distinguished from minor. The classic statement is Horace's, in *Satires* 1.4, where he reserves the name of poetry for inspired writing by a *mens divinior*. He disclaims the term for his satires, and mentions doubts about comedy too, on the ground of its closeness to ordinary speech.[58] Epic, tragedy, and elevated lyric, by contrast, give the inspired poet a more adequate opportunity. Although Horace does not value the genres *per se,* the passage has nevertheless authorized many subsequent rank-orderings of genres on a similar basis. Adrian Marino regards the division of genres into major and minor as "mistaken," since "it establishes a relative, transient, extra-aesthetic scale of values, of a purely historical significance."[59] But "extra-aesthetic" need not put us off: much of the best evaluative criticism is extrinsic.[60] Admittedly the scale of majority is relative. As we have seen, the generic paradigm alters very considerably from period to period. Each age—indeed, each movement—has its own high genres, even if these preferences remain unargued (as with the recent promotion of the social realistic novel). Changes in the paradigm are not random movements, however, so that we can to some extent make allowances for them. Moreover, contemplating earlier evaluations can improve our own perspective. Neither the earliest valuation nor our own is privileged, or above history. But unless we have incorporated relevant values of the past (whether by assimilation or rejection) we cannot hope to make an adequate evaluation of our own. Our own may or may not tend, that is to say, toward a less conditioned judgment. So in revaluing a minor writer, we should try to form not only a relative view, but one that takes the previous depreciation into account. Besides, some aspects of evaluation are unaffected by paradigm shift. Thus, a writer who chose the higher genres *of his own time* remains to that extent greater than another who confined himself to the genres then seen as less demanding. Of course, we may also have to consider his aspiration to modify the genres, or to challenge established values.

By a complementary Aristotelian principle, we judge by the criteria of an appropriate genre. So a work may be "good of its kind." This shibboleth is jeered at by those who are very sure that some kinds are better than others. But not to allow for genre at all would often mean applying generic rules inappropriately, as in James' notorious injustice to Fielding and Trollope.[61] Criticism of novels is particularly prone to inappropriate prescriptivism. One critic prescribes that novels must reflect "historical actuality," another that they should be unified, with single centers.[62] Generalizing the values of the verisimilar novel like this offends against the principle of judging by criteria appropriate to the genre. During the Milton controversy, similarly, *Paradise Lost* was sometimes criticized by canons more appropriate to short lyric genres than to epic, "as if all Poesy had one Character."[63] And it is the same with Leavis' comparison of Herrick and Marvell: a brief elegy of the former is found trivial beside a stanza from a heroic prospect poem by the latter. This is to forget that disparate genres offer different poetic pleasures:

> The wise, and knowing Critic will not say,
> This worst, or better is, before he weigh,
> Where every piece be perfect in the kind . . .
> (Ben Jonson *The Sad Shepherd* Prologue 43–46)

We need to be particularly on guard against a popular genre's imperialism, whereby its values expand to become general norms. In this way "dramatic" has come to be used as a universal criterion; and as a result a severe view is taken of masques, closet drama, Chapman's Byron plays, and other "nondramatic" drama.

However, Aristotle's program of evaluation by the criteria of the genre, and more especially its development by the Chicago School, runs into problems that some—notably E. D. Hirsch—have regarded as insuperable.[64] For a work's intrinsic aims are not given by the class. And genres have in any case no "definable essence or telos" that could be applied as a standard of judgment. We must at once agree that literature and its genres defy definition. But neither Hirsch nor (for that matter) any of the Chicagoans seem to have allowed for the possibility of adjusting criteria according to subgenre. Subgenres are not definable either, of course. But they have a near-inclusive relation to genre, so that criteria based on them have a superior relevance. Thus, even if we cannot define tragedy, we can say something about how Elizabethan revenge tragedy differs from some other subgenres. Approximate criteria based on an appropriate family of works, and on mores and standards shared by the author concerned, are closer to the mark, in practice, than others more extrinsic. At the very least—and this point is in itself sufficient to rebut the cruder versions of Crocian atomism—they enable us to recognize instances of incompetence in genre. For authors are sometimes ignorant, merely, of generic rules and models.

Other criteria in common use are best understood in terms of internal relations within a genre. These have to be seen historically. So Aristotle treats Sophoclean tragedy as the norm because it is "perfected." And Scaliger, in the first modern classic of evaluative criticism, similarly prefers Virgil to Homer by implicit criteria drawn from the more developed stage of epic. He does not examine the ground of his preference—any more than certain modern classicists, who reject generic stages later than the norm as decadent or "silver" or (in Curtius' term) "manneristic." The unexamined preference is for definitive, summational achievement. A contrasting value is originality. This is sometimes spoken of almost as an absolute quality possessed by a work in isolation. But of course it is meaningless apart from specific historical states of a genre. Clearer conceptions of generic development may lead to less simplistic views of the relative standing of works from different historical periods.

Originality is a developmental concept. We value mere novelties at a straw, by comparison with those seminal works that profoundly change their genre. This is made very clear in Ralph Cohen's discerning essay "Innovation and Variation," one of the very few diachronic treatments of originality. Cohen is able to show that the originality of *Cooper's Hill* can only be understood as Denham's response to previous georgic poems. The new type is set off from mere variations of the old by the "different concepts of experience"[65] that its forms imply. Cohen's distinction is a vital one, because the innovative or paradigmatic work is never absolutely original. Before it went partial or experimental attempts that are forgotten in the blaze of its success. Innovation and variation are not the only bases of formal value. Herrick's *Panegyric to Sir Lewis Pemberton* may be regarded as a high point of the estate poem, yet generically speaking it is not an innovative work. Its achievement is summational: as the finest and most definitive example of the genre it towers above such merely variational exercises as Carew's Saxham and Wrest poems. (Marvell's *Upon Appleton House* is rather to be grouped with prospect poems such as *Cooper's Hill* and *Windsor Forest*.) It is much more difficult, however, to compare the value of Herrick's poem with that of Jonson's *To Penshurst*, which also has both innovative and paradigmatic strengths. There seem to be independent grounds for value, according to whether a work comes early in its kind or late. Innovative, paradigmatic, and definitive works all have their places. Of course, they are not permanent places. For example, intensive imitation of a paradigm tends to reduce its originality in the eyes of critics of the next generation. Slavish imitations "gradually strip the model of its merit."[66] And it is for subsequent critics to assess the value of a *Lycidas,* in the face of a Johnson's disgust. Again, innovative or paradigmatic value is not incompatible with a certain dullness (or historical worthiness) in the eyes of posterity. It has a basis distinct from the more lasting value of the summational achievement. Definitive works are valued for qualities other than generic originality. They may even seem conventional—fulfilling rather than breaking rules. But this can be a deceptive matter. A classic work obeying obvious rules may break others less obvious.

The posterity of a work in literature and in criticism has a considerable bearing on its value. Continuing criticism, especially when it changes in response to newly discovered aspects, is a fairly dependable indication of worth. Certainly works that are not criticized and exercise no influence on their genre must have at best a slender reputation. In anomalous instances, generic influence may only be delayed (Sterne; Traherne; Herrick), but even then the reputation is liable to be uncertain. How are we to evaluate *Finnegans Wake* until we know whether it begins an emergent form, or is only an isolated tour de force?

In any full evaluation, many criteria will be balanced together: originality, definitiveness, elegance in variation, generic competence, generic height, and others of a broad-genre or extrinsic character. Excellence according to one may compensate for deficiency according to another, within the economy of genre. Thus, vagueness about conventions of genre can be forgiven in a writer who is effectively innovative, or who easily excels in realizing some of the qualities of the form (Whitman; Clare). And in any case "significant pieces of literature are worth much more than their kind."[67] The value of *Hamlet* has more to do with its profound exploration of life than with its contribution to revenge tragedy. In a sense it is worth more than the whole idea of revenge tragedy. Nevertheless, it is in relation to the forms of that genre, in the first place, that it exists and communicates its vision. It is indeed, for what that is worth, "good of its kind"; although we should want to add that it is so good as to transcend the ordinary values of that relatively low form of tragedy.

Conclusion

From the foregoing chapters, genre might almost be thought to embrace the whole of literary convention. And indeed all literature is organized generically, although not all to the same extent. (For example, many metrical structures have only a very broad significance for genre.) The field of genre being so large, and its role in literary change so central, the question naturally arises of its relation to the social and historical context. What causes genres to change? There are causes to be found—although not necessarily direct ones—in extraliterary events: pastoral was obviously affected by urban development; the factory novel has some connection with the Industrial Revolution. But literary and external histories need to be distinguished. The external has to do with social change and with changes of sensibility that matter deeply to the literary critic. Nevertheless, genre has its own history, too. There are literary laws of change, as we have seen, governing the formation and interaction of genres and the development of canons of genres. And individual works play a part too—especially originative and paradigmatic ones. In trying to account for generic change, therefore, it is not a good idea to turn immediately to explanation in terms of external causes, which may actually be quite remote. In any case, external causation is not in danger of neglect at present. Consequently, the emphasis of the present study has fallen on internal, mediated, or literary causes. This may seem strange to those who think of genres as public and external, in contrast to individual works. But a genre is public only comparatively. It is best thought of, perhaps, as a collective or group creative process; and as such it shares some of the elusiveness of a single work.

The present state of criticism seems not unhopeful from a generic standpoint. True, there have been decades of overconcentration on the novel, which has militated against the variety of imagination that the study of a range of genres fosters. (The novel, being postclassical, has not much tradition of genre criticism.) But there are signs now of a quickening interest in other prose kinds, such as short story, novella, and fabulation, as well as in subgenres of novel. A good deal of the best recent criticism has used a genre approach.

Some good critics have spoken of literature itself as moving away from genre. But that is at best a loose formulation. Much of the tenor of this book has gone to show that while literature may move away from the old genres, it cannot move away from genre altogether without ceasing to be literature. It would neither communicate with readers nor have leverage on existing values.

Another reason for reviving the criticism of genre in something like its traditional sense is that the interests of the critic and of the reader have tended in recent years to diverge. Genre criticism may return us to problems shared by readers and critics—especially the problem of identifying literary works' total forms. For genre is an organizing principle of the redundancies by which it is possible to break the hermeneutic circle and to reconstruct old or difficult works. Above all, dealing in terms of changing genres offers frequent reminders that works of literature come to us from literary communities, with which we in our turn have to form a relation.

NOTES

BIBLIOGRAPHY

INDEX

ABBREVIATIONS

AJP	*American Journal of Philology*
CL	*Comparative Literature*
CQ	*Critical Quarterly*
EC	*Essays in Criticism*
ELR	*English Literary Renaissance*
JEGP	*Journal of English and Germanic Philology*
MLR	*Modern Language Review*
MR	*Massachusetts Review*
N&Q	*Notes and Queries*
NLH	*New Literary History*
NYRB	*New York Review of Books*
OED	*Oxford English Dictionary*
PMLA	*Publications of the Modern Language Association*
PQ	*Philological Quarterly*
RES	*Review of English Studies*
SP	*Studies in Philology*
SR	*Southern Review*
TLS	*Times Literary Supplement*

Notes

1. Literature as a Genre

1. F. E. Sparshott *The Concept of Criticism* (Oxford 1967) 2-3.

2. *Pace* Hazard Adams *Interests of Criticism: An Introduction to Literary Theory* (New York 1969) 1.

3. Ihab Hassan *The Dismemberment of "Orpheus": Toward a Postmodern Literature* (New York 1971) 9; Jacques Rivière "Gratitude to Dada" in *The Ideal Reader* tr. Blanche A. Price (1962).

4. "The Death of Literature" *NLH* 3 (1971) 43.

5. *Poor Poll* 87-90.

6. Monroe C. Beardsley "The Concept of Literature" in *Literary Theory and Structure: Essays in Honour of William K. Wimsatt* ed. Frank Brady et al. (New Haven and London 1973) 36-37, in rebuttal of Colin A. Lyas "The Semantic Definition of Literature" *Journal of Philosophy* 66 (1969) 83.

7. Beardsley "The Concept of Literature" 24.

8. *Anatomy of Criticism: Four Essays* (Princeton 1957) 17. Cf. I. Christopher Butler "What Is a Literary Work?" *NLH* 5 (1973) 17-29.

9. For the distinction between main text (*Haupttext*) and side-text (*Nebentext*) see Roman Ingarden *Das literarische Kunstwerk* 30.6 (Tübingen 1965), tr. George G. Grabowicz as *The Literary Work of Art* (Evanston, Ill. 1973) 208-209, 377. Although its realizations (as distinct from its script) have no words, Beckett's play is probably best regarded as minimalist literature. It has a closer relation to other literary works than most mimes have, or films.

10. Beardsley "The Concept of Literature" 34; cf. Graham Hough *An Essay on Criticism* (London 1966) esp. ch. 9.

11. On Aristotle's position see Bennison Gray *The Phenomenon of Literature* De Proprietatibus Litterarum, ser. maior 36 (The Hague 1975) 37ff. For Sidney's see *A Defence of Poetry* in *Miscellaneous Prose of Sir Philip Sidney* ed. Katherine Duncan-Jones and Jan van Dorsten (Oxford 1973) 102. During the Middle Ages "the very words *story* and *history* had not yet been desynonymized" (C. S. Lewis *The Discarded Image* [Cambridge 1964] 179). Even today, uncertainty about borderline cases is common enough: Carlos Castaneda's *Separate Reality* was reviewed both as fiction and as non-fiction.

12. Tzvetan Todorov "The Notion of Literature" *NLH* 5 (1973) 7–8. The most absolute case for fiction as the basis of literature is probably Bennison Gray's. His argument is a powerful one, which clearly establishes fiction as a central characteristic of literature. But to make it a defining characteristic he must implausibly exclude from literature all "extended literature" and much writing in the central genres (didactic verse, *The Wasteland, Finnegans Wake,* etc.): see *The Phenomenon of Literature* 45, 65ff. See also Thomas J. Roberts *When Is Something Fiction?* (Carbondale, Ill. 1972); Laurence Lerner *The Truest Poetry* (London 1964); William Nelson *Fact or Fiction: The Dilemma of the Renaissance Storyteller* (Cambridge, Mass. 1933); and Herbert Lindenberger *Historical Drama* (Chicago 1975). The most interesting borderline examples are gathered by Gray.

13. "A literary work *purportedly imitates* (or reports) a series of speech acts, which in fact have no other existence." See Richard Ohmann "Speech Acts and the Definition of Literature" *Philosophy and Rhetoric* 4 (1971), cited in Beardsley "The Concept of Literature" 33. Cf. Hough *An Essay* 64–65. There is a more effective symposium on the subject in *Centrum* 3.2 (Minnesota 1975); see especially Martin Steinmann, Jr. "Perlocutionary Acts and the Interpretation of Literature" 112–116.

14. On the instrumental assumptions of Renaissance writers, see Robert M. Strozier "Roger Ascham and Cleanth Brooks: Renaissance and Modern Critical Thought" *EC* 22 (1972) 396–407; and Rosemond Tuve *Elizabethan and Metaphysical Imagery: Renaissance Poetic and Twentieth-Century Critics* (Chicago 1947) esp. ch. 14.

15. "The Notion of Literature" 15.

16. The last point is developed with amusing detail in Gilbert Highet *The Anatomy of Satire* (Princeton 1962) 3.3 "The Hoax as Satire."

17. "Some Aims of Criticism" in *Literary Theory and Structure* ed. Brady 53, rpt. as *The Aims of Interpretation* (Chicago and London 1976) ch. 8. Cf. the same author's "Privileged Criteria in Literary Evaluation" in *Problems of Literary Evaluation* ed. Joseph P. Strelka, Yearbook of Comparative Criticism 2 (State College, Pa. 1969) 22–34 (*The Aims of Interpretation* ch. 7); also Todorov "The Notion of Literature" 5. Todorov's main emphasis, however, is on the development of purely literary terms and methods of analysis, which would allow discussion of it as a separate intrinsic category. See the critique of this program in John Reichert "The Limits of Genre Theory" in *Theories of Literary Genre* ed. Joseph P. Strelka, Yearbook of Comparative Criticism 8 (University Park, Pa. and London 1978) 67ff. On the term "literature" see "La Définition du terme 'literature': Projet d'article pour un dictionnaire international des termes littéraires" in *Proceedings of the Third Congress of the International Comparative Literature Association* (The Hague 1962).

18. The terms *litteratura* and *litterae* in relevant senses can in fact be traced back to the second century A.D.: see René Wellek "What is Literature?" in *What is Literature?* ed. Paul Hernadi (Bloomington, Ind. and London 1978) 16ff. In English, "literature" goes back at least to 1761, sixty years before the *OED*'s first example.

19. Sidney *Defence* ed. van Dorsten 81, 92, 100.

20. So also Aristotle (see Gray *The Phenomenon of Literature* 37) and Sir Thomas Elyot (*The Book Named The Governor* ed. H. S. Croft 2 vols. [1880] 1.120)—but not, apparently, J. C. Scaliger, to judge by *Poetices Libri Septem* (Lyons 1561) 1.2, the (uncharacteristic) passage Sidney probably refers to in his *Defence* (ed. van Dorsten 100). These uses are much earlier than Wellek's eighteenth-century instances of what he

calls the "new aesthetic sense" of literature. However, his title of a work by Aurelio de Giorgi-Bertòla is a clinching example from the present point of view. The first version was entitled *Idea della poesia alemanna* (1779); the expanded version of 1784 changed "poesia" to "bella letteratura."

21. See Rosalie L. Colie *The Resources of Kind: Genre-Theory in the Renaissance* ed. Barbara K. Lewalski (Berkeley 1973) 20-21; also Bernard Weinberg *A History of Literary Criticism in the Italian Renaissance* 2 vols. (Chicago 1961) esp. chs. 13-14. On Aristotle's exclusion of Empedocles from poetry because he did not present a human action, see Gray *The Phenomenon of Literature* 37ff. Gray draws attention (41) to R. S. Crane's inconsistency in conceding the literariness of Lucretius. The Neo-Aristotelians' insistence on literature's indefinability is in Gray's view mere squeamishness about making exclusions from the category.

22. Hirsch "Some Aims of Criticism" 53.

23. Louis Kampf "Culture Without Criticism" *MR* 11 (1970) 624-644.

24. See, e.g., Francis Berry "The Present Willed Shortening of Memory" *NLH* 2 (1970) 56-63; and John Wain *A House for the Truth* (1972) 206.

25. See, e.g., G. Waldmann *Theorie und Didaktik der Trivialliteratur: Modellanalysen-Didaktikdiskussion-literarische Wertung, Krit. Information* 13 (1973).

26. "The Concept of Literature" 34.

27. See ibid. 28-29. For a strong critique of the language concept, see Gray *The Phenomenon of Literature* 26ff. Broader questions about literature's relation to language are discussed in Barbara Herrnstein Smith *On the Margins of Discourse: The Relation of Literature to Language* (Chicago and London 1978), and especially in André Lefevere *Literary Knowledge* (Amsterdam 1977) ch. 6.

28. Jean-Paul Sartre *What is Literature?* tr. Bernard Frechtman (1950) 10-11.

29. For the notion of foregrounding see Gerald L. Bruns *Modern Poetry and the Idea of Language: A Critical and Historical Study* (New Haven and London 1974) 78.

30. "The Semantic Definition" *Journal of Philosophy* 66 (1969).

31. Coleridge *Biographia Literaria* ed. J. Shawcross 2 vols. (Oxford 1907) 2.10; cited in Butler "What is a Literary Work?" 25.

32. See, e.g., "Littérature médiévale et expérience esthétique" *Poétique* 8 (1977) 322-336, a review article developed subsequently in "La Jouissance esthétique" *Poétique* 10 (1979) 261-274.

33. *The Rambler,* 23 March 1751.

34. Cf. the position in David Newton-de Molina *"Tempus edax rerum:* A Note on an Aspect of Frank Kermode's Theory of Fictions" *CQ* 12 (1970) 361-362.

35. See Hirsch "Some Aims of Criticism" 56; also *The Aims of Interpretation* ch. 6, a strong argument that "the values of literature are continuous with all other shared values of human culture." Nevertheless, attempts have been made to exclude evaluation from literary theory altogether, notably in Northrop Frye's *Anatomy of Criticism* and in Bennison Gray's *Phenomenon of Literature* (esp. 57ff.).

36. Hough *An Essay* 58. Cf. Beardsley "The Concept of Literature" 37-38: works can be literature by deficiency of illocutionary force or excess of semantic display (both departures, it is argued, from pragmatic function).

37. For textuality as a defining characteristic, see F. E. Sparshott "On the Possibility of Saying What Literature Is" in *What is Literature?* ed. Hernadi 9.

38. Todorov "The Notion of Literature" 14.

39. On the positive harmfulness of a unified account of literature, see Sparshott "On the Possibility of Saying What Literature Is" 9.

40. Butler "What is a Literary Work?" 29. On literature as institution, see Claudio Guillén *Literature as System* (Princeton 1971) index, s.v. *Institutions;* H. Levin *The Gates of Horn* (New York 1963) 16–23; F. Jameson "Magical Narratives: Romance as Genre" *NLH* 7.1 (1975) 135–163.

2. Ancient Misapprehensions

1. Colin Cherry *On Human Communication* (New York 1961) 18–19.

2. On situation of utterance, see John Lyons *Introduction to Theoretical Linguistics* (Cambridge 1968) 275ff.

3. E. E. Cummings *Complete Poems* 2 vols. (1968) 2.662. On Cummings' consistent but idiosyncratic grammar, see Norman Friedman *E. E. Cummings: The Art of his Poetry* (London and Baltimore 1960). On abrogation of linguistic rules in modern poetry, see Samuel R. Levin *Linguistic Structures in Poetry* Janua Linguarum, ser. min. 23 (The Hague 1973); and idem *The Semantics of Metaphor* (Baltimore 1977). And on grammaticality in literature, see J. P. Thorne "Stylistics and Generative Grammars" *Journal of Linguistics* 1 (1965), rpt. in *Linguistics and Literary Style* ed. D. Freeman (New York 1970); idem "Poetry, Stylistics and Imaginary Grammars" *Journal of Linguistics* 5 (1969), rpt. in *Literaturwissenschaft und Linguistik* 2.2 *Zur linguistischen Basis der Literaturwissenschaft* 1, ed. J. Ihwe (Frankfort 1971); and idem "Generative Grammars and Stylistic Analysis" in *New Horizons in Linguistics* ed. J. Lyons (Harmondsworth 1970).

4. Bennison Gray to the contrary; see *The Phenomenon of Literature* De Proprietatibus Litterarum, ser. maior 36 (The Hague 1975) 30. This is not to deny the validity of Hirsch's argument about synonymity in *The Aims of Interpretation* (Chicago and London 1976) ch. 4. But even if propositional synonymity of literary works were to occur in practice, this option (or neglect) on the writer's part would affect the meaning, considered as a literary communication. The negligence would be part of his stance.

5. "Information Theory and Literary Genres" in *Zagadnienia Rodzajów Literackich* 4.1 (6) (Lodz 1961) 31–48; developing a concept of code set out by Mukařovský: see *Theories of Literary Genre* ed. Joseph P. Strelka, Yearbook of Comparative Criticism 8 (University Park, Pa. and London 1978) 257. A partial exception must be made for the semiotic contribution by Thomas G. Winner, "Structural and Semiotic Genre Theory" (in the same volume), which does recognize the diachronic variation of genre.

6. *Pace* Arthur K. Moore *Contestable Concepts of Literary Theory* (Baton Rouge 1973) 161n. Although Croce's theory has lost its relevance, it was historically justified. On Thibaudet's and similar views, see Adrian Marino "A Definition of Literary Genres" in *Theories of Literary Genre* ed. Strelka 52.

7. "Tradition and the Individual Talent" *Selected Essays* (London 1951) 15. Here again the communication theory analogy breaks down. In telecommunication's simpler sequentiality, modulating a signal fortunately has no such repercussions.

8. *Validity in Interpretation* (New Haven and London 1967) 50, 81.

9. Hough *An Essay on Criticism* (London 1966) 83.

10. Cornelis F.P. Stutterheim "Prolegomena to a Theory of the Literary Genres" *Zagadnienia Rodzajów Literackich* 6.2 (11) (Lodz 1964) 18–19.

11. Compare John Reichert "The Limits of Genre Theory" in *Theories of Literary Genre* ed. Strelka 76.

12. This point is developed in Chapter 3. Theorists nevertheless frequently speak of defining individual genres and even literature itself. On some of the reasons why the latter enterprise is foolish, see E. D. Hirsch "What Isn't Literature?" in *What Is Literature?* ed. Hernadi (Bloomington, Ind. and London 1978) 24–34.

13. Lines 56–57; *Ben Jonson* ed. C. H. Herford, P. and E. M. Simpson, 11 vols. (Oxford 1925–1952) 7.10. This remarkable passage (ll. 31–66) is relevant in its entirety.

14. George Watson *The Study of Literature* (1969) 86. On the fragmentary character of eighteenth-century genre theory, see Ralph Cohen "On the Interrelations of Eighteenth-Century Literary Forms" in *New Approaches to Eighteenth-Century Literature* ed. Phillip Harth (New York and London 1974) 33–78. The point about the disparity of medieval genre criticism is qualified in Chapter 7; but it remains true of secular literary theory, with the exception of a few genres such as the *epistola*.

15. Claudio Guillén is unfair to Scaliger, however, when he compares him unfavorably with Minturno and denies that he made any "attempt to adjust traditional systems to the masterpieces of his own age"; see Claudio Guillén *Literature as System* (Princeton 1971) 404 [hereafter referred to as Guillén]. In fact, although Scaliger was primarily concerned with the ancient paradigmatic authors, he was also keenly interested in new generic forms. He draws attention in this regard to the achievements of "magnus vir Sanazarus" (*Poetices* 150.a.1) and claims to have extended the subject matter of pastoral.

16. This influence is one of the themes of Rosalie L. Colie *The Resources of Kind: Genre Theory in the Renaissance* ed. Barbara K. Lewalski (Berkeley 1973).

17. Nicholas Rowe "Some Account of the Life etc. of Mr William Shakespeare" (1709) in *Eighteenth Century Essays on Shakespeare* ed. D. Nichol Smith (Glasgow 1903) 10. For a shrewd defense of neoclassical drama criticism, revealing some of the issues underlying its prescriptions, see Thora B. Jones and Bernard de B. Nicol *Neo-Classical Dramatic Criticism 1560–1770* (Cambridge 1976).

18. *The Critical Works of John Dennis* ed. Edward Niles Hooker, 2 vols. (Baltimore 1939, 1943) 1.353.

19. Samuel Johnson "Preface to Shakespeare" (1765) in *Eighteenth Century Essays on Shakespeare* ed. Smith 131.

20. Guillén 128–129.

21. Bernard Weinberg *A History of Literary Criticism in the Italian Renaissance* 2 vols. (Chicago 1961) 2.1104.

22. "Heads of an Answer to Rymer" 6.40; *"Of Dramatic Poesy" and Other Critical Essays* ed. George Watson, 2 vols. (London and New York 1962) 1.218.

23. *L'Arte Poetica* (1564) Poetiken des Cinquecento 6 (Munich 1971) 35, discussing the "vitio di romanzi nell'interromper la narratione."

24. Probability as a rule of the novel was discussed by Hawthorne and James, as Hough notes (*An Essay* 112); but it was already implicit in eighteenth-century criticism.

25. *TLS* (9 May 1975) 520. Mixture of novel and essay has honorable precedents in Thackeray and Huxley, of course; Conrad's point is that the mixture is badly handled—as "jostled" implies.

26. F. R. and Q. D. Leavis *Dickens the Novelist* (1970) 113-114, 116. Compare the disapproval of melodrama in Wilkie Collins; see H. P. Sucksmith's introduction to Wilkie Collins *The Woman in White* (London 1975) vii, xvi. Prescriptive rules are more explicitly applied in Marxist criticism of novels. With poetry, modern prescriptiveness is sometimes very severe: a striking instance is John Barrell and John Bull's introduction to *The Penguin Book of English Pastoral Verse* (London 1975).

27. See Colie *Resources of Kind* 76ff.

28. *The Rambler* no. 125 (Tues. 28 May 1751) ed. W. J. Bate and Albrecht B. Strauss in *Works* Yale Edition vol. 4 (New Haven and London 1969) 300.

29. *The Critical Works* 1.406.

30. Ibid. 2.68. On the generic spirits, see Hooker's introduction, ibid. 2. lxxxvi, xc; also 2.198, 484 et passim.

31. See Guillén 377; cf. 111-112, 120. The idea occurs as early as Dante: see *De vulgari eloquentia* 2.9.2: "The term was invented . . . so that what the whole art of the *canzone* was to be contained within would be called a '*stanza*,' which is to say, a room, or receptacle, with a capacity for the whole art" (tr. Robert S. Haller *Literary Criticism of Dante Alighieri* [Lincoln, Neb. 1973] 50).

32. Guillén 129.

33. See Weinberg, index s.v. *Epic, Romance;* Guillén 108-109; Graham Hough *A Preface to "The Faerie Queen"* (1962) esp. chs. 1 and 3; and many studies of Spenser's use of classical and Renaissance Italian generic models, such as A. Bartlett Giamatti *The Earthly Paradise and the Renaissance Epic* (Princeton 1966).

34. Rosalie L. Colie *Shakespeare's Living Art* (Princeton 1974) 263, 266. See Weinberg, index s.v. *Guarini, Tragicomedy.*

35. T. S. Eliot, introduction to *Ezra Pound: Selected Poems* (rev. ed. 1948) x.

36. See Guillén 130-131.

37. Hassan *The Dismemberment of "Orpheus": Toward a Postmodern Literature* (New York 1971) 254 (cf. William Righter *Logic and Criticism* [1963] 120-122); René Wellek *Discriminations: Further Concepts of Criticism* (New Haven and London 1970) 225.

38. On the recurrence of modernism and its dependence on tradition, see J. V. Cunningham *Tradition and Poetic Structure: Essays in Literary History and Tradition* (Denver 1960) 106ff.

39. Robert Herrick *To M. Leonard Willan his peculiar friend,* in *Poetical Works* ed. L. C. Martin (Oxford 1956) 298.6.

40. See Weinberg 2.782-783.

41. On the paradigms, see further in Chapter 11.

42. *Anatomy* 22; cf. the more extreme stance of Louis Kampf in "Culture without Criticism" *MR* 11.4 (1970) 624-644.

43. On Fernand Braudel, see Guillén 386, 416.

44. See, e.g., *Resources of Kind* ch. 3; also 127—which, however, concedes too much to the idea of genre as conservative.

45. On the incorporation of the avant-garde in the contemporary literary estab-

lishment, see Gerald Graff *Literature Against Itself: Literary Ideas in Modern Society* (Chicago 1979).

3. Concepts of Genre

1. *An Essay on Criticism* (London 1966) 84.

2. Henry Home, Lord Kames *Elements of Criticism* 3 vols. ([Edinburgh 1762] facs. rpt. New York 1967) 3.219. See Adrian Marino in *Theories of Literary Genre* ed. Joseph P. Strelka (University Park, Pa. and London 1978) 49; John Reichert ibid. 65; and A. F. B. Clark *Boileau and the French Classical Critics in England (1660-1830)* (Paris 1925) 301. Voltaire's *Essai sur la poésie épique* gave an impulse in the same direction.

3. E. Donald Hirsch *Validity in Interpretation* (New Haven and London 1967) 50. Cf. Rudolf Carnap *The Logical Structure of the World* sects. 29, 30, 33, tr. Rolf A. George (Berkeley 1969) 51-54, 57-58. Paul Hernadi compares genres to Max Weber's "ideal types" in *Beyond Genre: New Directions in Literary Classification* (Ithaca and London 1972) 8. Klaus Hempfer *Gattungstheorie: Information und Synthese* (Munich 1973) attempts to avoid both nominalist and realist positions: see the revision by Paul Hernadi, *Comparative Literature* 28 (1976) 83-85.

4. Bennison Gray *The Phenomenon of Literature* (The Hague 1975) 56 regrets that Aristotle gives "non-defining characteristics and subspecies" of literature but "does not define the species."

5. See the survey by John Reichert in *Theories of Literary Genre* ed. Strelka 62-63. Reichert himself boldly rejects mutually exclusive categories, ibid. 65.

6. Claudio Guillén *Literature as System* (Princeton 1971) 121 [hereafter referred to as Guillén].

7. Francis Cairns *Generic Composition in Greek and Roman Poetry* (Edinburgh 1972) 6.

8. See Richmond Lattimore *Story Patterns in Greek Tragedy* (Ann Arbor 1969) 13n39.

9. *Heads of an Answer to Rymer* 12; *"Of Dramatic Poesy" and Other Critical Essays* ed. George Watson 2 vols. (London and New York 1962) 1.213.

10. A full bibliography is impossible here. Among many works worth consulting may be mentioned Willard Farnham *The Medieval Heritage of Elizabethan Tragedy* (Berkeley 1936); Fredson T. Bowers *Elizabethan Revenge Tragedy 1587-1642* (Princeton 1940); L. L. Brodwin *Elizabethan Love Tragedy 1587-1625* (London 1972); and, on English tragedy, J. V. Cunningham *Tradition and Poetic Structure* (Denver 1960) 170ff, 185.

11. Hernadi *Beyond Genre* 4.

12. Ludwig Wittgenstein *Philosophische Untersuchungen* (Frankfurt 1967) tr. G.E.M. Anscombe as *Philosophical Investigations* (Oxford 1953) sections 65-77.

13. Robert C. Elliott "The Definition of Satire" *Yearbook of Comparative and General Literature* 11 (1962); Maurice Mandelbaum "Family Resemblances and Generalization Concerning the Arts" *American Philosophical Quarterly* 2.3 (1965); Hough *An Essay* 86; Guillén 130ff.

14. See Gray *The Phenomenon of Literature* 49ff, 197ff.

15. Paul Delany *British Autobiography in the Seventeenth Century* (New York 1969) 1.

16. *The Rambler* no. 125 (Tues. 28 May 1751); *Works* vol. 4 ed. W. J. Bate and Albrecht B. Strauss (New Haven and London 1961) 300.

17. Yet it would be wrong to hold (with Gray) that the biological relation directly accounts for all family resemblance. After all, that partly extends to adopted children and to spouses exhibiting a marriage likeness.

18. Gordon Braden *The Classics and English Renaissance Poetry: Three Case Studies* (New Haven and London 1978) 137.

19. Abraham Cowley *Essays, Plays and Sundry Verses* ed. A. R. Waller (Cambridge 1906) 457.

20. Cf. Sol Worth "Seeing Metaphor as Caricature" *NLH* 6.1 (1974) 208–209.

21. Albert William Levi "Literature and the Imagination: A Theory of Genres" in *Theories of Literary Genre* ed. Strelka 18; Michael Riffaterre "The Stylistic Approach to Literary History" *NLH* 2.1 (1970) 52.

22. See Robert E. Scholes *Structuralism in Literature: An Introduction* (New Haven and London 1974) 128.

23. Guillén 121, 386.

24. Rosalie L. Colie *The Resources of Kind* (Berkeley 1973) 30.

25. See Bernard Weinberg *A History of Literary Criticism in the Italian Renaissance* 2 vols. (Chicago 1961) 2.774, 2.780.

26. Ibid. 2.770. Patrizi here uses *poesia* in a sense nearer to "poetry" than "imaginative literature": cf. and contrast "The Changing Paideia", Chapter 1 above.

27. Among many studies, see H. J. Chaytor *From Script to Print: An Introduction to Medieval Literature*(Cambridge 1945); Michael N. Nagler *Spontaneity and Tradition: A Study in the Oral Art of Homer* (Berkeley 1975); Bruce A. Rosenberg "The Genres of Oral Narrative" in *Theories of Literary Genre* ed. Strelka 150–165; and the special issue of *NLH,* vol. 8.3 (1977).

28. *The Study of Literature* (London 1969) 87.

29. On this polarity see, e.g., Brian Stock "Literary Discourse and the Social Historian" *NLH* 8.2 (1977) 183–194.

30. F.E. Sparshott *The Concept of Criticism* (Oxford 1967) 179–180.

31. See *The Classics and English Renaissance Poetry* 55–153.

32. Thomas Warton *Observations on the Fairy Queen of Spenser* 2nd ed. enl. 2 vols. (1762), facs. rpt. 2 vols. in 1 (Farnborough 1969) 1.9, 1.4.

33. Joseph Spence *Observations, Anecdotes and Characters of Books and Men* ed. James M. Osborn 2 vols. (Oxford 1966) sections 439–440.

34. *Lives of the English Poets* ed. George Birkbeck Hill 3 vols. (Oxford 1905) 3.254.

35. Ibid. 255, 257; 260, 270; 261; 267 (cf. 268–269).

36. *Prose Works* ed. W. J. B. Owen and J. W. Smyser vol. 2 (Oxford 1974) 57.

37. Letter to Eleanor Farjeon, cited in Edward Thomas *Poems and Last Poems* ed. Edna Longley (1973) 321.

4. Historical Kinds and the Generic Repertoire

1. Thomas G. Rosenmeyer *The Green Cabinet: Theocritus and the European Pastoral Lyric* (Berkeley and Los Angeles 1969) index s.v. *Hesiodic tradition;* John Taylor "The Patience of *The Winter's Tale" EC* 23 (1973) esp. 333.

2. René Wellek and Austin Warren *Theory of Literature* 3rd ed. rev. (New York 1962) 231.

3. Claudio Guillén *Literature as System* (Princeton 1971) 112-113.

4. *Poetics* 6, 1450a; but the whole section is relevant. The English equivalents given for Aristotle's terms are necessarily somewhat inexact. Very different translations have sometimes been made, as Northrop Frye's "theme" for *dianoia*.

5. E.g., Rosalie Colie's, in *The Resources of Kind* (Berkeley 1973) and *Shakespeare's Living Art* (Princeton 1974)—where, however, no consistent distinction is made between kinds and modes. Anyone working in this field is painfully aware of the variety of current nomenclature. To mention only two examples, readers should be watchful for Allan Rodway's use of several of the categorial terms in quite different senses in *The Truths of Fiction* (London 1970); and for *kind* as "presentational mode" (dramatic, lyric, etc.) in Ulrich Weisstein *Comparative Literature and Literary Theory: Survey and Introduction* tr. William Riggan (Bloomington, Ind. and London 1973).

6. On Menander, see Francis Cairns *Generic Composition in Greek and Roman Poetry* (Edinburgh 1972) 39.

7. *Satires* 2.1.1-2; Colie (*Resources of Kind* 12) thinks he was.

8. Incidental symbolism, of course, is not lacking in early picaresque: see Alexander A. Parker *Literature and the Delinquent* (Edinburgh 1967); and Javier Herrero "The Great Icons of the Lazarillo: The Bull, the Wine, the Sausage and the Turnip" *Literature and Ideology* 1 (1968). But the main generic features have a more direct and literal force. On picaresque, see further H. Sieber *The Picaresque: The Critical Idiom* (London and New York 1977); R. Bjornson *The Picaresque Hero in European Fiction* (Madison, Wis. 1977); and Alexander Blackburn *The Myth of the Picaro: Continuity and Transformation of the Picaresque Novel 1554-1954* (Chapel Hill 1979).

9. Tzvetan Todorov classes features as syntactic, pragmatic, or verbal.

10. *The Art of English Poesy* ed. Gladys Doidge Willcock and Alice Walker (Cambridge 1936) 38.

11. *Poetics* 12, 1452b, 17-24.

12. For many examples, see Alastair Fowler *Triumphal Forms* (Cambridge 1970).

13. *Poetics* 4, 1448b, 10ff.

14. Weisstein *Comparative Literature* 120.

15. See George Saintsbury *A History of English Prosody* 3 vols. (1906-1910) for numerous examples; also Derek Attridge *The Rhythms of English Poetry* (London, forthcoming).

16. Partly on that ground, Cairns denies it to be a genre (*Generic Composition* 92).

17. In "Nuns fret not at their convent's narrow room" and "Scorn not the Sonnet, Critic, you have frowned." See J. Hillis Miller "The Still Heart: Poetic Form in Wordsworth" *NLH* 2.2 (1971) 297-310.

18. See Weisstein *Comparative Literature* 122. But a sense of the "dimensional ground" returns: see Ian Reid *The Short Story* (London and New York 1977), ch. 4.

On the novella generally, see Mary Doyle Springer *Forms of the Modern Novella* (Chicago 1976); Robert J. Clements and Joseph Gibaldi *Anatomy of the Novella: The European Tale Collection from Boccaccio and Chaucer to Cervantes* (New York 1977).

19. "Tu dois sçavoir que toute sorte de Poesie a l'argument propre à son subject: l'Heroique, armes, assaults de villes, batailles, escarmouches, conseils et discours des capitaines.": Ronsard "Au Lecteur" before *Les Odes* (Paris 1587), cited in Colie *Resources of Kind* 24. Contrast Thackeray, who is equally clear about subjects for the kind of novel represented by *Vanity Fair:* "We do not claim to rank among the military novelists. Our place is with the non-combatants. When the decks are cleared for action we go below and wait meekly" (ch. 30).

20. *A Defence of Poetry* in *Miscellaneous Prose of Sir Philip Sidney* ed. Katherine Duncan-Jones and Jan van Dorsten (Oxford 1973) 94.

21. Colie *Resources of Kind* 28.

22. George Watson *The Study of Literature* (London 1969) 89.

23. On Milton, see John M. Steadman *Milton and the Renaissance Hero* (Oxford 1967); and Dennis H. Burden *The Logical Epic: A Study of the Argument of "Paradise Lost"* (1967). On the chivalric virtues, see Ernst Robert Curtius *European Literature and the Latin Middle Ages* tr. Willard R. Trask, Bollingen Series 36 (New York and London 1953) excursus 18 "The 'Chivalric System of the Virtues.' " On the sagas, see Hermann Pálsson "Icelandic Sagas and Medieval Ethics" *Medieval Scandinavia* 7 (1974). More generally, see *Concepts of the Hero in the Middle Ages and the Renaissance* ed. Norman T. Burns and Christopher J. Reagan (Albany 1975).

24. See, e.g., J. M. Nosworthy *Shakespeare's Occasional Plays: Their Origin and Transmission* (London 1965); Emrys Jones "Bosworth Eve" *EC* 25 (1975); C. L. Barber *Shakespeare's Festive Comedy* (Princeton 1959); Leslie Hotson *The First Night of "Twelfth Night"* (London 1954); Josephine Waters Bennett *"Measure for Measure" as Royal Entertainment* (New York 1966); and R. Christopher Hassel Jr. *Renaissance Drama and the English Church Year* (Lincoln, Neb. and London 1979).

25. For a definition of attitude, see Randolph Quirk et. al. *A Grammar of Contemporary English* (London 1972) 1.27. Some would introduce here the idea of "register" (Quirk 1.24), but that has proved a very loose concept.

26. Cairns *Generic Composition* 9.

27. On description, see Michael Irwin *Picturing: Description and Illusion in the Nineteenth-Century Novel* (1979). On naturalism of setting in melodrama, ghost stories, etc., see H. P. Sucksmith's introduction to Wilkie Collins *The Woman in White* (London 1975) xi–xii.

28. Letter to Raleigh. On a tradition of dividing the hero into practical and ethic parts, see James Nohrnberg *The Analogy of "The Faerie Queen"* (Princeton 1976) 58ff.

29. See, e.g., *Concepts of the Hero,* ed. Burns and Reagan; Steadman *Milton and the Renaissance Hero;* Mario Praz *The Hero in Eclipse in Victorian Fiction* (London 1956); Patricia Thomson *The Victorian Heroine: A Changing Ideal* (London 1956); Walter L. Reed *Meditations on the Hero: A Study of the Romantic Hero in Nineteenth-Century Fiction* (New Haven 1974); Mary Doyle Springer *A Rhetoric of Literary Character: Some Women of Henry James* (Chicago 1978); and Hans Robert Jauss "Levels of Identification of Hero and Audience" *NLH* 5.2 (1974) 283–317.

30. See Enid Welsford *The Fool: His Social and Literary History* (London 1935); William Willeford *The Fool and His Sceptre* (Evanston, Ill. and London 1969); Walter

Kaiser *Praisers of Folly: Erasmus, Rabelais, Shakespeare* (Cambridge, Mass. 1963); and many studies of the *Commedia dell'Arte,* such as Kathleen M. Lea *Italian Popular Comedy* 2 vols. (Oxford 1934); and Allardyce Nicoll *The World of Harlequin: A Critical Study of the Commedia dell'Arte* (Cambridge 1963). For other character types, consult Claude Aziza and Robert Sctrick *Dictionnaire des types et caractères littéraires* (Paris 1978).

31. Jean Chapelain "Letter or Discourse . . . to Monsieur Favereau . . ." in *The Continental Model: Selected French Critical Essays of the Seventeenth Century, in English Translation* ed. Scott Elledge and Donald Schier, rev. ed. (Ithaca and London 1970) 18. A similar contrast was made much earlier, by Minturno, Tasso, and others.

32. Ibid. 19–20.

33. Edmond Faral *Les Arts poétiques du 12ᵉ et du 13ᵉ siècle* (Paris 1962) 221–231, 285–293, cited in J. W. H. Atkins *English Literary Criticism: The Medieval Phase* (Cambridge 1943) 108. See James J. Murphy *Rhetoric in the Middle Ages: A History of Rhetorical Theory from Saint Augustine to the Renaissance* (Berkeley 1974) 172–173.

34. See, e.g., George Puttenham *The Art of English Poesy* (1589) bk. 3 chs. 5–6, discussed in Rosemond Tuve *Elizabethan and Metaphysical Imagery* (Chicago 1947) 240–243.

35. On his own line "Hail thou, who must God's wife, God's mother be!" Cowley comments *"God's Wife.* Though the word seem bold, I know no hurt in the figure. And *Spouse* is not a Heroical word" (*Davideis* bk. 2 n. 92; in *Poems* ed. A. R. Waller [Cambridge 1905] 321).

36. *Odyssey* 20.366–368; discussed in James Sutherland *A Preface to Eighteenth Century Poetry* (Oxford 1948) 88–89.

37. See, e.g., Tuve *Elizabeth and Metaphysical Imagery* ch. 9. esp. 224; Barbara K. Lewalski *Donne's "Anniversaries" and the Poetry of Praise* (Princeton 1973) ch. 1; O. B. Hardison *The Enduring Monument* (Chapel Hill 1962); Rosalie L. Colie *Paradoxia Epidemica: The Renaissance Tradition of Paradox* (Princeton 1966); John Arthos *The Language of Natural Description in Eighteenth-Century Poetry* (Ann Arbor 1949); Dorothy S. McCoy *Tradition and Convention: A Study of Periphrasis in English Pastoral Poetry from 1557 to 1715* (The Hague 1965); and (on anaphora in pastoral) Thomas G. Rosenmeyer *The Green Cabinet: Theocritus and the European Pastoral Lyric* (Berkeley and Los Angeles 1969) 307n65.

38. See, however, Roger Fowler *Linguistics and the Novel* (1977) for an exploration of uses of language that are carried furthest in novels.

39. See Frank Kermode "Novel and Narrative" in *The Theory of the Novel: New Essays* ed. John Halperin (New York and London 1974) 159ff.

5. Generic Names

1. Edmond Faral *Les Arts poétiques du 12ᵉ et du 13ᵉ siècle* (Paris 1962) 87.

2. See Gilbert Highet *The Anatomy of Satire* (Princeton 1962) index s.v. *Names.*

3. Ibid. 275n50.

4. *The Faber Book of Epigrams and Epitaphs* ed. Geoffrey Grigson (London 1977) no. 38 [hereafter referred to as Grigson].

5. Grigson nos. 24, 25, 46.

6. Walter de la Mare *Ding Dong Bell* (London 1924) 71.

7. Ibid. 64.

8. Here we must leave aside many interesting questions of a more specific character, such as whether Corinna alludes to Ovid's mistress only, or is meant also to suggest the lyric poetess.

9. *Mr.* Corydon, however, indicates mixture, since pastoral names are never surnames. On pastoral names in classical literature, the fullest treatment is C. Wendel *De Nominibus Bucolicis* (Leipzig 1900). On Mopsus, see Scaliger *Poetices* 7.d.2.

10. Thomas G. Rosenmeyer *The Green Cabinet* (Berkeley and Los Angeles) index s.v. *Theocritus: Idyll 11.*

11. William Diaper *The Complete Works* ed. Dorothy Broughton (London 1952) 301, 303, 306.

12. Ibid. xxvii.

13. Petrarch *Bucolicum Carmen* 6; see Helen Cooper "The Goat and the Eclogue" *PQ* 53 (1974) 369–370; and idem *Pastoral: Medieval into Renaissance* (Ipswich and To-towa, N.J. 1977) 191. On an earlier stage of the tradition, in Pomponius, see Ernst Robert Curtius *European Literature and the Latin Middle Ages* (New York and London 1953) 261. With the Spenser and Drayton examples compare Thomas Randolph's *Eclogue to Master Jonson* (1632), which has Tityrus to represent Jonson, Damon to represent Randolph himself.

14. On the names in *The Shepherd's Calendar* see the controversial study by Paul E. McLane *Spenser's "Shepherd's Calendar": A Study in Elizabethan Allegory* (Notre Dame 1961). On those in *Colin Clout's Come Home Again* see *Variorum Spenser,* supplemented by Leslie Hotson *Mr W.H.* (New York 1965) 193–200; S. Meyer *An Interpretation of Edmund Spenser's "Colin Clout"* (Notre Dame 1969); and Helen I. Sandison "Eglantine of Meliflure" *TLS* (6 July 1962) 493.

15. The innovations are not very radical. Considering those of Googe's names that are not obviously nuclear: Sirenus and Selvagia are in Sannazaro, Cornix suggests Petrarch's Volucer, while Faustus and Felix correspond to Petrarch's Festino and Mantuanus' Fortunatus. Pope's and Virgil's lists might be analyzed similarly.

16. *The Guardian* no. 40 (27 April 1713); *Prose Works of Alexander Pope* ed. Norman Ault vol. 1 (Oxford 1936) 98–99. Hobbinol was taken up again as a burlesque pastoral name in Somerville's *Hobbinol:* see John Chalker *The English Georgic* (London 1969) 188. Before Philips, it had been used as a "nuclear" English pastoral name in Shirley's *Triumph of Beauty,* and in Cotton's humorous lyric epistle *To My Friend Mr John Anderson From the Country* (where it keeps company with Winne, Besse, Jinne, Sisley, and Clout).

17. See *English Pastorals* ed. Edmund K. Chambers (London 1906) xlvi; John Gay *Poetry and Prose* ed. Vinton A. Dearing and Charles E. Beckwith vol. 2 (Oxford 1974) 513.

18. On romance names and naming see R. R. Bezzola *Le Sens de l'aventure et de l'amour* (Chrétien de Troyes) (Paris 1947), cited in John Stevens *Medieval Romance: Themes and Approaches* (London 1973) 117n8. There are several useful indexes of romance and heroic names, notably G. D. West *An Index of Proper Names in French Arthurian Verse Romances, 1150–1300* (Toronto 1969); idem *French Arthurian Prose Romances: An Index of Proper Names* (Toronto 1977); and George T. Gillespie *A Cata-*

logue of Persons Named in German Heroic Literature, 700-1600 (Oxford 1973). For an early discussion of names in epic, see Minturno, *L'Arte Poetica* (1564) 39.

19. On the proemial conventions of the novel, see Chapter 6 below.

20. See Rosenmeyer 107, commenting on Virgil's departure from the convention, in *Eclogues* 5, by introducing an unnamed character.

21. "An Essay on the New Species of Writing founded by Mr Fielding . . ." rpt. in *Novel and Romance 1700-1800* ed. Ioan Williams (London 1970) 153.

22. *The Rise of the Novel: Studies in Defoe, Richardson and Fielding* (London 1957) 19; the whole passage 18-21 is relevant. The same author's "Serious Reflections on *The Rise of the Novel" Novel* 1.3 (1968) 205-218 adds nothing on the present topic.

23. *Poetics* 9, 1451b, cited in Watt *Rise of the Novel* 19. Aristotle contrasts comedy, in this respect, however, with tragedy, where dramatists "keep to real names" (tōn genomenōn onomatōn antechontai).

24. Ian Watt "The Naming of Characters in Defoe, Richardson, and Fielding" *RES* 25 (1949) 332-338.

25. *Rise of the Novel* 105; cf. "Naming" 322.

26. Watt "Naming" 324.

27. *OED* 2; and cf. Moll Cutpurse, the notorious "roaring girl" of the early seventeenth century.

28. Watt "Naming" 334; 330.

29. Watt *Rise of the Novel* 20.

30. See Watt "Naming" 335-336. The book is the 1720 folio edition of Gilbert Burnet *History of His Own Time:* see *N&Q* ser. 9 no. 48 (26 Nov. 1898) 426.

31. On this point see Sir Alan Gardiner *The Theory of Proper Names* (Oxford 1940) 1-3, 25-28.

32. William Camden *Remains Concerning Britain* (1605), Library of Old Authors ed. (London 1870) 58. A little later, Witwoud was still a real-life name. And even in our own time, there are some factual names stranger than fiction. See, e.g., John Train *Remarkable Names of Real People* (New York 1977).

33. See James Nohrnberg *The Analogy of "The Faerie Queen"* (Princeton 1976) 683n53. However, book 6 is not alone in having allusions to prominent Humanist authors among its character names: we can add Dony (Antonio Francesco Doni).

34. *The Tender Husband* (1705) 2.1, cited in Watt "Naming" 326.

35. Watt argues that since the name "suggested 'vain amatorious romance,' rather than the pedestrian piety of the Andrews household," it implies social pretentiousness on the part of the parents ("Naming" 326). But the *Arcadia* was regarded as a serious book, and widely read by the devout.

36. Watt "Naming" 329. So Herbert Croft wrote, of Edward Young, "A writer does not feign a name of which he only gives the initial letter" (Samuel Johnson *Lives of the English Poets* ed. G. B. Hill 3 vols. [Oxford 1905] 3.381). Watt attributes the passage to Johnson, wrongly. Mary Coleridge is perceptive about incomplete names: "There is a charm about initials: they are rich in promise that the full-blown name hardly fulfils; they are at once intimate and mysterious" (*Chateau D.* in *Non Sequitur* [London 1900] 118).

37. As, e.g., with Maurice Baring's *C.* (1924): "I agreed that a biography was out of the question. We were too near the story; but we were, also, I thought and said, far too near to turn it into fiction" (xi).

38. Berger was no doubt also influenced by the tradition of political (and politic) anonymity, similarly exemplified by Costa-Gavras' *Z*.

6. *Generic Signals*

1. Ernst Robert Curtius *European Literature and the Latin Middle Ages* (New York and London 1953) 83–85. See also Alice S. Miskimin *The Renaissance Chaucer* (New Haven and London 1975) ch. 5, *"Auctoritee* and Modesty," on certain concepts of the poet entailed by Renaissance and medieval allusions.

2. On the *Book of the Duchess* as an allegory of consolation, see Russell A. Peck "Theme and Number in Chaucer's *Book of the Duchess"* in *Silent Poetry* ed. Alastair Fowler (London 1970) 73–115. *The Parlement of Foules* is a similar case: the reference to Cicero and Macrobius (31) shows that it is not an ordinary Valentide poem, but includes a didactic element: see J. A. W. Bennett *The Parlement of Foules: An Interpretation* (Oxford 1957) 18.

3. Vol. 1, chs. 6 and 7.

4. *The Complete Tales of Henry James* ed. Leon Edel vol. 10 (London 1964) 38.

5. E.g., Carl R. Proffer *Keys to "Lolita"* (Bloomington, Ind. 1968); Weldon Thornton *Allusions in "Ulysses": An Annotated List* (Chapel Hill 1968); Adaline Glasheen *Third Census of "Finnegans Wake"* (Berkeley 1977); Brendan O Hehir and John M. Dillon *A Classical Lexicon for "Finnegans Wake"* (Berkeley 1977); Louis O. Mink *A "Finnegans Wake" Gazetteer* (Bloomington, Ind. 1978). Joyce's aim of comprehensiveness makes him an extreme instance.

6. *The Honourable Schoolboy* (London 1977) 105, 333, 400.

7. *Broomsticks and Other Tales* (London 1925) 178, 183. Cf. John Ashbery's use of the fairy tale repertoire in *Self-Portrait in a Convex Mirror* (Manchester, England 1977) 67.

8. Ch. 10. For an interpretation of Hawthorne's fable see Frank Kermode *The Classic* (London 1975) ch. 3.

9. Kinbote's commentary on ll. 920 and 937; *Dunciad* A.1.72.

10. See the discussion of priority in Edward W. Said *Beginnings: Intention and Method* (New York 1975). Examples could, of course, be multiplied. But there are many in the critical literature already. See, e.g., H. D. Kelling's notice of Rabelais allusions in Swift: "Some Significant Names in *Gulliver's Travels" SP* 48 (1951) 761–778.

11. See, however, Dame Helen Gardner "The Titles of Donne's Poems" in *Friendship's Garland: Essays Presented to Mario Praz* ed. Vittorio Gabrieli 2 vols. (Rome 1966) 1.189–207; John Hollander *Vision and Resonance: Two Senses of Poetic Form* (New York 1975) ch. 10; Harry Levin "The Title as a Literary Genre" *MLR* 72 (1977) xxiii–xxxvi; Steven G. Kellman "Dropping Names: The Poetics of Titles" in *Criticism: A Quarterly for Literature and the Arts* 17.2 (Spring 1976) 152–167; and the generically oriented essay "Titles of Books" in Isaac D'Israeli *Curiosities of Literature* 3 vols. (London 1849). There is an early discussion of titling conventions in Aulus Gellius, Pref. 6.

12. Cf. Bergson, cited in Levin.

13. The comparable displacement of *roman* by *histoire, mémoire,* and *aventure* in

eighteenth-century France is discussed by Frédéric Deloffre *La Nouvelle en France à l'âge classique* (Paris 1967), cited in Levin xxix.

14. In the case of *Shirley,* however, we should not forget the presence of substantial romance elements.

15. "Naming" 331–332.

16. See Levin's fuller treatment of this point, xxxiii.

17. On the sources of Orwell's date, see R. E. F. Smith in *Journal of Peasant Studies* 4.1 (1976). The present rule applies only to full-length fiction of the modern and subsequent periods.

18. "Catch-22" perhaps alludes to the Russian idiom "twenty-two troubles." However, it is said that Heller originally called his book *Catch-18.*

19. See Donald J. Gordon *The Renaissance Imagination* (Berkeley 1975) 102.

20. C. J. Rawson's phrase. See his review of Miriam Lerenbaum *Alexander Pope's "Opus Magnum" 1729–1744* in *TLS* (30 Dec. 1977) 1525. Cf. Crabbe's use of "letter" as a part-name to suggest nonliterary informality.

21. John Hollander *Vision and Resonance* (New York 1975) 224.

22. Cf. ibid. 218, 219, 224. I have added further examples.

23. See James J. Murphy *Rhetoric in the Middle Ages* (Berkeley 1974) 204ff and index s.v. *Exordium.*

24. J. W. H. Atkins *English Literary Criticism: The Medieval Phase* (Cambridge 1943) 100–101; Edmond Faral *Les Arts poétiques du 12ᵉ et du 13ᵉ siècle* (Paris 1962) 200–203, 265–268 (Vinsauf *Poetria Nova* 87–202). Cf. John of Garland *Parisiana Poetria* 3: "The artificial beginning is when we start in the middle of the subject or at the end: we can do it in eight ways, and so this beginning has eight branches. The first branch or first type is when the artificial beginning is drawn either from the middle of the subject or from the end, without a proverb and without an example. The beginning is sometimes made with a proverb, which may concern the head of the subject, or the middle, or the end." Under a ninth type, it is noticed that "the ancients, Virgil and Lucan for instance, observed the artificial beginning by putting before the narration the proposition, the invocation, and the motivation of the plot [*causam historiae*]." *The "Parisiana Poetria" of John of Garland* ed. Traugott Lawler (New Haven and London 1974) 53, 57.

25. An earlier draft of *Anna Karenina* had an abrupt opening, inspired by the opening of one of Pushkin's *Belkin's Tales:* "The guests arrived at the country house."

26. See C. S. Lewis *The Discarded Image* (Cambridge 1964) 179.

27. *Discourses on the Heroic Poem* tr. and ed. Mariella Cavalchini and Irene Samuel (Oxford 1973) 115–116. See Gordon Braden *The Classics and English Renaissance Poetry* (New Haven and London 1976) 58 on the generic implications of changes in a single word in the epic *propositio.*

28. *L'Arte* 276.

29. See John Chalker *The English Georgic* (London 1969) 72.

30. Grigson's *Faber Book of Epigrams and Epitaphs* (London 1977), where over 80 epitaphs begin "Here . . ." Another formulaic opening for epitaphs is "Reader, stay [stop, pass on, etc.] . . ."

31. See A. J. Steele "La Fontaine: *Le Fermier, le Chien et le Renard*" in *The Art of Criticism* ed. Peter H. Nurse (Edinburgh 1969) 102–112.

32. *European Literature* 85–88.

33. On the conventions of the dream vision, see A. C. Spearing *Medieval Dream-Poetry* (Cambridge 1976); and cf. Donald R. Howard *The Idea of the Canterbury Tales* (Berkeley 1976) 194.

34. Frank Kermode *The Sense of an Ending: Studies in the Theory of Fiction* (New York 1967) 21.

35. Penelope Lively *The Road to Lichfield* (London 1977) 1; Paul Scott *Staying On* (London 1977).

36. On the connection with *Bartleby* see Richard W. Noland "John Barth and the Novel of Comic Nihilism" *Contemporary Literature* 7.3 (1966) 245.

37. *City Life* (New York and London 1971) 78. Cf. the novelistic application of the interview, as in Michael Wilding *Scenic Drive* (Sydney 1976) ch. 1.

38. *City Life* 73.

7. Mode and Subgenre

1. For a defense of the term "mode," see Paul Alpers "Mode in Narrative Poetry" in *To Tell a Story: Narrative Theory and Practice* Clark Library Seminar Papers (Los Angeles 1973). We shall not be concerned with uses of the term outside genre, such as Frye's grouping of heroes by mimetic "mode."

2. On the pastoral repertoire, see Charles W. Hieatt "The Integrity of Pastoral" *Genre* 5.1 (1972); and especially Thomas G. Rosenmeyer *The Green Cabinet: Theocritus and the European Pastoral Lyric* (Berkeley and Los Angeles 1969); they have little, however, to say about external forms. On pastoral generally, see W. W. Greg *Pastoral Poetry and Pastoral Drama* (London 1906); *English Pastorals Selected and with an Introduction* ed. Edmund K. Chambers (London 1906); William Powell Jones *The Pastourelle* (1931, rpt. New York 1973); William Empson *Some Versions of Pastoral* (London 1935); *English Pastoral Poetry: From the Beginnings to Marvell* ed. J. Frank Kermode (London 1952); W. Leonard Grant *Neo-Latin Literature and the Pastoral* (Durham, N.C. 1965); John Heath-Stubbs *The Pastoral* (London 1969); Harold E. Toliver *Pastoral Forms and Attitudes* (Berkeley 1971); Peter V. Marinelli *Pastoral* (London 1971); Laurence Lerner *The Uses of Nostalgia: Studies in Pastoral Poetry* (London 1972); Raymond Williams *The Country and the City* (London 1973); Renato Poggioli *The Oaten Flute: Essays on Pastoral Poetry and the Pastoral Ideal* (Cambridge, Mass. 1975); Helen Cooper *Pastoral: Medieval into Renaissance* (Ipswich and Totowa, N.J. 1977), with useful bibliography; Richard Feingold *Nature and Society: A Study of Later Eighteenth-Century Uses of the Pastoral and Georgic* (New Brunswick, N.J. 1977); and J. E. Congleton *Theories of Pastoral Poetry in England 1684–1798* (1952, rpt. New York 1968).

3. Jean Chapelain letter to Favereau, in Scott Elledge and Donald Schier *The Continental Model* (Ithaca and London 1970) 11. Cf. Cinthio, who applies "heroic" to romance and even biography, as well as epic.

4. Although the critical viewpoint may be interesting: see, e.g., David Lodge *The Modes of Modern Writing: Metaphor, Metonymy and the Typology of Modern Literature* (London 1977).

5. Rosalie L. Colie *The Resources of Kind* (Berkeley 1973) 67 and see ch. 2 passim.

For the encomiastic mode, see Barbara K. Lewalski *Donne's "Anniversaries" and the Poetry of Praise* (Princeton 1973); O. B. Hardison *The Enduring Monument* (Chapel Hill 1962); and James D. Garrison *Dryden and the Tradition of Panegyric* (Berkeley 1975). For the elegiac, see Abbie Findlay Potts *The Elegiac Mode: Poetic Form in Wordsworth and Other Elegists* (Ithaca 1967).

6. *Resources of Kind* 67.

7. For a list of the matters, as recognized by Scaliger in 1561, see *Poetices* (Lyons 1561) 3.99; p. 150.1.

8. *Il Verato secondo* (1593); see Bernard Weinberg *A History of Literary Criticism in the Italian Renaissance* 2 vols. (Chicago 1961) 2.684. Denores objected to the extension from eclogue to drama: see Weinberg 2.1075 and cf. 1082.

9. Rosalie L. Colie *Shakespeare's Living Art* (Princeton 1974) 244.

10. See S. L. Gilman *The Parodic Sermon in European Perspective: Aspects of Liturgical Parody from the Middle Ages to the Twentieth Century Beiträge zur Lit. des 15 bis 18 Jahrh.* no. 6 (Wiesbaden 1974); Colin J. Horne "The Phalaris Controversy: King *versus* Bentley" *RES* 22 (1946) 294 (on the satirical index); Gilbert Highet *The Anatomy of Satire* (Princeton 1962); Raman Selden *English Verse Satire 1590-1765* (London 1978).

11. See Jerome Mazzaro *Transformations in the Renaissance English Lyric* (Ithaca and London 1970) 157; also further refs. in note 47 below.

12. On the error of identifying medieval and nineteenth-century romance, see John Stevens *Medieval Romance* (London 1973) 20ff. For more synchronic but very interesting approaches see Northrop Frye *The Secular Scripture: A Study of the Structure of the Romance* (Cambridge, Mass. 1976); and B. E. Perry *The Ancient Romances: A Literary-Historical Account of Their Origins* (Berkeley and Los Angeles 1967).

13. *Resources of Kind* 112-114.

14. It would be tedious to catalogue more than token instances: English representatives alone run into three figures with some types. I take my examples from Sir Philip Sidney: (a) *Astrophil and Stella* 1; (b) ibid. 4; (c) ibid. 2; (d) ibid. 9, 11, 12, 29, 43, 77; (e) ibid. 73, 74; (f) ibid. 17; (g) ibid. 87-89; (h) ibid. 59; (i) "Leave me, O Love, which reaches but to dust."

15. Petrarch *Canzoniere* 151, 154. See the notes to *Astrophil and Stella* 7, 9 in *The Poems of Sir Philip Sidney*, ed. W. A. Ringler (Oxford 1962) 462-463; also Janet G. Scott *Les Sonnets élisabéthains* (Paris 1929) 42. For examples, see *Amoretti* 7-9; *Astrophil and Stella* 7, 26, 42, 48, 76.

16. *Les Blasons anatomiques du corps féminin . . . composez par plusieurs poètes contemporains* (1550) ed. A. [van] B[ever] (Paris 1907). See Hallett Smith *Elizabethan Poetry* (Cambridge, Mass. 1952) index s.v. *Blazons;* H. Weber *La Création poétique au XVIe siècle en France* 2 vols. (Paris 1956); and D. B. Wilson *Descriptive Poetry in France from Blason to Baroque* (Manchester and New York 1967), with many refs.

17. See Francis Cairns *Generic Composition in Greek and Roman Poetry* (Edinburgh 1972) 76. Longinus *On the Sublime* 10 discusses another example, Sappho's *Ode to Anactoria.*

18. See Jean H. Hagstrum *The Sister Arts* (Chicago and London 1958); also Marianne Albrecht-Bolt *Die Bildende Kunst in der Italienischen Lyrik der Renaissance und des Barock* (Wiesbaden 1976). Marvell uses "The Gallery" as title for an erotic poem

drawing on many visual art types for its images. On modern poems about paintings, see Eugene L. Huddleston and Douglas A. Noverr *The Relationship of Painting and Literature: A Guide to Information Sources* (Detroit 1978) 61-101 (bibliog. of poems) and 105-111, 121-128 (secondary sources).

19. W. S. Graham *Johann Joachim Quantz's First Lesson* in *Malcolm Mooney's Land* (London 1970) 56. On Auden's use of Brueghel, see John Fuller *A Reader's Guide to W. H. Auden* (London 1970) 121; on Brueghel poems generally, see Donald B. Burness "Pieter Brueghel: Painter for Poets" *Art Journal* 32.2 (Winter 1972-73) 157-162. Nemerov has said that Brueghel attracted him because he was a literary painter.

20. Williams' *Pictures from Brueghel* originally appeared in *Hudson Review* 13 (1960). John Berryman *Homage to Mistress Bradstreet* (London 1959) 35; Joseph Langland cited in Burness "Pieter Brueghel: Painter for Poets"; Howard Nemerov *The Collected Poems* (Chicago and London 1977) 257, 417, 429; J. Taylor in *MR* 8.2 (1967) 246; Michael Hamburger *Penguin Modern Poets* 14 (Harmondsworth and Baltimore 1969) 80; James Greene in *Lines Review* (1976) 9; Samuel Menashe *Fringe of Fire* (London 1973) 43. Exceptionally the work may be a tapestry or statue, as in Christopher Salvesen's *Five Gothic Bagatelles* in *New Departures* 2-3 (1960) 44-48. Saint Jerome: on Randall Jarrell's *Jerome*, see *The Biography of a Poem: Jerome* ed. Mary von Jarrell (New York 1971); for John Smith's see *Entering Rooms* (London 1973) 32. For many other items, see Huddleston and Noverr. Outstanding among more recent exemplars is Robert Fagles *I, Vincent: Poems from the Pictures of Van Gogh* Princeton Essays on the Arts 5 (Princeton 1978).

21. Robert Lowell *Epilogue* in *Day by Day* (London 1978); William Carlos Williams *The Hunter in the Snow, The Adoration of the Kings* and *Haymaking* in *Pictures from Brueghel* (New York 1962).

22. Cf. the conception of Dutch painting in Svetlana Alpers "Seeing as Knowing: A Dutch Connection" in *Humanities in Society* 1.3 (1978). Of 168 painting poems listed by Huddleston and Noverr, 20 treat Brueghel paintings, while 9 treat paintings by other old Dutch masters.

23. See Desmond Graham in *Stand* 18.3 (1977) 73 on Alasdair Maclean's poem on a similar subject.

24. *Implements in Their Places* (London 1977) 61.

25. *The Everlastings* (Garden City 1980) 31.

26. *Ambit* 66 (1976) 25.

27. Charles Causley *Collected Poems 1951-75* (London 1975) 283; Michael Shayer in *New Departures* 7-11 (1975) 49; Denise Levertov *The Freeing of the Dust* (New York 1975) 23.

28. *Implements in Their Places* 25-30.

29. Meyer H. Abrams *A Glossary of Literary Terms* rev. ed. (New York 1957) 58.

30. Northrop Frye *Anatomy of Criticism* (Princeton 1957) 310-312.

31. See Lewalski *Donne's "Anniversaries"* 226-235, esp. 232.

32. Malcolm Bradbury *Possibilities: Essays on the State of the Novel* (London 1973) 278-279. On the equal unreliability of formal categories, such as omniscient narration, see Meir Sternberg *Expositional Modes and Temporal Ordering in Fiction* (Baltimore and London 1978).

33. See René Wellek and Austin Warren *Theory of Literature* 3rd ed. (New York

1956) 216; Peter K. Garrett *The Victorian Multiplot Novel* (New Haven and London 1980); Ralph Freedman *The Lyrical Novel: Studies in Hermann Hesse, André Gide, and Virginia Woolf* (Princeton 1963); Robert Humphrey *Stream of Consciousness in the Modern Novel* (Berkeley 1954); Mus'ud Zavarzadeh *The Mythopoetic Reality: The Postwar American Nonfiction Novel* (Urbana 1976), J. Frank Kermode "Novel and Narrative" (on the detective story) in *The Theory of the Novel* ed. John Halperin (New York 1974); and Andrew Sanders *Victorian Historical Novels 1840–1880* (London 1978).

34. Henry James, cited in Martin Price "The Irrelevant Detail and the Emergence of Form" in *Aspects of Narrative* ed. J. Hillis Miller (New York 1971) 69.

35. "The Narrow Bridge of Art" in *Collected Essays* vol. 2 (London 1966) 224.

36. See Fredric Schwarzbach *Dickens and the City* (London 1978); Patrick Scott "The School and the Novel: *Tom Brown's Schooldays*" in *The Victorian Public School: A Symposium* ed. Brian Simon and Ian Bradley (London 1975); John Alcorn *The Nature Novel from Hardy to Lawrence* (London 1977); John Lucas *The Literature of Change: Studies in the Nineteenth-Century Provincial Novel* (Hassocks, England 1977); and Wendy A. Craik *Elizabeth Gaskell and the English Provincial Novel* (London 1975).

37. Bruce Merry *Anatomy of the Spy Thriller* (London 1977); Jerry Palmer *Thrillers: Genesis and Structure of a Popular Genre* (London 1978); Robert Lee Wolff *Gains and Losses: Novels of Faith and Doubt in Victorian England* (London 1977).

38. *Tristram Shandy,* end of 6.33; *Molloy* (New York 1955) 20. For fuller discussion of many *poioumena,* see Steven G. Kellman *The Self-Begetting Novel* (New York 1980).

39. Ibid. 94.

40. Here, however, there is mixture with another genre: the novel with historical characters, as in Aldridge's *One Last Glimpse.*

41. It is instructive to contrast Virginia Woolf's *A Room of One's Own,* which contains much material that could have gone to make a *poioumenon,* but where chaos is held more at arm's length, so that the effect remains that of an informal essay or lecture.

42. *Sartor Resartus* 2.9.

43. G. B. Tennyson *"Sartor" Called "Resartus"* (Princeton 1965) 173ff; George Levine *"Sartor Resartus* and the Balance of Fiction" *Victorian Studies* 8 (1964) 131–160; Morse Peckham *Beyond the Tragic Vision: The Quest for Identity in the Nineteenth Century* (New York 1962) 177ff; Gerry H. Brookes *The Rhetorical Form of Carlyle's "Sartor Resartus"* (Berkeley 1972).

44. Cited in Levine 156.

45. Melville on *The House of the Seven Gables,* cited in J. Frank Kermode *The Classic* (London 1975) 101.

46. In addition to those already noticed, one might mention Thomas Hinde *High,* Anne Roiphe *Torch Song,* Edward Candy *Scene Changing,* Thomas Williams *The Hair of Harold Roux,* James Purdy *Cabot Wright Begins,* John Irving *The World According to Garp,* and Jerome Charyn *The Catfish Man: A Conjured Life.* For many other titles see Kellman 144–145, where "reflexive fictions" are listed. However, Kellman's desire to trace an American tradition leads him to include items that have little to do with the self-begetting novel.

47. Medieval parody, however, has often the effect of gaiety and carnival rather

than satire: see P. Zumthor *Essai de poétique médiévale* (Paris 1972) 104-105. For pastiches, see the collection by Paul Reboux (Amillet) and Charles Muller, *A la Manière de* (Paris 1910-1913); for parody, burlesque, and similar forms, see Richmond P. Bond *English Burlesque Poetry 1700-1750* (Cambridge, Mass. 1932).

48. See the catalogue of any great library. Many elaborations of *Gulliver's Travels* have been reprinted in the Scholars' Facsimiles and Reprints Gulliveriana series. Among twentieth-century examples, Frigyes Karinthy's *Utazás Faremidóba Capillária* (Voyage to Faremido Capillaria) is outstanding. Among *Robinson Crusoe* elaborations, there are Michael Tournier's *Friday or the Other Island,* Derek Walcott's *Crusoe's Island,* Iain Crichton Smith's *Crusoe's Other Island,* and Elizabeth Bishop's *Crusoe in England.* Besides Marowitz's *Hamlet,* there are Gilbert and Sullivan's *Rosencrantz and Guildenstern,* Tom Stoppard's *Rosencrantz and Guildenstern Are Dead,* John Turing's *My Nephew Hamlet,* and Alethea Hayter's *Horatio's Version.* See Ruby Cohn *Modern Shakespeare Offshoots* (Princeton 1976). On the *Alice*s, see Martin Gardner *The Annotated Alice* (New York 1960). The outstanding *Huck Finn* is John Seelye's *The True Adventures of Huck Finn: As Told by John Seelye* (Evanston, Ill. 1970). And the best *Jane Eyre* is Jean Rhys' *Wide Sargasso Sea* (London 1966).

49. For an early anticipation, see [James White] *Original Letters, etc. of Sir J. Falstaff* (London 1796).

50. A few individual types have received attention. See Francis Berry *The Shakespeare Inset: Word and Picture* (London 1965); and, on framing, *Representation and Understanding* ed. Daniel G. Bobrow and Alan Collins (Edinburgh and New York 1975). Lyric applications of many constructional types are discussed in Robin Skelton *The Practice of Poetry* (London 1971).

51. *Night Light* (Middletown, Conn. 1967) 9.

52. Earl Miner *The Metaphysical Mode from Donne to Cowley* (Princeton 1969); cf. *Romanticism Reconsidered* ed. Northrop Frye (New York 1963), with the relevant review by Mark Roberts in *EC* 15.1 (1965) 118-130.

53. *The Archeology of Knowledge* tr. A. M. Sheridan Smith (London 1972) 23-24.

8. Generic Labels

1. On "imprecise" lexical categorization, see John Lyons *Introduction to Theoretical Linguistics* (Cambridge 1968) 426-427.

2. An exception is Allan Rodway and Brian Lee "Coming to Terms" *EC* 14 (1964) 109ff. There are, however, many nontheoretical dictionaries of terms, including those by Alex Preminger, J. A. Cuddon, Meyer H. Abrams, and (jointly) Karl Beckson and Arthur Genz. On the status of genre terms, see Robert Champigny "Semantic Modes and Literary Genres" in *Theories of Literary Genre* ed. Joseph P. Strelka (University Park, Pa. and London 1978) 94-111.

3. Dedication to Henry, Prince of Wales, *A Harmony of the Essays* ed. E. Arber (1895) 158-159, cited in Rosalie L. Colie *The Resources of Kind* (Berkeley 1973) 89.

4. Ibid. 14.

5. See, e.g., Antonio Sebastiano Minturno *L'Arte Poetica* (Venice 1564) 240ff.

6. See Harry Levin "The Title as a Literary Genre" *MLR* 72 (1977) xxvi.

7. Giordano Bruno *Eroici Furori* 1, cited in Colie *Resources of Kind* 111.

8. See Enid Welsford *The Court Masque* (1927, rpt. New York 1962) 44–45.

9. See Colie *Resources of Kind* 68–70; and J. C. Scaliger *Poetices* (Lyons 1561) 171. "Salt wit" and "salt of wit" were idiomatic from at least 1573, in referring either to pungency, sharpness, or epigrammatic point. See *OED* s.v. *Salt* adj. 5 and sb. 1.3c, with several quotations: esp. the following: *"salt,* a pleasant and merry word [i.e., saying] that maketh folk to laugh and sometimes pricketh" (1573); "salt and sharp quipping speeches" (Camden *Remains,* 1605); "So much and such savoured salt of wit is in his comedies . . ." (Epistle before Shakespeare *Troilus and Cressida,* 1609).

10. Ed. P. M. Zall (London 1972) 5. On *satura,* see Gilbert Highet *The Anatomy of Satire* (Princeton 1962) 231–232.

11. See Lyons *Introduction* 56–59; and idem *Semantics* vol. 1 (Cambridge 1977) 246.

12. See A. Hulubei *L'Eglogue en France au XVIe siècle, époque des Valois: 1515–1589* (Paris 1938), cited in Thomas G. Rosenmeyer *The Green Cabinet* (Berkeley and Los Angeles 1969) 8n23.

13. On the odelette form, see Gordon Braden *The Classics and English Renaissance Poetry* (New Haven and London 1978) 205ff; and Janet Smarr "Renaissance Anacreontics" *CL* 25 (1973) 221–239. Cf. Spenser's term *amoretti.* All such labels go back to Ovid's *Amores.*

14. *Institutio* 10.13.17; cf. Aulus Gellius *Noctes Atticae* pref. 6. See Hoyt Hopewell Hudson *The Epigram in the English Renaissance* (1947, rpt. New York 1966) 26.

15. Cf. also Florio, who makes Montaigne compare the casual unproportioned character of the *Essais* to the work of a painter who fills vacant spaces "with antike Boscage or Crotesko works; which are fantasticall pictures, having no grace, but in the variety and strangenesse of them" (1.27 "Of Friendship": the passage is not in Montaigne).

16. Scaliger *Poetices* 150.c.1. Cf. Jonson's note "To the Reader" before *The Underwood:* "With the same leave, the ancients called that kind of body *Sylva,* or *Hylē,* in which there were works of divers nature, and matter congested; as the multitude call Timber-trees, promiscuously growing, a *Wood,* or *Forest:* so am I bold to entitle these lesser Poems, of later growth, by this of *Under-wood,* out of the Analogy they hold to the *Forest,* in my former book, and no otherwise."

17. See *OED* s.v. *Divan* 6: "A Persian name for a collection of poems . . . From the original sense 'collection of written sheets.' "

18. Francis Cairns *Generic Composition in Greek and Roman Poetry* (Edinburgh 1972) 92, 113. On the repertoire of elegy, see George Norlin "The Conventions of the Pastoral Elegy" *AJP* 32 (1911) 294–312; H. M. Hall *Idylls of Fishermen* (New York 1914); *The Pastoral Elegy* ed. Thomas P. Harrison (Austin 1939); A. L. Bennett "The Principal Rhetorical Conventions of the Renaissance Elegy" *SP* 51 (1954) 107–125; G. Luck *The Latin Love Elegy* (London 1960); O. B. Hardison *The Enduring Monument* (Chapel Hill 1962), esp. ch. 6; Scott Elledge *Milton's "Lycidas": Edited to Serve as an Introduction to Criticism* (New York and London 1966); Christine M. Scollen *The Birth of the Elegy in France 1500–1550* Travaux d'Humanisme et Renaissance 95 (Geneva 1967); D. C. Mell *A Poetics of Augustan Elegy: Studies of Poems by Dryden, Pope, Prior, Swift, Gray, and Johnson* (Amsterdam 1974); J. E. Clark *Élégie: The Fortunes of a Classical Genre in Sixteenth-Century France* (The Hague 1975); Erick Smith *By Mourn-*

ing Tongues: Studies in English Elegy (Totowa, N.J. 1977); Ellen Zetzel Lambert *Placing Sorrow: A Study of the Pastoral Elegy Convention from Theocritus to Milton* (Chapel Hill 1978); Clifford Endres *Joannes Secundus: The Latin Love Elegy in the Renaissance* (Hamden, Conn. forthcoming); also the refs. in Chapter 11, notes 57, 58 below.

19. *Poetices* 52.d.1.

20. See Barbara K. Lewalski *Donne's "Anniversaries" and the Poetry of Praise* (Princeton 1973) 11–29. For the development of the elegy in France (where the grouping of elegy with epistle took quite a different shape), see Scollen *The Birth of the Elegy in France.*

21. Abbie F. Potts *The Elegiac Mode* (Ithaca 1967) 319.

22. *Fors Clavigera* 3.34.6.

23. For the term "narration" see, e.g., Jonson's "Conversations with Drummond" in *Works* ed. C. H. Herford and Percy and Evelyn Simpson vol. 1 (Oxford 1925) 133 l. 39.

24. See Bernard Weinberg *A History of Literary Criticism in the Italian Renaissance* 2 vols. (Chicago 1961) 1.400–401. Cf. Minturno *L'Arte* 240 "Epigramma è particella dell'Epica poesia," although this refers to epic in the sense "enarrative" (one of three broad divisions of literature: not lyric or dramatic but mixed).

25. On closure in epigram, see Barbara Herrnstein Smith *Poetic Closure: A Study of How Poems End* (Chicago 1968) 196–210.

26. *L'Arte* 240.

27. Cf. Colie *Resources of Kind* 67–68. On Estienne, see Rudolf Pfeiffer *History of Classical Scholarship 1300–1850* (Oxford 1976) 109. A complete Latin translation of the Planudean Anthology, by Eilhardus Lubinus, and partial translations by Grotius and others circulated or were published in the early seventeenth century. The fuller Palatine manuscript of the Greek Anthology was not copied until 1606, or edited until the eighteenth century.

28. See Rosenmeyer *The Green Cabinet* 58ff *et passim;* and C. W. Hieatt "The Integrity of Pastoral" *Genre* 5 (1972). On the term "idyll" and its creative misuse in the Renaissance, see Geoffrey H. Hartman *Beyond Formalism* (New Haven and London 1970) 177–178n.

29. See Scaliger *Poetices* 150.a.1; Richard F. Jones "Eclogue Types in English Poetry of the Eighteenth Century" *JEGP* 24 (1925) 34n; and W. W. Greg, *Pastoral Poetry and Pastoral Drama* (London 1906), Rosenmeyer *The Green Cabinet,* Helen Cooper *Pastoral* (Ipswich and Totowa, N.J. 1977) indexes, s.v. such appropriate topics as *Sannazaro, Fishing, Piscatory Eclogue,* etc. On the limited scope of pure pastoral, see Ralph Cohen "Innovation and Variation: Literary Change and Georgic Poetry" in *Literature and History* Clark Library Papers (Los Angeles 1974).

30. Medieval Lat. *aegloga,* Fr. *églogue:* see Helen Cooper "The Goat and the Eclogue" *PQ* 53 (1974) 26ff; and idem *Pastoral* index s.v. *Eclogue; Etymology.*

31. "An Essay on the New Species of Writing founded by Mr. Fielding . . ." rpt. Ioan Williams *Novel and Romance 1700–1800* (London and New York 1970) 152–153. On the term "novel," see Edith Kern "The Romance of Novel/Novella" in *The Disciplines of Criticism* ed. Peter Demetz et al. (New Haven and London 1968).

32. W. K. Wimsatt and C. Brooks *Literary Criticism: A Short History* (London 1957) 151.

33. *The Discarded Image* (Cambridge 1964) 31.

34. *The "Parisiana Poetria" of John of Garland* ed. T. Lawler (New Haven and London 1974) 101.

35. Ibid. 103.

36. See ibid. 99.

37. *Ars Versificatoria* 4.16; see Edmond Faral *Les Arts poétiques du 12ᵉ et du 13ᵉ siècle* (Paris 1962) 184.

38. See Donald R. Howard *The Idea of the "Canterbury Tales"* (Berkeley 1976) 57.

39. On the various *artes praedicandi,* esp. Thomas of Salisbury's, see James J. Murphy *Rhetoric in the Middle Ages* (Berkeley 1974) ch. 6. esp. 317-325. On epistolary rhetorics, see ibid. ch. 5.

40. On this distinction, see John D. Peter *Complaint and Satire in Early English Literature* (Oxford 1956); and John H. Fisher *John Gower: Moral Philosopher and Friend of Chaucer* (New York 1964) 3, 36, 153, 206.

41. See, e.g., F. C. Gardiner *The Pilgrimage of Desire: A Study of Theme and Genre in Medieval Literature* (Leiden 1971); and Edmund Reiss "The Pilgrimage Narrative and the *Canterbury Tales" SP* 67 (1970) 295-305. On medieval terminology generally, see J. W. H. Atkins *English Literary Criticism: the Medieval Phase* (Cambridge 1943); D. W. Robertson "Some Medieval Literary Terminology, with Special Reference to Chrétien de Troyes" *SP* 48 (1951) 669-692; Murphy *Rhetoric in the Middle Ages;* Paul Strohm *"Storie, Spelle, Geste, Romaunce, Tragedie:* Generic Distinctions in the Middle English Troy Narratives" *Speculum* 46 (1971) 348-359; Johannes A. Huisman "Generative Classifications in Medieval Literature" in *Theories of Literary Genre* ed. Strelka 123-149; and A. J. Minnis "The Influence of Academic Prologues on the Prologues and Literary Attitudes of Late-Medieval English Writers" *Medieval Studies* 43(1981)342-383. Individual terms are interestingly discussed in Rosemary Woolf *The English Religious Lyric in the Middle Ages* (Oxford 1968); and Pamela Gradon *Form and Style in Early English Literature* (London 1971).

42. See, e.g., Paull F. Baum *Chaucer: A Critical Appreciation* (Durham, N.C. 1958) 74-84; Robert O. Payne *The Key of Remembrance: A Study of Chaucer's Poetics* (New Haven and London 1963); Alan Gaylord *"Sentence* and *Solaas* in Fragment VII of the *Canterbury Tales" PMLA* 82 (1967) 226-235; S. S. Hussey *Chaucer: An Introduction* (London 1971).

43. *Idea of the "Canterbury Tales"* 31, 34-35.

44. *The "Parisiana Poetria"* ed. Lawler 102; see n. to 371.

45. Cf. H. J. Chaytor *From Script to Print* (Cambridge 1945) 74.

46. As Alastair J. Minnis argues in "Discussions of 'Authorial Role' and 'Literary Form' in Late-Medieval Scriptural Exegesis" *Beiträge zur Geschichte der Deutschen Sprache und Literatur* 99 (1977) 37-65, an article to which the present section owes many debts. See also idem "Late-Medieval Discussions of *Compilatio* and the Rôle of the *Compilator*" in the same journal, 101 (1979) 385-421; idem "Literary Theory in Discussions of *Formae Tractandi* by Medieval Theologians" *NLH* 11.1 (1979) 133-145; and idem "The Influence of Academic Prologues."

47. The list could be greatly extended. See Minnis "Discussions of 'Authorial Role'" 47-48; also M. B. Parkes "The Influence of the Concepts of *Ordinatio* and

Compilatio on the Development of the Book" in *Medieval Learning and Literature: Essays Presented to R. W. Hunt* ed. J. J. G. Alexander and M. Gibson (Oxford 1975) 115–141.

48. See Minnis "Discussions of 'Authorial Role' " 59.

9. The Formation of Genres

1. Francis Cairns *Generic Composition in Greek and Roman Poetry* (Edinburgh 1972) 34. For classical predecessors of the novel, see Ben Edwin Perry *The Ancient Romances* (Berkeley and Los Angeles 1967); and Arthur Heiserman *The Novel before the Novel* (Chicago 1977).

2. Cairns *Generic Composition* 69.

3. Many studies of origins have been attempted. See, e.g., Claude Luttrell *The Creation of the First Arthurian Romance: A Quest* (Evanston, Ill. and London 1974).

4. See, e.g., Richmond Alexander Lattimore *Story Patterns in Greek Tragedy* (Ann Arbor 1964) 9ff. On the use of mythic material by modern writers, see John Vickery *The Literary Impact of "The Golden Bough"* (Princeton 1973).

5. For a sympathetic interpretation of these, see Geoffrey H. Hartman *Beyond Formalism* (New Haven and London 1970) esp. xii, 9, 29.

6. Cf. John Casey *The Language of Criticism* (London 1966) ch. 7. See W. K. Wimsatt "Northrop Frye: Criticism as Myth" in *Northrop Frye in Modern Criticism* ed. Murray Krieger (New York and London 1966) 75–107; and Roy H. Pearce *Historicism Once More: Problems and Occasions for the American Scholar* (Princeton 1969).

7. See Ulrich Weisstein *Comparative Literature and Literary Theory* (Bloomington and London 1973) 114; Robert E. Scholes *Structuralism in Literature* (New Haven and London) ch. 3; Paul Hernadi *Beyond Genre* (Ithaca and London 1972) 91–92. On the riddle see, e.g., Michele de Filippis *The Literary Riddle in Italy to the End of the Sixteenth Century* (Berkeley 1948).

8. "The Notion of Literature" *NLH* 5.1 (1973) 15.

9. See F. W. Bateson *The Scholar-Critic* (London 1972) 62–65.

10. Cairns *Generic Composition* 129.

11. *Poetices* 152.b.1 and 153.b.1.

12. *Paradise Lost* 1.503–505; cf. the British matters introduced soon after, 1.579–587, the passage omitted by Bentley as "Romantic trash." On the epic catalogue, see T. W. Allen "The Homeric Catalogue" *Journal of Hellenic Studies* 30 (1910); H. E. Wedeck "The Catalogue in Late and Medieval Latin Poetry" *Medievalia et Humanistica* 13 (1960); Cedric H. Whitman *Homer and the Heroic Tradition* (Cambridge, Mass. 1967) index s.v. *Catalogue of Ships;* Michael O'Connell "History and the Poet's Golden World: The Epic Catalogues in *The Faerie Queen*" *ELR* 4.2 (1974) 241–267; and Gordon M. Braden "Riverrun: An Epic Catalogue in *The Faerie Queen*" *ELR* 5.1 (1975) 25–48.

13. See Ralph Cohen *The Art of Discrimination* (Berkeley 1964) 19ff; John Chalker *The English Georgic* (London 1969) ch. 4.

14. See Weisstein 102; Dámaso Alonso "Tradition or Polygenesis" *Modern Humanities Research Association Bulletin* (November 1960).

15. For refs. on the country house poem see Alastair Fowler *Conceitful Thought*

(Edinburgh 1975) ch. 6; and James Turner *The Politics of Landscape* (Cambridge, Mass. 1979).

16. Perhaps not quite seriously, however. See *Stories and Verse* ed. W. L. Renwick (Edinburgh 1964) 254.

17. *Essay on Manners;* cited in Peter Burke *The Renaissance* (London 1964) 7.

18. "Assembly" is used informally, without implying that works of art are assemblages rather than organizations. For generic transformation, see Chapters 10 and 11.

19. See Muriel C. Bradbrook *The Growth and Structure of Elizabethan Comedy* (London 1955) pt. 1; Brian Jeffery *French Renaissance Comedy 1552-1630* (Oxford 1969) 100.

20. Cf. E. E. Kellett *The Whirligig of Taste* (London 1929) 20.

21. See Enid Welsford *The Court Masque* (Cambridge 1927) 125.

22. See Dwight L. Durling *Georgic Tradition in English Poetry* (New York 1935) ch. 2; and Chalker *The English Georgic.*

23. Cf. Rosalie L. Colie *The Resources of Kind* (Berkeley 1973) 82.

24. Tzvetan Todorov "The Origin of Genres" *NLH* 8.1 (1976) 161.

25. See Victor Erlich *Russian Formalism: History—Doctrine* (The Hague 1955) 227.

26. Thomas G. Rosenmeyer *The Green Cabinet* (Berkeley and Los Angeles 1969) 6.

27. *The Life of Lord Herbert of Cherbury* ed. J. M. Shuttleworth (London 1976) 101.

28. *A Preface to Paradise Lost* (London 1942) 12.

29. Discussion of this topic goes back to Macrobius. Among recent treatments, see Georg N. Knauer *Die Aeneis und Homer* (Göttingen 1964); Brooks Otis *Virgil: A Study in Civilized Poetry* (Oxford 1964); Kenneth Quinn *Virgil's Aeneid: A Critical Description* (London 1968); and, on Virgil's awareness of epic values, Davis Harding *The Club of Hercules* (Urbana 1962) 31-32.

30. For the "Homeric duplex" see James Nohrnberg "The *Iliad*" in *Homer to Brecht* ed. Michael Seidel and Edward Mendelson (New Haven 1977) 14.

31. J. C. Scaliger *Poetices* (Lyons 1561) 5, esp. ch.3, 216-245.

32. Ibid. 118.a.2.

33. "Pastoralia," ibid. 3.94; 150.a.1.

34. Northrop Frye *Anatomy of Criticism* (Princeton 1957) 60.

35. See esp. *Daniel Deronda* ch. 16. The motif obviously could be traced in comedy also, from Menander through Shakespeare and Molière (*L'Avare*) to Wilde and Shaw. (*Heartbreak House* is an interesting case of a work that presses "beyond" romance: in it the story of the foundling in an antique chest is shown to be false.)

36. On Virgil's Latin predecessors, see Otis ch. 2.

37. See *Three Gothic Novels* ed. M. Praz (Harmondsworth 1968) 17.

38. See Erlich 220.

39. René Wellek "The Concept of Evolution in Literary History" in *Concepts of Criticism* ed. Stephen G. Nichols, Jr. (New Haven and London 1963) 44, 51. The analogy is defended in Michael T. Ghiselin "Poetic Biology: A Defense and Manifesto" *NLH* 7.3 (1976) 493-504; and in Alastair Fowler "The Life and Death of Literary Forms," a fuller version of the present passage, in *New Directions in Literary History* ed. Ralph Cohen (1974) 84-88.

40. Cf. Eliseo Vivas "Literary Classes: Some Problems" *Genre* 1 (1968) 101.

41. René Wellek *Concepts of Criticism* 44.

42. Ibid. 55. To do justice to Wellek's consistency, he considers the evolutionary character of history itself problematic: see ibid. 53n.

43. Sir Kenneth Clark *Civilisation: A Personal View* (London 1969) overstates this point.

44. On the psychology underlying cosmic number symbolism in the Renaissance, see William Kerrigan "The Articulation of the Ego in the English Renaissance" in *The Literary Freud: Mechanisms of Defence and the Poetic Will* ed. Joseph H. Smith, Psychiatry and the Humanities vol. 4 (New Haven and London 1980) 292, 299–300.

45. The current term "romantic epic" is something of a misnomer, since the structure is more romance than epic in all but a few instances such as Trissino's *L'Italia Liberata da Gothi*. However, the term may reflect regrouping. From one standpoint Ariosto's form is tertiary epic, just as Scott's "historical romance" is now called historical novel.

46. Watson smiles at Fielding's idea of the genre of *Tom Jones*. But perhaps Fielding knew quite well what he was about, in assembling diverse generic ingredients. On the development of romance into novel, see Henry Knight Miller "Augustan Prose Fiction and the Romance Tradition" in *Studies in the Eighteenth Century* ed. R. F. Brissenden and J. C. Eade vol. 3 (Canberra 1976) 241–255.

47. The analogy rejected by Wellek, *Concepts* 40, 44–45.

48. Like some of the epics mentioned by W. Macneile Dixon in *English Epic and Heroic Poetry* (London 1912) 11.

10. Transformations of Genre

1. For different categories see, e.g., Francis Cairns *Generic Composition in Greek and Roman Poetry* (Edinburgh 1972) 99.

2. See C. L. Barber *Shakespeare's Festive Comedy* (Princeton 1959); Leslie Hotson *The First Night of "Twelfth Night"* (London 1954).

3. Cf. Cairns *Generic Composition* 123.

4. For many examples of aggregation in round numbers, see Ernst Robert Curtius *European Literature and the Latin Middle Ages* (New York and London 1953) 505–509. On the organization of Boccaccio's aggregate, see Janet Levarie Smarr "Symmetry and Balance in the *Decameron*" *Mediaevalia* 2 (1976).

5. See Godfrey Frank Singer *The Epistolary Novel* (Philadelphia 1933, rpt. 1963); also *The Novel in Letters* ed. Natascha Würzbach (Coral Gables, Fla. 1969). For modern examples, see *TLS* (9 Feb. 1973) 153.

6. Petrarch's *Canzoniere* used a calendrical structure that became a paradigm for Spenser and others: see Thomas P. Roche "Shakespeare and the Sonnet Sequence" in *English Poetry and Prose, 1540–1674* ed. Christopher Ricks (London 1970); idem "The Calendrical Structure of Petrarch's *Canzoniere*" *SP* 71 (1974); and Philip Blank *Lyric Form in the Sonnet Sequences of Barnabe Barnes* (The Hague 1974). There were other calendrical models, notably the early fourteenth-century *Sonetti dei Mesi* of Fulgore da San Gemignano.

7. See Alastair Fowler *Triumphal Forms* (Cambridge 1970) ch. 9; Roche "Sonnet Sequence" 105–106; and Rosalie L. Colie *The Resources of Kind* (Berkeley 1973) 104. By contrast, nineteenth-century sequences tend to be congeries of individual lyric poems. D. G. Rossetti, e.g., "certainly never professed, nor do I consider that he ever wished his readers to assume, that all items [in *The House of Life*] had been primarily planned to form one connected and indivisible whole." W. M. Rossetti *Dante Gabriel Rossetti as Designer and Writer* (1888) 181–182.

8. Some of these plans have survived, such as John Philips' for *Cider,* which is particularly interesting in view of the work's generic originality (see John Chalker *The English Georgic* [London 1969] 45).

9. See Cairns *Generic Composition* 119.

10. Cf. Colie *Resources of Kind* 85; Geoffrey H. Hartman *Beyond Formalism* (New Haven and London 1970) 177–180.

11. On the modified limerick, see Martin Gardner *Scientific American* (April 1977) 134.

12. Cairns analyzes many such variations in *Generic Composition* chs. 8–9.

13. "Parody as a Literary Form: George Herbert and Wilfred Owen" *EC* 13 (1963) 306. See also Colie *Resources of Kind* 57; Lily B. Campbell *Divine Poetry and Drama in Sixteenth-Century England* (Cambridge 1959); and Barbara K. Lewalski *Protestant Poetics and the Seventeenth-Century Religious Lyric* (Princeton 1979).

14. See Claudio Guillén *Literature as System* (Princeton 1971) 146–158.

15. See Cairns *Generic Composition* 129ff. The process was well understood in the Renaissance. See, e.g., Thomas Watson's note to *The . . . Passionate Century of Love* (1582) no. 96: "In this Passion, the Author is scoffing bitterly at Venus, and her son Cupid, alludeth unto certain verses in Ovid, but inverteth them to an other sense, than Ovid used, who wrote them upon the death of Tibullus."

16. Cf. Colie *Resources of Kind* 93–94.

17. On Milton and Christian epic, see Campbell *Divine Poetry;* Barbara K. Lewalski *Milton's Brief Epic* (Providence and London 1966); and Dennis H. Burden *The Logical Epic* (London 1967) 9–13, 63–64, et passim.

18. Those of Bembo, Della Casa, Milton, and others approached the loftier ode. Colie (*Resources of Kind* 106–107) quotes Vauquelin de la Fresnaye: "Si tu fais un Sonnet ou si tu fais un Ode, / Il faut qu'un mesme fil au sujet s'accommode" and "on peut le Sonnet dire une chanson [canzone] petite." Cf. Minturno *L'Arte* 240ff, on the "Somiglianza tra il sonetto, e la Canzone."

19. For European practitioners see Colie *Resources of Kind* 106. The theorist Minturno himself wrote spiritual sonnets.

20. For a dramatic instance, see George Peele, *Old Wives' Tale* (1595) l. 698; for a fine elegiac version, William Cartwright *To the Memory of a Shipwrackt Virgin* in *The Plays and Poems of William Cartwright* ed. G. Blakemore Evans (Madison, Wis. 1951). This particular antigenre has outlived the primary genre: there is an example in *Concrete Poetry: An International Anthology* ed. Stephen Bann (London 1967) 155.

21. E.g., Johnson related *The Village* to pastoral. For a contrary view, that Crabbe's originality lies outside the pastoral tradition, see Dennis H. Burden "Crabbe and the Augustan Tradition" in *Essays and Poems Presented to Lord David Cecil* ed. W. W. Robson (London 1970) 77–92.

22. *The Village* 1.17–20. On Johnson's contribution to these lines, see Burden "Crabbe" 80–81.

23. *The Parish Register* 1.26. Cf. the allusion in *The Village* bk. 1: "He, 'passing rich with forty pounds a year?' / Ah! no; a shepherd of a different stock, / And far unlike him, feeds this little flock."

24. *The Spirit of the Age* in *Complete Works* ed. P. P. Howe vol. 11 (London 1932) 167.

25. *The Village* bk.1 ad fin.

26. Burden "Crabbe" 87.

27. The excellent phrase is Hazlitt's—who did not mean it approvingly. Cf. Burden "Crabbe" 92.

28. Contemporary review of *Tristram Shandy;* in Ioan Williams *Novel and Romance 1700–1800* (London 1970) 239.

29. But contrast the view in Peter Conrad *Shandyism* (London 1978).

30. For James and Besant see James "The Art of Fiction" in *Selected Literary Criticism* ed. Morris Shapira (London 1963) 93f; for Forster's low regard for story, *Aspects of the Novel* (London 1927) 41.

31. A. Walton Litz "The Genre of *Ulysses*" in *The Theory of the Novel* ed. John Halperin (New York and London 1974) 116, 118.

32. Ibid. 115, 118, 120.

33. J. Fletcher *The Novels of Samuel Beckett* (London 1964) 76–77, quoting Christine Brooke-Rose "Beckett and the Anti-Novel" *London Magazine* 5 (1958). John Chalker "The Satiric Shape of *Watt*" in *Beckett the Shape Changer* ed. Katherine Worth (London 1975) sets Beckett in a satiric context. Antinovel often overlaps with satire, but need not do so. Satire in the ordinary sense may not be the best key to Beckett's work.

34. For the tapestry poem see *Variorum Spenser* 1.386; for triumphs, Fowler *Triumphal Forms;* and for many other inclusions, James Nohrnberg *The Analogy of "The Faerie Queen"* (Princeton 1976).

35. On the encyclopedic character of epic, see Northrop Frye *Anatomy of Criticism* (Princeton 1957) 324. On inclusion, see below, Chapter 12.

36. See John Steadman *Epic and Tragic Structure in "Paradise Lost"* (Chicago 1976); and *The Poems of John Milton* ed. John Carey and Alastair Fowler (London 1968) 421–422, 852–853 (n. to 9.6), 966 (n. to 10.773). See also Colie *Resources of Kind* 119.

37. Colie lists some of these, enjoying the artificiality with which they are inset; see *Resources of Kind* 119f; A. K. Nardo "The Submerged Sonnet as Lyric Moment in Miltonic Epic" *Genre* 9.1 (1976) 21–35; *The Poems of John Milton* ed. Carey and Fowler 683 (n. to 5.153–208).

38. See Thomas G. Rosenmeyer *The Green Cabinet* (Berkeley and Los Angeles 1969) 121. Cf. the epitaph to Eurymedon, by Theocritus or Leonidas of Tarentum.

39. Formerly attributed to Wyatt; see *Collected Poems* ed. Kenneth Muir and Patricia Thomson (Liverpool 1969) 439. Cf. S.H.'s *On Cleveland* in *The Poems of John Cleveland* ed. Brian Morris and Eleanor Withington (Oxford 1967) xxi–xxii; and Mildmay Fane's epitaph on Ben Jonson, *He Who Began from Brick and Lime,* in *Ben Jonson and the Cavalier Poets* ed. Hugh Maclean (New York 1974).

40. The satiric possibility is realized in "On I.W.A.B. of York," attributed to Cleveland in *Minor Poets of the Caroline Period* ed. G. Saintsbury 3 vols. (Oxford 1905-1921) 3.71.

41. See, e.g., Cairns *Generic Composition* 161, 167. George Puttenham treats triumphals, genethliaca, and epithalamies as "poetical rejoicings": see *The Art of English Poesy* 1.23, ed. Gladys D. Willcock and Alice Walker (Cambridge 1936) 46.

42. This problem is discussed in Colie *Resources of Kind* 112-114.

43. *The Shakespearian Inset* (London 1965). There is a large literature on the play-within-a-play: see, e.g., Robert Egan *Drama Within Drama* (New York 1975); and James L. Calderwood *Shakespearian Metadrama* (Minneapolis 1971). For the psychology of framing, see Erving Goffman *Frame Analysis: An Essay on the Organization of Experience* (New York 1974). Many aspects are discussed in *Representation and Understanding* ed. Daniel Bobrow and Alan Collins (London 1976).

44. Cairns is rightly careful to distinguish inclusion from generic mixture: see, e.g., *Generic Composition* ch. 7, esp. 158-159.

45. Ben Jonson *Horace, "Of the Art of Poetry"* ll. 124-125, translating 89; *Works* ed. C. H. Herford, Percy Simpson and Evelyn M. Simpson 11 vols. (Oxford 1925-1952) 8.311. Cf. the classic statement in Cicero *De Optimo Genere Oratorum* 1: "In tragedy the comic is a fault, and in comedy the tragic displeases." *Ancient Literary Criticism* ed. D. A. Russell and M. Winterbottom (Oxford 1972) 250.

46. Ulrich Weisstein *Comparative Literature and Literary Theory* (Bloomington and London 1968) 99-100, instancing the Romantic ideal of *Gesamtkunstwerk,* and citing Behrens and Ehrenpreis.

47. See Cairns, *Generic Composition* 158-159 and ch. 7 passim.

48. E.g., Minturno *L'Arte* 3-4, which probably underlies Colie *Resources of Kind* 21—a passage not concerned with the problem of distinguishing between inclusion and modulation.

49. *Miscellaneous Prose* ed. Katherine Duncan-Jones and Jan van Dorsten 94. See Colie *Resources of Kind* 28.

50. *The Works of Michael Drayton* ed. J. W. Hebel et al. 5 vols. (Oxford 1941) 2.346: "Some [odes] transcendently lofty, and far more high than the Epic (commonly called the Heroic Poem) witness those of the inimitable Pindarus ... Others, among the Greeks, are amorous, soft, and made for Chambers, as others for Theatres; as were Anacreon's, the very Delicacies of the Grecian Erato." It is not clear how far Drayton is identifying *ballad* and *balade:* "the last Ode of this Number, or if thou wilt, Ballad in my Book: for both the great Master of Italian Rhymes, Petrarch, and our Chaucer, and other of the upper House of the Muses, have thought their Canzons honoured in the Title of a Ballad; which, for that I labour to meet truly therein with the old English Garb, I hope as able to justify, as the learned Colin Clout his Roundelay."

51. The subtitle of *Rubenus,* on which see Colie *Resources of Kind* 94. Cf. Shakespeare's criticism of the pedantic classifications that were failing to keep pace with the movement, in Polonius' speech, *Hamlet* 2.2.377ff.

52. *The Works of Thomas Nashe* ed. McKerrow and F. P. Wilson vol. 2 (Oxford 1958) 209, 227, 234f, 241, 320; cf. 292 "elegiacal history." In the seventeenth century, the heyday of sophisticated generic mixture, its terminology was even used as meta-

phor. So in *Philaster*, Bellario entering with a masque says "I should / Sing you an Epithalamion of these lovers," and the king's response is to promise, in effect, a tragic wedding masque: "I'll provide a Masque shall make your Hymen / Turn his saffron into a sullen coat, / And sing sad Requiems to your departing souls."

53. *A Treatise De Carmine Pastorali*, pref. to Thomas Creech's translation of the *Idylliums* of Theocritus (1684) ed. J. E. Congleton, Augustan Rpt. Soc. series 2, no. 3, pub. 8 (Ann Arbor 1947) 27, 28.

54. "Pref. of 1815"; *The Prose Works* ed. W. J. B. Owen and Jane W. Smyser 3 vols. (Oxford 1974) 3.28 or *Wordsworth's Literary Criticism* ed. W. J. B. Owen (London 1974) 177.

55. *Anatomy* 312, 313.

56. Ibid. 246.

57. For Du Bellay and others who related sonnet and epigram, see Colie, *Resources of Kind* 68, quoting de la Fresnaye: "Et Du Bellay quitant cette amoureuse flame, / Premier fist le Sonet sentir son Epigramme." Also idem *Shakespeare's Living Art* (Princeton 1974) 82-85, esp. 83, quoting Sébillet's 1548 statement that the sonnet "suit l'epigramme de bien près, et de matière, et de mesure: Et quant tout est dit, Sonnet n'est autre chose que le parfait épigramme de l'Italien, comme le dizain du François." However, several of these passages connecting sonnet and epigram come in the context of equally close comparisons with other neighboring kinds. Even Lorenzo de'Medici, e.g., says that the sonnet tercet is "quasi simile all'eroico" (*Scritti d'Amore* ed. G. Cavalli [Milan 1958] 114). The theorists' difficulty lay in the fact that the sonnet was a modern vernacular kind only, without a place in the ancient system.

58. *L'Arte* 240-242.

59. Marot, e.g., called some of his sonnets epigrams: see M. Praz *The Flaming Heart* (New York 1958) 208; Colie *Shakespeare's Living Art* 77-79, 89.

60. See Colie *Resources of Kind* 68, 75; idem *Shakespeare's Living Art* 79.

61. Cf. Colie *Shakespeare's Living Art* 93; idem *Resources of Kind* 69.

62. See Colie *Shakespeare's Living Art* 72.

63. As Rosalie Colie notices: see *Resources of Kind* 69f; *Shakespeare's Living Art* 79.

64. Colie *Shakespeare's Living Art* 75: a superior formulation to the idea of compromise in *Resources of Kind* 75.

65. See Colie *Shakespeare's Living Art* 73, 76.

66. See J. W. Lever *The Elizabethan Love Sonnet* (London 1956) 31, 45, 51-52. Contrast, however, such instances as Jonson *Epigrams* 103, a "sonnet" in distichs.

67. *The Poems of Sir John Davies* ed. Robert Krueger (Oxford 1975) 164-167; see Colie *Shakespeare's Living Art* 78-79, 90-92. Cf. Jonson *Epigrams* 56.

68. Cf. Colie *Shakespeare's Living Art* 90, where she does not, however, explain "sullenness." See *OED* s.v. *Sullen* 3 "melancholy," citing *Othello* 3.4.51 (Q1): "a salt and sullen rheum" and 4 "of a dull colour."

69. See *OED* s.v. *Passion* 6d: "A poem, literary composition, or passage marked by deep or strong emotion"; citing Watson 1582; *Midsummer Night's Dream* 5.1.321, etc.

70. Ed. A. B. Grosart (1881) 62: "Upon a finical ass, I wrote a kind of Epigrammical sonnet in this manner." The sonnet that follows is satirical throughout.

71. Tasso, however, thought the final line the best place: see Colie, *Shakespeare's Living Art* 85, 88.

72. *Character of Several Authors* in *Works* ed. J. Sage and T. Ruddiman (Edinburgh 1711) 226; contrast the theory in *The Works of Michael Drayton* 5.139. Drayton's editors seem not to have appreciated that any generic question was involved, although they note that the sonnets added in 1619 are "the sonnets of a satirist."

73. Besides *Resources of Kind* and *Shakepeare's Living Art*, see Colie " 'All in Peeces:' Problems of Interpretation in Donne's *Anniversary Poems"* in *Just So Much Honour* ed. Amadeus P. Fiore (University Park, Pa. 1971). See also Susan Snyder *The Comic Matrix of Shakespeare's Tragedies* (Princeton 1979).

74. *Defence* ed. van Dorsten 114-115. See Marvin T. Herrick *Tragicomedy: Its Origin and Development in Italy, France, and England* (Urbana 1955); Madeleine Doran *Endeavours of Art* (Madison, Wis. 1954).

75. Dean Frye "The Question of Shakespeare's 'Parody' " *EC* 15 (1965) argues in particular against the tendency automatically to treat Shakespeare's comic subplots as parodies of the main plots.

76. Cf. Colie *Shakespeare's Living Art* 276: "Polixenes cannot recognize the theoretical force of Guarini's dictum that the shepherd's life is ennobling, whether engaged in by shepherds or by nobles seeking some recreation from their busy life."

77. *Defence* ed. van Dorsten 114; see *An Apology for Poetry* ed. G. Shepherd (London 1965) 135 ll. 36, 39nn.

78. *Mimesis: The Representation of Reality in Western Literature* tr. Willard R. Trask (Princeton 1953) 312ff. *Henry IV* part 1 is not a fair example, since it is concerned precisely with Hal's social mixing. Different style levels are certainly used in Shakespeare's comic subplots as well as in comic scenes in the tragedies.

79. John Marston *The Malcontent* ed. George K. Hunter (Manchester 1975) introd. 62.

80. *Ars Poetica* 220-233; *De Poeta* (1559) 125-126; *L'Arte Poetica* (1564) 163.

81. Cyrus Hoy *The Hyacinth Room: An Investigation Into the Nature of Comedy, Tragedy, and Tragicomedy* (London 1964) 210ff. See also Alvin Kernan *The Cankered Muse: Satire of the English Renaissance* Yale Studies in English 142 (New Haven and London 1959).

82. "To the Reader" before *The Faithful Shepherdess;* in *The Dramatic Works in the Beaumont and Fletcher Canon* ed. Fredson Bowers vol. 3 (Cambridge 1976) 497. See Hoy *The Hyacinth Room* 213.

83. See Hoy *The Hyacinth Room* index s.v. *Beckett;* and p. 8, where the modern tragicomedy genre is adumbrated through examples. See also Karl S. Guthke *Modern Tragicomedy* (New York 1966).

84. Guthke *Modern Tragicomedy* 211.

85. Although it itself may derive from earlier dramatic skits: see Gilbert Highet *The Anatomy of Satire* (Princeton 1962) 232-233. On the dangers of mixture with realistic fiction, see ibid. 158.

86. Philip Henderson, introd. to *Shorter Novels: Elizabethan and Jacobean* vol. 1 (London 1929) xxi.

87. John Carey "Sixteenth and Seventeenth Century Prose" in *English Poetry and Prose, 1540-1674* ed. Ricks (London 1970) 378.

88. *Sartor Resartus* 1.4, 2.5, 2.9; ed. W. M. Hudson (London 1967) 25, 104, 146; cf. 230, where "New England Editors" comment on the "burlesque style."

11. Generic Modulation

1. Barbara H. Smith *Poetic Closure* (Chicago 1968) 31.

2. For many ancient examples of modulation, see Francis Cairns *Generic Composition in Greek and Roman Poetry* (Edinburgh 1972) chs. 6 and 7.

3. *European Literature and the Latin Middle Ages* (New York and London 1953) 260.

4. See ibid., index s.v. *Biblical poetics.*

5. See Helen Cooper *Pastoral* (Ipswich and Totowa, N.J. 1977); and idem "The Goat and the Eclogue" *PQ* 53(1974)363–379 with refs. For bibliography on the pastoral mode, see above, Chapter 6 note 1.

6. See, e.g., E. Faye Wilson "Pastoral and Epithalamium in Latin Literature" *Speculum* 23 (1948) 35–57; and Marc M. Pelen *The Marriage Journey: Dream Vision Romance Structures and Epithalamic Conventions in Medieval Latin and French Poems and in Middle English Dream Poems* (diss. Princeton 1973) 704.

7. On the allegorical mode, see C. S. Lewis *The Allegory of Love* (Oxford 1936); Angus Fletcher *Allegory: The Theory of a Symbolic Mode* (Ithaca 1964); Northrop Frye "Allegory" in *Encyclopedia of Poetry and Poetics* ed. Alex Preminger et al. (Princeton 1965); John MacQueen *Allegory* (London 1970); Gay Clifford *The Transformations of Allegory* (London 1974); Maureen Quilligan *The Language of Allegory: Defining the Genre* (Ithaca and London 1979).

8. "Allegory" in *Encyclopedia of Poetry and Poetics* 12.

9. See Lewis *Allegory of Love* 78–82; F. J. E. Raby *A History of Secular Latin Poetry in the Middle Ages* 2 vols. (Oxford 1934) 1.100; William H. Stahl "To a Better Understanding of Martianus Capella" *Speculum* 40 (1965) 102–115; and William H. Stahl et al. *Martianus Capella and the Seven Liberal Arts* vol. 1 (New York and London 1971) 55–71 et passim.

10. Stahl *Martianus Capella* 26n, 27n, listing examples of the symposium genre, from Plato and Xenophon to Aulus Gellius.

11. On the journey as an allegorical feature, see Fletcher *Allegory* 151ff, developing Lewis *Allegory of Love* 69.

12. The evidence for the existence of a consciously recognized dream-poem kind is reviewed in Spearing *Medieval Dream-Poetry:* see esp. 2ff.

13. *Form and Style in Early English Literature* (London 1971) 374.

14. Ibid. 376.

15. Lewis *Allegory of Love* 249–250, a view followed by Derek A. Pearsall, ed. *"The Floure and the Leafe" and "The Assembly of Ladies"* (London and Edinburgh 1962) 52: "In 'The Assembly of Ladies' the use of convention is automatic and superficial, the author's real interests lying elsewhere."

16. As most critical comments on the poem imply it to be.

17. Ed. Pearsall, lines 17–21.

18. See, e.g., Rosalie L. Colie *The Resources of Kind* (Berkeley 1973); idem *Shakespeare's Living Art* (Princeton 1974) ch. 2 (where many contemporary comments are noticed); and Mario Praz *The Flaming Heart* (Garden City 1958) 191–263 passim.

19. *Choice, Chance and Change* (1606); ed. Alexander B. Grosart (London 1881) 62.

20. *The Art of Poetry* ll. 329-346, in *The Poems of John Dryden* ed. James Kinsley 4 vols. (Oxford 1958) 1.341.

21. Contrast Peter Hughes "Restructuring Literary History: Implications for the Eighteenth Century" *NLH* 8.2 (1977) 265, putting the change later and treating it as a breakdown of genre.

22. See Francesco Robortello and Tomaso Correa, cited in Colie *Shakespeare's Living Art* 82n; and Minturno, ibid. 83-84. For Minturno, see esp. *L'Arte Poetica* (1564) 279: "Talvolta materia gli diede l'Historia; talvolta e la Tragedia, e la Comedia; nè una volta l'Epica Poesia." Cf. Colie *Resources of Kind* 106-107, on similar receptiveness in the sonnet, at an earlier period. To the genres extended to the sonnet, one might add georgic—as in Fulgore da San Gemignano's calendrical *Sonetti dei Mesi*.

23. See above, Chapter 6.

24. *Resources of Kind* 25-26; cf. 29-30.

25. E.g., 188.1 and 4.

26. See Antoinette B. Dauber "Herrick's Foul Epigrams" *Genre* 9.2 (1976) 87-102. Among the kinds used are: sonnet (*The Poetical Works of Robert Herrick* ed. L. C. Martin [Oxford 1956] 11.1, 15.3, 47.2), valediction (14.3, 42.4), satiric instructions to painter (38.2), New Year poem (126.3), ode (198), Anacreontic ode (39.3, 178.2, 187.1, 191.4, 217.2, 238.3 etc.), epithalamium (53.2, 112.3, 124.3, 261.4), estate poem (146.1), eclogue (183.2), prospective poem (234.3), dialogue (248), and hymn (259.2, 260.5, 296.3).

27. See Janet Smarr "Renaissance Anacreontics" *CL* 25(1973) 224.

28. On the extension to epithalamium, see David M. Miller *The Net of Hephaestus: a Study of Modern Criticism and Metaphysical Metaphor*. De Proprietatibus Litterarum, ser. maior 11 (The Hague and Paris 1971) 146ff. Another aspect of the epigrammatic repertoire, extreme elision, was not much extended until the minimal poetry of the twentieth century.

29. Praz *The Flaming Heart* 206ff; idem *Studies in Seventeenth-Century Imagery* rev. ed. (Rome 1964) ch. 1; Joseph A. Mazzeo *Renaissance and Seventeenth-Century Studies* (New York and London 1964) ch. 3, esp. 52ff; and George Williamson *The Proper Wit of Poetry* (London 1961) 94 et passim.

30. *The Flaming Heart* 207.

31. Ibid. 218. Frequently Elizabethan sonnets, too, had epigram sources: see, e.g., J. W. Lever *The Elizabethan Love Sonnet* (London 1956) 63, 66.

32. *The Poems of John Cleveland* ed. Brian Morris and Eleanor Withington (Oxford 1967) 48. The structure as well as the conceits is close-knit: numerologists will notice, e.g., that "centre" comes in the center line of the poem. For a discussion of Donne's love poems as Roman elegies, see Earl Miner *The Metaphysical Mode from Donne to Cowley* (Princeton 1969) 220ff.

33. *The Spectator* no. 62 (11 May 1711) ed. Donald F. Bond 5 vols. (Oxford 1965) 1.267.

34. E.g., "You write with ease, to show your breeding; / But easy writing's vile hard reading." From Sheridan's *Clio's Protest:* see *The Faber Book of Epigrams and Epitaphs* ed. Geoffrey Grigson (London 1977) no. 346 [hereafter referred to as Grigson].

35. A good beginning is made by Brian Vickers in *Francis Bacon and Renaissance Prose* (Cambridge 1968) ch. 3.

36. Ibid. 74.

37. *Resolves: Divine, Moral, Political* (1628) 1.70: "Of Poets and Poetry" ed. O. Smeaton (London 1904) 192.

38. *Religio Medici* 1.37, in *Works* ed. G. Keynes 4 vols. (London 1964) 1.48.

39. Ibid. 1.35, in *Works* 1.258.

40. Nor with other widespread seventeenth-century transformations, such as the encomiastic. For the extension of the repertoire of encomium to funeral elegy and ode see, e.g., Dryden *Upon the Death of the Lord Hastings* and John Oldham *To the Memory of My Dear Friend, Mr Charles Morwent.*

41. A. Fleming (1589); J. Brinsley (1620); T. May (1628).

42. "An Essay on Virgil's *Georgics*" (1697), in *Eighteenth-Century Critical Essays* ed. Scott Elledge 2 vols. (Ithaca 1961) 1.2.

43. Ibid. Cf. *The Spectator* no. 417 (28 June 1712) ed. Bond 3.565: "Virgil . . . in his *Georgics* has given us a Collection of the most delightful Landskips that can be made out of Fields and Woods, Herds of Cattle, and Swarms of Bees."

44. The development of English georgic is traced in D. L. Durling *Georgic Tradition in English Poetry* (London 1935); John Chalker *The English Georgic* (London 1969); Ralph Cohen *The Art of Discrimination* (Berkeley 1964); and idem *The Unfolding of "The Seasons": A Study of James Thomson's Poem* (London, 1970).

45. See Chalker *English Georgic* 28, 187. The *locus classicus* for the introduction of political matter was Virgil *Georgics* 4.4ff: "Maecenas, read this other part, that sings / Embattled Squadrons and advent'rous Kings: / A mighty Pomp, though made of little Things" (tr. Dryden).

46. *Winter,* 1744, ll. 389–393; see Chalker *English Georgic* 136.

47. Chalker *English Georgic* 67ff.

48. Ibid. 75–76. The game laws of the time carried strong political implications: see Edward Palmer Thompson *Whigs and Hunters: The Origins of the Black Act* (London 1975).

49. Lines 1248, 1251, 1258–59. The Chatsworth section is 1252–1473.

50. Cf. Chalker *English Georgic* 170. Perhaps the origin of this feature lay in a neighboring didactic form, the Art of Poetry (Oldham, Dryden, Pope).

51. Not only in *The Creation* but in *Prince Arthur:* "He spread the airy Ocean without shores, / Where birds are wafted with their feather'd oars." This passage is justly noticed for its illustrative effect by Johnson (*Lives of the English Poets* ed. G. B. Hill 3 vols.[Oxford 1905] 2.255). Milton's melopoeia would be modeled primarily on Virgil's.

52. Wordsworth's interests extended backward to the seventeenth-century origins of descriptive poetry. For his reading of *To Penshurst,* e.g., see Dorothy Wordsworth *Journal* 11 Feb. 1802.

53. Contrast, however, Northrop Frye *Anatomy of Criticism* (Princeton 1957) 246.

54. Geoffrey Tillotson treats it as mock heroic and mock pastoral. But these are common ingredients of English georgic. Among other things, the poem teaches how to study. As to the mode, the common description "novel in verse" testifies to its obviousness. See Geoffrey and Kathleen Tillotson *Mid-Victorian Studies* (London 1965) 124ff. As Tillotson notes, the subtitle of *The Bothie* was *A Long-Vacation Pastoral.*

55. Used even of people and things: e.g., Keats *The Cap and Bells* 4, in *The Poetical Works* ed. H. W. Garrod rev. ed. (Oxford 1958) 396: "While little harps were touch'd by many a lyric fay"; and Browning *Balaustion's Adventure: Including a transcript from Euripides* (1871) l. 186: "Strangers, greet the lyric girl!"

56. René Wellek and Austin Warren *Theory of Literature* rev. ed. (New York 1956) 231–232.

57. J. C. Scaliger *Poetices* (Lyons 1561) 169.c.2. For Tomaso Correa *De Elegia* (Bologna 1590), developing Scaliger's description, see Bernard Weinberg *A History of Literary Criticism in the Italian Renaissance* 2 vols. (Chicago 1961) 1.231. Cf. Abbie F. Potts *The Elegiac Mode* (Ithaca 1967) 36ff et passim; also Wesley Trimpi *Ben Jonson's Poems* (Stanford 1962) 228–229. For refs. on elegy, see above Chapter 8 note 18.

58. Scaliger *Poetices* 169.c.2. Cf. Potts 39, 42, 49; also Maurice Bowra *Early Greek Elegists* (Cambridge, Mass. 1938) 107. Cf. Joseph Trapp *Lectures on Poetry* (1742) 169: "With this Kind of Poem, every Thing that is epigrammatical, satirical, or sublime, is inconsistent. Elegy aims not to be witty or facetious, acrimonious or severe, majestic or sublime; but is smooth, humble, and unaffected." Cited in Ian Jack "The Elegy as Exorcism: Pope's 'Verses to the Memory of an Unfortunate Lady'" in *Augustan Worlds: Essays in Honour of A. R. Humphreys* ed. J. C. Hilson et al. (Leicester 1978) 78.

59. See Potts *Elegiac Mode* 36ff, 55, 232. For revelations in Propertius, see ibid. 51.

60. As Scaliger observes, perhaps already working toward a concept of mode: "Epicedia quoque, et Epitaphia, et Epistolae hoc genere Poematis recte conficiuntur" (169.d.2).

61. Potts *Elegiac Mode* 235.

62. For the two senses of "elegiac," see Stephen F. Fogle, in *Encyclopedia of Poetry and Poetics* 216.

63. Cf., e.g., Geoffrey H. Hartman "Self, Time, and History" in *The Fate of Reading and Other Essays* (Chicago and London 1975) 284ff, on Wordsworth's self-building. On Wordsworth's internalizing use of Minucius Felix and the dialogue form, see Alan G. Hill "New Light on *The Excursion*" *Ariel* 5 (1974) 37–47.

64. See Donald S. Hair *Browning's Experiments with Genre* (Toronto 1972) index s.v. *Lyric;* also 8, on a new, personal conception of lyric in the nineteenth century.

65. The improved, 1846 text; see *The Poetical Works of Walter Savage Landor* ed. Stephen Wheeler 3 vols. (Oxford 1937) 3.77.

66. This is a question not discussed by Potts, who treats elegy and epigram indifferently. As her title indicates, she is solely concerned with elegy as a mode.

67. Greek Anthology 7.80; Cory *Ionica* (1858), rpt. as Grigson no. 183.

68. Ed. Wheeler 2.479; Grigson no. 450.

69. Ed. Wheeler 3.44; Grigson no. 443.

70. Ed. Wheeler 2.465–466.

71. Ibid. 2.476; Grigson no. 440.

72. Ed. Wheeler 3.372; Grigson no. 442.

73. For the relation of elegy and romance, see Patricia A. Parker *Inescapable Romance: Studies in the Poetics of a Mode* (Princeton 1979) index s.v. *Deferral.*

74. See Geoffrey Tillotson *Essays in Criticism and Research* (Cambridge 1942) 67; Bernard Groom *The Diction of Poetry from Spenser to Bridges* (Toronto 1955) 148.

75. As Potts perhaps hints, *Elegiac Mode* 3.

12. Hierarchies of Genres and Canons of Literature

1. "Literary Fashions" in Isaac D'Israeli *Curiosities of Literature* 3 vols. (London 1849).

2. B. Fabian and Siegfried J. Schmidt rightly draw attention to the "eminently canonizing effect" of the Cambridge Bibliographies: see the latter's "Problems of Empirical Research in Literary History" tr. P. Heath *NLH* 8.2 (1977) 218. But what else did they expect? Any useful bibliography is bound to exert such an effect.

3. See J. Carter *Taste and Technique in Book Collecting* (Cambridge 1948) 60ff, on the effect of biliophily. Claudio Guillén *Literature as System* (Princeton 1971) 398-399 touches on the influence of anthologies, a subject on which fundamental work remains to be done.

4. This method of censorship conveniently allows control of future publication. For the earlier period, see F. S. Siebert *Freedom of the Press in England, 1476-1776* (Urbana 1952) and (on the Inquisition) *Erasmus Newsletter* 8 (1976) 5 and Paul F. Grendler *The Roman Inquisition and the Venetian Press, 1540-1605* (Princeton 1978). For the more modern, S. Hynes *The Edwardian Turn of Mind* (Princeton 1968); and D. Thomas *A Long Time Burning* (London 1969). There is an early attack on bookstall censorship in A. T. Quiller-Couch *Adventures in Criticism* (London 1896) 279ff.

5. On "unwritten poetics" see Renato Poggioli *The Spirit of the Letter* (Cambridge, Mass. 1965) 343-354; Guillén *Literature as System* 125-126.

6. *Elizabethan Critical Essays* ed. G. Gregory Smith 2 vols. (Oxford 1904) 1.255; *Miscellaneous Prose of Sir Philip Sidney* ed. Katherine Duncan-Jones and Jan van Dorsten (Oxford 1973) 98; *Critical Essays of the Seventeenth Century* ed. J. E. Spingarn 3 vols. (Oxford 1908-9) 2.295; *The Art of Poetry* l. 590 in *The Poems of John Dryden* ed. James Kinsley, 4 vols. (Oxford 1958) 1.348.

7. Sir John Harington *A Brief Apology* in *Elizabethan Critical Essays* ed. Smith 2.209; Pope *An Essay on Criticism* l. 419.

8. Edward Phillips *Critical Essays* ed. Spingarn 2.266.

9. *A Discourse Concerning Satire* in *"Of Dramatic Poesy" and Other Critical Essays* ed. George Watson 2 vols. (London and New York 1962) 2.82.

10. "On the Interrelations of Eighteenth-Century Literary Forms" in *New Approaches to Eighteenth-Century Literature* ed. Phillip Harth (New York and London 1974) 35-36.

11. J. C. Scaliger *Poetices Libri Septem* (Lyons 1561) 144.a.1.

12. As the continuation makes clear: "Epica Poesia, a cui non fa mestiere ne canto, ne rappresentatione." See Antonio Sebastiano Minturno *L'Arte Poetica* (1564) 281.

13. Minturno *L'Arte Poetica* 3. For epic in the sense *genus mixtum* cf. Diomedes' classification, cited below.

14. Ed. van Dorsten 94.

15. Of *Dramatic Poesy* in *Critical Essays* ed. Watson 1.7.

16. The classification made popular by Diomedes. This sense of "epic" is missed by commentators and is not in the *OED*.

17. *A Discourse Concerning Satire* in *Critical Essays* ed. Watson 2.149.

18. Cohen "On the Interrelations" n. 12.

19. Ibid. 35.

20. Preface to *Theatrum Poetarum* in *Critical Essays* ed. Spingarn 2.266. For a discussion see Cohen "On the Interrelations" 36. On epionic verse, see Scaliger *Poetices* 67.

21. See Guillén *Literature as System* 403ff; Ernst Robert Curtius *European Literature and the Latin Middle Ages* (New York and London 1953) 440ff; Charles Trinkaus "The Unknown *Quattrocento* Poetics of Bartolommeo della Fonte" *SR* 13 (1966) 87.

22. Cicero *De Optimo Genere Oratorum* 1.1; Horace *Ars Poetica* 73-98 (where the sequence may be determined by metrical considerations rather than a hierarchical principle of arrangement), 220-294; Quintilian *Institutio Oratoria* 10.1.46-100, the sequence used in considering Greek authors. (The Latin series reverses the orders of tragedy and comedy, and omits pastoral.) Quintilian already notices a change in iambic, which he regards as no longer a completely separate form of composition: see further in Guillén *Literature as System* 399ff. Since the *Institutio* turns immediately to authors of history and other "extraliterary" genres, the paradigm is not for Quintilian a closed canon. The same point could be made about Dionysius Halicarnassus.

Diomedes (see further in Curtius *European Literature* 440) lists the following species of *genus enarrativum* (*exegeticon vel apangelticon*, i.e., interpretative, descriptive, or narrative): *angeltice* (preceptive); *historice* (narrative, genealogical, etc.); *didascalice* (didactic). As in Aristotle, the *genus commune* (*coinon vel micton*) is the presentational mode in which both poet and characters speak.

Sidney *Defence* ed. van Dorsten 81: "The most notable be the heroic, lyric, tragic, comic, satiric, iambic, elegiac, pastoral, and certain others, some of these being termed according to the matter they deal with, some by the sorts of verses they liked best to write in." From the fuller review of "the special kinds" of poetry at 94ff, it is clear that by "elegiac" Sidney means "lamenting elegiac."

Harington *A Brief Apology* in *Elizabethan Critical Essays* ed. Smith 2.209-210, where the purpose of defending against the charge of lewdness may influence the arrangement of genres. "Mourning elegy" shows that "elegy" is used in something like its later sense, rather than to imply elegiac meter or include amatory elegy.

Meres *Palladis Tamia* in *Elizabethan Critical Essays* ed. Smith 2.319; Phillips' preface to *Theatrum Poetarum* in *Critical Essays* ed. Spingarn 2.266; Dryden *The Art of Poetry* in *The Poems of John Dryden* ed. Kinsley 1.332-361.

23. *Reason of Church-Government* in *Complete Prose Works* ed. Don M. Wolfe et al. 8 vols. (New Haven 1953-) 1.813-816. Not, however, Jacopo Mazzoni's different scheme in *Della defesa della "Commedia" di Dante* (Cesena 1688): see *Literary Criticism: Plato to Dryden* ed. A. H. Gilbert (New York 1940) 382. On tripartite ordering of the genres see further Guillén *Literature as System* 390-419. On tragedy and comedy as higher genres, see *Theories of Literary Genre* ed. Joseph P. Strelka (University Park, Pa. and London 1978) 199.

24. See *Theories of Literary Genre* ed. Strelka 400-401; and cf. Curtius *European Literature* 441 on Diomedes' six *qualitates carminum*. On seventeenth-century revaluation of Horace as a lyric poet, see Valerie Edden " 'The Best of Lyric Poets' " in *Horace* ed. C. D. N. Costa (London and Boston 1973) 135-159. By the 1650s, however, lyric could already be disparaged: see, e.g., *Naps upon Parnassus* cited in Gordon Braden *The Classics and English Renaissance Poetry* (New Haven and London 1978) 244.

25. Peter Hughes "Restructuring Literary History" *NLH* 8.2 (1977) 265.

26. Sidney *Defence* ed. van Dorsten 95. Cf. Puttenham cited in Cohen "On the Interrelations" 39.

27. Besides the notorious dismissal of pastoral in connection with *Lycidas, Lives of the English Poets* ed. G. B. Hill 3 vols.(Oxford 1905) 1.163-164, see Hill's index s.v. *Pastoral poetry: Johnson's contempt for it.* Outgoing forms are often treated with acerbity: one might compare Johnson on alliteration.

28. When Sidney (*Defence* ed. van Dorsten 95) speaks of iambic poetry as bitter rather than satiric he may refer to *fel* epigram.

29. *Elizabethan and Metaphysical Imagery* (Chicago 1947) 242.

30. Dryden *The Art of Poetry* ll. 336-346 ed. Kinsley 1.341. On the deletion of the sonnet, see Johnson *Dictionary* s.v. *Sonnet* ("It is not very suitable to the English language, and has not been used by any man of eminence since Milton") and *Sonneteer* ("A small poet, in contempt"). On the epigram, Johnson notes that Warton "observes very justly, that the [Saint Cecilia's Day] odes both of Dryden and Pope conclude unsuitably and unnaturally with epigram" (*Works* ed. Hawkins et al. vol. 15 ed. Gleig [1789] 473).

31. *An Essay on the Genius and Writings of Pope* in Scott Elledge, ed., *Eighteenth-Century Critical Essays* 2 vols. (Ithaca 1961) 2.718, 763. On the *Dunciad* as true epic, see Aubrey Williams *Pope's "Dunciad": A Study of Its Meaning* (Baton Rouge 1955) 131ff. On the bearing of satire's mixture on its hierarchical status, see Cohen "On the Interrelations" 43.

32. See Cohen "On the Interrelations" 39-40, citing Addison and Tickell.

33. *Defence* ed. van Dorsten 80.

34. Cf. Rosalie L. Colie *The Resources of Kind* (Berkeley 1973) 86-87. The rise of georgic may seem incompatible with a thesis of James Turner's *Politics of Landscape* (Oxford and Cambridge, Mass. 1979), that manual labor was undervalued in seventeenth-century literature. But sometimes georgic was elevated by excluding the details of work—which appear more fully, if under symbolic guise, in devotional works (see Turner 172).

35. The view taken by L. Lipking in an important study, *The Ordering of the Arts in Eighteenth-Century England* (Princeton 1970) 365-366. For the Warton passage, see Elledge 2.719-720.

36. *An Essay* Elledge 762.

37. *Lives* ed. Hill 3.251.

38. Ibid. 2.295, 3.242; *Dictionary; Rambler* no. 158.

39. H. Blair *Lectures on Rhetoric and Belles Lettres* 2 vols. (Edinburgh 1783): Lecture 19, "General Characters of Style."

40. Ibid. Lecture 40, "Didactic Poetry—Descriptive Poetry."

41. *The Prose Works of William Wordsworth* ed. W. J. B. Owen and Jane W. Smyser 3 vols.(Oxford 1974) 3.27.

42. *Praeterita* vol. 2 (Orpington 1887) ch. 4.

43. James, preface to *The Ambassadors,* last paragraph; Kermode *The Classic.*

44. *Anatomy of Criticism* (Princeton 1957)18.

45. See Colie *Resources of Kind* 92, 98-99.

46. See, e.g., Elizabeth W. Bruss' illuminating study *Autobiographical Acts: The Changing Situation of a Literary Genre* (Baltimore and London 1976).

47. Marilyn Butler *Maria Edgeworth* (Oxford 1972) 347-348.

48. *The Life of Mr John Milton* in *Milton: The Critical Heritage* ed. J. T. Shawcross (London 1970) 104. *Paradise Regained* was the second work of Milton's to receive critical treatment at full length, from R. Meadowcourt (1732).

49. G. A. Wilkes *"Paradise Regained* and the Conventions of the Sacred Epic" *English Studies* 44 (1963); Barbara K. Lewalski *Milton's Brief Epic* (Providence and London 1966).

50. *The Art of T. S. Eliot* (London 1949) 3.

51. Some other influences on taste are studied in Ernest Edward Kellett *The Whirligig of Taste* (London 1929) and in B.S. Allen *Tides in English Taste 1619-1800: A Background for the Study of Literature* 2 vols. (New York 1958). But histories of reception and reputation in English literature are needed for most periods.

52. Johnson *Lives* ed. Hill 1.235.

53. 1861, more than twenty printings; 1891, more than twenty printings; etc.

54. Harmondsworth 1956, with eleven printings by 1971.

55. *A New Canon of English Poetry* ed. James Reeves and Martin Seymour-Smith (London 1967), being specifically designed to go outside the "Oxgrave" canon, is hardly comparable with the anthologies discussed here. It does not itself offer a canon, but only supplements, in large part from Trumbell Stickney. Nevertheless it, too, is guided by generic considerations: its choices are "mostly short" and exclude ballads.

56. In prose fiction the length to be considered is not only that of the complete work, but of its component parts. Short chapter divisions are at present in favor, because of the prominence of such forms as antinovel, experimental novel, *poioumenon,* and mosaic fiction.

13. Systems of Genres

1. See René Wellek *Discriminations* (New Haven and London 1970) 234; Paul Hernadi *Beyond Genre* (Ithaca and London 1972) 187-205.

2. See Claudio Guillén *Literature as System* (Princeton 1971) 393, 396-397; Hernadi *Beyond Genre* 54-55; and Chapter 12 above. The division goes back to Plato *Republic* 392C-D; and it is still used by Klaus Weissenberger in "A Morphological Genre Theory" in Joseph P. Strelka *Theories of Literary Genre* (University Park, Pa. and London 1978) 229-253.

3. Frye's theory of four radicals is criticized by Hernadi *Beyond Genre* 141-144; and Robert E. Scholes *Structuralism in Literature* (New Haven and London 1974) 124. See also Guillén *Literature as System* 387.

4. In *De Poeta* (1559) and more fully in *L'Arte* (1564). Guillén *Literature as System* 389ff, 394 is not firm enough in correcting Behrens (*Die Lehre von der Einteilung der Dichtkunst*) on this point.

5. See Hernadi *Beyond Genre* 23-37, with refs.; Wellek *Discriminations* 236-240.

6. Cornelis F. P. Stutterheim "Prolegomena to a Theory of the Literary Genres" *Zagadnienia Rodzajów Literackich* 6.2(11)(Lodz 1964)11-12 traces some of the confusions to differences between English and German.

7. Wellek *Discriminations* 236ff, 251; see also Hernadi *Beyond Genre* 12, 48-49, 56, 58 (on Guérard's lyric "spirit"), and 68-69. What would Wellek say about John Richetti's lapse in *Defoe's Narratives* (Oxford 1975)16: "The novel is aware."

8. *Literature as System* 389-398, with many refs. For a criticism of Guillén, see

David Newton-de Molina "Here is No Continuing City" *EC* 23 (1973) 179-186.

9. Again the point is Goethe's. For a fuller treatment see Hernadi *Beyond Genre* 35, 37, 41, 159; Ulrich Weisstein *Comparative Literature and Literary Theory* (Bloomington and London 1968)119; Guillén *Literature as System* 115.

10. See Weisstein *Comparative Literature* 108; Hernadi *Beyond Genre* 162, 189, 191, and appendix passim.

11. See Guillén *Literature as System* 117-118.

12. See Hernadi *Beyond Genre* 14. And cf. ibid. 51, 187ff; and Guillén *Literature as System* 395.

13. *Literature as System* 114. Weisstein (*Comparative Literature* 109) objects to treating the didactic as a representative mode, on the ground that it is distinguished by purpose. But this has little force; purpose is not the only *differentia* of the didactic.

14. See Hernadi *Beyond Genre* 88-89, 150.

15. See M. A. K. Halliday "Language Structure and Language Function" in *New Horizons in Linguistics* ed. John Lyons (Harmondsworth 1970) 141.

16. Susanne K. Langer *Feeling and Form* (1953) 266, 411ff; see Hernadi *Beyond Genre* 106.

17. See the critique in Hernadi *Beyond Genre* 99-100; also John Reichert in *Theories of Literary Genre* ed. Strelka 64 (showing that Aristotle himself held that the same work could be both mimetic and didactic).

18. See above, Chapter 12; and Guillén *Literature as System* 403-404.

19. Weisstein *Comparative Literature* 108.

20. *Ars Versificatoria* 2.5-80; Edmond Faral *Les Arts poétiques du 12ᵉ et du 13ᵉ siècle* (Paris 1962) 153.

21. Cf. Rosalie L. Colie *The Resources of Kind* (Berkeley 1973) 10. Epic and tragedy are interchangeable in such schemes, while satire and pastoral converge in medieval practice. Comedy, of course, was upwardly mobile.

22. John of Garland *The "Parisiana Poetria"* ed. Traugott Lawler (New Haven and London 1974) figs. 3 and 4, and p. 239, with refs. See also Faral *Les Arts poétiques* 87; Ernst Robert Curtius *European Literature and the Latin Middle Ages* (New York and London 1953) 231-232; and Guillén *Literature as System* 409ff. As Lawler notes, John of Garland's own version of the *rota* replaced the old shepherd-farmer-soldier triad with a new triad: peasants-city dwellers-courtiers.

23. "The Answer of Mr Hobbes to Sir William Davenant's Preface Before Gondibert" in *Critical Essays of the Seventeenth Century* ed. Joel E. Spingarn 3 vols. (Oxford 1908-1909) 2.55.

24. Such as Petersen's. See Weisstein *Comparative Literature* 113; Hernadi *Beyond Genre* 57.

25. *Anatomy of Criticism* (Princeton 1957) 162ff; see Hernadi *Beyond Genre* 136f. For a sharp critique of the seasonal scheme see W. K. Wimsatt "Northrop Frye: Criticism as Myth" in *Northrop Frye in Modern Criticism* ed. M. Krieger (New York and London 1966) 75-108.

26. See Scholes *Structuralism in Literature* 119; and cf. the similar critique by Todorov, discussed by Christine Brooke-Rose in "Historical Genres/Theoretical Genres" *NLH* 8.1 (1976) 146-148.

27. *Anatomy* 33, 34.

28. Frye's subsequent statement in "Reflections in a Mirror" in *Northrop Frye* ed. Kireger 142–144 attempts to put his view of the relation of history and literary history on a less unsatisfactory footing.

29. *Anatomy* 52.

30. "Utopian History and the *Anatomy of Criticism*" in *Northrop Frye* ed. Krieger 68–69.

31. *Structuralism in Literature* 132ff.

32. Ibid. 136.

33. Ibid. 134.

34. See the sharp review by David Newton-de Molina in *MLR* 69 (1974) 134–137.

35. The diagram is from Hernadi *Beyond Genre* 166, but appeared originally in *College English* (October 1971) 24.

36. The diagram receives some approval from David Newton-de Molina in *MLR* 69 (1974) 136.

37. *Beyond Genre* 153. On factor analysis and mapping, see *Pattern Recognition: Ideas in Practice* ed. Bruce G. Batchelor (New York and London 1978); *Pattern Recognition: Introduction and Foundations* ed. Jack Sklansky (Stroudsburg, Pa. 1973); *Frontiers of Pattern Recognition: The Proceedings* ed. Satoshi Watanabe (New York 1972).

38. With the grand exception of Paul Zumthor: see especially his *Essai de poétique médiévale* (Paris 1972). However, Zumthor's system does not so much organize the traditional genres as replace them with a coaxial classification of such categories as "high courtly lyric"—in accordance with a poetic in which authorial individuality with respect to specific genres has little place.

39. *Anatomy* 308.

40. *The Modes of Modern Writing* (London 1977), based on a dichotomy of Jakobson's. See the review by Frederick M. Keener *EC* 29 (1979) 254.

41. See Ian Reid *The Short Story* (London and New York 1977) 28; where, however, the example of *The Prelude* (in which "spots of time" are by no means presented as pure lyric) is misapplied.

42. Ibid. 40, 46.

43. Angus Fletcher (*Northrop Frye* ed. Krieger 121–122) describes Frye's thinking about the order of literature as spatial. But the best in Frye has nothing to do with this (significantly, he himself makes no use of diagrams); only a few passages, such as *Anatomy of Criticism* 17, lend support to Fletcher's observation.

44. *Structuralism in Literature* 137.

45. Cf. William Righter's critique of Frye in "Myth and Interpretation" *NLH* 3.2 (1972) 334: "Literature, insofar as it is an intelligible whole, is so by accumulation and continuity, not through any internal logic pertaining to an 'order of words.'" The relativity is stressed and probably overstressed by Tzvetan Todorov, where he argues for a subjective basis to the choice of the *differentiae* distinguishing genres that were once thought of as "natural" forms. He suggests arranging these properties according to whether they arise from syntactic, pragmatic, or verbal aspects. See "The Origin of Genres" *NLH* 8.1 (1976) 162–163.

46. See John Lyons *Introduction to Theoretical Linguistics* (Cambridge 1968) 431, and F. R. Palmer *Semantics: A New Outline* (Cambridge 1976) 74–76, on the complica-

tions of color words. Even ordering them by three dimensions (hue, brightness, saturation) involves oversimplifying.

47. Even, for example, such a fundamental quality as alterity. See John A. Burrow's discussion of the difference between French and British culture in this regard, in *NLH* 10.2 (1979) 385-390.

48. *Structuralism in Literature* 138.

49. *Beyond Genre* 168.

50. See, e.g., his "O literaturnoj èvoljucii" *Na literaturnom postu* 4 (1927), tr. C. A. Luplow in *Readings in Russian Poetics: Formalist and Structuralist Views* ed. Ladislav Matejka and Krystyna Pomorska (Cambridge, Mass. and London 1971) 66-78.

51. Patricia A. Parker *Inescapable Romance: Studies in the Poetics of a Mode* (Princeton 1979).

52. The term used for similars by Scholes: see, e.g., *Structuralism in Literature* 134.

53. Cited in Johnson *Dictionary* s.v. *Pastoral*.

54. Cf. the different sorts of semantic antynomy; on which see Lyons *Introduction* 463; Palmer *Semantics* 78-82.

55. See the discussion in John Stevens *Medieval Romance* (London 1973), esp. 80, 90.

56. Cf. Ralph Cohen "Innovation and Variation" in *Literature and History* (Los Angeles 1974) 24ff; Thomas G. Rosenmeyer *The Green Cabinet* (Berkeley and Los Angeles 1969) index s.v. *Hesiodic tradition*.

57. "A Discourse on Pastoral Poetry" in *The Prose Works of Alexander Pope* ed. Norman Ault (Oxford 1936) 298.

58. Cf. here Pope's criticism of the length of Spenser's eclogues, ibid. 301.

59. Ibid. 301-302.

14. Genre in Interpretation

1. Cf. Paul Hernadi *Beyond Genre* (Ithaca and London 1972) 7-9, esp. 7: "The study of genres must not become an end in itself but rather serve as a means toward the fuller understanding of individual works and of literature as a whole."

2. Claudio Guillén *Literature as System* (Princeton 1971) 107ff.

3. On the debate on intentionalism, see the refs in note 36 below.

4. "The Hermeneutics of Literary Indeterminacy: A Dissent from the New Orthodoxy" *NLH* 10.1 (1978) 78.

5. See Walter A. Davis *The Act of Interpretation: A Critique of Literary Reason* (Chicago and London 1978) 52. The utopian solution Davis proposes—preliminary agreement on aesthetic definitions of the entities to be looked for—does not come to grips with the actual phenomena of reading and criticizing.

6. Monroe C. Beardsley *Aesthetics: Problems in the Philosophy of Criticism* (New York 1958) 144.

7. W. K. Wimsatt *The Verbal Icon: Studies in the Meaning of Poetry* (1954, rpt. New York 1958) ch. 1 n. 7; this chapter was written in collaboration with Monroe C. Beardsley.

8. See E. Donald Hirsch *Validity in Interpretation* (New Haven and London 1967) 220-221.

9. Ibid. 237ff.

10. Beardsley *Aesthetics* 144.

11. Hirsch *Validity in Interpretation* 222.

12. Ibid.

13. Francis Cairns *Generic Composition in Greek and Roman Poetry* (Edinburgh 1972) 6; cf. Ulrich Weisstein *Comparative Literature and Literary Theory* (Bloomington and London 1968) 103.

14. See, e.g., Walter Allen *The English Novel* (London 1954) 57.

15. See John Chalker *The English Georgic* (London 1969) 172.

16. Guillén *Literature as System* 108. Cf. Graham Hough *An Essay on Criticism* (London 1966) 61–62.

17. "The Rise of Hermeneutics" tr. Frederic Jameson *NLH* 3.2 (1972) 243. For a useful survey of early hermeneutic theory, see Kurt Müller-Vollmer *Towards a Phenomenological Theory of Literature: A Study of Wilhelm Dilthey's "Poetik"* (The Hague 1963). See also David Couzens Hoy *The Critical Circle: Literature and History in Contemporary Hermeneutics* (Berkeley 1978); R. E. Palmer *Hermeneutics* (Evanston, Ill. 1969); André Lefevere *Literary Knowledge* (Amsterdam 1977), esp. ch. 8; and Josef Bleicher *Contemporary Hermeneutics: Hermeneutics as Method, Philosophy and Critique* (London 1980).

18. This institutional aspect of criticism militates against the totally free grouping according to similarity imagined by Popper. See Hernadi *Beyond Genre* 4–5.

19. See ibid. 2.

20. Ralph Cohen "Innovation and Variation" in *Literature and History* (Los Angeles 1974) 10.

21. F. R. Palmer *Semantics: A New Outline* (Cambridge 1976) 57, in rebuttal of the Sapir-Whorf hypothesis.

22. Cf. C. G. Jung *Psychology and Alchemy* tr. R. F. C. Hull (London 1953) 84.

23. William Righter *Logic and Criticism* (London 1963) 122.

24. Cf. John M. Ellis *The Theory of Literary Criticism* (Berkeley 1974) 228–229.

25. Morris Weitz *Hamlet and the Philosophy of Literary Criticism* (London 1965) 49ff. Cf. Daryl J. Gless *Measure for Measure: The Law and the Convent* (Princeton 1979), which shows how much reconstruction of *Measure for Measure* must depend on recognizing its relation to antimonastic satire.

26. See, however, the attempt at a *rapprochement* in Helen Gardner *The Business of Criticism* (Oxford 1959) 45ff.

27. F. E. Sparshott *The Concept of Criticism* (Oxford 1967) 179–180.

28. F. W. Bateson's term; see René Wellek "The Literary Theories of F. W. Bateson" *EC* 29 (1979) 117.

29. Carlyle *Sartor Resartus* 3.3.

30. See Harry Caplan "The Four Senses of Scriptural Interpretation and the Medieval Theory of Preaching" *Speculum* 4 (1929) 282–290.

31. Frank Kermode *The Classic* (London 1975) 40, 44.

32. "The Rise of Hermeneutics" 243. For a defence of Dilthey against Heidegger, see E. D. Hirsch "Faulty Perspectives" *EC* 25 (1975) 164.

33. See James Nohrnberg "Pynchon's Paraclete" in *Pynchon: A Collection of Critical Essays* ed. Edward Mendelson (Englewood Cliffs 1978) 147–161, which already de-

velops the apocalyptic connections of Pynchon's work, discovered in its Biblical symbolism.

34. For an early instance of changed grouping and uncertainty about generic identity, see Cairns *Generic Composition* 96-97, discussing Roman treatment of triumph poems as dithyrambs. Aristotle shows dissatisfaction with generic grouping on a metrical basis, without seeming to realize that the metrical markers had become inadequate because of changes in the genres. See Rosalie L. Colie, *The Resources of Kind* (Berkeley 1973) 9.

35. Wolfgang Iser "Indeterminacy and the Reader's Response in Prose Fiction" in *Aspects of Narrative* ed. J. Hillis Miller (New York and London 1971) 42. Iser's thesis is developed at length in *The Act of Reading: A Theory of Aesthetic Response* (Baltimore and London 1978) index s.v. *Indeterminacy* and *Gaps*. The question whether modern literature calls for reader participation in a fundamentally new way is discussed in Charles Altieri "The Hermeneutics of Literary Indeterminacy" *NLH* 10.1 (1978) 88f.

36. Iser *The Act of Reading* 178. It is unfortunate that much modern Continental theory is still occupied with reaction to Ingarden, whose version of intentionalism, though powerful, hardly represents the contemporary intentionalist position. For some modern developments see *On Literary Intention* ed. David Newton-de Molina (Edinburgh 1976); idem the "Critical Challenges: The Bellagio Symposium" issue, *NLH* 7.1 (1975); and the "Literary Hermeneutics" issue, *NLH* 10.1 (1978).

37. Kermode *The Classic* 129, of *Wuthering Heights* (a significantly special case, in which plurality is contingent on the incompletely revised state). Cf. ibid. 108-109, 113-114, 130-133.

38. The notion of "gaps" or "places of indeterminacy" (*Unbestimmtheitsstellen*) derives from Ingarden, who developed it with a different purpose altogether, to circumscribe the area of the reader's discretion. See Iser *The Act of Reading* 170 et passim.

39. Kermode *The Classic* 130.

40. See ibid. 78, 135; and cf. "A Surplus of Signifier," the critical review by Oliver Taplin in *EC* 26 (1976) 342.

41. Davis *The Act of Interpretation* 161.

42. Altieri "The Hermeneutics of Literary Indeterminacy" 90.

43. Hough *An Essay* 72.

44. In spite of his claim to advance a "Jungian formulation."

45. See John Lyons *Introduction to Theoretical Linguistics* (Cambridge 1968) 412, 414n, 426 on this limited indeterminacy.

46. Ambrose Bierce *An Heiress from Redhorse* in *In the Midst of Life* (London 1892).

47. Hirsch *Validity in Interpretation* 255.

48. See Altieri "The Hermeneutics of Literary Indeterminacy" 89.

49. Kermode *The Classic* 75-76; and cf. 74, 131-133. On Kermode's polarities, see Taplin "A Surplus of Signifier" 339. See also E. D. Hirsch's review of *The Genesis of Secrecy* in *NYRB* (14 June 1979) 18-20.

50. Altieri "The Hermeneutics of Literary Indeterminacy" 87-88; cf. 85-90 passim.

51. Cited in Walter de la Mare *Lewis Carroll* (London 1932) 53.

52. Altieri "The Hermeneutics of Literary Indeterminacy" 90.

53. See Taplin "A Surplus of Signifier" 343.

54. Hirsch "Faulty Perspectives" 167; see also idem "Privileged Criteria in Literary Evaluation" *Problems of Literary Evaluation* ed. Joseph P. Strelka, Yearbook of Comparative Criticism no. 2 (State College, Pa. 1969) 22–34; idem "Literary Evaluation as Knowledge" Wisconsin Studies in Contemporary Literature no. 9 (1968) 319–331; and idem "The Paradoxes of Perspectivism" *Lebendige Form: Festschrift für Heinrich E.K. Henel* ed. Jeffrey L. Sammons and Ernst Schürer (Munich 1970) 15–20.

55. See Martin Steinmann, Jr. "Cumulation, Revolution, and Progress" *NLH* 5.3 (1974) 477–490.

56. Jean Starobinski "On the Fundamental Gestures of Criticism" tr. Bruno Braunrot *NLH* 5.3 (1974) 491–514.

57. On the possibility of valuable misunderstanding, see E. Donald Hirsch "Some Aims of Criticism" in *Literary Theory and Structure: Essays in Honour of William K. Wimsatt* ed. Frank Brady et al. (New Haven and London 1973) 51–52.

58. *Satires* 1.4.39–69. See C. O. Brink *Horace on Poetry: Prolegomena to the Literary Epistles* (Cambridge 1963) 161–163.

59. Adrian Marino "Toward a Definition of Literary Genres" in *Theories of Literary Genre* ed. Strelka 53.

60. See Hirsch "Privileged Criteria" 31–33.

61. See Robert E. Scholes *Structuralism in Literature* (New Haven and London 1974) 131.

62. E.g., Hough *An Essay* 117: "Any criticism of the novel which neglects its ties with historical actuality is false to the novel's real values, and empty when it should be full." The whole chapter, ibid. 111–120, makes the prescriptions of the verisimilar novel usefully explicit. For the requirement of unicentrality, see, e.g., Alan Friedman's criticism of *Nostromo* in *The Turn of the Novel* (New York 1966).

63. Prologue to *The Sad Shepherd* l. 56. This point is well brought out by Paul Alpers in *Twentieth-Century Literature in Retrospect* ed. Reuben A. Brower, English Studies 2 (Cambridge, Mass. 1971) 197ff.

64. See Hirsch "Privileged Criteria" 30. For the genre theories of the Chicago School, see, e.g., R. S. Crane *The Languages of Criticism and the Structure of Poetry* (Toronto 1953); *Critics and Criticism* ed. R. S. Crane (Chicago 1952); Elder Olson *On Value Judgement in the Arts* (Chicago 1976).

65. Cohen "Innovation and Variation" 9.

66. See Emil Staiger "The Questionable Nature of Value Problems" in *Problems of Literary Evaluation* ed. Strelka 207.

67. Colie *Resources of Kind* 128.

Bibliography

Abrams, Meyer H. *A Glossary of Literary Terms.* Rev. ed. New York 1957.

Adams, Hazard. *Interests of Criticism: An Introduction to Literary Theory.* New York 1969.

Allen, Beverly Sprague. *Tides in English Taste, 1619-1800: A Background for the Study of Literature.* 2 vols. Cambridge, Mass. 1937, rpt. New York 1969.

Altieri, Charles. "The Hermeneutics of Literary Indeterminacy: A Dissent from the New Orthodoxy." *New Literary History* 10.1 (1978) 71-99.

Assembly of Ladies, The: see Pearsall, Derek A.

Atkins, J. W. H. *English Literary Criticism: The Medieval Phase.* Cambridge 1943.

Auerbach, Erich. *Mimesis: The Representation of Reality in Western Literature.* Tr. Willard R. Trask. Princeton 1953.

Barber, C. L. *Shakespeare's Festive Comedy: A Study of Dramatic Form and Its Relation to Social Custom.* Princeton 1959.

Barthelme, Donald. *City Life.* New York and London 1971.

Bateson, F. W. *The Scholar-Critic: An Introduction to Literary Research.* London 1972.

Beardsley, Monroe C. *Aesthetics: Problems in the Philosophy of Criticism.* New York 1958.

———— "The Concept of Literature." In *Literary Theory and Structure: Essays in Honour of William K. Wimsatt.* Ed. Frank Brady et al. New Haven and London 1973.

Berry, Francis. *The Shakespearean Inset.* London 1965.

Bond, Donald F., ed. *The Spectator.* 5 vols. Oxford 1965.

Bradbrook, Muriel C. *The Growth and Structure of Elizabethan Comedy.* London 1955.

Braden, Gordon. *The Classics and English Renaissance Poetry: Three Case Studies.* Yale Studies in English 187. New Haven and London 1978.

Brady, Frank; Palmer, John; and Price, Martin, eds. *Literary Theory and Structure: Essays in Honour of William K. Wimsatt.* New Haven and London 1973.

Brooks, Cleanth: *see* Wimsatt, William K., and Brooks, Cleanth.

Brunetière, Ferdinand. *L'Evolution des genres dans l'histoire de la littérature.* Paris 1890.

Burden, Dennis H. *The Logical Epic: A Study of the Argument of "Paradise Lost."* London 1967.

———— "Crabbe and the Augustan Tradition." In *Essays and Poems Presented to Lord David Cecil* ed. W. W. Robson. London 1970.

Burness, Donald B. "Pieter Brueghel: Painter for Poets." *Art Journal* 32 (Winter 1972-73) 157-162.

Butler, I. Christopher. "What is a Literary Work?" *New Literary History* 5 (1973) 17–29.

Cairns, Francis. *Generic Composition in Greek and Roman Poetry.* Edinburgh 1972.

Campbell, Lily B. *Divine Poetry and Drama in Sixteenth-Century England.* Cambridge 1959.

Capella, Martianus: *see* Stahl, William H., et al.

Chalker, John. *The English Georgic: A Study in the Development of a Form.* London 1969.

Chambers, Sir Edmund, ed. *English Pastorals Selected and with an Introduction.* London 1906.

Choice, Chance and Change. Ed. Alexander B. Grosart. London 1881.

Cleveland, John. *The Poems of John Cleveland.* Ed. Brian Morris and Eleanor Withington. Oxford 1967.

Cohen, Ralph. *The Art of Discrimination: Thomson's "The Seasons" and the Language of Criticism.* Berkeley 1964.

―――― "Innovation and Variation: Literary Change and Georgic Poetry." In *Literature and History* papers read at a Clark Library Seminar, 3 March 1973, by Ralph Cohen and Murray Krieger. Los Angeles 1974.

―――― "On the Interrelations of Eighteenth-Century Literary Forms." In *New Approaches to Eighteenth-Century Literature* ed. Phillip Harth. New York and London 1974.

Colie, Rosalie L. *The Resources of Kind: Genre Theory in the Renaissance.* Ed. Barbara K. Lewalski. Berkeley 1973.

―――― *Shakespeare's Living Art.* Princeton 1974.

Collins, Wilkie. *The Woman in White.* Ed. H. P. Sucksmith. Oxford English Novels. London 1975.

Cooper, Helen. "The Goat and the Eclogue." *Philological Quarterly* 53 (1974) 363–379.

―――― *Pastoral: Medieval into Renaissance.* Ipswich and Totowa, N.J. 1977.

Critical Essays of the Seventeenth Century. Ed. Joel E. Spingarn. 3 vols. Oxford 1908–1909.

Cunningham, J. V. *Tradition and Poetic Structure: Essays in Literary History and Criticism.* Denver 1960.

Curtius, Ernst Robert. *European Literature and the Latin Middle Ages.* Tr. Willard R. Trask. Bollingen Series 36. New York and London 1953.

Davis, Walter A. *The Act of Interpretation: A Critique of Literary Reason.* Chicago and London 1978.

Dennis, John. *The Critical Works.* Ed. Edward Niles Hooker, vol. 1: 1692–1711; vol. 2: 1711–1729. Baltimore 1939, 1943.

Dilthey, Wilhelm. "The Rise of Hermeneutics." Tr. Fredric Jameson. *New Literary History* 3.2 (1972) 229–244.

Dorsten, Jan van: *see* Sidney, Sir Philip.

Drayton, Michael. *The Works of Michael Drayton.* Ed. J. William Hebel, Kathleen Tillotson, and Bernard H. Newdigate. 5 vols. Oxford 1931–1941.

Dryden, John. *The Poems of John Dryden.* Ed. James Kinsley. 4 vols. Oxford 1958.

―――― *"Of Dramatic Poesy" and Other Critical Essays.* Ed. George Watson. 2 vols. London and New York 1962.

Duncan-Jones, Katherine: *see* Sidney, Sir Philip.

Durling, Dwight L. *Georgic Tradition in English Poetry.* New York 1935.

Eighteenth Century Essays on Shakespeare. Ed. D. Nichol Smith. Glasgow 1903.

Elizabethan Critical Essays. Ed. G. Gregory Smith. 2 vols. Oxford 1904.

Elledge, Scott, ed. *Eighteenth-Century Critical Essays.* 2 vols. Ithaca 1961.

Elledge, Scott, and Schier, Donald. *The Continental Model: Selected French Critical Essays of the Seventeenth Century, in English Translation.* Rev. ed. Ithaca and London 1970.

Encyclopedia of Poetry and Poetics. Ed. Alex S. Preminger. Princeton 1965.

Erlich, Victor. *Russian Formalism: History—Doctrine.* Ed. Cornelis H. van Schooneveld. Slavistic Printings and Reprintings 4. The Hague 1955.

Faber Book of Epigrams and Epitaphs, The. Ed. Geoffrey Grigson. London 1977.

Faral, Edmond. *Les Arts poétiques du 12ᵉ et du 13ᵉ siècle.* Paris 1962.

Fernandez, Roman. *Messages.* First series. Paris 1926.

Fletcher, Angus. *Allegory: The Theory of a Symbolic Mode.* Ithaca 1964.

Fowler, Alastair. *Triumphal Forms.* Cambridge 1970.

———— "The Life and Death of Literary Forms." *New Literary History* 2.2 (1971) 199-216. Reprinted in *New Directions in Literary History.* Ed. Ralph Cohen. London 1974.

Frye, Northrop. *Anatomy of Criticism: Four Essays.* Princeton 1957.

Fubini, Mario. *Critica e poesia.* Bari 1966.

Garland, John of: *see* John of Garland.

Gradon, Pamela. *Form and Style in Early English Literature.* London 1971.

Graham, W. S. *Implements in Their Places.* London 1977.

Gray, Bennison. *The Phenomenon of Literature.* De Proprietatibus Litterarum, series maior 36. The Hague 1975.

Greg, Walter W. *Pastoral Poetry and Pastoral Drama: A Literary Inquiry, with Special Reference to the Pre-Restoration Stage in England.* London 1906.

Grigson, Geoffrey, ed. *The Faber Book of Epigrams and Epitaphs.* London 1977.

Grosart, Alexander B., ed. *Choice, Chance and Change.* London 1881.

Guillén, Claudio. *Literature as System: Essays toward the Theory of Literary History.* Princeton 1971.

Halperin, John, ed. *The Theory of the Novel: New Essays.* New York and London 1974.

Hardison, O. B. *The Enduring Monument.* Chapel Hill 1962.

Hartman, Geoffrey H. *Beyond Formalism: Literary Essays 1958-1970.* New Haven and London 1970.

Hassan, Ihab. *The Dismemberment of "Orpheus": Toward a Postmodern Literature.* New York 1971.

Hernadi, Paul. *Beyond Genre: New Directions in Literary Classification.* Ithaca and London 1972.

————, ed. *What is Literature?* Bloomington, Ind. and London 1978.

Highet, Gilbert. *The Anatomy of Satire.* Princeton 1962.

Hirsch, E. Donald. *Validity in Interpretation.* New Haven and London 1967.

———— "Faulty Perspectives." *Essays in Criticism* 25 (1975) 154-168.

———— "Privileged Criteria in Literary Evaluation." In *Problems of Literary Evaluation.* Ed. Joseph P. Strelka. Yearbook of Comparative Criticism 2. State College, Pa. 1969.

———— "Some Aims of Criticism." In *Literary Theory and Structure: Essays in Honour of William K. Wimsatt.* Ed. Frank Brady et al. New Haven and London 1973.

———— *The Aims of Interpretation.* Chicago and London 1976.

Hollander, John. *Vision and Resonance: Two Senses of Poetic Form.* New York 1975.

Hotson, Leslie. *The First Night of "Twelfth Night."* London 1954.

Hough, Graham. *A Preface to "The Faerie Queen."* London 1962.

———— *An Essay on Criticism.* London 1966.

Howard, Donald R. *The Idea of the Canterbury Tales.* Berkeley 1976.

Hoy, Cyrus. *The Hyacinth Room: An Investigation into the Nature of Comedy, Tragedy and Tragicomedy.* London 1964.

Huddleston, Eugene L., and Noverr, Douglas A. *The Relationship of Painting and Literature: A Guide to Information Sources.* Detroit 1978.

Hughes, Peter. "Restructuring Literary History: Implications for the Eighteenth Century." *New Literary History* 8.2 (1977) 257–277.

Hugo, Victor. Preface to *Cromwell.* 1827.

Ingarden, Roman. *Das literarische Kunstwerke.* Tübingen 1965. Tr. George G. Grabowicz as *The Literary Work of Art.* Evanston, Ill. 1973.

Iser, Wolfgang. *The Act of Reading: A Theory of Aesthetic Response.* Baltimore and London 1978.

Jauss, Hans Robert. *Literaturgeschichte als Provokation der Literaturwissenschaft.* Konstanz 1967.

———— "Levels of Identification of Hero and Audience." *New Literary History* 5.2 (1974) 283–317.

———— "Littérature médiévale et expérience esthétique." *Poétique* 8 (1977) 322–336.

———— "La Jouissance esthétique." *Poétique* 10 (1979) 261–274.

John of Garland. *The "Parisiana Poetria" of John of Garland.* Ed. with introduction, translation, and notes by Traugott Lawler. Yale Studies in English 182. New Haven and London 1974.

Johnson, Samuel. *Lives of the English Poets.* Ed. George Birkbeck Hill. 3 vols. Oxford 1905.

Jolles, André. *Einfache Formen: Legende, Sage, Mythe, Rätsel, Spruch, Kasus, Memorabile, Märchen, Witz.* Rev. ed. Halle 1956.

Jonson, Ben. *Ben Jonson.* Ed. C. H. Herford, Percy Simpson, and Evelyn M. Simpson. 11 vols. Oxford 1925–1952.

Kaiser, Walter. *Praisers of Folly: Erasmus, Rabelais, Shakespeare.* Cambridge, Mass. 1963.

Kellett, Ernest Edward. *The Whirligig of Taste.* London 1929.

Kellman, Steven G. *The Self-Begetting Novel.* New York 1980.

Kermode, J. Frank. *English Pastoral Poetry from the Beginnings to Marvell.* Life, Literature, and Thought Library. London 1952.

———— *The Classic.* London 1975.

Krieger, Murray, ed. *Northrop Frye in Modern Criticism.* Selected papers from the English Institute. New York and London 1966.

Kinsley, James, ed. *The Poems of John Dryden.* 4 vols. Oxford 1958.

Landor, Walter Savage. *The Poetical Works.* Ed. Stephen Wheeler. 3 vols. Oxford 1937.

Lattimore, Richmond Alexander. *Story Patterns in Greek Tragedy.* Ann Arbor 1964.

Lemon, Lee T., and Reis, Marion J., eds. *Russian Formalist Criticism: Four Essays.* Regents Critics Series. Lincoln, Neb. 1965.

Lever, J. W. *The Elizabethan Love Sonnet.* London 1956.

Levin, Harry. "The Title as a Literary Genre." *Modern Language Review* 72 (1977) xxiii–xxxvi.

Lewalski, Barbara Kiefer. *Milton's Brief Epic: The Genre, Meaning and Art of "Paradise Regained."* Providence and London 1966.

—— *Donne's "Anniversaries" and the Poetry of Praise: The Creation of a Symbolic Mode.* Princeton 1973.

Lewis, Clive Staples. *The Allegory of Love.* Oxford 1936.

—— *The Discarded Image: An Introduction to Medieval and Renaissance Literature.* Cambridge 1964.

Lodge, David. *The Modes of Modern Writing: Metaphor, Metonymy and the Typology of Modern Literature.* London 1977.

Lukács, Georg. *Der historische Roman.* 1937. Tr. H. and S. Mitchell as *The Historical Novel.* London 1962.

Lyas, Colin A. "The Semantic Definition of Literature." *Journal of Philosophy* 66.3 (1969) 81–95.

Lyons, John. *Introduction to Theoretical Linguistics.* Cambridge 1968.

Marino, Adrian. "Towards a Definition of Literary Genres." In *Theories of Literary Genre.* Ed. Joseph P. Strelka. Yearbook of Comparative Criticism 8. University Park, Pa. and London 1978.

Matejka, Ladislav, and Pomorska, Krystyna, eds. *Readings in Russian Poetics: Formalist and Structuralist Views.* Cambridge, Mass. and London 1971.

Meredith, George. *An Essay on Comedy and the Uses of the Comic Spirit.* London 1897.

Milton, John. *The Poems of John Milton.* Ed. John Carey and Alastair Fowler. London 1968.

Miner, Earl. *The Metaphysical Mode from Donne to Cowley.* Princeton 1969.

Minnis, A. J. "Discussions of 'Authorial Role' and 'Literary Form' in Late-Medieval Scriptural Exegesis." *Beiträge zur Geschichte der Deutschen Sprache und Literatur* 99 (1977) 37–65.

—— "The Influence of Academic Prologues on the Prologues and Literary Attitudes of Late-Medieval English Writers." Forthcoming in *Medieval Studies.*

Minturno, Antonio Sebastiano. *De Poeta* (*1559*). Facs. ed., Poetiken des Cinquecento 5. Munich 1970.

—— *L'Arte Poetica* (*1564*). Facs. ed., Poetiken des Cinquecento 6. Munich 1971.

Morris, Brian, and Withington, Eleanor, eds. *The Poems of John Cleveland.* Oxford 1967.

Murphy, James J. *Rhetoric in the Middle Ages: A History of Rhetorical Theory from Saint Augustine to the Renaissance.* Berkeley 1974.

Nashe, Thomas. *The Works of Thomas Nashe.* Ed. Ronald B. McKerrow and re-ed. F. P. Wilson. 5 vols. Oxford 1958.

Newton-de Molina, David, ed. *On Literary Intention: Critical Essays.* Edinburgh 1976.

Nohrnberg, James. *The Analogy of "The Faerie Queen."* Princeton 1976.

Northrop Frye in Modern Criticism. Ed. Murray Krieger. Selected papers from the English Institute. New York and London 1966.

Otis, Brooks. *Virgil: A Study in Civilized Poetry.* Oxford 1964.

Palgrave, Francis Turner. *The Golden Treasury of the Best Songs and Lyrical Poems in the English Language.* Cambridge and London 1861.

Palmer, F. R. *Semantics: A New Outline.* Cambridge 1976.

Pearsall, Derek A., ed. *"The Floure and the Leafe" and "The Assembly of Ladies."* London and Edinburgh 1962.

Perry, Ben Edwin. *The Ancient Romances: A Literary-Historical Account of Their Origins.* Berkeley and Los Angeles 1967.

Poggioli, Renato. *The Oaten Flute: Essays on Pastoral Poetry and the Pastoral Ideal.* Cambridge, Mass. 1975.

Pope, Alexander. "A Discourse on Pastoral Poetry." *The Prose Works of Alexander Pope Newly Collected and Edited by Norman Ault.* Vol. 1: *The Earlier Works, 1711–1720.* Oxford 1936.

Potts, Abbie Findlay. *The Elegiac Mode: Poetic Form in Wordsworth and Other Elegists.* Ithaca 1967.

Praz, Mario. *The Flaming Heart: Essays on Crashaw, Machiavelli, and Other Studies in the Relations between Italian and English Literature from Chaucer to T. S. Eliot.* Garden City 1958.

Preminger, Alex S., ed. *Encyclopedia of Poetry and Poetics.* Princeton 1965.

Puttenham, George. *The Art of English Poesy.* Ed. Gladys Doidge Willcock and Alice Walker. Cambridge 1936.

Reid, Ian. *The Short Story.* The Critical Idiom 37. London and New York 1977.

Ricks, Christopher, ed. *English Poetry and Prose, 1540–1674.* Sphere History of Literature in the English Language. Vol. 2. London 1970.

Righter, William. *Logic and Criticism.* London 1963.

Roche, Thomas P., Jr. "Shakespeare and the Sonnet Sequence." In Christopher Ricks, ed. *English Poetry and Prose, 1540–1674.* London 1970.

Rosenmeyer, Thomas G. *The Green Cabinet: Theocritus and the European Pastoral Lyric.* Berkeley and Los Angeles 1969.

Scaliger, Julius Caesar. *Poetices Libri Septem.* Lyons 1561. Facs. ed. August Buck. Stuttgart-Bad Cannstatt 1964.

Schiller, Friedrich. "Über naive und sentimentalische Dichtung." *Die Horen* nos. 11–12 (1795–1796).

Scholes, Robert E. *Structuralism in Literature: An Introduction.* New Haven and London 1974.

Sidney, Sir Philip. *The Poems of Sir Philip Sidney.* Ed. William A. Ringler. Oxford 1962.
—— *Miscellaneous Prose of Sir Philip Sidney.* Ed. Katherine Duncan-Jones and Jan van Dorsten. Oxford 1973.

Smarr, Janet Levarie. "Renaissance Anacreontics." *Comparative Literature* 25 (1973) 221–239.

Smith, Barbara Herrnstein. *Poetic Closure: A Study of How Poems End.* Chicago 1968.

Smith, G. Gregory, ed. *Elizabethan Critical Essays.* 2 vols. Oxford 1904.

Smith, D. Nichol, ed. *Eighteenth Century Essays on Shakespeare.* Glasgow 1903.

Sparshott, F. E. *The Concept of Criticism.* Oxford 1967.

Spearing, A. C. *Medieval Dream-Poetry.* Cambridge 1976.

Spectator, The. Ed. Donald F. Bond. 5 vols. Oxford 1965.

Spenser, Edmund. *The Works of Edmund Spenser: A Variorum Edition.* Ed. Edwin Greenlaw et al. 10 vols. Baltimore 1932–1957.

Spingarn, Joel E., ed. *Critical Essays of the Seventeenth Century.* 3 vols. Oxford 1908–1909.

Stahl, William H., et al. *Martianus Capella and the Seven Liberal Arts.* Vol. 1: *The Quadrivium of Martianus Capella.* New York and London 1971.

Staiger, Emil. *Grundbegriffe der Poetik.* Rev. ed. Zurich 1963.

Steadman, John M. *Milton and the Renaissance Hero.* Oxford 1967.

Stempel, W. D. "Pour une description des genres littéraires." Actes du XIIe congrès international de linguistique romane. Bucharest 1968. Rpt. *Beiträge zur Textlinguistik.* Munich 1970.

Stevens, John. *Medieval Romance: Themes and Approaches.* London 1973.

Strelka, Joseph P., ed. *Problems of Literary Evaluation.* Yearbook of Comparative Criticism 2. University Park, Pa. and London 1969.

———— *Theories of Literary Genre.* Yearbook of Comparative Criticism 8, University Park, Pa. and London 1978.

Stutterheim, Cornelis F. P. "Prolegomena to a Theory of the Literary Genres." *Zagadnienia Rodzajów Literackich* 6.2 (11) (Lodz 1964) 5-24.

Sucksmith, H. P., ed. *The Woman in White.* By Wilkie Collins. Oxford English Novels. London 1975.

Todorov, Tzvetan. "The Notion of Literature." Tr. Lynn Moss and Bruno Braunrot. *New Literary History* 5.1 (1973) 5-16.

Tuve, Rosemond. *Elizabethan and Metaphysical Imagery: Renaissance Poetic and Twentieth-Century Critics.* Chicago 1947.

Turner, James G. *Politics of Landscape: Rural Scenery and Society in English Verse 1630-1660.* Oxford and Cambridge, Mass. 1979.

Tynjanov, Jurij. "O literaturnoj èvoljucii." *Na literaturnom postu* 4 (1927). Tr. C. A. Luplow as "On Literary Evolution." In Ladislav Matejka and Krystyna Pomorska, eds. *Readings in Russian Poetics: Formalist and Structuralist Views.* Cambridge, Mass. and London 1971.

Variorum Spenser: see Spenser, Edmund.

Viëtor, Karl. "Probleme der literarischen Gattungsgeschichte." *Deutsche Vierteljahrsschrift für Literaturwissenschaft und Geistesgeschichte* 9 (1931) 425-447.

Weinberg, Bernard. *A History of Literary Criticism in the Italian Renaissance.* 2 vols. Chicago 1961.

Weisstein, Ulrich. *Comparative Literature and Literary Theory: Survey and Introduction.* Translated by William Riggan in collaboration with the author. Bloomington, Ind. and London 1968. Originally published as *Einführung in die Vergleichende Literaturwissenschaft.* Stuttgart 1968.

Wellek, René. *Concepts of Criticism: Essays.* Ed. Stephen G. Nichols, Jr. New Haven 1963.

———— *Discriminations: Further Concepts of Criticism.* New Haven and London 1970.

Wellek, René, and Warren, Austin. *Theory of Literature.* Rev. ed. New York 1956.

Welsford, Enid. *The Court Masque: A Study in the Relationship between Poetry and the Revels.* 1927. Rept. New York 1962.

Williams, Ioan. *Novel and Romance 1700-1800: A Documentary Record.* 1970.

Wilson, D. B. *Descriptive Poetry in France from Blason to Baroque.* Manchester and New York 1967.

Wimsatt, William K., and Brooks, Cleanth. *Literary Criticism: A Short History.* New York 1957.

Wordsworth, William. *The Prose Works of William Wordsworth.* Ed. W. J. B. Owen and Jane Worthington Smyser. 3 vols. Oxford 1974.

Index

209–210; encomiastic, 197, 218; era of, 213–214; external structure of, 183–184; *fel, acetum, sal* topics in, 184, 229; fetid, 198, 229; fourteen-line, 57; generic labels for, 131–132; Greek, 138, 211; Herrick's, 114, 197–198; in the hierarchy, 213–214, 217, 218, 219, 220, 221, 222–223, 229, 231; "I write" formula, 198; length of, 183; liminal, 198; love, 76, 137, 138; lyric, 139, 254; *mel,* 208, 229–230; Metaphysical style, 198–199; Minturno on, 183; modal extensions of, 108; modern, 63, 128, 134; modulation through, *see* epigrammatic modulation; names in, 76; nomenclature of, 136, 137–138; on a historical personage, 114; opening formula of, 101; origins of, 153; "overwhelming Parnassus," 196; place in education, 196; plain diction of, 138, 198, 199, 201, 202; pointed *concetti,* 198, 199; relabeling as lyric, 137–138; religious and sacred, 171, 198; Renaissance, 137, 176, 196–197; satiric, 222, 252; size of, 63; sonnet and, 71, 138, 139, 171, 176, 183–185, 216, 221, 251–252; subepigram, 199; subgenres of, 114; terseness of, 137; titles of, 96; tradition and poems on art, 115; transformation of, 171, 176; Tudor, 51, 134; wit in, 198, 199, 200, 201, 222
epigrammatic modulation: by assimilation, 197–198; by contribution, 197, 198–200; contrasted with inclusion, 199; diastole of, 197–198; diminished versions of other genres in, 197–198; early 18th century, 195; effect of, 196, 202; effect on elegy, 199–200; effect on essay, 200–201; effect on prose, 200–202; in Herrick, 197–198; late 16th century, 195; 17th century, 196; systole of, 198–200; vogue in, 195–196
epilogue, 60
episode, 61
epistle: Augustan satiric verse, 66; elevation of the, 187; Renaissance, 207; size of, 64; use of term, 39; verse, 66, 68, 70, 108
epistolary: modulation, 108; novel, 33, 120; rhetoric, 146, 303
epitaph: as miniature tragedy, 197; Caroline, 58; Elizabethan, 58; inset in, 179; Johnson on, 52–53; medieval, 144; names in, 76; occasion of, 153; opening formulas and topics, 101; Renaissance, 207; size of, 63; social function of, 7; subject of, 65; transformation of, 144; use of term, 141; Virgilian, 144; Wordsworth on, 53

Epitaph of Sir Thomas Gravener, Knight, 179
epithalamium: biblical, 192; division of, 61; epigram in, 198; extension of, 192; insets in, 179; in *silva,* 134, 135; journey in, 193; *kēroi* in, 59, 152; medieval view of, 143, 144; occasion of, 67, 152, 162; Renaissance, 162; social function of, 7; transformation of, 144, 192
epode, 143
epodon, 143
epoenetic, 219, 220, 221
epyllion, 51, 94, 109, 232
Essais, 4
essay: as a universal, 238; assembly of, 157; critical, 227; didactic verse, 211; elegiac modulation of, 210; epigrammatic modulation of, 200–201; familiar, 157, 166, 210, 227; informal, 92; in 19th century, 11; in systems of genres, 255; mixture of novel and, 28, 190, 286; modal extensions of, 108–109; philosophical, 238; relation to central genres, 5, 11; size of, 63; status of nontechnical, 11, 12; titling of, 92; treatises viewed as, 12–13; uses of term, 131, 135
estate poems, 154, 155, 156, 171, 203, 275
Estienne, Henri, 137, 222, 223, 302
Euripides, 27, 164; *Iphigenia in Taurus,* 40
evaluation, 256, 272–276
Evans, Stuart, *Caves of Alienation,* 124
Evanthius, 145, 146
excellence criterion, 17
exode, 61
exordium, 73, 88, 89–90, 102, 103, 104
expository: aspects of 18th-century English georgic, 60; prose, 7, 12, 248; writing becoming literary, 12–13
extended literature, 7
external: features of genres, 260; form, 107, 111, 119, 183, 192; structure, 60–61, 73, 106, 108

fable, 64, 91, 101–102
fabliau, 64, 152, 180
Fainlight, Ruth, *All Those Victorian Paintings,* 117
Fairfax, Thomas, 224
fairy tale, 63, 82, 90–91, 99–100, 150, 151
Fall of the Nibelungs, The, 160
family resemblance theory, 40–44, 58
Fanshawe, Sir Richard, 232
Faral, Edmond, 240
Farjeon, Eleanor, 53, 288
farrago, 110, 119, 132, 189–190
fashion, 213–214
Faulkner, William, 237